Frie

C000001156

FOR KING AND COUNTRY

FOR KING AND COUNTRY

The Letters and Diaries of John Mills,
Coldstream Guards, 1811-14

'I myself keep a diary, merely to mark the day.
Some years hence I shall look over it with pleasure.'

John Mills, Castello de Vide, May 28th 1812

Edited by

Ian Fletcher

SPELLMOUNT
Staplehurst

British Library Cataloguing in Publication Data:
A catalogue record for this book is available
from the British Library

Copyright © Ian Fletcher 1995
Photographs © G.M.H. Mills

ISBN 1-873376-22-7

First published in the UK in 1995 by
Spellmount Ltd
The Old Rectory
Staplehurst
Kent TN12 0AZ

3 5 7 9 8 6 4 2

The right of Ian Fletcher to be identified
as the author of this work has been asserted by him
in accordance with the Copyright, Designs
and Patents Act 1985

All rights reserved. No part of this publication may be
reproduced, stored in a retrieval system or transmitted in
any form or by any means, electronic, mechanical, photocopying, recording or
otherwise, without prior permission in writing from
Spellmount Limited,
Publishers.

Printed and bound in Great Britain by
T.J. Press (Padstow) Ltd
Padstow, Cornwall

CONTENTS

ILLUSTRATIONS

1. John Mills. Watercolour study by Sir William Hayter, 1832, for his House of Commons painting.
2. Sarah Charlotte Mills. Oil painting by Sir Francis Grant RA.
3. Fuentes de Oñoro, May 3rd-5th 1811. This was JM's first action in the Peninsula.
4. 'Troops bivouacked near the village of Villa Velha, on the evening of the 19th of May 1811, showing the various occupations of an encampment.' This marvellous painting by Major Thomas St Clair gives some idea of the day to day life of Wellington's men.
5. The battle of Salamanca, fought on July 22nd 1812.
6. The interior of the castle of Burgos during Wellington's abortive siege in September and October 1812.
7. William Mills. Oil painting by George Romney, 1789.
8. Elizabeth Mills. Oil painting by George Romney, 1789.
9. John Mills' Military General Service Medal, with clasps for Fuentes de Oñoro, Ciudad Rodrigo and Salamanca.
10. Filly, 'Kate'. Oil by J.F. Herring, 1832. Bred at Bisterne in 1829 she finished 10th in the Derby and 4th in the Oaks, 1832.
11. John Mills' yacht, 'Julia', winning her 11th cup at Cowes Regatta, August 7th 1828.
12. Arthur Wellesley, 1st Duke of Wellington. After a painting by Goya.
13. Sir Thomas Graham, Lord Lynedoch. After a painting by Sir Thomas Lawrence. Graham commanded the 1st Division of the army for a while.
14. John Mills, on horse, partly shown by Richard Dighton, c1840.
15. 'The House of Commons, 1833.' Painting by Sir George Hayter. JM stands on the extreme left of the picture, back row. On the right, with a blue sash across his white waistcoat, stands Wellington.
16. Detail from the same. The Duke of Richmond, of Waterloo Ball fame, stands, bottom left, with the Marquess of Anglesey behind him at his left shoulder.
17. John Mills, on his grey hunter, hunting with the Quorn at Quenby Hall in Leicestershire. Oil painting by John Ferneley, 1819.
18. Bisterne Manor, near Ringwood, Hampshire, John Mills' home.

Picture Credits

1, 2, 7, 8, 9, 10, 11, 14, 17 and 18, courtesy of G.M. H. Mills; 3, 4, 5, 6, 12 and 13, author's collection; 15 and 16, courtesy of the National Portrait Gallery, London.

MAPS

ACKNOWLEDGEMENTS

I wish to express my most sincere thanks to Major John Micklethwait Mills, OBE, DL, and Major General Giles Hallam Mills, CB, CVO, OBE, without whose help and co-operation this volume would not have been possible. My thanks also go to the late Colonel Paul Adair, a former Guardsman himself, and former curator of the Guards Museum, London, for his earlier work on John Mills, to Paul Chamberlain, for his expert help in matters relating to the prisoner-of-war exchange system, to Carole Stacey, who cast her expert eye over the manuscript, and to Tony Hawkins for answering one or two of my more obscure queries. Thanks also go to the National Portrait Gallery for the Hayter painting of the House of Commons. The maps of Ciudad Rodrigo, Badajoz, the Salamanca forts and Burgos appear courtesy of Jamie Wilson of Spellmount Ltd.

Finally, when we consider the very trying nature of the campaign in the Iberian Peninsula, the miseries of the cold, wet winters and the hot, stifling summers, let alone the rigours and dangers of the war itself, it is quite remarkable that men like John Mills were able to produce first-rate legible accounts of the campaign in which they were participating. Therefore, I have to pay a great debt of gratitude to JM for leaving us this most fascinating insight into the Peninsular War. I am sure that this remarkable man would feel more than satisfied that, some 184 years on, his letters and diaries, begun in 1811, had at last found a wide audience.

Ian Fletcher,
Rochester, 1995.

JOHN MILLS OF BISTERNE MANOR, HAMPSHIRE AND HIS IMMEDIATE FAMILY

*denotes mentioned in Letters

JOHN MILLS I (1677-1717) = Sarah Best
Court of Chancery Official

REV JOHN MILLS II = Sarah Wheler
(1712-1791) Rector of Barford

William Mills I = Selina Salter
(1714-1782)
East India Trade
Glyn's Bank dsp
dau. of Sir John Salter, Lord Mayor of London

WILLIAM MILLS II = Elizabeth Digby*
(1750-1820)
(?-1828)
Purchased Bisterne 1792.
MP for Coventry 1808-12

Charles Mills I* = Jane Digby*
(1755-1826)
MP for Warwick 1802-26 dsp

Rev Francis Mills* = Catharine Mordaunt*
(1759-1851)
Rector of Barford, founder of Pillerton Manor, Warwickshire and Bude Haven, Cornwall branches of Mills family now extinct in the male line

---

JOHN MILLS III* = Sarah Charlotte Micklethwait
(1789-1871)
referred to as JM in letters and diaries

William Mills III* = Charlotte Hare
(1791-1838)
58th Regt. in Peninsula
Major in 22nd Light Dragoons
This branch is now extinct in the male line

Charles Mills II*
Glyn Mills (1792-1872)
Baronet 1868. The later barony of Hillingdon is now extinct

Francis *
(1793-1854)
died unmarried
Collector of pictures

JOHN MILLS IV* = Louisa Entwhistle
(1836-1899)
See epilogue

REV CECIL MILLS = Anne Nicolls
(1839-1908)
Rector of Barford
Inherited Bisterne from JOHN IV, his brother

Edward Mills* = Frances Wingfield
(1801-1865)
Their only daughter married Lt Col C R Hon
Edward Cooper of Markree Castle, Ireland

Charlotte Mills* = Henry C. Compton*
(1788-1855)

Selina Mills
(1797-?) married
C.H. Bracebridge, Atherstone
Hall, Warwickshire. They
chaperoned Florence
Nightingale and worked with
her at Scutari, 1854-55

Major JOHN MILLS VI = Prudence Cooper-Key
(1919-) OBE, DL

SIR JOHN MILLS V = Carola Tuck
(1879-1972)
See Epilogue
(1889-1995) dau. of Judge S.P. Tuck
Annapolis, Maryland USA

Giles Mills = Emily Tuck
(1922-)
Major General
CB, CVO, OBE
KStJ & RJ3
dau. of Capt W.H. Tuck USNR
Baltimore, Maryland USA
Resident Governor HM Tower of London,
1979-1984

Julian Mills = Diana Russell-Wood
(1926-)

Foreword

John Mills and his Forebears

by
Major John Micklethwait Mills OBE, DL,
and
Major General Giles Hallam Mills, CB, CVO, OBE.

Although the Mills family have been active in many facets of Hampshire life for 200 years, their origins lay in Warwickshire and their early success in the city and fortunate marriages.

The great-grandfather of our John Mills (JM) was John Mills I (1677-1717). He prospered in the office of the Six Clerks in Chancery and probably acquired the patronage of the appointment of the Rector of Barford in Warwickshire. JM's grandfather, the Reverend John Mills II (1712-1791) began a 160-year period of successive Mills Rectorships of Barford and married Sarah, the granddaughter of Admiral Sir Francis Wheler. A great aunt Harriet Mills married General George Scott (1732-1811), Colonel of the 58th Regiment, which appears in our story.

Most importantly, however, JM's great uncle William I (1714-1782) married Selina, daughter and heiress to Sir John Salter, Lord Mayor of London. Salter introduced William to the profitable East India Company trade and left him property at Walthamstow. In 1722 he was able to help save Glyn's Bank from collapse on the promise that he and Reverend John II's second son, Charles Mills I (1755-1826) became directors of what was to be Glyn Mills. When William I died childless in 1782, his heir to Reverend John II's eldest son, and JM's father, William II (1750-1820) had the money to invest in a country estate.

In 1786 William Mills II married the fourth daughter, Elizabeth, of the Hon. Wriothesley Digby. His brother Charles I, the banker, married her youngest sister Jane, but they had no children. That the brothers were well established in Warwickshire is shown by the fact that William II was MP for Coventry 1808-1812 and Charles I MP for Warwick 1802-26. Both were early members of the Woodmen of Arden, the prestigious Warwickshire Archery Society, and had registered their arrows with the family demi-lion crest, millrind and blue and silver colours. That the Digbys were a Dorset family may have drawn William II to search for a property in Wessex. In 1792 John Compton put Bisterne Manor, near Ringwood in Hampshire, on the market and William II bought the estate, while Compton concentrated his resources on Minstead Manor in the New Forest.

The twin manors of Bisterne and Minstead had been in one ownership since before the Norman Conquest. The Bettesthorne (old spelling of Bisterne) heiress had brought them to the Berkeleys in 1399, and the Berkeley heiress to the Comptons a century later, so this is the only recorded sale. The Compton descendants have retained Minstead, and, as will be seen in many of the letters, William II's eldest daughter, Charlotte Mills, JM's favourite sister, married John Compton's heir, Henry, and the two families have remained close friends. Although the Bisterne farms were leased to tenants, William II immediately began to show himself a forward looking landlord. In 1794 he was a founder member of the South Avon and Stour Agricultural Society, the oldest of its kind in England, and introduced the swede turnip to the area; probably he influenced his tenants to adopt the ecologically sound Norfolk four-course rotational system of farming, which was written into all tenancies until the exigencies of World War II forced intensive arable farming. William also started the tree planting, which his descendants adopted as a conscientious annual programme to this day.

The subject of this book, John Mills III (JM), was born in 1789, the year of the fall of the Bastille, and died in 1871, as the exiled Napoleon III arrived in England. His life thus covered the whole development of the Industrial Revolution and the expansion of democracy. Service in the Peninsular War widened his horizons, but his character, whose diversity of interests made him fully at home in the Regency Age, was already largely formed.

He was three when William, his father, bought Bisterne, and it is rather touching that, when asked whom he would like to invite to his first birthday party in his new home, he could only suggest the classical children shown clambering over a lion in the carved chimney piece in Bisterne's dining room. By the time he joined the army, however, he had made a wide circle of friends and his interest in people individually and collectively was a notable aspect of his character, so well shown in Beau Brummel's circle after the war.

He had learnt to ride and shoot — salmon fishing on the Avon was developed in the next generation. Reporting to his father on Spanish crops and sending seed samples home indicate his agricultural interest; he was a keen observer of birds (see his excellent description of a Black-bellied Sandgrouse in his Diary, August 6th 1812) and of trees and plants. He had developed an appreciation of architecture and pictures, displayed in his visit to Madrid and elsewhere. He was politically aware and his letters show that he had a clear grasp of, and decided views on, the military strategy and tactics of the Peninsular campaigns.

He was educated at Harrow and Christ Church, Oxford, before volunteering for the army. He was clearly irked by the fact that his next brother, William III (1791-1838), was his senior in the 58th Regiment by volunteering from school and takes every opportunity to decry his service on base duties in Portugal. He seems to have preferred the next brother, Charles II, (1792-1872), who followed his uncle, Charles I, into Glyn Mills, becoming a Baronet, since he entrusted him with all his finances.

JM's father purchased for him a commission as an Ensign in the 2nd or Coldstream Guards on December 21st 1809. There he would have been trained by a Drill Sergeant until passed fit to carry out simple guard and other duties at St James's Palace under the eye of the Adjutant. In December 1810 he received orders to proceed with a draft of Coldstreamers to Lisbon. At this time Wellington was holding the nearby Lines of Torres Vedras while, until February 1811, Marshal Massena was struggling to maintain his starving army in a land laid waste by both sides.

A marked difference between the letters and diaries of officers in the two World Wars and those of JM from the Peninsula is that no guardsman, except his soldier servant, is mentioned by name. This derives not from any aloofness on his part; years later he was writing warmly to the young keeper friend, Daniel, of his boyhood, offering him his fare to visit Bisterne from the Midlands. Indeed, he spent many nights in bivouac with the guardsmen of the 5th Company, 1st Battalion Coldstream Guards, but the then organisation of the infantry and the duties assigned an Ensign allowed no permanent relationship with them. The 95th and 5/60th, deployed in small parties of riflemen on the outposts, had necessarily started to develop a platoon organisation; otherwise the infantry normally fought in mass. A battalion consisted of ten companies, of which only the light company was detached to support the 5/60th Riflemen. The captain commanding a company was responsible to the commanding officer for every aspect of its administration and tactical command. Although it could be temporarily divided into two halves, one under his lieutenant, the ensigns had no specific responsibilities for the care of soldiers.

The reader will note that JM is from time to time assigned a party of men, never the same ones, to command for a specific task. These included night picquets to give warning, and work on trenches or protection of those working, usually at night, in a siege as at Ciudad Rodrigo and Burgos; at Fuentes de Oñoro he commanded a burial party which allowed him to use his French on Massena's officers, similarly employed. At the attempted storming of Burgos he was allotted fifty men to command with scaling ladders and no doubt, as the surviving officer, gave the order to withdraw.

Lack of forage forced armies, deprived of fodder for cavalry or artillery horses, mules and oxen, to spend long months in winter quarters. The Guardsmen were no doubt delighted to rest and stay warm in their billets, mending and cleaning their kit under their NCOs, after exhausting summer marches. JM could thus easily obtain leave to go shooting for the company officers' mess or to canter off on his horse 'Docktail' to races, hunts, games of cards, billiards, balls and dinner parties.

These social contacts will be useful to him at Almack's or White's Club after the war, but we see them becoming tedious in his second year overseas. The thrusting young officer, who goes forward to snipe the French, besieged in the forts at Salamanca, becomes bitter at the waste of life and failure at Burgos and even cynical about Wellington's leadership and motives. He is heartily glad to be posted back to home duties. The final letters from Holland in 1813 and 1814 see him well content to remain in warm billets and it was indeed the extreme cold which saw him invalided back, probably with pneumonia. Otherwise our story might have ended in the ruins of Hougoumont.

In the Epilogue we shall trace his development from regency dandy to a responsible Hampshire country gentleman.

Major John Micklethwait Mills
OBE, DL

Major General Giles Hallam Mills,
CB, CVO, OBE.

Introduction

On May 28th 1812, Ensign John Mills, of the 1st Battalion Coldstream Guards, came in from the fiery Portuguese sun and sat down at his portable writing desk in his quarters at Castello de Vide, a few miles north of Portalegre. After dipping his quill into the ink which he made from wine mixed with gunpowder, he began to write a letter to his mother in England. Towards the end of the letter he drew her attention to a book by Captain William Stothert, of the 3rd Foot Guards, which had recently been printed in England and which was a narrative of the campaigns of 1809, 1810 and 1811. 'I am told it is a miserable performance', he wrote, and went on to add, 'I keep a private diary myself, merely to mark the day. Some years hence I shall look over it with pleasure.' It might amuse John Mills, or JM as we shall call him, that today, some 184 years on, his letters and diaries, written beneath the blistering heat of the Iberian sun or on a wet November day on the road from Burgos, were being scrutinised by a generation of military historians seeking to discover what life was really like behind the mask of martial magnificence that was Wellington's campaign in the Peninsula between 1808 and 1814.

Of course, Peninsular War memoirs are plentiful enough although in recent years good, extensive, contemporary memoirs have become few and far between and the Napoleonic student has become used to a diet of facsimiles and reprints. JM's letters and diaries, therefore, represent a refreshing break from this trend and offer us a candid glimpse into the life of a subaltern during one of the British army's most successful campaigns.

The early nineteenth century saw a marked increase in literacy throughout Britain and this has left us a crop of diaries, letters and memoirs the like of which had never been seen before. It is upon these reminiscences that we base a great deal of our research into the Napoleonic Wars. As far as Britain was concerned the bulk of these memoirs naturally allude to the Peninsular War, it being a tale of triumph for the British army for the greater part of its six years duration. However, many of the memoirs have to be used with care owing to the fact that they were written many years afterwards, not only with the benefit of hindsight but also when the memory had began to blur somewhat. Some were dictated to be written up by a third party while some were edited many years after, either by a third party or by a member of the correspondent's family. Here, we come across another problem as, with the benefit of hindsight, some editors, keen to place their ancestor's deeds in greater light, were apt to bend the truth slightly.

Much of this has to do with the appearance in the mid-1830s of Napier's

History of the War in the Peninsula, surely one of the great works of English literature. Napier, an eye-witness himself with the 43rd Light Infantry, brought the war to life for thousands of avid readers, prompting scores of veterans, who realised they had lived through something very special, to put pen to paper recalling their own experiences. Naturally enough, Napier's work induced many veterans, whose own recollections had begun to fade, to believe that they actually saw or took part in many of the events described by him, which was not always the case.

To understand this we have to appreciate that during the Peninsular War one of the main sources of information for those soldiers who could read was the English press whose news in turn derived usually from Wellington's own despatches. Now, for the ordinary soldier who had little time or inclination to digest the events taking place around him, some battles must surely have blurred into one another. Napier's history unlocked the fading memories of more than a few old soldiers but these memories, in some cases, sadly, were based more upon old yarns spun round the fireside, prompted more by a drop of ale or gin than by personal experience. The subject is dealt with in depth by Sir Charles Oman, in his *Wellington's Army, 1809-1814*, where he quite accurately describes these veterans' 'artless tales' as having, 'all the characteristics of the memoirs of the prince of their tribe — the delightful but autolatrous Marbot.'[1] As for those memoirs written up after the war, Oman also makes the point that, 'an officer writing of Corunna or Talavera with the memory of Vittoria and Waterloo upon him, necessarily took up a different view of the war from the man who set down his early campaign without any idea of what was to follow.' One of JM's comrades, John Stepney Cowell, was one of the former kind. His *Leaves from the Diary of an Officer of the Guards* is a wonderful book, full of anecdotes and vignettes of campaign life in Spain and Portugal. But when one comes across him referring to events such as Waterloo it puts the work into perspective as being a rather retrospective look at the war.[2] Even some of the best memoirs, such as Grattan's *Adventures with the Connaught Rangers*, need a degree of care as Grattan is often to be found describing events to which he was not a witness. At the storming of Badajoz, on April 6th 1812, he describes the assault on the breaches by the 4th and Light Divisions and the escalade of the San Vincente bastion by Leith's 5th Division whereas his own unit was engaged at the time in escalading the castle. In fact, Grattan may not have seen any of these for he himself was wounded whilst in the act of attempting to blow up the dam at the San Roque. Grattan claims this happened at around 2am on April 7th, after the castle had fallen, but it is quite possible that, having been detailed to blow up the dam, he did not take part in the main attack on the castle itself.[3]

Another problem when dealing with Peninsular War memoirs is that few correspondents were willing to level any criticism at any former comrade still

[1] Oman, *Wellington's Army, 1809-1814*, p.3. Baron Marbot was the bragging, exaggerating and often inaccurate hero of his own memoirs. It is said that Conan Doyle based his *Adventures of Gerard* novels upon him.

[2] John Stepney Cowell's *Leaves from the Diary of an Officer of the Guards*, was published in London in 1854.

[3] Grattan, *Adventures with the Connaught Rangers, 1809-1814*, p.205.

living whilst any criticism of Wellington was almost unheard of. From the moment of his great triumph at Salamanca until his death some forty years later, Wellington's influence on British society was immeasurable, whether it be as commander of the forces, as a politician or merely as elder statesman. If a problem arose whether it be political, military or even how to rid the Great Exhibition building of unwanted sparrows, it was not unusual for the advice of the great Duke to be sought. Not all of this influence and guidance was for the good, however, as the Duke set himself firmly against reform, something which, for example, held the progress of the British army in check. Indeed, when Wellington died the army is said to have breathed a great sigh of relief, as if it could 'get on with its job' without interference from the great old man. This legacy became sadly apparent two years later when Britain's army, still to emerge from the Duke's shadow, suffered an almost total breakdown during the cold, bleak winter landscapes of the Crimea.

A small, but perhaps significant pointer to attitudes in the army in post-Wellington Britain, can be gauged by a look in the Army Lists of the period. As anyone who has consulted these volumes will know, the era of the mid-nineteenth century carried biographies of officers with extensive military careers. It is worth noting how certain criticisms of Wellington, absent in many pre-1852 biographies, begin to creep in after his death. As we shall see, JM was certainly not one to hold back when criticising Wellington, particularly after Burgos. 'If ever a man ruined himself,' he wrote, 'the Marquis has done it; for the last two months he has acted like a madman.' Beresford is called 'the most noted bungler that ever played at the game of soldiers' and later 'a military delinquent', following his handling of the battle of Albuera.

With these points in mind any letters that were written on campaign become all the more important as accurate reflections of events and attitudes of the day. JM's diary kept during the Peninsular War lists everything from the lengths of marches, to battles and sieges, to the local agriculture, people, the guerrillas, and his thoughts on Wellington and other Allied commanders. As far as JM was concerned the war was changing from one day to the next. He was not writing with the benefit of hindsight. One day Wellington is all-conquering, the next he is an ass. On another occasion, the British army has all but defeated the French but on the next there seems no hope at all and an evacuation appears likely.

The letters and diaries appear almost exactly as they were written by JM whilst on campaign. Naturally, the punctuation has been altered slightly to improve the flow of the story although care has been taken to avoid too many changes. As with many writers of the period commas and full-stops were in short supply, and they chose instead to employ scores of dashes throughout their correspondence. I have also sought to standardise place names. For example the village of Nave de Haver appeared as 'Nave de Haver', 'Naval de Azar' and 'Navi di Avil'. Elsewhere, I have inserted — very occasionally — names within square brackets in order to clarify a statement. Other than these few points, JM's correspondence appears as it was written. The letters have been arranged to fall chronologically into the diaries. As such, many of them repeat what JM had written in his diary but with a great deal of expansion. This again gives them a sense of immediacy as he recounts to his relatives and friends the events that were unfolding around him, often correcting in his letters entries made in his diaries as a result of hearing more news on the particular event. It also illustrates the subtle difference between the letters and the diaries. It is easy to imagine JM writing entries in his diary, often hurriedly, as can be judged from some written during the siege of Burgos or during the retreat from there, but mainly at the end of the day, perhaps while on picquet duty. Compare this with the apparently easy pace at which the letters are written, probably while off duty in the comfort of his quarters.

JM had been commissioned as an ensign in the Coldstream Guards on December 21st 1809. The 1st Battalion of his regiment had fought at Talavera five months earlier, on July 27th-28th, and, while it passed away the winter months on the Portuguese-Spanish border, JM began a year-long period of training as an officer in His Britannic Majesty's regiment of Coldstream Guards.

The regiment had a long and distinguished history dating back to 1650. In fact, its origins give grounds for its claim to be the oldest regiment in the British regular army, claims imbued perhaps in the regimental motto, Nulli Secondus, 'second to none'. The regiment had seen active service in the Dutch wars of 1665 and 1672, a company had been sent to Tangier in 1680, while the 18th century had seen the Coldstream fighting at Gibraltar and in the wars of Spanish and Austrian Succession, as well as the Seven Years War. During the latter part of the century the Coldstream had seen action in America during the War of Independence and in the Low Countries at the start of the Napoleonic Wars, while the early years of the 19th century saw the Coldstream fighting in Egypt and at Copenhagen.

When the Peninsular War broke out in 1808 the men of the Coldstream Guards found themselves kicking their heels in frustration as other regiments were sent to Portugal. This was probably a blessing, however, because following Sir Arthur Wellesley's victories at Roliça and Vimeiro in August 1808 two senior British officers arrived to concoct the now notorious Convention of Cintra, which allowed the defeated French troops of Junot to escape with their arms and equipment and with all accumulated plunder. To rub salt into the wound, the French troops were conveyed out of Portugal in the ships of the Royal Navy. Wellesley was recalled and the British army placed under the command of Sir John Moore who soon afterwards found himself in the midst of the terrible retreat to Corunna. The Coldstream Guards were thus spared the harrowing ordeal endured by the British army which by now included the 1st Foot Guards who had arrived in the Peninsula in September 1808.

The 1st Battalion Coldstream Guards finally sailed from England on January 15th 1809 with a strength of 33 officers and 1,120 rank and file,[1] as well as 17 women who had been lucky enough to be allowed to accompany their husbands to Spain. The journey was an eventful one, however, as a series of storms forced the transports to seek shelter at Cork. It was not until February 25th that the fleet finally resumed its voyage, arriving at Lisbon on March 13th. The light

[1] Mackinnon, *Origin and Services of the Coldstream Guards*, II, 103.

company of the battalion did not arrive until April 6th having been driven into Waterford by the storms. Upon arrival, the battalion was brigaded with the 1st Battalion 3rd Foot Guards in the 1st Division of Wellesley's army, along with some companies of the 5/60th Royal Americans, a crack unit armed with Baker rifles which acted as skirmishers on the fringes of the 1st Division.

It was not long before the Coldstream saw action, at the crossing of the Douro on May 12th 1809 and at Salamonde four days later when the Guards came up with and attacked the rearguard of Soult's retreating French army. The Coldstream fought its first major battle at Talavera on July 27th-28th 1809 at which it suffered casualties of 3 officers and 33 men killed and 10 officers and 253 men wounded. There were to be no further actions for another fourteen months as Wellington's army kept its vigil on the Portuguese border in anticipation of Massena's invasion. The French finally broke through in the summer of 1810, prompting Wellington to begin his withdrawal to the Lines of Torres Vedras, stopping only to fight at Busaco along the way on September 27th 1810. The Coldstreamers were present at the battle but did not take part in any of the fighting. The retreat finally ended when Wellington's army withdrew into the Lines themselves to sit and watch while Massena's army starved in front of them.

It was during the year-long period between the Christmases of 1809 and 1810 that JM was learning not only the art of soldiering but also how to conduct himself in the most prestigious corps of fighting men in the British army, the Foot Guards, dubbed 'The Gentlemen's Sons' by the rest of Wellington's army in the Peninsula. The nickname 'The Gentlemen's Sons' derived, of course, from the predominance of titled officers and sons of the landed gentry amongst the Guards regiments for when it came to the composition of the officer corps the Guards were unrivalled. They came only from the higher echelons of society, from the landed gentry and from the families of successful merchants and tradesmen.[1] Of all the titled officers serving in the British army at the outbreak of the Peninsular War, either in the cavalry and infantry, nearly a third could be found in the three regiments of Foot Guards.[2]

That only the well-connected or titled could afford to join this socially exclusive military assembly was reflected in the high prices paid for commissions in the Guards. When JM's father bought him an ensigncy in the Coldstream he would have paid well above the asking price for the equivalent rank in a Line regiment. For example, in the Guards, a lieutenant-colonelcy cost £6,700, a majority £6,300, a captaincy £3,500 and a lieutenancy £1,500. The equivalent ranks in the Line regiments would cost £3,500, £2,600, £1,500 and £550 respectively. The rates of pay differed in similar fashion. A major in the Foot Guards received £1 4s 6d per day, a captain 16s 6d, and a lieutenant 7s 10d. Their

---

[1] The term 'tradesmen' should not be confused with the present-day meaning of the word. By definition, a tradesman in the early part of the nineteenth century might be a banker, a lawyer or an accountant.

[2] Fortescue, *A History of the British Army*, X, 205. According to Fortescue's figures, there were 2 officers bearing hereditary or courtesy titles in the Household Cavalry, 29 in the Line Cavalry, 3 in the Royal Engineers and Royal Artillery, 49 in the Foot Guards and 75 in the Line Infantry regiments.

equivalents in the Line regiments received 16s, 10s 6d, and 6s 6d per day.[1]

When JM joined the Coldstream Guards one of his first priorities would have been the purchase not only his service uniform but also his undress uniform and his full dress uniform, worn to the various functions held at Windsor or St James's and at parades such as Trooping the Colour. These uniforms were paid for by the officers themselves with no recompense from the government. JM's full dress uniform consisted of a long tailed scarlet coat with a scarlet collar laced with gold all round. The coat had dark blue lapels with broad gold lace button-holes or loops which were spaced in pairs in the Coldstream fashion. The cuffs were dark blue and had two bands of gold lace around them. The turnbacks were of white kerseymere and were laced and edged in dark blue with embroidered skirt ornaments. The respective regimental star was set in a half-wreath of laurel on blue cloth.

JM's second uniform was his undress uniform, a plain scarlet coat with dark blue lapels, collar and cuffs. The dark blue lapels were laced all round in gold, the collar likewise. The cuffs were round and also edged with gold lace. Like all Guards officers' coats, the buttons were at regimental spacing on the lapels which was, for the Coldstream, in pairs. The skirts of the coat had laced diamond decorations at the hips, the pockets were laced gold all round with gold and the turnbacks were of white kerseymere edged gold with sycamore seed shaped blue patches upon which were embroidered sprays of palm leaves.

The third uniform was the service dress, worn on campaign. This was in effect a version of the undress coat. The jacket was scarlet with dark blue lapels, collar and cuffs, all edged with gold lace. The buttons were of regimental spacing, in pairs, and the regimental star was used as skirt ornaments. Up until 1812 the officers of the light infantry company wore short skirted jackets, the coat up until 1812 having long skirts. However, after this date short skirts were introduced for all officers which, judging from JM's reaction, was met with some apprehension; 'We are all in consternation at the idea of the dress of the army being altered from cocked hats and coats to caps and jackets. Ye heavens, what will become of crooked legs, large heads, and still larger hinder parts?'

This reference to caps refers to the change in alteration in headdress for when JM joined the Coldstream Guards officers still wore the bicorn or cocked hat for full dress, undress and service dress. Worn 'fore and aft' the hat was made from felt, had gold edging and tassels although on active service the edging was of black tape. Plumes were of cut feathers, colours as for infantry shakos, and were secured by a small black cockade with a gold lace loop running down from it. However, in 1812 officers of all regiments of the army were expected to wear the 'stove-pipe' shako, already worn by other ranks and light infantry officers. Introduced in 1806, the shako was cylindrical in shape and was made of strong felt. The shako plate was brass and bore the Royal Cypher within the garter, the Crown above, the Royal Lion below and trophies on either side. The officers wore cut feather plumes on their shakos, the colours being the same as the Line regiments which, in JM's case, was white over red for a battalion company.

[1] Haythornthwaite, *Wellington's Military Machine*, p.26.

JM would also have worn a single breasted waistcoat of white face cloth with a high collar and short skirts, two pockets with outside flaps and three or four buttons at the hip. As an ensign, he would have worn a single gold epaulette on his right shoulder with the garter star embroidered upon it. His sash was made of crimson silk and was 6 inches wide and some 7 feet 4 inches long, with a 10-inch tassel fringe.

On campaign Wellington's men wore grey-blue trousers, usually over half boots with a grey strap under the instep, while during the summer months many took to wearing white trousers. Many officers wore blue-grey overalls, reinforced around the bottoms with leather cuffs. White kerseymere breeches also saw widespread use. At Court, or on full dress parade, white silk stockings were worn with shoes or, alternatively, white linen gaiters with black buttons and strap and a buckle below the knee. The gaiters reached 4 inches above the knee. JM had a variety of boots to choose from, such as Hessian boots, hussar boots, top boots or half boots. Given his country background JM may have opted for top boots.

His white leather shoulder belt was fastened with a very attractive gilt plate bearing the regimental badge. When on duty a gilt gorget was worn also, bearing the Royal coat of arms with the Coldstream regimental badge on either side while the gorget itself was decorated with two dark blue rosettes.

When JM arrived in the Peninsula in 1811 he found himself posted to the 5th Company of the battalion which was significant in that, although he makes no mention of it, he may have held either of the regiment's two Colours at some point, it being placed between the 4th and 5th companies. The Colours of an infantry regiment were its greatest possessions, serving not only as a rallying point in the heat of battle but also as the symbol of regimental pride in which was embodied the spirit of the regiment. To lose one's Colours to the enemy was as great a disaster as a regiment could suffer and to ensure maximum protection the Colours were held by an ensign who was in turn guarded by two sergeants. The Colour itself measured 6 feet 6 inches wide by 6 feet deep and was mounted on a pike 9 feet 10 inches long. On the top of the pike was a spearhead and a metal ferrule. In a strong wind it required great strength to hold it upright, the more so since the ensigns carrying them were generally fairly young men. In order to combat this, therefore, a good deal of the Colour would have been wound round the pike.

The Coldstream Guards, like all British infantry regiments, had two Colours, namely, the King's Colour and the Regimental Colour, the latter having the regiment's battle honours upon it. When JM joined his battalion in Portugal in April 1811 he would have found the Regimental Colour bearing the honour 'Egypt', awarded after the Egyptian Campaign of 1801. The Coldstream Guards were awarded the battle honour in 1807 and a Sphinx was added to the Colour. The Sphinx was silver, and was mounted on a plinth inscribed with Egyptian hieroglyphics within a circular wreath of golden laurels with red berries. Between the tips of the wreath was the word, 'Egypt', in gold roman capitals. On June 20th 1811, shortly after JM's arrival, the Coldstream Guards were awarded the battle honour 'Lincelles' but, like the honours 'Talavera' and Barrosa' which were awarded on February 12th 1812, it was not added to the Colour until 1814 by which time the war was over.

JM's period of training at home would have involved much drilling, based upon the 1792 *Rules and Regulations for the Formations, Field Exercise, and Movements of His Majesty's Forces*, written by Colonel (later General Sir) David Dundas. The battalion was the unit upon which all training centred, it being divided into ten companies; eight centre or battalion companies, one grenadier company and one light company. Each battalion was commanded by a lieutenant colonel. There were also two majors per battalion, ten captains, one to each company, and 20 subalterns, half of them being ensigns and the others being lieutenant-captains. These lieutenant-captains were the result of a peculiarity of the Foot Guards known as 'double-ranking' whereby the officers of the Guards held both regimental and army ranks. This dated back to 1687, when a captain in the Guards was ranked as a lieutenant colonel, and to 1691, when lieutenants in the Guards were ranked as captains. This meant, of course, that a captain in the Guards could exchange into a Line regiment as a lieutenant colonel.

During his period of training JM would have come to terms with the normal marching rate, known as the 'ordinary step' which was 70 paces per minute of 30 inch length. The 'quick step' was 108 paces, also of 30 inches length, used when deploying from column into line and vice versa. This was the step used on the parade ground. The quickest step was used mainly for wheeling or making up time and was 120 paces per minute, each of 20 inches length. He would also have learned to use the standard British infantry weapon of the age, the 'Brown Bess' musket. This musket, with a 42-inch barrel and firing a .75 calibre ball weighed 10lbs 4½ ounces and involved a number of movements before it could be fired which, for a trained soldier, could be three times a minute. Clumsy to load and slow to fire, this musket nevertheless swept the French from many a dusty battlefield in the Peninsula. It was a weapon which JM would rarely have used on campaign, if at all, but being the sportsman that he was, he did have his own sporting gun which he used to supplement his often meagre rations. And during the siege of the forts at Salamanca he went forward into advanced positions with other officers and took pot shots at the French defenders.

The weapon which JM would have carried with him throughout the Peninsula was the 1796-pattern infantry officers' sword. This most elegant-looking sword had a straight blade measuring 32 inches, a brass knuckle-bow guard, a ball pommel and side shells, all gilded, and a grip bound with silver wire. He would have carried it in a black leather scabbard with brass mounts either in frogs or on slings.

The cost of all his equipment and his three fine uniforms would have been great enough but, as well as this, JM would have been expected to pay even higher mess bills during the course of a year, all of which necessitated the need for a considerable private income. Then there were the London clubs, fashionable haunts of the rich, famous and powerful that became meeting places for the Guards. Amongst the most prominent were White's, Boodle's, Brooks's, Arthur's and Graham's. Here, the Guards mixed with politicians and socialites, indulging in various card games such as whist, faro and macao. These clubs were concentrated in the west end of London, mainly in the Piccadilly area, and entry into White's in particular was very difficult indeed. As we shall see in the Epilogue of this book, JM's connections with White's extended well beyond his military career. It was an expensive business being an officer in the Guards but in spite of this, however, the clamour for commissions in the Guards was often intense and the rate of purchase the highest in the army.[1]

As with all of Wellington's British troops the Guards were fiercely loyal to their regiments, a loyalty born out of comradeship and of the sharing of the hardships of campaign life. But it was also a loyalty, of course, to king and country that bound the officers of the Guards together in a bond of unrivalled *esprit de corps,* for the aristocratic and land-owning Guards had much to lose should the spectre of republicanism materialise at home in the shape either of Napoleon or of anarchy and revolution. After all, revolution had only recently swept away the aristocracy in France and, with the beheading of Louis XVI, the rest of Europe trembled lest the winds of change blew over their own lands. The legacies of the Industrial Revolution in England had created an undercurrent of revolutionary fervour in Britain, stirred up by the displaced workers, the poor and the homeless, who looked to France for inspiration. Fortunately for Britain, there was an even stronger loyalty to king and country, for the great majority of Britons had no desire to see their green, pleasant and happy land trodden underfoot by the Corsican upstart. Moreover, the many broadsheets and satirists of the day did their job well, providing savage-looking cartoons to a genuinely worried British public illustrating the terrible and disturbing consequences of a successful invasion by Napoleon who was quickly transformed into the greatest bogey man before Hitler this nation has ever known, an ogre whose shadow was cast over the British Isles for nigh on twenty years.[2] It was, therefore, such threats both from without and within that bound the Guards together in a bond of loyalty and allegiance to king, country and regiment at the end of the 18th and beginning of the 19th centuries.

That the officers of the Guards were able to command more respect from their men as a result of their upbringing is borne out by one of the Peninsular War's most lauded diarists, John Kincaid, of the 95th Rifles, who regretted the fact that more aristocratic families of England did not send their sons into the army as they seemed to be able to command more willing obedience from their men with less effort than others. Echoing these thoughts a century later, J.W. Fortescue, the great historian of the British army, went on to say that, 'no one who knows anything of the subject will dispute the advantage which the habit of command, inherited through many generations and acquired in childhood, may confer upon a man.'[3]

[1] Nearly 50% of all commissions in the Foot Guards were bought compared to 17.7% in the Line regiments. See Glover, *Wellington's Army in the Peninsula*, p.86.
[2] For an expert treatment of the British press at the time of Napoleon's threatened invasion the reader should consult Peter Lloyd's *The French Are Coming! The Invasion Scare 1803-05.*
[3] Fortescue, *History of the British Army*, X, 205.

Having availed himself of twelve months' training at the capable hands of the highly-rated NCOs of the Guards[1] JM finally received a posting to the 1st Battalion Coldstream Guards serving in Portugal. He set sail from England in December 1810 with Edward Harvey, fellow Coldstream officer, as well as a draft of the regiment and the following month arrived at Lisbon where, as he says, he remained in anticipation of joining his battalion. However, when it became clear that the Coldstream would not be marching south he set out in company with another young ensign, James Bradshaw, who had joined the Coldstream just two weeks after him. On April 18th 1811 the two young men finally arrived at Puebla where they found their battalion. That night JM dined with Charles White, a fellow ensign who had been with the Coldstream in the Peninsula since December 1809. White would not have 'talked shop', certainly not over dinner, but presumably pointed out the best areas for sport, for the following day JM went out shooting, 'but killed nought'.

Barely three weeks later JM saw his first action, at Fuentes de Oñoro on May 3rd-5th 1811. The battle lasted three days during which the French commander, Marshal Andre Massena, pushed Wellington hard in an effort to relieve the beleaguered French garrison stranded at Almeida. During the battle JM watched as the light companies of the Coldstream Guards and 3rd Foot Guards took the brunt of some fierce fighting on the right of Wellington's line. He appears to have taken the enemy shelling of the Guards in his stride and, as he himself says, 'I never was better in my life.' This would indicate that he had adapted quickly to the hot Portuguese climate which, even in the relatively short time he had been in the country, had tanned him to the colour of, 'a dark boot top.....two degrees darker than mahogany.'

JM's own story of his two years in the Peninsula begins, however, on the long, dusty road from Lisbon to Puebla. The first entry in his diary is dated April 1st and reads, 'Made a fool of; I sent the servants by water to Villa Franca and walked to Saccavem.' We cannot be sure whether the joke was intentional, although I suspect it was, but it does set the tone for the greater part of JM's story, that of a fine, good-humoured young officer, with the instincts of a sportsman in search of his quarry, with an eye for the wildlife and agriculture of the two Iberian countries, but above all with a sense of duty, for King and Country.

[1] Wellington's own views as to the merits of the Guards' NCOs were recorded by the Earl of Stanhope, many years after the war. 'The Guards are superior to the Line, not as being picked men like the French — for Napoleon gave peculiar privileges to his guardsmen and governed the army with them — but from the goodness of the non-commissioned officers. They do in fact all the commissioned officers in the Line are expected to do — and don't do it. This must be as long as the present system lasts — and I am all for it — of having gentlemen for officers; you cannot require them to do many things that should be done. They must not speak to their men for instance — we should reprimand them if they did....Now all that work is done by the non-commissioned officers of the Guards. It is true that they regularly get drunk once a day - by eight in the evening, and go to bed soon after, but then they always took care to do first whatever they were bid. When I had given an officer in the Guards an order, I felt sure of its being executed; but with an officer in the Line, it was, I will venture to say, a hundred to one against its being done at all.' Stanhope, *Notes of Conversations with the Duke of Wellington, 1831-1851*, pp.17-18.

Chapter One

Fuentes de Oñoro

When JM finally caught up with the Coldstream at Puebla he did so at a time when the topsy-turvey nature of Wellington's Peninsular campaign had begun to settle down. Wellington had arrived in Portugal in 1808 as Sir Arthur Wellesley but, soon afterwards, saw his victories at Roliça and Vimeiro diminished by the Convention of Cintra. The following year the expulsion from Portugal of Marshal Soult after the victory at Oporto, which Wellesley followed up with his success at Talavera, again had the gloss taken from them somewhat by the subsequent retreat to Portugal. The period between the battles of Talavera — after which Wellesley was created Lord Wellington — and Busaco and, in fact, right up until Massena's eventual withdrawal from in front of the Lines of Torres Vedras in November 1810, was one of the most difficult of the war for Wellington as the clamours for a return to England grew ever louder in his ears. There was much 'croaking' even in his own camp amongst his officers who saw no point in remaining in the hot, uncomfortable country any longer than was necessary. Fortunately, Wellington decided, and convinced his government, that it was indeed necessary to remain and was to prove his point over the next four years of almost unbroken success. The tide had begun to turn in Wellington's favour in October 1810 when Massena's army arrived in front of the Lines of Torres Vedras. These Lines had been constructed in secret the previous year and consisted of a series of natural barriers, hillforts and redoubts, most of which were mutually supporting. The forts were manned by Portuguese militia and by other auxiliary forces while the regular troops remained within the Lines, ready to be brought to any point being threatened by the French at any given time. The French made no serious effort to break through, however and, while Wellington's troops remained on the alert in their camps, well fed and supplied through Lisbon by the ships of the Royal Navy, Massena's disheartened and demoralised troops starved as they stared in bewilderment at the impenetrable obstacles constructed in front of them. By March 1811 Massena had finally had enough and he began his retreat to Spain, followed all the way by Wellington's men who hustled and harried the French rearguard all the way to the Spanish frontier. The French troops exacted a terrible retribution on the Portuguese people as whole villages were burned to the ground and their inhabitants slaughtered. This trail of devastation was seen by JM as he made his way to Puebla, which he finally reached on April 18th. Just three weeks later he found himself in the midst of his first battle, Fuentes de Oñoro, which marked Massena's desperate attempt to relieve the French garrison at Almeida. JM's story begins here, just prior to the battle, on the road to join his regiment.

April 1st. Made a fool of; I sent the servants by water to Villa Franca and walked to Saccavem.

April 2nd. To Azambuja through Villa Franca. Missed my servants and baggage. Got some chocolate at a Pot house then went forward. I was more surprised than pleased at hearing of my baggage that night. Dined with Colonel Fuller. Slept on the floor.

April 3rd. Rode over to Alcoentre in hopes of finding my baggage as that place is on the road to Coimbra, which road I thought they had taken. I heard nothing of them and returned to Azambuja. Wild scenery.

April 4th. Intended to have remained, but at 12 o'clock the German Light Brigade[1] came in and as General Alten seemed to wish for our quarters, Bradshaw and myself walked to Cartaxo. I got quarters at the Signal House.[2] Tried to prig an ass but would not do.[3]

April 5th. To Santarem. I wandered about in search of the Juis de Tora, who gave me a wretched billet. Not hearing any tidings of our baggage, Bradshaw bought a pony and we set off for Pernes. Our baggage consisted of a valise with two shirts, 2 stockings, a haversack with some chocolate, 6 cakes of soup. Got to Pernes after dark. Bad road. Found a hospitable priest. Played baggaman with a suckling pig[4] and beat him. Soup for supper, salt fish, rice dressed with butter. Two good beds. NB — always remember his kindness.

April 6th. To Thomar, through Torres Novas — 27 miles. The road is much cut up by the army that advanced. There are dead horses in numbers. Large convent at the entrance to Thomar which is a fine town. I found Fuller and dined with him. A Commissary introduced us to a lawyer who gave a bed between Bradshaw and myself.

April 7th. To Abacos 16m. A very bad road. It is a miserable place, and I almost starved. Some of the Regiment of Guides[5] turned out. Fine scenery. Springs of

[1] This 'brigade' consisted of the 1st and 2nd Light Battalions, King's German Legion, which had landed at Lisbon on March 21st. The two battalions were to form part of the newly formed 7th Division. The brigade was commanded by Charles Alten. See Oman, *Wellington's Army, 1809-1814*, p.357.

[2] This Signal House, as JM calls it, may possibly have been one of the old medieval *atalaias*, or watchtowers, that were used as semaphore stations. These telegraph stations were used extensively during the Peninsular War by Wellington and proved most effective except in bad weather when the signals were obscured. See Ward's, *Wellington's Headquarters*, pp.126-128.

[3] ie to steal a donkey. Most officers, even junior ones, soon found themselves in need of more than a donkey or two on which to transport their baggage. As we shall see, JM soon acquired quite a sizeable collection of animals for himself. Such were the numbers of these horses and donkeys that Wellington was forced to restrict each subaltern to just one each, a rule that was flouted with temerity by the Guards. (See also JM's Journal, June 13th 1811).

[4] A 'suckling pig' was a 19th century description of a naive fellow.

[5] The Corps of Guides was a small body of men raised by the Quartermaster General for the purpose of acting as interpreters and guides. By the end of the war, however, the corps was also involved in the gathering and transmission of intelligence, and even in the preparation of maps. In June 1809 Wellesley had written, 'I have been endeavouring to form a corps of guides — that is to say, one of officers and non-commissioned officers, who should be interpreters between our people and those of the

water, bathed in the evening. Slept on a bench.

April 8th. To Espinhal. Road tolerable. It rained a little. Espinhal is a good town but a little destroyed. Got good quarters in a library.

April 9th. To Ponte de Murcello. Walked. We did not set off till 11 o'clock as it rained. Road mountainous, the scenery bold and fine. We intended to go to St Michael de Rogans, but found ourselves at St Philip of the same name and then were obliged to go on to Ponte de Murcello. Near that place we crossed the end of the Sierra and the bridge being broken, crossed the Elva by a bridge of boats. About two miles before we came to Foz de Pograno, we passed over the river Sierra by a bridge of boats, the French having broken that one too. The village was called Foz d'Arouce. We saw great quantities of dead jackasses which the French had killed. They lost a great number of men here in passing the river. In this day's march and in the preceding and subsequent ones, we saw vast quantities of dead horses.[1] Got to Ponte de Murcello at eight o'clock, dark. Ate some bread and cheese and slept in the corner of a very dirty room.

April 10th. To Riba on the Mondego. Rainy day. Went to Moita, but not finding a Commissary turned about and went two miles back to Riba. The stores for the army come up there. We saw three hundred carts loaded with bread and corn. The village being full of stores, I got a quarter on the hill. Turned out a guide

---

country, who must show them their roads. We have got some officers, but we want non-commissioned officers. I shall be very much obliged to you if you will allow us to have José Bannas, corporal in the 2nd company of grenadiers of the 13th Regiment, and eight or ten sergeants, corporals, or steady soldiers, men of good character, who can speak either English or French, to make of them sergeants or corporals of guides. They will have with us the pay and allowances of British cavalry.' (*Despatches*, Wellesley to Beresford, 2nd June 1809, IV, 356). The corps was raised by the master cypher breaker, George Scovell, in September 1808 and served throughout the Corunna campaign. The corps was re-formed again in May 1809 with a strength of 8 officers and 34 NCOs and men, and by the beginning of the Vittoria campaign had grown to 12 officers and 193 NCOs and men and, as well as British and Portuguese, numbered amongst its ranks French deserters and Spanish guerrillas. Scovell, commanding the Guides, was also in charge of the Military Post Office. (See also Ward, *Wellington's Headquarters*, pp.125-126).

[1] When Massena's army retreated from Santarem following its failure to penetrate the Lines of Torres Vedras it left in its wake a trail of devastation and ruin, the path of the French retreat being marked by the smouldering remains of Portuguese villages. Added to these were the dead bodies of hundreds of Portuguese peasants who had died at the hands of Massena's murderous soldiers. Captain William Stothert, of the 3rd Foot Guards, wrote on April 15th 1811, 'The most barbarous excesses were committed by the enemy throughout his whole line of march, and the inhabitants, who from age or sickness, were unable to quit their houses, became victims to the horrid brutality of the French soldiery. There is no atrocity of which these unprincipled ruffians have not been guilty; every crime that stains the black catalogue of human cruelty having been committed on the persons and property of the poor wretches who had the misfortune to fall into their hands. The prospect before the advanced guard, was always that of burning villages, of plundered cottages, of murdered peasants. The roads were covered with the dying and the dead — with cannon, baggage and ammunition, which the enemy could not carry off; with mutilated cattle, with everything, in short, that could create horror and disgust, that could make the heart feel sentiments of indignation against the barbarous enemy, and of pity for the suffering and ravaged natives.' (Stothert, *A Narrative of the Principal Events of the Campaigns of 1809, 1810 and 1811 in Spain and Portugal*, pp.240-241.)

who said he was a Volunteer.[1] However, he being civil, we let him share our house. We got some meat for the first time since leaving Thomar.

April 11th. To a village out of the road, a league from Moita. The farmer was very civil.

April 12th. To Naveira. I saw two hundred French prisoners who had been taken at Sabugal.[2] They complained of their army not having been paid for 13 months. They told us of the birth of the King of Rome.[3]

April 13th. To Lambego. Country flat. Tolerable quarters.

April 14th. To Celorico. Got quarters at Lord Wellington's. The town is somewhat less destroyed than I expected. We heard of our baggage being at Coimbra, and determined to wait for it. It is a large town, but irregularly built.

April 15th. Halted. Bathed in the river. The weather is extremely hot. Branch came up on his way to Lisbon.

April 16th. Halted. As the baggage is not coming up, I fixed to set off the next day. Slept all the time here in some old tapestry, which made a good bed.

April 17th. To a village, a league beyond Guarda. The country between Celorico and Guarda is very fine and rich. There is a tremendous hill before we got to Guarda, which we ascended by a diagonal road about a mile in height. Guarda is a place of great strength, rocky ground on all sides and entered by a gateway, but not fortified. The rain obliged us to take shelter in a desolate village. I was obliged to sit up, the house being so small. A man stole every inch he had.

[1] Volunteers were, in effect, 'gentlemen rankers' who came out to the Peninsula at their own risk and served in the ranks of any given battalion on the chance of being gazetted to it without purchase. They were armed with muskets but wore better quality uniforms than the rank and file and messed with the regular officers of the battalion. One such notable 'volunteer' was George Hennell, of the 43rd Light Infantry, whose letters appeared under the editorship of Michael Glover as, *A Gentlemen Volunteer: The Letters of George Hennell from the Peninsular War, 1812-13*.

[2] The battle at Sabugal was the last in a series of actions that took place during Massena's retreat. Fought on April 3rd 1811, and involving the Light Division, it was later described by Wellington as, 'one of the most glorious actions British troops were ever engaged in.' This, however, was no thanks to Sir William Erskine, commanding the Light Division in Robert Craufurd's absence. Massena occupied a position behind the Coa river with Reynier's corps, some three divisions strong, positioned at Sabugal. The Light Division was ordered to attack Reynier, on the French left flank, but amidst a dense fog Erskine led part of the Light Division too far to the east leaving the rest of the division groping in the fog. Both brigades of the Light Division eventually emerged only to find themselves in the midst of Reynier's three divisions and heavy fighting ensued. Erskine played little part in the battle, the fighting being handled by the division's fine battalion commanders. At one point Sydney Beckwith's brigade took on all three enemy divisions and for a while pushed them back. When Reynier spotted the rest of the Allied force through the fog he withdrew having suffered 760 casualties. The Light Division lost just 179 men. Wellington was driven to despair by the bungling Erskine who had been foisted on him by the Horse Guards and who was generally regarded as being insane. Indeed, he committed suicide in 1813.

[3] Napoleon's son, Napoleon-François-Charles-Joseph, Prince Imperial, King of Rome and Duke of Reichstadt, was born on March 20th 1811. His birth was greeted in Paris with a 101-gun salute. He later became an officer in the Austrian army. He died in 1832.

April 18th. To Puebla, where I found the Regiment.[1] I dined with White, and was happy to arrive at the end of my journey.
April 19th. Halted. Went out shooting but killed nought. April 20th. Halted. April 21st. Halted. My baggage came up.

Puebla, on the frontier of Spain,
21st April 1811.

My Dearest Mother,

At length we have got to the place of our destination. We set out from Lisbon on the 31st of March. The next day our servants who were with our baggage, mistook their way, and Bradshaw and myself had to fight our way here without anything in the world but a shirt apiece, besides the things we had on. We are in hourly expectation of their arrival as we have heard of them upon the road. They went by way of Coimbra, we went by another route. We stayed at Lisbon longer than we imagined, in expectation of the army halting. When we found that not probable we proceeded in chase of them.

At Lisbon I met with Wheler Hood, who was particularly kind to me. He is now coming up to the army. We did propose coming together, but I was obliged to set off sooner than I expected. We spent our time pleasantly enough at Lisbon. Being Lent it had a sombre appearance. The Opera was open twice a week for the performance of a serious opera. There was no good woman singer, and but one fine man. After the Opera there was a Ballet the style of which I cannot say I admired. It consisted chiefly of men dressed in large trousers, who jumped in the most grotesque way. This the Portuguese think uncommonly fine. Their Opera house is about the same size, but infinitely finer than ours. There is a magnificent Box, the Centre for their Prince Regent, which has a fine effect. It is shockingly lighted. During the ten days I was at Lisbon I seldom dined at home. The Minister, Mr Stuart, makes a point of keeping an open table, to which the English are invited. Desborough is with him and I was surprised to recognise an Oxford acquaintance. I went to one Portuguese Ball, in the style of an English one, that is to say they had English Country dances. I was unfortunate enough to have the honour of the hand of a plump backed Spanish girl; her first debut in the fashionable world, she thought it necessary to attempt the English steps, which were not quite in the style of Mr Jenkins. The Ladies were dressed in the English costume. There are multitudes of English at Lisbon, Officers and others, indeed it somewhat resembles an English colony. Some of the shops are kept by English people, and you generally see, translated into our language, the articles they sell over the door. The Portuguese men all wear snuff coloured great coats, which they put on as cloaks. They are extremely indolent, and as dirty. The women are certainly not pretty nor do the men seem to pay

---

[1] After spending the second week of April 1811 in various camps the 1st Battalion Coldstream Guards 'moved, for the convenience of quarters, to Puebla.' (Mackinnon, *Origin and Services of the Coldstream Guards*, II, 155.)

them much attention. We set out on our way to the army on Sunday the last day of March. We went by way Villa Franca, Azambuja, Cartaxo, Santarem, Pernes, Torres Nova, Thomar, Espinhal, Ponte Murcello, Maceira, Celorico, through Guarda to this place, Puebla, which is about a league in Spain. I assure you we had not a very pleasant journey of it, Bradshaw and myself being almost all the way by ourselves, neither of us understanding the language;[1] we were in bed but twice in the 18 days. The country through which we passed was entirely despoiled. You can form no idea of what a ruined country this is; the houses in the towns and villages are most of them unroofed and not a vestige of anything that can be called furniture in them. They have burned all the houses that will burn, and the others that have no wood in them the French have entirely gutted. When we were upon our journey the inhabitants of the different towns were beginning to return to them from the mountains. They appeared nearly famished — such a scene of distress you cannot imagine.

One division of the French army retreated by the route we came. The rest of their army went by way of Coimbra, though not through that place; for the inhabitants had broken down the bridge. I am inclined to think that the number of prisoners and killed on the part of the French is not so great as is generally represented. At least I know we were told that several hundred had fallen belonging to the division whom we (B and myself) followed. I am sure that they did not lose ten. The other divisions being more closely followed certainly lost more, but two hundred in prisoners and killed until the affair of Sabugal is putting it at the outside.[2]

Lord Wellington is gone into the Alentejo, I hear very much displeased with the operations there. We expect to remain here till Almeida surrenders. There is a report today that it has done so.[3] The French have got several cars

---

[1] The complexities of the Spanish and Portuguese languages appear to have defeated even the most determined of Wellington's officers. Those officers who had daily business with the local people, such as the commissaries, engineers, Staff Corps, etc, would have needed to know a little of the language but the majority seem to have survived in blissful ignorance of it. William Guthrie's *Historical and Commercial Grammar*, published in 1770, provided Wellington's men with a useful guide to the Portuguese language while Mordente's *Spanish Grammar* was a common companion to many officers. The problems faced by Wellington's officers are dealt with extensively in Brett-James's superb *Life in Wellington's Army*, pp.135-144.

[2] Oman estimates Massena's loss to be at around 25,000 men. His strength in September 1810 was 65,050 and on April 15th 1811 was 39,546. Between these two dates he had received two drafts of 3,225 men, and had sent back two columns of sick totalling about 3,000 men. Of Massena's 25,000 casualties, 8,000 were taken prisoner by Wellington in the hospital at Coimbra in October 1810 and a further 2,500 were killed in action. The rest died not by the sword but from hunger. A further 5,872 of Massena's 14,000 horses were lost as well as almost all of his wheeled vehicles. See Oman, *A History of the Peninsular War*, IV, 202-203.

[3] The report of Almeida's surrender was not true. Almeida was a strong fortress on the Portuguese border opposite Ciudad Rodrigo. It was garrisoned by a Portuguese force under the command of a British officer, Lieutenant Colonel William Cox, and was more than adequately stocked with ammunition and provisions. In August 1810 it was besieged by Ney although Wellington was confident that it could hold out for at least a month. However, on August 26th, when the French siege guns opened fire for the first

loaded with provisions into the place before we got there and it must be reduced by starvation, as we have no heavy artillery with us.[1] We are in the advance. The greatest part of the army is in Portugal. You will I am afraid be tired of my writing to you of sieges and armies, but I really have nothing else to tell you of and I am afraid it has not the recommendation of being news, for in London they know much better what is doing than we do.[2] Everything is unreasonably dear here. Bread three shillings a loaf for which in England you would give eighteen pence. English cheese three shillings a pound, their own not eatable. The wine is execrably bad and the roads much the same. I am afraid you will have a good deal of postage to pay for this scrawl.[3] But a private hand is the worst of all hands. I am now messing with Steele. We live very comfortably and get a very good sheep for three dollars. Paulet Mildmay is very well, and I think much grown.

     Your ever affect. Son, John Mills.

April 22nd to 26th. Halted.
April 27th. Moved to Nave de Haver in consequence of information that the enemy were in motion. We remained on the ground some time and then moved back to Almedilla.

time, a shell caused an explosion in the main powder magazine, shattering the town and killing 500 of the defenders. The place surrendered on August 28th and was subsequently garrisoned by a French force under General Antione Francois Brennier.

    [1] JM is only partially correct here and has, perhaps, confused Almeida with Ciudad Rodrigo. It is true that Wellington possessed no guns with which to breach the walls of Almeida, which had been repaired by Brennier, and was left with no other choice but to starve it into submission. However, no convoy managed to penetrate the Allied blockade there. On the other hand, such a convoy did manage to enter Ciudad Rodrigo on April 13th, due entirely to Sir William Erskine who failed to intercept it, much to Wellington's great annoyance. 'Sir William Erskine did not send a detachment over the Agueda in time, as I had desired him, and the consequence was that the French got their convoy into Ciudad Rodrigo yesterday morning.' (*Despatches*, Wellington to Beresford, 14th April 1811, VII, 467). Little wonder, therefore, that when writing to Robert Craufurd upon the latter's return from leave (Erskine was in temporary command of Craufurd's Light Division), an exasperated Wellington said, 'You will find your division on your old quarters, Gallegos, and the sooner you can come up to them the better.' (*Despatches*, Wellington to Craufurd, 14th April 1811, VII, 464).

    [2] Such was the amount of information published in the newspapers at home — the result of letters written by serving officers — that in August 1810 Wellington was forced to issue a General Order, urging the correspondents to refrain from communicating such information as it gave the game away to the enemy. Indeed, it is said that the French gleaned more information from the English press than they did from their own intelligence system, bedeviled as it was by the Spanish and Portuguese guerrillas.

    [3] British troops in the Peninsula enjoyed a concessionary postage rate of one penny per letter. However, scores of letters were sent home without the sender having paid any postage. Indeed, by 1814, when Lisbon ceased to be the postal station for the army, almost £200 was still owing in unpaid postage. From JM's comment it appears that the recipient often paid the postage upon receipt of the letter. For a treatment of Wellington's postal system see, 'The Postal Service of Wellington's Army in the Peninsula and France, 1809-1818.' by Peter B. Boyden, in Alan J. Guy's *The Road to Waterloo*, pp.149-155.

28th to May 1st. Halted.

May 2nd. To Nave de Haver. Bivouacked in an open field.

May 3rd. We remained at Nave de Haver in position until twelve o'clock. Heard some firing, and saw French columns advancing. We moved off to the rising ground opposite to Fuentes de Oñoro and saw the light troops engaged about a mile in our front.[1] Remained under arms till dark. Bivouacked.

May 4th. There was firing at daylight which continued till ten o'clock. About two, I went into the village of Fuentes, close to the French sentries. The town much destroyed and I saw but few dead.[2] Bivouacked.

May 5th. At daylight, we heard three or four shots. At eight o'clock, we moved off about half a mile on our right. The Guards formed the right of the line. We saw the troops engaged in the plain below us. The French cavalry charged the Chasseurs Britanniques,[3] who fired a volley which dispersed them. Our troops then retired in good order, and formed at the left of the line. At ten o'clock, the French guns advanced to about seven hundred yards in our front, and fired grape, canister and round shot till tea. The French cavalry advanced upon us with the intention of charging us. They continued to advance to within two hundred yards of us till the guns in our front fired a volley at them which made them retire. About one, our picquet which had been sent in front to the village of Fuentes came in, attended by some French cavalry, who cut them down

[1] The battle of Fuentes de Oñoro, fought on May 3rd-5th 1811, was ostensibly an attempt by Massena to relieve the beleaguered fortress of Almeida. The village of Fuentes de Oñoro was the centre of Wellington's position and it was here that Massena launched his attack on the afternoon of May 3rd. The Coldstream Guards — part of the 1st Division — occupied a position on the right of the Allied line but saw no real fighting. The action was confined to the village itself which was assaulted with great vigour by Massena whose battalions took the village several times, only to be swept out again after bloody fighting. The light companies, seen by JM, were probably those holding the village. In fact the majority of the 2,260-strong force there were light infantry; the light companies of Nightingale's, Howard's and Löwe's brigades of the 1st Division, and Mackinnon's, Colville's and Power's brigades of the 3rd Division. They were commanded by Colonel Williams of the 5/60th who was seriously wounded during the day.

[2] There was very little fighting on May 4th and, in fact, a truce had been agreed upon in order to allow the dead and wounded to be carried away. During the evening the French held a grand parade while the phlegmatic British sat and watched. As one of Mills' comrades put it, 'The moon rose, the bivouac fires were trimmed, the cigar smoked, and our soldiers sank to rest.' (Cowell, *Leaves from the Diary of an Officer of the Guards*, p.84.)

[3] The regiment of Chasseurs Britanniques was one of the foreign corps serving with Wellington's army. Formed ten years earlier, it consisted largely of former prisoners of war and deserters from the French army. A large proportion were Italians and Swiss while the officers themselves were French royalists. At Fuentes de Oñoro the Chasseurs acquitted themselves well when they unleashed a shattering volley to see off Montbrun's cavalry who were attempting to get in amongst Houston's retreating 7th Division. The Chasseurs, commanded by Lieutenant Colonel Eustace, lost 58 men during the day and were mentioned by Wellington in his despatch. (*Despatches*, Wellington to Lord Liverpool, 8th May 1811, VII, 530.) Unfortunately, it was one of the few occasions where the unit did distinguish itself as it proved largely unreliable. It also had an alarming rate of desertion and as such was never trusted to undertake any outpost duties.

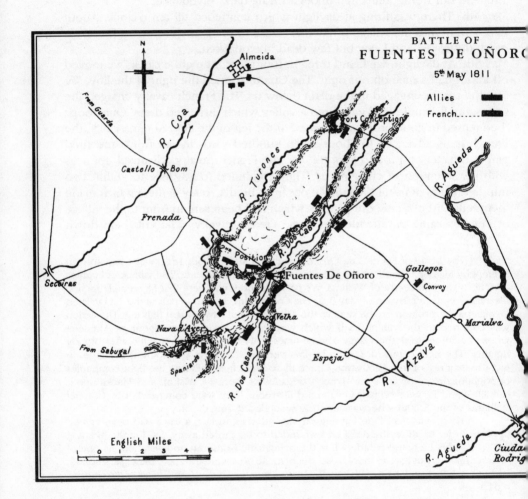

BATTLE OF
FUENTES DE OÑORO

5th May 1811

Allies
French

within fifty yards of our regiment. The picquet had almost all their men killed or wounded.[1] At four, the firing from their guns ceased but our guns continued a partial firing. At six, all firing ceased. The French retired to their old position and we kept ours. In this affair, we lost seventeen hundred and fifty men. The Brigade of Guards had 134 rank and file killed and wounded. One officer was killed, 1 wounded and 2 prisoners. It was an extremely hot day and between the firing, lemonade was sold. Slept out the whole time.[2]

May 6th. We were under arms at daylight and expected a general engagement. In the night we threw up a breastwork in our front. The French remained quiet for the whole day. I was ordered out to a burying party but did not find more than six bodies. Five French officers came out and talked on different subjects. I saw a dressing gown and purple pillow but could not pick it up. They talked of engaging the next day.[3] The weather intensely hot. Bivouacked. Fine night.

May 7th. We remained on our ground. The French made no move. Intensely hot. Bivouacked. Fine night.

May 8th. In the morning the French closed to their right, as we thought with an intention on Almeida. In the evening we could perceive them rebuilding their army and pass before Massena. I constructed a hut to keep out the sun. This night was as cold as the preceding had been hot. The door of the hut faced to the wind — a mistake in architecture. Bivouacked.

[1] When Craufurd's Light Division reached the village of Fuentes de Oñoro the skirmishers of the 1st Division opened fire on the enemy cavalry who were in hot pursuit. The initial volleys threw the cavalry back but the picquets of the Brigade of Guards, under the command of Lieutenant Colonel Hill, of the 3rd Foot Guards, were taken in flank by the French 13th Chasseurs and were badly cut up losing 80 men killed and wounded. Hill was taken prisoner with Ensign Stothert, of the Coldstream, and nineteen other men. During the fight Captain Home, of the 3rd Foot Guards, was attacked by three of the Chasseurs, one of whom grabbed Home's water bottle, the strap of which snapped, while another tore an epaulette from his uniform. The third Frenchman thrust at Home with his sabre but the brave Guards officer almost pulled the man from his horse. As the Frenchman rode off Home grabbed the man's prized cross of the Legion of Honour before turning to his cheering comrades with his prize. See Cowell, *Leaves from the Diary of an Officer of the Guards*, pp.89-91. Also, Stothert, *A Narrative of the Principal Events*, pp.245-246.

[2] Total casualties for the Brigade of Guards were; Coldstream Guards, 4 men killed and one officer, Captain Harvey, and 51 men wounded. Ensign Stothert (not to be confused with Captain Stothert of the 3rd Foot Guards, author of *A Narrative of the Principal Events*), and 7 men taken prisoner. The 3rd Foot Guards lost 5 men killed and one officer, Captain Clitheroe, and 52 men wounded. Lieutenant Colonel Hill, along with twelve men, were taken prisoner.

[3] This mutual respect between the British and French soldiers lasted throughout the Peninsular War and there are countless instances of fraternisation recorded in the journals and letters of Wellington's men. Of course, the vast majority of meetings occurred during the quieter moments of the war, usually when picquets met. But even during pitched battles British and French soldiers found time during a lull in the fighting to meet and talk to each other. During the battle of Talavera, on July 28th 1809, the men of both sides quenched their thirst in the Portina brook which separated the two armies, while truces were declared at Busaco and Fuentes de Oñoro in order that the wounded might be brought in. There was no such relationship between the armies of France and the two Iberian countries however.

Camp near to Fuentes de Oñoro
(Fountain of Honour)
Wednesday 8th May 1811.

My Dearest Mother,

You will at the time you receive this, likewise receive the newspaper accounts of what has taken place here within these few days. I never was better in my life, and thank God I have my head on my shoulders. My last letter was dated from Puebla; soon after that we moved to Almedilla, where we were kept in constant alarm. On the night of the 2nd we marched to Nave de Haver. On the 3rd we marched here. That evening there was a good deal of fighting; we were not engaged. On the 4th there was but little done. On the 5th the action began. We the Guards were cannonaded by grape, round shot and shell from ten o'clock in the morning till four in the evening. The Guards formed the right of the army, where they intended to attack us. Their line of cavalry at two o'clock formed to charge us and it was an anxious moment. When they came near us they thought better of it and turned about, so that we never fired a shot at them. In the evening they withdrew. Our loss in killed and wounded amounts, I understand, to fifteen hundred. The Guards lost one officer killed, two wounded and prisoners. I will not attempt to give you any account of the action — the newspapers will do it much better than I can.

The enemy failed, for their object was to drive us away from our position and relieve Almeida — in this they failed. On the 6th and 7th nothing was done. This morning I understand their whole force is marched off. Their cavalry is now moving, and I understand they are retreating. Since the 1st we have slept in the field without a tree to shelter us, or anything but a greatcoat to cover us, the baggage being sent to the rear. The weather has luckily been fine. We have been in a constant state of alarm expecting every moment to engage, the enemy not being more than a mile from us. The 5th was a very trying day for us. Their cannon played most furiously upon us, and had Lord Wellington not ordered our men to lie down we should have been entirely cut to pieces.[1] Our loss has been on the whole not so great as might have been expected. I have given you a brief account of what has befallen us. I am afraid it is not a clear one for we are still on the alert, and really my head is so bewildered I hardly know what I am writing. Where the enemy have retreated to nobody knows. We imagine that Almeida has surrendered,[2] but even if it has, God knows what will be done. We

---

[1] The effects of enemy round shot could be quite devastating. Cowell, of the Coldstream, recalled that on one occasion during the battle a round shot came bouncing in, missed the ranks of the Coldstreamers and fell in amongst a group of staff officers. The shot took the head off General Howard's horse, killed that of his aide-de-camp Captain Battersby, took off the leg of Major Stewart of the 92nd, and knocked over two private soldiers before 'hopping' on like a cricket ball. 'This shot may be fairly said to have done its duty,' (Cowell. *Leaves from the Diary*, p.95.)

[2] A false assumption on JM's part. Almeida was still in possession of the French although the commanding officer, Brennier, was busy making preparations to make good his escape along with his men, Massena having given up all hope of revictualling the place.

could not attack them on account of their vast superiority of cavalry. Their Imperial Guards were to have charged us. *Gardes contre Gardes.*[1]

I had some conversation yesterday with some French officers who came out to me as I was employed in burying the dead. They were extremely polite, talked much of their own cavalry and lamented their being obliged to leave Salamanca, where they said the women were so beautiful. The nights have, fortunately for us, been very fine, or we could never have stood it. We are under arms every morning at three, and till this moment have expected an attack every hour.

The loss of the French must have been very considerable. Neither side can claim a victory. We had little the best of it, as we kept our position and a village in our front which the French took six times, and we as often retook. Some officers we took on the 3rd complained much of the conduct of their men; on the 5th the men certainly behaved well. They had five thousand cavalry, we not more than one thousand, and I am sorry to say that number is diminished.[2] Should you see I. Hulse tell him that Clitheroe is not badly wounded, the shot went through his mouth and he is doing well. Harvey who went out with me is wounded in the head with a sabre but slightly. Had you known in England that the two armies were within a mile of one another for five days, you would not have imagined it would have ended as it has.

I never was better in my life. Before we came into the field I was not quite right, but since, I have not even had a cold. I am tanned to the colour of a dark boot top, and my hands from not wearing gloves to two degrees darker than mahogany.[3] We have been very well supplied with bread, chocolate and lemonade, which have been the three articles of sale here, and at this moment I hear a man crying lemonade, which appears a little out of character for a field of battle.[4] I have just been looking at the enemy; they seem to be retreating to-

---

[1] Wellington's Foot Guards never came into contact with the Imperial Guard at Fuentes de Oñoro. They would have to wait until June 18th 1815 when the two elite units came face to face for their momentous clash at Waterloo.

[2] Things were not as bad as JM thought. Wellington's cavalry numbered some 1,854 men at Fuentes de Oñoro of whom 157 became casualties. Overall losses on the Allied side were 1,804 all ranks, while Massena lost 2,844. See Oman, *A History of the Peninsular War,* IV, 619-624.

[3] Life as a soldier in Spain and Portugal was hard on the men of all nations fighting there and in the days before sun lotions the problems presented by over-exposure to the fierce summer sun were very great indeed, particularly on units just arrived in the theatre of war. Umbrellas were a great favourite amongst the officers of the Guards as a means of protection. Some cavalry regiments took to wearing oak branches in their helmets to provide some shade whilst several officers wore wide-brimmed hats, notably Sir Thomas Picton who suffered badly from the glare of the sun. One of the earliest methods used to alleviate sunburn, adopted in August 1808, involved the placing of a leaf between the teeth and lower lip. This cured the painful and unsightly problem experienced by the inflammation of the under-lip which then burst, the ensuing trickle of blood adding a copper hue to the victim's chin. The problems of life on the march are dealt with in Brett-James's *Life in Wellington's Army,* pp.23-37.

[4] These camp followers, known as sutlers, were a necessary evil during the Peninsular War as they enabled many a soldier to obtain food, drink and other items that were otherwise unobtainable at times, notably when the commissariat broke down or

wards Ciudad Rodrigo. They are now about three miles off with their faces that way. We are not yet attempting to follow them, and should be inclined to think that we shall not. The troops we have with us are healthy and we were anxious to have a brush with the French. Cannon played furiously on us; at one time they were within three hundred yards of us, and if we had not been ordered to lie down we must have lost all our men. The shots that went over our heads hit the poor Scotch men and killed a great many. I believe it was the Scotch Regiment, the 72nd.[1] The news I have given you I am afraid is not cheering or entertaining but really I am quite puzzled. Please send to Nollis to say that Paulet is quite well.

Give my kindest love to all my friends, and believe me, My Dearest Mother, Ever truly yours. John Mills.

when supplies were late coming up. Naturally, these sutlers did their very best to relieve the British troops of their money and the letters and diaries of Wellington's men are littered with complaints about extortionate prices. The officers of the Guards appear to have made great use of them, their private incomes allowing them to purchase all manner of goods despite the high prices.

[1] JM is mistaken here. The 72nd never served in the Peninsula. The three Scottish battalions numbered amongst the 70s were the 1/71st, the 1/74th and the 1/79th, all of which saw much fighting at Fuentes de Oñoro. The 79th, in particular, was involved in some very bitter fighting in the village and lost 281 during the battle. It is very likely, however, that the battalion JM refers to is the 1/92nd, part of Howard's brigade of the 1st Division, which occupied a position behind the Guards.

Chapter Two

Portugal

Following the battle of Fuentes de Oñoro the opposing armies slipped into a period of manoeuvring and counter manoeuvring astride the Spanish-Portuguese border. In the south, Beresford lay siege to the French-held fortress of Badajoz but, on May 12th, he was forced to abandon the siege in order to march against Soult who was approaching from the south with a French relieving army. The battle of Albuera, on May 16th, was one of the bloodiest of the Peninsular War and the Allied victory there is entirely due to the guts of the British soldier who, locked in a titanic struggle with his French counterpart, refused to buckle in spite of some of the most tremendous punishment meted out by the French in the whole war.

The sieges of Badajoz in May and June 1811 resulted in dismal failures and Wellington returned north to blockade Ciudad Rodrigo. There was a great deal of manoeuvring in that area, culminating, on September 27th, with Marmont's lost opportunity at Fuenteguinaldo, when, faced by just 15,000 of Wellington's men he refused to attack, thinking that the bulk of Wellington's army lay out of sight on the reverse slope of the British commander's position.

The campaigning year ended with Rowland Hill's outstandingly successful attack on Girard at Arroyo dos Molinos on October 28th, which resulted in the capture of over a thousand prisoners, including high-ranking officers. This operation effectively closed what had been a year of consolidation for Wellington who would shortly begin to turn his thoughts to the great fortresses of Ciudad Rodrigo and Badajoz. For JM the year was also one of consolidation as he learned the art of soldiering on active service, experienced the rigours of marching and came to terms with the world of billets and bivouacs which was a far cry from that he had been used to at St James's or Windsor. His story resumes four days after Fuentes de Oñoro with the French moving off towards Ciudad Rodrigo.

May 9th. The French seemed in motion, as we learn, since the cavalry retreated in the evening to Ciudad Rodrigo. I saw their wounded go off. Bivouacked.

May 10th. In the morning their whole force retired. We were unable to follow from our want of cavalry. In the evening some of our troops marched off. I had an attack of the ague. Bivouacked.

May 11th. Moved to Puebla. Saw innumerable eagles and vultures. Felt unwell.

May 12th to 24th. Halted. Ponte de Ceima, 2 leagues north of Castello Branco,

May 25th. At three o'clock we received an order to march. Went to Souto, three leagues, and bivouacked in a chestnut grove. At Alfaiates, the right wing of the battalion lost the left.

May 26th. At three o'clock we marched through Sabugal to Penamacor, 6 leagues. The road was very bad and the day so hot, that the men were beat. The country about Penamacor is very rich. The men are in a convent.

May 27th. Received orders to march back at daylight to Sabugal. Rainy day.

May 28th. To Nave — 2 leagues. Quarters.

May 29th. To Puebla, through Albegueria, 4 leagues.

May 30th. I went over to Guinaldo to see what they called a Bull fight. There was nothing but cows and oxen. At night I went to a Ball there, and invited all the company to a Ball and supper at Puebla on the 4th.

May 31st. Made preparations for the Ball. White, Masters and myself are stewards. Ordered the Ball, 60ft by 20ft. The supper room is 52 by 14. The rafters were fir, and the seat of young oak. There are 28 men at work.

June 1st and 2nd. Work continued.

June 3rd. The whole was roofed in and completed. The German band has been procured. Tents are pitched round for different occupations.

June 4th. Busy all the morning. At seven Don Julian appeared.[1] The bands played God Save the King. The Ball commenced with fandangos — Spanish country dances — and Waltzes, till eleven. There are 120 people. At 11, seventy sat down to supper. Colonel Fermor is at the head of the table. He gave Ferdinand the seventh; Don Julian then gave George 3rd. Don Julian's health was afterwards drunk. I made a Spanish lady tipsy. At twelve orders came to march at three. I danced after supper and there was a considerable scramble for the remains of the same. The Spaniards went home at one. There were forty subscribers at 7 dollars each — £70.[2]

[1] Don Julian Sanchez was one of the foremost guerrilla leaders in the Peninsula. A retired regular soldier he worked closely with Wellington and his mounted units did fine work, particularly at Fuentes de Oñoro in 1811. Perhaps his most notable coup came on October 15th 1811 when he captured General Renaud, governor of Ciudad Rodrigo, who was inspecting the garrison's herd of cattle, which he also carried off. In 1813 his guerrillas were converted into two regular cavalry units. Nicknamed 'El Charro', a monument to his memory stands in Ciudad Rodrigo just inside the site of the Great Breach facing the cathedral.

[2] The Ball held at Puebla on June 4th is well documented by the officers of the Coldstream Guards. George Percival wrote an account of it in a letter to his aunt on June 18th 1811. (*MSS letters of 29th Sept. 1810 to 11th June 1814, written to his aunt Mrs Charles Drummond in London by Lt & Capt G.H. Percival, Coldstream Guards, from the Peninsula, 1810-11 and the Low Countries, 1813-14*. National Army Museum, London).

June 5th. We marched at daybreak to Almedilla and remained there all day. Played cricket.[1]

June 6th. At daybreak we marched to Souto, and to the same chestnut trees we had been to on the 25th. The day was hot. We heard that the enemy were advanced upon us, and saw three wounded dragoons. The baggage is beyond the Coa through Sabugal. Bivouacked.

June 7th. Marched at daylight to a position on the left bank of the Coa, about a mile through Sabugal. We passed the Coa by the bridge at that place. When we got upon our ground, we heard that the French had gone off in the direction of Ciudad Rodrigo. The men were allowed to leave their arms. Steele and myself who had messed together since joining the regiment got under a chestnut tree, in which the country abounds about here. Bivouacked. A fine night. The day was very hot, and a strong dew at night.

June 8th. Expected to halt all the day. I sold a mare, bought off Mildmay, to a sutler for twenty dollars. I bought tea, snuff and tobacco of which things I stood much in need. At three, much are the vicissitudes of a soldier's life, we received orders to march 3 leagues to Nermas. We got there after dark, and I was much hurt at finding the tobacco I had bought would not smoke. Bivouacked. Bad night.

June 9th. To Pedrogão, 4 leagues. We left Penamacor on our left. The country about it most luxurious. Bivouacked. Fine night.

June 10th. Halted. The weather till this time has been very hot. Some corn has been cut which I appropriate to my own use. Bivouacked. Fine night.

June 11th. Before daylight we marched to Ponte de Cernas (Escallias de Sema). I got a place in a garden. Fine night.

June 11th 1811.

My Dearest Mother,

You have not heard from me for some time, and as you will hear of the different movements of the army you may perhaps like to know in which I am con-

---

John Stepney Cowell, in his *Leaves from the Diary of an Officer of the Guards*, pp.120-122, also wrote an account of the Ball. The Guards constructed a huge hut for the occasion, the floor of which was covered with grass. For supper the officers pooled their rations whilst punch was made in camp kettles. The Ball ended in the early hours of June 5th when an order arrived for the Brigade of Guards to march. See also JM's letter to his mother, June 11th 1811.

[1] All manner of sports were played in the Peninsula by Wellington's men including cricket. In August 1810, while Ney's troops were laying siege to Almeida, the British troops close by played cricket. Surgeon Charles Boutflower, of the 40th, wrote, 'We amuse ourselves in this place chiefly at cricket, and from the ground where we play we can distinctly see the fire from the garrison of Almeida. From the spirit with which the officers in general enter into this game one would hardly suppose there was an enemy within a hundred leagues of us.' (Boutflower, *The Journal of an Army Surgeon*, p.53.) One wonders what sort of bats, stumps and balls were used. The game was later played before a crowd of bewildered French onlookers on the Champs Elysee during the Occupation of Paris in 1815.

cerned. It is now seven o'clock; we march at 3 in the morning, therefore I have only half an hour while the light lasts to write. On the 5th of June the French moved down a strong body of cavalry and infantry to drive in our advanced posts. The Coldstream were the farthest advanced. We, and indeed the whole army, retreated through Alfaiates to Sabugal, on the Coa. There the army waited expecting the French to advance. This they did not do, but went off and it is supposed are on their way to succour Badajoz. Consequently we are moving down in a parallel line. We are never shut into quarters, but take our abode under a tree if we are lucky enough to find one. As yet I have not suffered from it, and am quite well. The weather is luckily fine. The days are so hot that we march sometimes at twelve o'clock at night.

For these summer movements, bivouacking does not much signify, but I am afraid that in winter we shall feel it, and all the houses being burnt, there is no alternative. Lord Wellington has left us, and is near Badajoz.[1] General Sir Brent Spencer commands.

I must tell you of a Ball and Supper we gave at Puebla, to Don Julian, and the Spanish ladies about there.[2] There were three stewards, one of whom was your humble servant. We had two temporary huts built; the dancing sixty foot by twenty, with a recess for the Band, which was German. The other fifty-two by eighteen for a supper room. It was made of the branches of oak. The dancing room was lighted by small lamps hung amongst the leaves, a transparency at each with George III and Ferdinand VII. Our Colours stood at the end. The Supper consisted of mutton, trout, cherries, puddings, cakes, sweetmeats, etc., etc., and though from this bill of fare you would imagine it was not fine; yet the table was so covered, that people flattered us by saying that it really looked uncommonly well. It answered our purpose, for it delighted the natives. Behind the Supper room, tents were pitched, each for a different occupation — lamplighter, fruit, meat, confectionery, wine. I forgot to say that the whole was built, even the tables made, without a single nail — so much for the ingenuity of

---

[1] The fortress of Badajoz lies on the Guadiana river and commanded the southern corridor between Spain and Portugal. The town was enclosed within nine bastions connected by strong walls and was protected by three outworks. The fortress had fallen to the French in March 1811 when its governor, Imaz, had given the place up to Soult. This followed a vigorous defence by the former governor, Menacho, who was killed during a sortie on March 3rd. Fortescue, in his *History of the British Army*, VIII, 38, condemned Imaz for his conduct. 'It was amazing good fortune for Soult that Menacho's successor should have been so incompetent.' Wellington had sent Beresford to lay siege to the place in May 1811, although this lasted just a few days on account of Beresford having to march south to fight the French relieving army under Soult at Albuera. The siege resumed in June 1811 but again this proved unsuccessful. The governor, Armand Phillipon, proved a brave and resourceful commander, as Wellington would again find to his cost in March and April 1812. In June 1811 the outwork, Fort San Christobal, was chosen as the point of attack but the two assaults on the place were driven back with heavy loss. By mid-June, the armies of Soult and Marmont were approaching, forcing Wellington to raise the siege having lost nearly 500 men. The relieving forces entered Badajoz on June 20th 1811.

[2] See also JM's Journal for June 4th 1811.

our men.[1] The dancing commenced at seven, about a hundred and thirty persons, waltzes, boleros, etc., till eleven. Supper; toasts innumerable. In the middle of it orders came to march at three. We took no notice to the strangers, who separated at two o'clock highly delighted. It went off uncommonly well. Don Julian told us that the French in Ciudad Rodrigo had made several enquiries about it. I am inclined to think they disturbed us on purpose. We cannot form a conjecture as to what will be our plan of operations. It is supposed that Badajoz must have fallen today, if so, we shall not go down. It is so dark, I have not light to see to write any more, but thought you would be glad to have even a line.

Remember me most kindly to all friends, cousins, relations, fathers, brothers, sisters, etc. and believe me, most affect. yours, John Mills.

Marmont commands the French army here. Massena is gone to Paris. I have just heard we halt tomorrow; if we do I shall tear this and write at length. This work is very harassing. We are not secure of marching at a moment's notice nor have we been for a month. This is the second trip within a fortnight to this neighbourhood. Adieu.

June 12th. To Sarnadas through Castello Branco, 5 leagues. This town is less destroyed than I have yet seen that the French have been through. I saw two Convents. There was all sorts of English manufacture to be sold there. Linen drapery of all kinds. We halted near the town for a few hours, then moved on to Sarnadas where we bivouacked. Fine night.

June 13th. Halted, and heard that it was probable we should not be wanted in the Alentejo. The French are supposed to be moving the force they had in the north of Portugal to the relief of Badajoz. Marmont commands that army in the absence of Massena, who is reported to have gone to Paris in disgrace.[2] Bivouacked. Fine night. My Stud at this time consists of a horse, Docktail, who was taken from the French at Salamonde[3] — a great favourite. Two mare mules —

---

[1] Ensign Rees Gronow, of the 1st Foot Guards, thought the British soldier to be infinitely inferior to his French counterpart when it came to the building of huts and bivouacs. He claimed that the English soldier was content to make use of any old building or house, rather than construct anything for themselves. He compared this to the habit of the French soldiers who constructed huts made from branches and formed them into streets and squares with ditches to drain off any rain water. See Raymond (Ed), *The Reminiscences and Recollections of Captain Gronow*, p.319. The Foot Guards certainly appear to have outdone themselves at the Ball at Puebla on June 4th.

[2] On May 10th 1811 General Foy arrived at Ciudad Rodrigo bearing Napoleon's orders relieving Massena of his command of the Army of Portugal. Marshal Auguste Marmont, Duke of Ragusa, assumed command instead. Exhausted by years of campaigning Massena nevertheless felt ill-treated and protested, claiming that others, including Foy himself, had transmitted a false picture of his late campaign. The accusation was unfounded and in fact Napoleon had decided as early as April 20th, possibly even April 16th, to replace him with a younger general. See Oman's *History of the Peninsular War*, IV, 295-296 & 357-368 for an analysis of Massena's recall.

[3] Following Wellesley's brilliant operation to cross the Douro at Oporto on May 12th 1809, the Brigade of Guards found itself in the vanguard of the British army pursuing Soult's retreating French. On May 16th the British troops came upon the French

Bess and Jenny. Both are very quiet. A small he mule, Turpin; a rogue, he carries
William. Mare mules carry the baggage and I ride Docktail. My servants consist
of William, a private servant, Duckworth, a soldier servant who looks after the
animals, Joseph, a Portuguese boy under him.[1] We contrive to get grass for the
animals, and some straw as the corn is now cut.

June 14th. The 4th and 5th companies marched to a village a mile from Villa
Velha, situated in the mountains. The cork trees are in great perfection. Our
Patrone made us a present of some honey.

June 15th. We marched at two o'clock to Villa Velha. From thence about half a
mile to the banks of the Tagus. We were delayed here some time, as there were
but two boats joined together to pass an army of 30,000 men. Got over about
eleven. The ground rising from the banks is rocky and steep. We ascended a
wretched road for two leagues after passing the ferry.[2] There are no trees; brush

rearguard at Salamonde and in the ensuing fight the light companies of the Coldstream
and 3rd Foot Guards led the attack against the French left flank. Following this the rest of
the two Guards battalion clashed with and broke the French 4th Léger, considered to be
one of the stronger enemy regiments, who fled in disorder. In their flight over the Ponte
Nova, a narrow bridge with no parapets, the French panicked and struggled with each
other, scores drowning as they fell into the water below. In his despatch to Castlereagh,
Wellesley wrote, 'The brigade of Guards were at the head of the column, and set a
laudable example; and in the affair with the enemy's rearguard on the evening of the
16th, they conducted themselves remarkably well.' (*Despatches*, Wellesley to Castlereagh,
18th May 1809, IV, 317.)

[1] An indication of the large amount of baggage carried by the officers of the
Guards can perhaps be illustrated by a passage in the memoirs of Francis Seymour
Larpent, Wellington's Judge Advocate. He said that the 'Gentlemen's Sons' would never
learn how to be 'killed properly' if they were continually nursed up in the rear, as a result
of having insufficient means of conveying their baggage, Wellington having limited the
number of mules per subaltern to just one. This meant of course that if an officer chose
to ride he could carry none of his own baggage and if, on the other hand, he decided to
carry his equipment he had to walk, with the result that he was often unfit for duty when
he came into quarters. This rule was particularly hard on the officers of the Guards, most
of whom had several mules and horses on campaign with them. Indeed, Larpent claimed
that even the most junior Guards subaltern had as many animals as any staff officer ought
to have had. He went on, 'He [the Guards officer] carries his bed out to the guardhouse,
and has his canteen fit to give a dinner and every luxury, whereas one set of canteens per
company would, in my opinion, be a liberal allowance. Their General has given them a
week to comply with this order, but somehow or other they will contrive, probably, to
evade it or they will be the most miserable animals in existence. Whilst they were in
camp, they left one officer with the men in camp, and the rest got into houses, whilst in
many instances even the generals in other divisions commanding brigades were out
under canvas, or at most in huts.' (Larpent, *The Private Journal of Sir F. Seymour Larpent,
Judge Advocate General*, II, 54.)

[2] The pontoon bridge at Villa Velha was a major crossing point over the Tagus for
the British army in the Peninsula as it allowed relatively easy access between the north
and south banks of the river. The French, on the other hand, had no bridge lower down
the river than the old Roman bridge at Almaraz and as such had to undertake long
detours and spend much longer in shifting their forces from the northern to the southern
theatre of war and vice versa. The pontoon bridge and the river crossing are featured in
several contemporary pictures, notably that done by Captain Thomas St Clair, whose
watercolours are amongst the finest records of the operations in the Peninsula.

wood (hollow) at bottom consisting of gum trees and a few other shrubs. Mr Johnson, an officer of the artillery, was drowned in attempting to ford the river. Passed through Niza. I saw four flat-bottomed boats on carriages drawn by eight oxen. They were going to Villa Velha to construct a bridge. The sailors appeared much amused at us. The baggage was left behind at the ford and was not to pass till the rear of the division, consequently we had nothing to eat. Bivouacked about a mile from Niza.

June 16th. Marched at two in the morning to Portalegre. As you approach this town which is situated on the side of a hill, the country appears particularly fertile. The vineyards which are very numerous here looked uncommonly well. The town is the only one in Portugal that the French have not been in. There are two squares, the houses are generally clean and the quarters remarkably good. We are much crowded as there are already 10,000 men in the town, and room is left for the 6th Division.[1] Everything of English manufacture is to be had, which considering the gypsy life we have been leading is delightful. I dined with Robert Digby of the 52nd, and enjoyed some champagne which he gave us. Our baggage not yet arrived. The fleas are very numerous and in motion.[2]

June 17th. Halted. I dined with Walcott at the artillery barracks. The baggage came up.

June 18th. Halted. On this day was decided a question between Sir G. Stirling, Coldstream, and Captain Home, 3rd Guards. Sir B. Spencer and General Campbell decided that a superior officer of a different (or even of the same regiment) had no right to put an inferior officer under arrest whilst the his/inferior's commanding officer was on the ground. Thunder and rain.

---

[1] In June 1811, the 6th Division, commanded by General Alexander Campbell, consisted of Hulse's brigade (the 1/11th, 2/53rd, 1/61st, one company of the 5/60th), Burne's brigade (2nd and 2/36th), and Eben's Portuguese brigade (the 8th and 12th Line). See Oman, *Wellington's Army, 1809-1815*, p.351 & 356.

[2] When each regiment or draft arrived in Portugal one of the first things noted by the men was the extremely dirty nature of Lisbon and its inhabitants. After a few months of campaigning, however, British soldiers — officers and men alike — found that they too were not to be spared the attentions of fleas and other such insects. One of JM's comrades, John Rous, was a young man of just eighteen when he arrived in the Peninsula, and in his first letter home was moved to write, 'I am bitten all over by the fleas and bugs.' (Fletcher (Ed), *A Guards Officer in the Peninsula*, p.31.) For some, however, these pests proved more than just a nuisance. Ensign Rees Gronow recalled the tragic story of a fellow officer in the 1st Foot Guards in the Peninsula. The officer was Sir Thomas Styles, a young man who had been at school at Eton with the poet Shelley and whom Gronow said, 'shone to advantage on parade and at the mess-table.' But on campaign it proved a different story. Styles arrived at Lisbon in 1813 to find that his battalion was in the Pyrenees and so had to undergo the long journey through Portugal and Spain and by the time he reached his battalion was in a poor state. He was exhausted and said he was in such a state he thought he could not survive for much longer. Gronow went on, 'Observing that something extraordinary had happened, he was pressed to be more explicit, and to tell what had occurred to make him so miserable. He replied, with a very grave countenance, that the fleas and vermin on the march had nearly driven him mad and that when the peasant girls observed him scratching himself, they would laugh, and shaking their petticoats over pails full of water, would tell him how much more they were to be pitied than he.' The regimental surgeon, Bacot, thought that Styles was suffering from

June 19th. We marched at three o'clock to a cork wood near Assumar. There was no water near and what we did get was very bad. Bivouacked.

June 20th. Halted. At night it lightened and I was afraid of rain, which however did not happen. Bivouacked.

June 21st. Halted. A Mail arrived from England which brought the Gazette's account of the action of Fuentes de Oñoro. I borrowed Fuller's tent which was fortunate as it rained. I increased my establishment by Moore, a batman. Bivouacked.

June 22nd. Halted. Forty of the 11th Lt. Dragoons, which had but just joined, and twenty of the German Hussars were taken near Elvas by a strong patrol of the enemy.[1] Bivouacked.

June 23rd. Marched at 3 to St Olaia. The men were ordered to hut themselves. Cold wind. The long grass is so much burnt up that the men are obliged to clear the ground for cooking, for fearing of setting fire to it.[2] I built a hut and bivouacked.

June 24th. Halted. I saw a stubble field on fire and one old woman putting it out. Hot sun and cold wind. The draft from Cadiz came up.[3] There are quails in abundance. Bivouacked.

June 25th. Halted. I received a mail in eleven days from London. Bivouacked.

June 26th. Halted and bivouacked.

'brain fever' and confined him to his bed and told his servant to keep watch over him. During the night, however, he fell asleep at which Styles got up, unlocked his trunk, took out his razors and cut his own throat from ear to ear. Raymond (Ed), *The Reminiscences and Recollections of Captain Gronow*, pp.331-332.

[1] On June 22nd a French cavalry force under Latour-Maubourg, consisting of four squadrons of dragoons and Polish lancers, forded the Guadiana and advanced towards Elvas. The Allied cavalry screen here was provided by the 2nd Hussars KGL and the 11th Light Dragoons. Upon being attacked the small force of the 2nd Hussars, instead of retiring, engaged the French but after initial success were badly mauled losing 25 men. Having scattered the hussars, Latour-Maubourg turned to his right and found himself in the rear of the picquet of the 11th Light Dragoons, under Captain Lutyens, who apparently mistook the French for Portuguese. Lutyens realised just who they were when it was too late and was forced to cut and hack his way out. In the ensuing melee, the light dragoons cut their way through the first French line only to fall in with the second, much stronger, line. The entire squadron, save Lieutenant Binney who escaped, was taken. Oman, in his *History of the Peninsular War*, IV, 448, gives 65 casualties, Fortescue, *History of the British Army*, VIII, 235, gives 90, whereas Long's account in *Peninsular Cavalry General — The Correspondence of Lieutenant General Robert Ballard Long*, (Ed. T.H. McGuffie), p.119, gives 134. See also Beamish's *History of the King's German Legion*, II, 5-8, and *Despatches*, Wellington to Lord Liverpool, 27th June 1811, VIII, 57. It is curious that Fortescue (*History of the British Army*, VIII, 234n) actually gives the date of the fight as being June 23rd, following Wellington's despatch. Oman gives June 22nd and as JM does likewise I would suggest that the date of the fight was June 22nd.

[2] The tinder-dry nature of the ground was often a great problem when lighting fires for cooking and great care had to be taken. After the battle of Talavera, on July 28th 1809, scores of badly wounded men, unable to drag themselves away from the battlefield, were consumed by fire when the tall dry grass ignited.

[3] The draft of the Coldstream Guards arrived on June 25th consisting of Captain the Hon. John Walpole, Ensign G.H.M. Greville, 3 sergeants and 95 rank and file. See Mackinnon, *Origin and Services of the Coldstream Guards*, II, 164.

June 27th.   Halted. I went to General Nightingale's sale.[1] Wrote to England.
Bivouacked.

St. Olaia, 3 leagues from Elvas,
27th June 1811.

My Dearest Mother,

I wrote you a letter a fortnight ago, which I could not seal having neither wafers
nor sealing wax; but as it contained no secrets I sent it open; I am afraid it may
not have arrived safe, therefore I write you a few lines by this mail to let you
know how we are going on. I must first acknowledge the receipt of two letters,
which I have lately received from you. The date of the first I forget but the
second is the 27th of May. Many thanks for your congratulations — before I
close this dispatch I expect to have another from you, as I hear that another mail
is arrived, in eleven days from London to this place, which is 150 [miles] from
Lisbon, and the travelling in this country is not quite so expeditious as in England. In my last letter, which was I believe from Ponte de Carnao, I gave you an
account of the Ball we gave to Don Julian. We were then on our march to this
part of Portugal in consequence of a similar movement of the French, we crossed
the Tagus at Villa Velha, and wonderful to say, the whole army had but one
small boat to cross in. We then marched to Portalegre, where we halted two
days. I saw Robert Digby there, and dined with him.[2] I conferred the same
honour on Yeomans Walcott, who is with the Horse Artillery.

We marched on to this place, where the whole army is concentrated. The
French are about four leagues from us on the other side of the Guadiana. Their
cavalry crossed that river in force a few days ago, and took sixty of the 11th
Light Dragoons who had just come from England.[3] The 11th, you may remember, quartered at Ringwood. An amateur, son of Mr. Gray, the Jeweller, was
captured a few days ago; the French sent him in, desiring that he might be
exchanged for a Colonel of theirs, at the same time professing their ignorance of

[1] General Miles Nightingale, often called Nightingall, was posted to the 1st Division on January 23rd 1811 and commanded a brigade at Fuentes de Oñoro. He left the
army in June 1811, bound for Bengal. Such sales were normally as a result of the death
of an officer although it appears on this occasion that Nightingale must have had an
excess of equipment which he had no desire to take with him to India. While personal
and sentimental items of dead officers were usually preserved for the dead man's family
other items of equipment, such as his baggage, would be auctioned and the proceeds —
after the deduction of funeral expenses — would be forwarded to his family. John Rous,
a comrade of JM in the Coldstream, bought a tent for fifteen guineas at one such sale in
November 1812. See Fletcher (Ed), *A Guards Officer in the Peninsula*, p.39.

[2] Robert Digby was a cousin through JM's mother. He was serving in the 52nd
Light Infantry at the time.

[3] The 2nd Hussars KGL had only arrived in the Peninsula on April 15th 1811 and
the 11th Light Dragoons on June 1st of the same year. In his despatch of June 27th 1811
Wellington himself wrote, 'The loss of the picquet of the 11th Light Dragoons and that
sustained by the 2nd Hussars, were disagreeable circumstances; but they tend to show
the difference between the old and new troops.' (*Despatches*, Wellington to Lord Liverpool, 27th June 1811, VIII, 58.) See also JM's Journal for June 22nd 1811.

what description of man an amateur was, as they had none in their army. Lord Wellington has sent Mr. Gray Junr. back again, with his respects and they may keep him.[1] As I predicted, I have just received two letters from you of the 3rd and 10th of June. All your letters have arrived safe; when you go to Bisterne you may direct them under cover to the Adjutant. I am delighted to hear of Sir John Dalrymple's good fortune, and only hope he may succeed in Edinburgh. The weather is now most dreadfully hot; so far it suits the Fresco amusement of bivouacking. Pray excuse the ink, for it is made with gunpowder and wine. The fields are burnt up to a stick and great caution must be used in lighting fires for it is no uncommon thing to have a camp on fire. The harvest is nearly all in. We are all here much surprised at the Vote of Thanks to Genl. Beresford — Good John Bull, how easily art thou duped. Genl. Beresford is the most noted bungler that ever played at the game of soldiers, and at Albuera he out-bungled himself. Lord Wellington riding over the ground a few days after with Beresford observed that there was one small oversight; that his right was where his left should have been.[2] I have learned one thing since I have been in this country, and that is to know how easily England is duped; how completely ignorant she is of the truth of what is going on here, and how perfectly content she is, so long as there is a long list of killed and wounded. At Fuentes, the French completely turned our right; Lord Wellington in his dispatch slightly notices it, and would lead you to think that the troops on the right were withdrawn rather, than as was the case, driven in; And then they give him what he himself never dreamt of claiming, a victory.[3] Our Foreign Troops, Germans and French, have

[1] Gray was probably one of the many 'volunteers' who served with Wellington's army in the hope of obtaining a commission in the field. See JM's Journal for April 10th 1811 for a definition of this status.

[2] The battle of Albuera was fought on May 16th 1811 and was one of the bloodiest battles of the Peninsular War. The brutal bludgeoning match cost the Allied army, under Beresford, some 6,000 casualties, while Soult lost between 7-8,000 men. Much of this was due to Beresford's poor dispositions. The ground at Albuera is fairly flat and undulating and the heights or hills mentioned in various accounts are nothing more than gentle crests. Beresford chose to throw his army across the main road from Albuera to Badajoz, ignoring the rising ground to the south of the town, and when a massive French infantry attack struck the right flank of his position British and Spanish troops were forced into a nightmare of shot, shell and close quarter musketry in order to drive the French from it. The resulting Allied victory was due almost entirely to the stubbornness of the British infantry who refused to yield an inch of their hard-won ground until Soult's Frenchmen finally gave way themselves. Wellington considered Blake's inability to move south when the initial French attack began — Beresford had ordered him to do so upon seeing the French advance — as being one of the main causes of the trouble but added later, when riding over the field himself with Charles Stewart, that, 'Beresford, on the evening of the 15th seems not to have attempted to take up the ground in the manner which might have rendered it very formidable, but — like a Spanish army and officers — as the high road led from Albuera to Badajoz, he placed his army across it, as if this alone could stop the foe. From this period to the commencement of the battle, his right seems to have been placed where his left should have been.' Charles Stewart to Castlereagh, 22nd May 1811. (Quoted in Fortescue, *History of the British Army*, VIII, 189-190.)

[3] JM was not afraid to criticise Wellington, or any other commander for that matter, albeit in private. Very few writers were willing to come out into the open and do the same, particularly in the post-Waterloo era when Wellington's fame was at its height. This is an example of the value of letters and diaries written as the events themselves

been deserting in numbers lately. Fifty of the Chasseurs Britanniques went over in a body a few nights ago and a night or two afterwards, the same number of Germans under the pretence of going for water, played the same trick.[1] Our army is tolerably healthy. The Portuguese have a great many sick; in consequence of their being more employed in this neighbourhood; which is reckoned not so healthy as the north. It lies very low, and is more subject to Agues. It is quite the reverse of the other side of the Tagus. It is a much more fertile country, and has been but little ravaged by the French. The roads are uncommonly good. About Castello Branco there are immense tracts covered with the gumcistus, it is reckoned a rare plant in England is it not. Paulet Mildmay is not yet returned from Coimbra — he will soon go home now, for I believe that Col. Smyth is going out; he will then be the first for promotion. Marmont commands the French army. Soult is second in command, though much the senior officer. They are estimated at about 50,000. Their superiority of cavalry is so great, that until we get some more we shall not be able to do anything.[2] The allied infantry

unfolded, without having the benefit of hindsight and when the war was still precariously balanced. Wellington's despatch to Castlereagh, see *Despatches*, 8th May 1811, VII, 528-534, informing him of the battle of Fuentes de Oñoro, does indeed gloss over the turning of his right flank on May 5th, which it undoubtedly was, intense French pressure causing Wellington to re-align his position. The manoeuvre, when executed, was skilfully done, but it forced him into giving up his communications with the River Coa.

[1] The Chasseurs Britanniques deserted to the enemy at an alarming rate (See JM's Journal for May 5th 1811, note 17). Wellington recorded the desertions in a despatch to Lord Liverpool, *Despatches*, 13th June 1811, VII, 11-12. 'I beg to inform your Lordship that, since the commencement of the siege of Badajoz, fifty-two of the Chasseurs Britanniques have deserted, notwithstanding that we have with the army only a selection of that corps; 686 who are suspected being left behind at Lisbon. The inconvenience of the desertion of the soldiers of this army is very great, because it is almost the only mode by which the enemy can acquire intelligence; but, besides the inconvenience which all must feel, the disgrace is no trifle, and it would be very desirable if these corps could be relieved by others. I much fear from all that I hear that the recruiting of these corps has not been as the Government intended, and that prisoners have been enlisted, as well as deserters, into the Chasseurs Britanniques and the Brunswick Legion.'

[2] It was not until the Vittoria campaign of 1813 that Wellington, who had suffered from a woeful shortage of cavalry from the moment he had arrived in the Peninsula in 1808, was able to compete with the French with an equal number of cavalry. Even so, Wellington considered this arm of his army to be inferior to its French counterpart owing to the British cavalry's exasperating habit of riding hell for leather at everything in its path and getting out of control, often with disastrous consequences. Indeed, in a letter to Lord Russell, written in 1826, Wellington wrote, 'I considered our cavalry so inferior to the French from want of order, that although I considered one of our squadrons a match for two French, yet I did not care to see four British opposed to four French, and still more so as the numbers increased, and order (of course) became more necessary. They could gallop, but could not preserve order.' (Quoted in Oman, *Wellington's Army, 1809-14*, p.104.) On June 18th 1812, a week after Slade's disastrous affair at Maguilla, which cost him 166 casualties, Wellington claimed that it was occasioned by, 'the trick our officers have acquired of galloping at everything, and their galloping back as fast as they gallop on the enemy. They never consider their situation, never think of manoeuvring before an enemy.....The Royals and the 3rd Dragoon Guards [involved in the fight] were the best regiments in the cavalry in this country, and it annoys me particularly that this misfortune has happened to them. I do not wonder at the French boasting of it; it is the greatest blow they have struck.' (*Despatches*, Wellington to Hill, 18th June 1812, IX, 238.)

is nearly if not quite equal to theirs. Our cavalry is in bad order and few in number; not amounting English and Portuguese to more than 3,000, theirs to 7,000. The Polish Lancers who did so much execution at Albuera, have long lances, with white flags at the end, against a retreating foe they may do something; but against cavalry they are nothing.[1] A report is just circulated that Badajoz has fallen or rather that the enemy has evacuated it. I do not credit the report for are we not more than three leagues from it, and must have heard the explosion.[2] Wheler Hood is now going home; I am sorry to lose him, but am rejoiced at his good fortune. We have so large an army in this immediate neighbourhood that provisions are difficult to be got — a little mutton, and some bread is all we can boast of. You would be surprised with this little how nice a dinner we contrive to make. Our cooks are very clever hands at it, and when we are in quarters where vegetables and poultry are to be got, can turn out a very respectable dinner.[3] Everything is enormously dear, even bread and the common necessaries of life are three times as much as in England. In the unsettled state we are now, the officers of the company live together; Steele and myself domesticate — in quarters we live separately — and always dine amongst each other. Steele and myself have two beautiful goats, who are now boring me to give them

---

[1] The regiment which did so much execution at Albuera was the 1st Lancers of the Vistula. Supported by the French 2nd Hussars, the Poles fell upon Colborne's brigade, the 1/3rd, 2/48th, 2/66th and 2/31st, at the very moment that a violent thunderstorm began, the inky black skies opening up with torrents of rain and stinging hailstones. The British infantrymen's muskets were quickly rendered useless and as the rain lashed down into their faces they failed to see the French cavalry that were bearing down upon them using the sudden downpour as a screen. Caught in line and unable to form square the infantry were an easy target for the cavalry who were armed with the lance, a fearsome weapon seldom seen by the British and a superb killing instrument that enabled the bearer to kill with little danger to himself. It was also a weapon from which there was little escape, it being just as easy to thrust down and kill someone on the ground as it was to kill a man standing. The Polish lancers attacked with extreme violence and when they withdrew just a few minutes later some 1,300 out of Colborne's 1,600 men had been either killed or wounded, only the 1/31st managing to form square in time to avoid adding to the carnage. In spite of their undoubted advantage with the lance the Poles were by no means invincible and in fact Beresford himself parried a lancer's thrust at Albuera before throwing his would-be assailant to the ground.

[2] JM was right. Badajoz had not fallen and had certainly not been evacuated by the French.

[3] Keeping a good table appears to have been a major priority with the Guards. On January 11th 1813, John Rous, of the Coldstream, wrote to his mother, 'Fish is to be got in plenty, which I can assure you makes a great addition to our dinner. Nobody dines out without considering that fish in the first course and a roast turkey in the second is what he may reasonably expect, besides which we have plenty of woodcocks. This is merely to give you an idea of the living of the Guards when compared to that of the Line, who live on a pound of tough beef and a pound and a half of bread (per diem) commonly called ration, a thing not known to us when in quarters.' (Fletcher (Ed), *A Guards Officer in the Peninsula*, p.48.) This tradition was maintained by the Guards even in the terrible trenches of the First World War. In October 1916, Lieutenant Brian Lawrence, of the Grenadier Guards, sat down with three other officers to a dinner of, 'thick soup, fish cakes, curried prawns and rice, cutlets and mashed potatoes and beans, trifle, cheese souflet, dessert, coffee, port and brandy,' (Fletcher (Ed), *Letters From the Front*, p.23.)

some biscuit. We have got a hut under an old Cork tree, like the Patriachs of old with our servants, horses, mules, &., &., round us. This seems charming but I prefer the dirtiest house to the neatest hut, made of boughs.[1] You would be surprised in how short a time our men build one of these huts. There is an abundance of timber about, and no crusty farmers to prevent your maiming their trees.

I shall send by Wheler Hood some wheat, peculiar I fancy to this country. It is bearded and the beards black. He will send it to Portman Square.[2] Will you tell my father I have sent it to him, and wish it may thrive as well at Bisterne as it does here. I envy your summer at Bisterne; I wish you may have as fine weather as we have now, it would suit your donkey cart. Remember me most kindly to Charlotte. Tell her the next letter I write to Manor House shall be to her, and tell her to give my compliments to Master Jacky.[3] Col. Smyth is going to marry one of the Miss Wilsons, of Yorkshire; a large fortune.

Your ever affect. Son, John Mills

P.S. 1500 of the enemy's cavalry crossed the Guadiana yesterday morning, but have retired.

June 28th. A mail from England in eleven days. Some guns fired in the morning, which proved to be alarm guns from Campo Mayor and Elvas. Breakfasted at Barbassina with the 13th Dragoons, and from thence to Elvas. On the left it is commanded by Fort de Lippe, considered the most perfect fortress in the world. On the right is Fort St Lucie, much weaker than Elvas, and in fact the only available place. De Lippe is about half a mile, the other about two hundred yards from Elvas, which is very strong and has six royal bastions. These three forts rise from an immense plain and are only to be taken by blockade. Elvas is a very large town and the dirtiest in Portugal. It is manned by some Portuguese regiments of the line, one company of British Artillery and by townsmen, the most wretched drillers I ever beheld. We had not time to go round De Lippe.

---

[1] JM's sentiments were echoed by one of his comrades, John Stepney Cowell, who, when the Coldstream were billeted at St Olaia in the summer of 1811, found himself in a hut which had been constructed for the battalion. Such was the heat of the sun that the men were forced to remain inside. This, however, had the adverse effect as the men had yet to master the art of building huts from branches. 'The heat was excessive, our shelter from its intenseness inadequate; large plains, dotted and interspersed with olive-trees, afforded more dust than shade; our huts were not constructed of the best materials to defend us from the sun's scorching blaze; soon after daybreak they became little hothouses, or rather ovens, from whence came forth for parade an almost baked battalion.' (Cowell, Leaves from the Diary of an Officer of the Guards, p.133.)

[2] Portman Square was the Mills family town house, occupied for the London season and for William Mills to attend the House of Commons.

[3] 'Master Jacky' was Charlotte's eldest son, John Combe Compton, born in 1811. Sadly he died on February 7th 1812. Charlotte eventually bore twelve children, of whom ten survived to adult life.

There is a fine view of Badajoz which is about 3 leagues off. The French are in possession of Badajoz. Returned to dinner and bivouacked.

June 29th. Went to the village to see Crofton. Got some dollars from the Provost. Bivouacked.

June 30th. Bought some small articles at a sale of the Germans. Went to see Crofton. Bivouacked. The French are moving off in two columns.

July 1st. Rode with Percival to a garden nearby, bought some apricots and took as many more. The trees are uncommonly fine. Bivouacked.

July 2nd. The cavalry made a reconnaissance to Badajoz. The French have moved in the direction of Seville. Heard that the prisoners we lost at Fuentes have been rescued near Salamanca by the natives.[1] Bivouacked.

July 3rd. Rode with Bradshaw to the same garden. All the apricots had gone, but we got some fine plums. Bivouacked.

July 4th. A Mail to England. Wrote to Davies and Ramsden. Dined with Rose at the garden. Had some venison for dinner, which was rather high. Saw a lady riding astride. Bivouacked.

July 5th. Bought a mule off Smyth, and exchanged Bess with Crofton for a fan. Bivouacked.

July 6th. Rode with Dawkins and Allix to De Lippe and Elvas. De Lippe mounts 230 guns, 8 of them 24-pounders — the rest are small. The garrison is 900 and two companies of artillery. There is a tank of water within it that contains water for 6 months for 5,000 men. The fortifications are not extensive but are prodigiously strong. Rode on to Elvas. Drank some porter and ate some bread and cheese. Rode back through Headquarters. Money came up. Bivouacked.

July 7th. Lord Wellington was to have been at church but did not come. Digby rode over. Bivouacked.

July 8th. A mail arrived from England up to the 27th. Steele took my batman, Moore, dismissed his servant and made William our Major Domo. Lord Wellington showed our division to the Prince of Orange. Bivouacked.

July 9th. Digby dines with us. Bivouacked.

July 10th. Stayed at home. Steele built another hut. The weather has been very hot. The grass is all burnt up. Bivouacked.

July 11th. Thunder and lightning, but no rain. Got 200 dollars. Wrote to Charles. Dined with Percival. Bivouacked.

July 12th. Thunder as yesterday. Dined by myself. Bivouacked.

July 13th. Sat at home. Heard that Digby Mackworth was taken prisoner at Alberquerque, to which place he had gone contrary to advice. The French were in possession of the town and consequently took possession of him.[2] The grass is entirely burnt up, and I am obliged to send 10 miles for forage. The days and nights are intensely hot. Bivouacked.

[1] There is no reason to doubt that some, at least, of the Coldstreamers taken prisoner at Fuentes de Oñoro had been freed by the Spaniards. As far as the officers were concerned, however, this was not the case. Ensign William Stothert remained as a prisoner-of-war until the end of the Peninsular War in 1814.

[2] See JM's letter to his Mother, August 6th 1811, for more on the subsequent fate of Digby Mackworth.

July 14th. This was as hot a day (barring the hot Tuesday and Wednesday in July 1800) as I ever felt. The sun is very hot from seven in the morning till six at night. The heat of Lisbon is more oppressive than this, arising not so much from the heat of the sun as from a volcanic feel in the air. The Prince of Orange is appointed as extra aide de camp to Lord Wellington, with the rank of lieutenant colonel in the army. I heard of the melancholy death of Colonel Bevan of the Queen's. He had conceived himself alluded to in Lord Wellington's dispatch relative to the escape of the garrison of Almeida. He constantly applied for a Court of Inquiry and was as constantly refused. It preyed upon his spirits and he blew his brains out.[1] Got four loads of good forage. Bivouacked.

July 15th. Began building a hut, as I find the hut I am in is extremely hot. Lord Wellington is not well. The report of our going into quarters is revived. Bivouacked.

July 16th. An aide de camp of Marmont is taken by the guerrillas. The Spanish muleteers make a great noise in rear of my tent, dancing and singing at night, accompanying their discordant voices with the tops of kettles after the manner of tambourines. The right of Marmont's division of the French army is upon Merida, and in that neighbourhood. Soult with the remainder is at Seville. Bivouacked.

July 17th. Sent William over to General Hill to enquire about Mackworth. He did not get back until one in the morning. Bivouacked.

July 18th. My hut is completed at last. The bât and forage money has arrived.[2]

---

[1] Colonel Bevan was actually in command of the 4th (King's Own) Regiment in front of Almeida when the beleaguered garrison of the town was led to safety by its resourceful commander, Brennier, on the night of May 10th 1811. Having placed several mines about the place Brennier personally led his 1,400 men out of the town towards the bridge over the Agueda at Barba del Puerco. In spite of coming under heavy fire from the various British units deployed round the place to stop such an eventuality, Brennier and his men managed to escape back to Massena's camp with the loss of 360 killed, wounded and taken prisoner. His baggage was lost also. Brennier was promoted general of division by Napoleon for his conduct. The escape was facilitated by a great deal of ill-fortune and bad management on the part of the British whose operation was commanded by the unfortunate (again) Sir William Erskine. Wellington was naturally furious and as Fortescue points out, practically turned Fuentes de Oñoro into a defeat. (Fortescue, *History of the British Army*, VIII, 178.) In his despatch of May 15th 1811, *Despatches*, VII, 565-567, Wellington wrote, 'I have never been so much distressed by any military event as by the escape of even a man of them [the garrison].' He went on, 'if the 4th Regiment [under Bevan] had....not missed their road, the garrison must have laid down their arms.' Bevan was not the chief culprit, however, and the army itself believed Erskine to have been responsible. Bevan took his commander's rebuke to heart and with the prospect of a possible court martial looming he shot himself a short while afterwards, much to the regret of the army. Bevan was not the only officer to have either committed suicide or to have got himself shot on having incurred Wellington's wrath. Lieutenant Colonel Sturgeon, of the Staff Corps, is said to have purposely got himself killed at Vic-en-Bigorre on March 19th 1814 having fouled up the organisation of the military post-office following the battle of Orthes the previous month. See also Oman, *History of the Peninsular War*, IV, 348-356, for further analysis of the incident and its aftermath.

[2] According to the *Regulations for the Issue of Bât and Forage*, issued in May 1809, an allowance of 6d per day was payable to all British officers on active service overseas. This covered rations of forage for the animals carrying their baggage. Accord-

July 19th. Dined with Sullivan. The 1st Division of cavalry was reviewed.[1] Bivouacked.

July 20th. The other divisions marched off. Bivouacked.

July 21st. The same dull routine as usual. Bivouacked.

July 22nd. Little or no variation. Bivouacked.

July 23rd. Marched to Assumar. Got quarters in the town with Burgess. Our hostess was young, pretty and agreeable, and by far the most intelligent Portuguese I have met with. She seemed sorry to lose us.

July 24th. Marched into Portalegre. There was a great scramble for quarters. I got a very indifferent one near the jail without any furniture in it.

July 25th. After a rustication of a month, I can hardly persuade myself that I am under a roof. The sun is most tremendously hot.

July 26th. My house is next door to the jail. The jailer's daughter is very pretty. The conscripts for the Portuguese army I see are brought in in irons, and are forwarded from jail to jail till they arrive at their regiments. Above a thousand have deserted lately. One regiment that was 1,200 strong is now 500.[2] A promenade in the evening at the convent of St Bernado. Lord Wellington and his staff were there.

July 27th. Great change of quarters. Dined with Wedderburn.

July 28th. Lord Wellington gave a grand dinner and Ball in honour of the Battle of Talavera.[3] Walcott dined with me. I was too unwell to dine at the table.

July 29th. Kept my bed. Received orders to march on the 31st to Castello Branco.

July 30th. Everyone seems au desespoir at leaving this place; we are just beginning to enjoy ourselves and should have been well pleased to stay another month. I got leave from Fuller to stay two days longer.

ingly, a lieutenant colonel, commanding a battalion, was entitled to ten rations, whereas a captain comanding a company was allowed five. An ensign, like JM, would have been allowed just one ration. In addition to this payment the officers received an advance of 200 days bât and forage money — £3.15s in JM's case — as well as an allowance called baggage money. These last two payments were paid when a battalion was sent overseas.

[1] The 1st Cavalry Division consisted of the 1st Dragoons and 12th Light Dragoons, under Slade, the 13th and 16th Light Dragoons, under George Anson, the 11th Light Dragoons and 1st Hussars KGL, under Victor Alten, and Madden's Portuguese. See Oman, *Wellington's Army, 1809-1814,* p.352.

[2] Unlike Britain, Portugal operated a system of conscription which perhaps accounts for the reluctance on the part of the Portuguese conscripts. Wellington was not unaware of the problem, as he pointed out to Lord Liverpool in August 1811. 'Your Lordship is probably not aware that the whole military force of Portugal is raised by a conscription, not very different from that which prevails in France, and that according to the ancient constitution of Portugal, every individual is obliged to serve in the regular army, in the militia or in the ordenza, as an Officer or soldier.....the people of Portugal, in general, are agriculturalists, and, like those of the same description in all other countries, are very little disposed to military service....they are very much addicted to desertion (not to the enemy) in their own country, as well as in Spain.' (*Despatches,* Wellington to Lord Liverpool, 4th August 1811, VIII, 172.)

[3] Never one to need an excuse to give a party, Wellington nonetheless often held such parties on the anniversary of a battle. Vimeiro, Busaco, Fuentes de Oñoro, Albuera, Badajoz and Salamanca were all celebrated in the years following the battles. See Brett-James' *Life in Wellington's Army,* pp.120-130, for accounts of these parties.

July 31st. The division marched. White and Barrow, having escorted the regiment some distance out of the town, returned, breakfasted and dined with me. The French say they have some 60,000 fresh men at Bayonne. I hear, too, that we are going to beseige Ciudad Rodrigo.

August 1st. Bradshaw and myself dined together at Raikes's old quarters. The town seemed very dull. I bid adieu to the beautiful Menualla and prepared to start the next morning.

August 2nd. To Niza. The morning is so hot that a hen which was on my baggage died of heat. The view as we left Portalegre was beautiful. The sun has just risen and the vineyards and gardens shed a most delightful perfume. At Niza we heard of poor Dalling's death. Nothing ever struck me more. 5 leagues.

August 3rd. To Sarnadas, where we found the brigade. They were bivouacked in the old place. I was delighted to find Paulet Mildmay, who was just returned from Coimbra. I breakfasted and dined with him. Near Niza I overtook some pontoons on artillery carriages. They think we are going to beseige Rodrigo.

August 4th. To Castello Branco. I have seen the heroine of Saraggosa. She is little and ugly, and dresses as a man in a captain's uniform with a sword. She has two little badges upon her arm; what was on them I did not see.[1] I got a most excellent quarter in town. The patrone was a shrewd fellow. Mildmay stayed with me. In the evening we walked around the Bishop's Garden.

August 5th. To Escallias de Sema. I got a dirty quarter in the village. I left William behind at Castello Branco as he was unwell, but expect him up. There has been a skirmish at Alfaiates with the Dragoons. We had one killed and 14 wounded.

August 6th. Halted. Dalling's things were sold. I bought a blue great coat.[2] Mail from England.

In Camp near Castello Branco,
August 6th 1811.

My Dear Mother,

When I last wrote to you we were quietly encamped at St. Olaia where we remained till the 23rd of July. We then moved to Portalegre where we all expected to remain some time. It is a delightful place and after being encamped so long we enjoyed ourselves, and looked forward with great pleasure to the time we should spend there. But such is the uncertainty of all our doings here, that we received orders to march on the 31st, and retraced our steps across the Tagus, through Castello Branco, to this camp where we are halting for a day; and I believe no one soul knows what we are going to do. Various are the conjectures, amongst others that we are going to besiege Ciudad Rodrigo. Our army is I am afraid not healthy: and ten thousand Portuguese troops have des-

---

[1] See also JM's letter to his Mother, August 27th 1811.

[2] Captain Edward Dalling, of the Coldstream, had died on July 31st 1811. This was obviously a sale of his effects. The blue coat mentioned was probably a greatcoat, worn over the uniform in cold weather. The Coldstreamers' greatcoats became so worn out and threadbare that they left them in the breach at Ciudad Rodrigo after the storming of the place in January 1812.

serted within two months. I am glad of it. The fewer we have of them the better.[1]
There was a skirmish on the 3rd at Alfaiates near Sabugal, between our dragoons and the French, so that some part of the French force at all events, has re-
entered Portugal.

Paulet Mildmay will be in England by Christmas. The death of Capt. Dalling
gives him his lieutenancy; but he must wait till he is relieved — he is just
returned from Coimbra, where he was for some time with a detachment; he is as
you may imagine, delighted at the prospect. Three mails are arrived from England and I have no doubt but I shall find a letter from you. But by some mismanagement they are wandering about the country in search of us. The weather is,
and has been for some time, so intensely hot, that it is utterly impossible to
move out in the middle of the day. The Portuguese say that nothing but an
Englishman or a dog ever think of it. I have had a little bilious attack but am
now quite well. You have before this, I dare say heard of Digby Mackworth
being a prisoner, I am afraid it was his own fault, and that his curiosity led him
too far — do not be afraid that I shall ever commit myself in that way, the
Beaux[2] are quite terrible enough at a distance, my *curiosity* never would lead
me very near them. I wrote to Gen. Hill whose aide-de-camp he was to enquire
about him. He said there were some hopes of an exchange; but that must now
be at an end: from the subsequent movements of the armies.[3]

---

[1] JM's opinion of the Portuguese soldier is typical of the British who initially
regarded their allies as lazy, dirty brutes who cared more for their stomachs than fighting
the French. The Portuguese fought with great distinction at Busaco on September 27th
1810, however, and by the end of the Peninsular War had certainly proved their worth to
earn the grudging respect of their British allies. Indeed, on July 25th 1813 Wellington
wrote to Lord Liverpool, 'the Portuguese are now the fighting cocks of the army,' although he added, 'I believe we owe their merits more to the care we have taken of their
pockets and bellies than to the instruction we have given them.' (*Despatches*, Wellington
to Lord Liverpool, 25th July 1813, X, 569.)

[2] ie the French.

[3] The fate of Lieutenant Digby Mackworth can be followed in *Despatches*, VIII,
217, passim. In a tantalising glimpse into the civilities that existed between the two
opposing armies, Wellington wrote to Marmont on August 22nd 1811 offering to exchange Captain d'Artillerie Gravelle for him. (Incidentally, in the same letter Wellington
enquires about the possibility of the release, through exchange, of Captain Lutyens, of
the 11th Light Dragoons, taken prisoner on June 22nd 1811. See note 15 above). Marmont
replied by asking for a certain Captain Larchier in exchange for Mackworth, although this
was refused by Wellington on the grounds that he was not of equivalent rank. Eventually,
Mackworth was given his cartel in exchange for a Lieutenant Miramom, who was a
French prisoner in England. This, in effect, secured his release in lieu of the correspond-
ing release of a French prisoner. The question of parole for prisoners was evidently a
source of great anguish to Wellington who complained about the number of French
prisoners allowed to return to France from England on parole and who never returned.
The same indulgence, he said, had never been extended to British officer prisoners in
France. He added, 'I am sorry to add to this statement, that in the course of three years,
during which I have been opposed to the French armies in the Peninsula, the French
generals have not allowed one Officer to come back upon his parole, excepting Lieut.
Mackworth, who was allowed to return by the Maréchal Duc de Raguse.' (*Despatches*,
Wellington to Hill, 8th November 1811, VIII, 390.) The system of prisoner exchange
dated back to 1781 during the American War of Independence when both sides came to

The difference between this part of Portugal and the Alentejo is very different. This has been so often wasted by the enemy and received a fraternal hug from our army, that there is now, scarce anything for either party to exercise their talent upon. A very shrewd Portuguese I met with a day or two ago said: it makes very little difference to us, whether it is an English and Portuguese, or a French army, which is quartered upon us — the French take everything they can find — your soldiers do the same — the only difference is that you are the civilest of the two. Hood is of course arrived — I never saw anyone more delighted in my life. I hope he may now remain for some time. If I don't send you this scrawl I amy not have an opportunity for some time — they have just sent to say that a Mail is going this moment, so pray excuse this shabby note; I intended it for a long one, but am cut short, with love to all.

Believe me, Ever affect. yrs. John Mills.

August 7th. To Michael d'Arez. I found William there who had been wandering about the country since we left Castello Branco. Wyndham passed through; he breakfasted with me. I took him to dine at Masters'.

August 8th. To Pedrogão. I lost my watch which Paulet luckily found. Bivouacked. 2 leagues.

August 9th. To Val de Lobo, 4 leagues. Left Penamacor on the right. I got under a fig tree near Crofton and Mildmay. Bivouacked. 4 leagues.

August 10th. Halted. There is nothing to be got. It is a village in the mountains, which are if possible worse than those in the plains. At night, not being very well, I got into a hovel.

August 11th. I felt melancholy this day. It was my birthday and the first I had ever spent out of England. We marched, the brigade only, to Penamacor, 2 leagues, where we expect to remain for some little time. My quarters are bad but I do not think it worth while to change. There is a fine view from a large convent and the country below is fertile.

August 12th. No-one seems to know what we are about to do. Headquarters are at Gallegos, near Ciudad Rodrigo. The French are, I hear, at Madrid. If so, we must be waiting for the battering train to beseige Rodrigo.

August 13th. A Market begins to be established, which always happens even in the most desolate parts when troops have been a day or two in the place. Rice, tobacco, rum and other small things are the articles for sale. Butter is almost

an arrangement for the exchange of prisoners involving men of similar rank. Problems arose, of course, when one side had a preponderance of a particular rank. In the Peninsula, local agreements were made whereby a British colonel might be exchanged for two French captains. Once a prisoner was given his parole he agreed not to bear arms against his former captors until the exchange had been completed. Such were the courtesies and formalities of these arrangements that it is recorded that some British prisoners were allowed to leave the camp at Verdun, in France, to return to England in order to arrange their own exchange. However, on their failure to make such an arrangement they returned to France to resume their life as a prisoner-of-war! Digby Mackworth himself was acting as Hill's ADC which probably accounts for the commander-in-chief's involvement. Mackworth later served as ADC to Hill during the Waterloo campaign.

always to be met with even in the smallest places. It is sold for about four shillings a pound. The natives make none. Cows are seldom seen, goats are used as a substitute.

August 14th. Fuller and Peacocke had a shot at each other without effect. The difference was then adjusted.[1]

August 15th. I heard a noise like a dustman's bell and looking out of the window I saw the following procession. First was a boy with a bell, two men in white singing, a man carrying a picture of a martyr or something of the sort, the clergyman and a bier in which was the body of a man. His face was uncovered and the rest of his body was covered with a brown cloth. They do no use coffins.

August 16th. The grapes are just getting ripe. They are not very high flavoured. The vineyards about here are very much out of order and appear not to have been pruned this year. The vines are about five feet high and planted at intervals of about a yard. This is a stupid place and very little is to be procured. Rose, Fremantle and Mildmay dined with me.

August 17th. Colonel Douglas passed through with despatches for Lord Wellington. He brings intelligence of three more heavy regiments of cavalry being on their way out which will complete our force and make it nearly equal to the French.[2] I rode out about the neighbouring vineyards.

August 18th. An officer and twenty men of the 11th Light Dragoons were surprised and taken about four leagues in front of us two days ago. This is the second time within two months that this has happened to the same regiment.[3] A mail is gone through to Headquarters but we have not as yet got our letters.

August 19th. I am in anxious expectation of letters, which have arrived but have not yet come here.

[1] The two officers in question were Lieutenant Colonel Joseph Fuller, of the Coldstream, and Colonel Warren Marmaduke Peacocke, also of the Coldstream and Commandant of the British Army at Lisbon. A good account of the duel exists in Cowell's *Leaves from the Diary of an Officer of the Guards*, pp.143-144. 'One of them established himself at the village of Pedrogão, in some hovel, more convenient-looking than ordinary. The other, of senior rank, arrived later, but, on doing so, turned out the first possessor. Warm expressions passed in consequence; and the following day, while on the march, the ejected party rode up to, and remonstrated with the ejector. The latter coolly assured him that, "so far from relinquishing his right to what he had done now, he should continue to act in the same manner on all future occasions." The other replied that, in such a case, he "sheltered himself under his rank as senior officer, to be guilty of a dirty and ungentlemanlike action." This, of course, was a *closer* to the conversation at the time. After some little delay, these two men went out; the junior fired at the senior, the senior at the junior, and so ended this stupid and ill-occasioned dispute.' Wellington, of course, set himself against such duels in the army but he himself 'went out' with Lord Winchelsea in 1829.

[2] These three cavalry regiments were probably the 4th Dragoon Guards, who arrived on August 15th, the 3rd Dragoons, who arrived on August 20th, and the 5th Dragoon Guards, who arrived before October 1st. See Oman, *Wellington's Army, 1809-1814*, p.352.

[3] A picquet of the 11th Light Dragoons was taken at San Martin de Trebejos, near the Puerto de Perales, on August 14th 1811, by French cavalry on a reconnaissance from Plasencia.

August 20th. Mail arrived from England. A letter arrives from Ramsden. A mail has likewise been sent to England. I wrote to Charlotte,[1] Charles and Ramsden.

Penamacor,
August 20th 1811.

My Dearest Charlotte,

Your letter which I received by the last mail has put me in mind of writing to you; one thing or another had made me postpone it, but it had long been my intention. I am anxious to know whether Harry[2] received a letter of mine of the 21st of June; you do not mention it and I am afraid it may have miscarried. I must begin with giving you an account of the military operations of the army. Headquarters are at Gallegos, a small village on the frontier of Spain, near Almeida. Ciudad Rodrigo is invested.[3] The battering train from Lisbon, which comes by way of Oporto, and so up the Douro, is expected at the beginning of September; the siege will then be undertaken in form, and the French are likely enough to try to raise it. With the reinforcements which are on their way up, we shall be quite strong enough even in the point of cavalry to meet them. Ciudad Rodrigo is by no means a strong place. It is surrounded by a very high wall but has no ditch. It stood three weeks of siege against the French. Since they have had possession of it, I have no doubt but they have made it stronger and if we take it in a month it will be as much as we shall be able to do.[4]

Our division is posted here; I believe in order to be able to move north or south as occasion may require. The 5th is at Castello Branco and watches the great road from Spain into Portugal, which runs through that place. Nobody seems to know where the French are or what they are about; report says they are at Madrid. This I am inclined to doubt, as an advanced party of theirs three nights ago carried off a picquet of an officer and twenty men of the 11th Dragoons from a small village in our front, called St. Martino — it is about three leagues from here. I dare say you all think that we are always near the enemy; and that there is some fighting every day. No, we keep ourselves very quiet, and seldom see a Frenchman. We have however, the consolation of never knowing what we are going to do, or when we are going to march; An order comes in the middle of the night, to march in half an hour; our things are packed up and we

---

[1] Charlotte Mills (1788-1855) was JM's favourite sister. She was a year older than him and was married to Henry Combe Compton (1789-1866), of the Manor House, Minstead, near Lyndhurst. His father, John Compton, sold Bisterne, the manor linked to Minstead since Saxon days, to William Mills, JM's father, in 1792. It had always previously passed through heiresses.

[2] JM's brother-in-law, Henry Combe Compton.

[3] This was actually a blockade, rather than a regular siege. Wellington began his blockade in August but by the end of September was forced to withdraw to Alfaiates as a result of an advance by Marmont who succeeded in revictualling Ciudad Rodrigo.

[4] In fact, JM was being rather pessimistic here, for when Wellington laid siege to Ciudad Rodrigo in January 1812 he took the place in just eleven days of open trenches, from January 8th until the town fell on January 19th.

find some other habitation, sometimes better, sometimes worse than we have left. No one place has any attraction for us and we change our abode from the south to the north, with the greatest indifference. In this uncomfortable gipsy life it is pleasant to think of the scenes that are past, and our friends though at a distance, are associated with past events. The greatest luxury here is to have all your little comforts about you — any place is then tolerable and you are perfectly independent.

I carry about a portable table and stool, on which I am now writing. The Mules which carry your baggage are the only things which cost nothing. You send them out to forage and though it is not lawful to take corn, bat and straw come under no act — the advice I would give anybody coming out to this country would be precisely the reverse of what was given me — I would say, bring out as many little comforts as you can. The state of the country, so ruined by contending armies, affords you none and they are not to be purchased here. The articles of life are all enormously dear; full three times as much as they were two years ago. Bread is fully four times as dear as in England and is getting dearer every day.

The Portuguese live incredibly hard; they have constantly on the fire an earthen pot into which they put a few leaves, and water. Those that can afford it add a little oil to this mess; when it is sufficiently boiled they put it into a plate, and the family assemble round it, each with a spoon, and a small bit of bread. They have always one of these pots on the fire; and will devour the contents seven or eight times a day. Both men, women and children seem to have no occupation.

The soil is delightful, and at two periods of the year, they have some employment sowing and reaping. The friendly interposition of allies as well as the enemy frequently save from the last — a fat English farmer would be mad at the approach of an army; they shrug their shoulders and say nothing. The consequence is, that the quantity of land in cultivation is very small, and in a short time a field of corn will be quite a sight. Immediately about this place there are a great many vineyards. Few of them have been pruned, and consequently bear but little. The vines are trained to poles about five feet high: the grapes are now almost ripe; they are about as high flavoured as the outdoor grapes in England. Portugal generally speaking, is a wild but not picturesque country. There is no character in their cottages, and chapels that are frequently built on rocks, look more like a hideous white summer house than anything else. The rivers are few and even the most considerable are generally dry in summer. Lakes they have none. It has all the desolate appearance of Scotland without its sublimity; and those spots which have been reserved by nature from the general waste, to supply the wants of the people, bear the sad marks either of the indolence of the Nation, or the ravages of war.

The climate is by no means a delightful one. We are apt to complain of the fickleness of our own; but a fine day doubly repays a bad one, and holds out the greater inducement to enjoy it. The laws of weather are here fixed. There is the wet, and the dry season. For more than two months I have seen but one shower of rain — three hours in the evening is all that can be enjoyed of this mass of sunshine — and this will be all repaid by several months of wet. Until you have left it, you know not the delights of England.

Now that I have formally introduced myself to you as a correspondent, I intend from time to time to write to you. In return I expect to hear from you. It will be no excuse to say you have nothing to write about. I shall be delighted to hear of the most indifferent things; even a detail of the thoughts and actions of the Walcott family would be amusing. I saw that bright luminary, Mr Yeomans at Portalegre, he is a volunteer in the service of his country;[1] his own troop being stationed at Lisbon, his aspiring genius could not brook the inactivity of remaining there, so he took up his sword and marched to the army. Genl. Graham, of some notoriety in the fighting world, has joined the army, and takes command of this, the 1st Division. Lord Wellington likes him much; he is like him. An active, enterprising man, Lord W. has never once been to bed since he came to this country. He dresses himself at night, and lies down in a cloak — I do not find that he recommends this same exercise to his staff, or the rest of the army. It may suit such aspiring heroes, but I am a plain man, and prefer dressing in the mornings.[2] Paulet Mildmay is returning from Coimbra, where he was for two months, with a detachment of sick; he is now on the point of returning home. I am sure you will like him as much as ever; he is the same good humoured excellent fellow that he was. I have got a dear old pet brown goat, which would suit your little boy. She is quite a parlour boarder — I dare say you are surprised at the idea of drinking goat's milk; it is really not so bad, and the animal besides being more portable, eats much less than a cow.

Should we advance into Spain, I will tell you all about this race of people; possessing much more character in their manners and costume, than their neighbours, and differing very materially from them in everything but indolence. The

[1] Yeomans Walcott was noted in an earlier letter, June 27th 1811. A Royal Artillery officer, Walcott had been stationed at the artillery barracks at Christchurch and must have been known to Charlotte as well as JM who had dined with him.

[2] Wellington's sleeping habits were not quite as spartan as JM would have us believe, although it is recorded that he slept in his cloak on many occasions. He did, in fact, possess a brass-framed chair which converted into a camp bed by way of an extension to the seat, made of canvas, with legs, which could be folded forward, almost in the manner of a modern sun-lounger. Proof that Wellington did sleep in a bed comes from the pen of John Stepney Cowell, who recalled a dinner party held in 1810 at which a friend, Mr Sudenham, who was visiting headquarters, remarked, 'With the details you have to think of, the numerous affairs, both political and diplomatic, you have to provide for, added to the military responsibility you have to bear, I cannot conceive how you can sleep in your bed?' Wellington simply replied, 'When I thrown off my clothes I throw off my cares, and when I turn in my bed it is time to turn out.' (Cowell, *Leaves from the Diary of an Officer of the Guards*, p.37.) James Thornton, Wellington's cook, recalled the tent arrangements in camp before Badajoz. 'The tent the Duke occupied to sleep in was enclosed in a large Marquee, the Marquee serving for a sitting and dining room; the gentlemen of the staff had a tent each, smaller than the Marquee. I had a round tent to sleep in, the Butler one also, my two Assistants had one between them, the Duke's footmen and all the staff servants had one tent for two servants, all the servants' tents were round ones, the gentlemen's small Marquees — the Duke's tent was very near the others, they were all pitched in one field.' (*Your Most Obedient Servant: James Thornton, Cook to the Duke of Wellington*, p.105.)

natural antipathy of the one nation to the other is very great. The Spaniards, who in different occupations follow the army, carry firearms to protect them from the Portuguese. Let my mother know you have heard from me. I was obliged to leave off in the middle of the last letter I wrote her but as she will hear of me from you I shall defer making her reparation till the next post. I was not surprised to hear of General Scott's death. None will regret it much and he had arrived at a good old age, and if he could, would have no right to complain.[1]

The gay world seems at last to have recovered the shock of the Prince's fête. For some time after, nothing was to be heard but accounts of streams of water in the middle of a table, with fish and weeds congenial to the soil and tubs of shoes, which the anxiety of spectators had induced to leave behind.

August 21st. Masters dined with me. My establishment is not flourishing in a way, William being obliged to go to hospital at Castello Branco.
August 22nd. Dined with Masters. We played cards in the evening at Raikes's.
August 23rd. Dined with General Campbell, who is not what the world would call a wag.
August 24th. I took a ride to a neighbouring vineyard. The grapes are now ripe. The road out of the town is so bad that it is a service of danger.
August 25th. A usual ride to the usual vineyard.
August 26th. A mail has arrived from England; letters from Bisterne and Charles. The weather is now really cold, so sudden a change from extreme heat.
August 27th. Wrote to my Mother, and to Francis. I gave a card party but was obliged to break it up soon on account of our marching in the morning.

                                                                 Penamacor,
                                                           August 27th 1811.

My Dearest Mother,

Luckily you have very good eyes or I am sure you would not be able to read my letters; I really feel ashamed to send a shabby letter so many miles, and not being able to get large paper, I am reduced to contract a hand which in its best days is not remarkable for its exuberance. We have been here since my Natal day, the 11th of this month,[2] and are likely to stay some little time longer; this of course is merely conjecture for humbug is the great system here as well as elsewhere; and however unimportant the matter, the greatest mystery envelops it. However, ten thousand fresh [French] troops have arrived at Vittoria; a town as you will see by the map, on the great north road into Portugal; and it is conjectured that they have a design upon Oporto.

[1] General Scott (1732-1811) was a natural son of the 2nd Duke of Buccleuch and was brought up by him. He married JM's aunt, Harriet Mills.
[2] JM's birthday, August 11th. He was now 22 years old.

Our movements will be regulated by theirs, and Oporto being a town but little inferior to Lisbon, will I have no doubt be protected. Our army is healthy, considering the season of the year. The men who have lately come out from England have suffered, as they always do considerably.[1] The French, who deal a good deal in round numbers reckon that if they take the field in the Spring with their battalions eight hundred strong, that if they have four hundred at the end of the campaign, they are well off — of course all casualties are included. They certainly do lose more men in proportion than we do. Their movements are quicker, and more harassing and if a man lies down from fatigue, the Spaniards are sure to kill him. I attempted to argue the point with a man of Don Julian's Corps who murdered sixteen large carts full of wounded after the Battle of Fuentes [de Oñoro]. Instead of being ashamed of it, he considered it as a great feat; nor could I persuade him that the situation of a wounded man differed materially from another. He said that the wounded were Frenchmen, and that he was justified in killing them wherever he could find them. No wonder then if the French hang them.

The battering train is on its way to Ciudad Rodrigo which I hope will be ours ere long. It is only defended by a Moorish wall; and a garrison of twelve hundred men.[2] The information Lord Wellington gets by his spies is remarkably good. There is a man at Salamanca whom the French have never been able to discover, that regularly sends accounts. When Marmont's headquarters were there he even related conversations which took place at his table.[3] Both sides

[1] Adjusting to the climate was often a major problem for new battalions upon arrival in the Peninsula. On October 1st 1812, the 1st Battalion 1st Foot Guards arrived at Corunna to join Wellington's army with the 3rd Battalion, which had been at Cadiz, coming up in the following month. Within the space of just one month, however, the two battalions, which had formed the 1st Brigade of Guards, had been laid low with sickness. The returns for November 25th 1812 show a total of 696 sick out of 2,541, a ratio of one in four. By February 1813 the situation had become so bad that Wellington ordered the 1st Foot Guards to Oporto to recuperate. In March there were still just 355 and 430 men fit for active service in the 1st and 3rd Battalions respectively and it was not until June 24th 1813 that the brigade was strong enough to begin its march from Oporto to rejoin Wellington's army. See Hamilton, *The Origin and History of the First, or Grenadier Guards*, II, 448-450. Sickness amongst newly-arrived battalions was one of the reasons why Wellington introduced his so-called 'Provisional Battalions'. Rather than send his veteran battalions that had been weakened by continual action home to England to recruit, Wellington preferred to keep them in the Peninsula to form Provisional Battalions. See also Oman, *Wellington's Army, 1809-1814*, pp.187-188.

[2] JM was not too wide of the mark here. By the time Wellington laid siege to the town in January 1812 the garrison had grown to around 1,800 all ranks, of which 1,500 were infantry.

[3] It is highly probable that this man was Dr Patrick Curtis, Regius Professor of Astronomy and Natural History at the University of Salamanca and Rector of the Irish College there. Curtis had entered the college in 1769 and ran his own intelligence service from beneath the noses of the French. Captain William Tomkinson, of the 16th Light Dragoons, wrote in his journal on June 21st 1812, 'In Salamanca I became acquainted with a priest, who was much with Lord Wellington, and had sent him nearly all the information he received from Salamanca. He was a superior, quiet sort of person; and during the time the enemy occupied the place, was on such terms with them as not to be suspected.' (Tomkinson, *The Diary of a Cavalry Officer in the Peninsular War and Wat-*

depend upon it, know nearly the situation of the other. They used to be very far
superior to us in espionage, but we are improving in this, as well as in other
matters. We are beginning to grumble a little about our pay. We are two months
in arrears, instead of being one in advance.[1] To the men this is a serious evil, as
there are many little necessaries they are deprived of, amongst others, salt, to
those who have never been in want of it, this may seem a trifle. Those only who
have been without it, know its importance. The French I believe have had very
little, if any pay, for two years. But they take what they want; and it does not so
much signify. We don't do the same; because we are in a friend's country and
the want of money is seriously felt. Give me an enemy's country to make war in.
If they get paid at all, they think themselves lucky; But an ally knows you must
buy his bread and makes you pay his price, instead of yours. You see what
Piratical ideas campaigning gives.

I saw the Heroine of Saraggosa the other day, a heroine of all people in
the world ought to be beautiful and I really should have thought it incumbent
upon me, to have fallen in love with her; But nature has bestowed upon her, a
visage so much in opposition to my ideas of beauty that with all my previous
determination I could not do it. She was dressed in a jacket, turned up with red,
and upon her arm she had two badges; resembling those you see at Westminster Bridge upon the arm of a Waterman. She had half boots, and pantaloons. I
saw her two days after; she had doffed the pantaloons, and assumed petticoats
— I had forgot to mention, a huge cutlass, which hung by her side.[2] The dress

erloo Campaign, 1809-1815, p.167.) Jock Haswell, in his The First Respectable Spy: The
Life and Times of Colquhoun Grant, Wellington's Head of Intelligence, pp.175-181, gives
a good account of Curtis' activities including an interview with Marmont. Wellington
himself, without mentioning names, gives an alluring glimpse into the business in a
despatch to Charles Stuart on June 1st 1812. 'I have long had in contemplation the means
of obtaining intelligence from distant and various parts of the Peninsula, and I had settled
a plan with that view with our principal correspondent at Salamanca, who is certainly the
best of the whole class. In searching for correspondents at Madrid, he has fallen in with
the persons with whom you correspond in that city.' (Despatches, Wellington to Charles
Stuart, 1st June 1812, IX, 198.)

[1] Pay was a subject close to the hearts of all of Wellington's men, and every other
army too. On August 1st 1811 the men had been paid only up until June 24th of the same
year, whereas they ought to have been paid up until August 24th. The officers' bât and
forage allowance which was due in March of that year had yet to be paid either, while
the Spanish muleteers were six months in arrears. See Despatches, Wellington to Lord
Liverpool, August 1st 1811, VIII, 161. This was a major headache for Wellington who
wrote in the same despatch, 'I did not think it necessary to trouble your Lordship upon
that subject [ie the want of money]; nor should I do so now, if I did not feel the utmost
anxiety upon it, particularly as these wants will materially affect any prospect we may
have of carrying on the war offensively.' The shortage of money resulted from a problem
between Spain and her colonies and, secondly, American ships who, after having brought
corn to Lisbon, required payment by specie rather than by the usual method of taking its
equivalent value in English-made goods. This latter problem was due to the trade dispute
between Britain and America, President Madison having imposed a ban on trade between the two countries. See also Fortescue, History of the British Army, VIII, 342-344.

[2] The 'Heroine of Saragossa', as JM calls her, was Augustina Zaragoza, who rose to
fame during the two French sieges of Saragossa in 1808 and 1809. The girl had groped
her way through smoke and dust to seize the linstock from a dying gunner before firing

of the Spaniards is particularly picturesque — they are much addicted to gaudy colours; but there is a vast deal of taste in the arrangement of them. The Portuguese on the contrary, have a very sombre appearance. The women when they go out wear a black cloak, on their heads a clean white handkerchief; the men in the hottest weather wear a snuff coloured cloak, which they wrap round them, and look precisely like assassins. Even the little boys wear a cocked hat. I am much mistaken if they do begin to feel themselves a little squeezed by the fraternal hug we have given them. One of the great systems of this war, is to eat up a country. The word itself sounds horrid, but the eating up is done to render it useless to the enemy. You then retire or advance, and find some other country to be devoured. This cannibal like system may suit us, who are sure to find some other place, when we have devoured the one we are in. But it does not suit the natives, who are to live for ten months in a country, which the General prides himself upon having picked to the bone — the little money they may have gained will not as in England purchase bread — that is all gone; and if some little should remain, the owner will not part with it, not knowing where to get more. The people know that they must lose all their grain and cattle upon the eating system, and who can wonder then that they should be tired of the war and after all it makes not the smallest difference to them, whether the House of Braganza or of Bonaparte is upon the throne. The voice of the people would if they were to open their mouths, call for rest upon any terms. It is the voice of the grandees you hear, who do not suffer the privations to the same extent, and are influenced by different motives. I am much amused by Taylor's zeal and shall be much mistaken if his return be not as precipitate, as his advance. A bivouac in a wet night would settle his ardour.

I received yesterday a letter from you of the 5th of August. I wish the weather there may be as fine as it is here. We are on top of a high hill; and get a little breeze which we have not had before for some time. We have had but one shower of rain for three months and that was two months ago — it would really be a pleasing variety. The grapes are ripe; and the morning's ride is generally to a vineyard. They are small black grapes without much flavour. I have found a few Frontiniac — water melons are in abundance — I think them but an indifferent fruit. Cucumbers are also in great plenty — the bon vivants take out the seeds, and stuff them with forced meat so you see we are not starving. Paulet Mildmay expects soon to be relieved by Beckford, he will then not be long before he is in England — at least it will not be his fault if he is. He will be a great loss to us here and as great a gain in England. My servant, whom I

a 24-pounder gun into the ranks of approaching French infantry. Her actions encouraged the wavering defenders who forced the oncoming French to retire with heavy loss. She was immortalised in Byron's *Childe Harolde's Pilgrimage*, in which she is described as having, 'long looks that foil the painter's power.....her fairy form, with more than female grace.' Byron's image of the girl, and certainly that in several romantic paintings, is not how she appeared in real life if JM's description of her is to be believed, and there is no reason why it should not be. She managed to escape from Saragossa when the place surrendered in February 1809 and lived for many years afterwards. She is buried in the Portillo Church in Saragossa. See also Rudorff's *War to the Death: The Sieges of Saragossa, 1808-1809,* for her adventures during the siege.

brought with me is ill, and I have been obliged to send him to the hospital at Castello Branco. I hope he will be soon well enough to join me, for I am at sixes and sevens without him. When you do not hear from me, and want to know in what part of the country I am in, look in the newspapers for the 1st Division — The Guards are in it.[1] Whenever circumstances will allow it, we are at Headquarters. But that is not always the case, as for instance now. Lord Wellington is at Guinaldo, a village on the frontiers, a league in front of Puebla de Azura; where the regiment was when I joined it and for some time after. We are favourites with his Lordship; who always makes a point of inviting a certain number of us to dinner, when we are with him — of course the others are jealous of us. William's old regiment, the 58th, is at Lisbon being deemed unfit from bad conduct for service.[2] The old General[3] would not have liked to hear this account of his gallant crew but it is so. I have heard nothing of Digby Mackworth; so I imagine he is by this time in France — I am afraid it was in some degree his own fault.

I hear a most deplorable account of Miss Long's fete at Wanstead; amongst other complaints that there was a lack of eatables. That might be excusable here, by not at Wanstead. One really would imagine that there had been an army there upon the eating principle; besides those who were there, who seemed to have been inclined, had it been in their power, to pursue the same. The next time you write will you send me some black ribbon for shoes strings, and a few shirt buttons — both of these articles rarely to be met with here.

Believe me, Most truly yours, John Mills.

August 28th. To Val de Rosa. By way of shortening the road we went a league round. I got an indifferent quarter.

August 29th. To Sabugal. The town is in a much worse state than when we were last here. Few of the houses have floors and the one I am in has such large holes in it, that I am afraid of breaking my leg.

August 30th. Moved in the evening to St Bartholemew, a most romantic village. The streets were covered with trellis work of vines. The houses were so extremely bad that I borrowed Raikes's tent and pitched it under some very fine chestnut trees. The night was beautifully serene. Bivouacked.

[1] On August 27th 1811, the composition of the 1st Division of the army was as follows: Campbell's brigade, the 1/Coldstream, 1/3rd Foot Guards, 1 coy 5/60th, Stopford's brigade, 2/24th, 2/42nd, 1/79th, 1/26th, 1 coy 5/60th, and Löw's brigade, 1st, 2nd and 5th Line KGL. The division had been commanded by Spencer until August 9th when Sir Thomas Graham was appointed to command. See Oman, *Wellington's Army, 1809-1814*, pp.351 & 353.

[2] William Mills (1791-1839) was JM's nearest younger brother. Not going to university, he was commissioned in the 58th Regiment and joined its 2nd Battalion in Portugal well before JM joined the Coldstream. He seems to have annoyed JM by boasting about his campaigning upon return to England, as JM makes a series of patronising comments.

[3] This was their uncle, General Scott, who was colonel of the 58th Regiment from 1787 to 1811. He must have granted his nephew, William, a commission. See also JM's letter to Charlotte, August 20th 1811.

August 31st. Halted. I rode over to Sabugal and there heard that we were to march tomorrow morning. Bivouacked.

September 1st. To Novinha — 2 leagues. There is little shade and the water is bad. Bivouacked.

September 2nd. Marched at three o'clock to Nave de Haver, 4 leagues, through Villa Mayor. Near that place we heard two shots which proved to be the sentence of a Court Martial upon a man of the Chasseurs Britanniques for desertion.[1] This being the first day of shooting, I thought often of my friends in England. I drank a bumper to my brother sportsmen and envied them.

September 3rd. Wrote to H. This is indeed a horrid place. Mounted main guard.

Nave de Haver, Nr Almeida.
September 3rd 1811.

My Dear Harry,

On coming in yesterday from a long and hot march, I received a long letter from Manor House, the joint composition of diverse hands — yours occupying the greater extent of paper, shall be answered first. I thought of you often in the course of yesterday and drank your health in a bumper. We halted for half an hour, and heard two shots fired, which I immediately declared to be at partridges but found it to be at an unfortunate member of the army who was shot for desertion. I wrote to Charlotte from Penamacor, since which we have moved up here — for what purpose we are at a loss to conjecture. The general opinion seeming to be now, that we shall not undertake the siege of Ciudad Rodrigo. If not all must be over for this campaign, and a miserable end it is. It was begun by a retreat of the enemy as fine as any on record. We then fought to save Almeida; succeeded for the moment, but allowed the garrison to escape, and even suffered them to take prisoners some of the besieging army. I would rather have the credit of that one enterprise, than all the Laurels put together, of all the campaigns in this country. We then fought the battle of Albuera — The most sanguine even doubt the victory claimed, even as related in the Gazette account, and even that account is questionable as there is a dispute between Beresford and the Spaniards as to whether Blake did, or did not occupy the hill which cost us so many lives.[2] We then besieged Badajoz, found there were in the

[1] See also JM's letter to his Mother, June 27th 1811.

[2] At the battle of Albuera, on May 16th 1811, General Joachim Blake commanded three Spanish divisions totalling nearly 11,000 troops. When the battle began Blake was convinced that the main French attack would be delivered from the east against the centre of the Allied position, which was the town of Albuera itself. However, at about 9am a massive French attack developed to the south, the French troops debouching from thick woods which had covered their advance. The alarmed Beresford immediately ordered Blake to face south to meet them, the British 2nd Division being sent in support. Beresford then rode off in blissful ignorance for Blake, still convinced that the main French attack would be delivered from the east, virtually ignored the order and instead deployed just four of his battalions to meet the attack from the south. In the struggle that followed heavy casualties were sustained by Allied troops, in driving the French back.

whole battering train but seven straight guns and twice attempted to storm. The first time, the breach was not practicable — the next the ladders were two feet too short. On the approach of the enemy the siege was given up.[1] This is all that has been done. We have lost more men from sickness than in any former campaign, have harassed them more and have worked up the cavalry till half of them are unfit for duty and have lost several picquets of them in a most disgraceful way, and yet we shall be told that the army has covered itself with glory, and that in the end the French must be beat. More money must be granted to carry on the expense of the war and England must be drained to support it. At the end of a few years, people will open their eyes, and see they have been humbugged and even now, if they would divest themselves of prejudice and think for themselves they would see their error. Lord Wellington is a great General, but beats even the Dean of Ch Ch at humbug.[2]

The body of the French are now at Truxillo, on the road to Madrid. But their patrols come very near us, though the armies are so far distant. They are fond of doing this, as it obliges us to keep strong picquets out in front and their superiority in cavalry enables them to do it without working up their horses. In England it may be no difficult matter to bring a horse round; but here it is the work of time. The supplies of corn are very irregular and they have to go long distances for straw — not as in England for litter, but as a substitute for hay — and this too must be carried upon the sick horse so that it is next to impossible to get them round. However, most of our Dragoons, and all the artillery drivers will sell their corn. Mares stand the work better than horses. Lord Wellington rides nothing else. I think you have been very lucky about selling Johnny; he was a nice little horse but at all events you got his value. Old Morant did not think very highly of him.[3] I am anxious to hear how you succeed at this moment in your shooting and likewise hope to hear of Jack Early's being in limbo at Winchester;[4] he disgraces the dignity of vengeance. Morant really ought not to continue the farm to the old one.[5] Lord Tweedale by way of a wise thing had brought out a pack of hounds to hunt in the winter months. If you were to see

[1] The second siege of Badajoz had begun on May 29th 1811 but was a far from satisfactory affair. The two chosen points of attack were the castle, part of the town itself, and the fort San Christobal, which lay on the left bank of the Guadiana. The old siege guns used during the siege proved totally inadequate and when an attempt to escalade the San Christobal was made on June 10th the ladders proved far too short, the tenacious defenders beating off the attack with ease. Of the 400 or so men used in the assault 139 became casualties. The castle, on the other hand, was breached on June 10th but when Wellington received news of the imminent junction in the area of the armies of Marmont, Soult and D'Erlon he called off the operation and the Allied army withdrew into Portugal.

[2] JM had been an undergraduate at Christ Church, Oxford.

[3] The 'old' is presumably ironic, as this is John Morant (1787-1857). He owned not only Brockenhurst Park but also the Manor House, Ringwood. As such, the Morants were the landlords of the northern farms on the present Bisterne estate until outlying lands were exchanged with JM in the 1800s.

[4] This is probably a reference to the County Jail at Winchester. There was a tenant named Early on the estate the Morants bought at Ringwood. It would have been only too easy for the tenant's son, Jack, to net the nearby Bisterne partridges on stubbles at night.

[5] ie Jack's father, Early senior.

this country you would really pity him. I think it will generally end in a red herring.

In all human probability we shall winter in the north of Portugal — if so I shall be in the way of procuring port wine. If you should care to have a pipe, I daresay I could get you a good one. The price used to be £30; I fancy it is now raised, but not more than £40 — at all events it must be cheaper than you can buy in London. The country wine is vile; we pay here $6 a bottle for Port — what an imposition.

I wish you were in this country to see the grapes; a vineyard would be a delightful thing to meet with in a hot September day. You eat as many for nothing, as Mr. Owen would charge you five guineas for. If I had a dog here I could kill a great deal of game quails and hares are in abundance. But few of the Spanish Pointers will hunt, and none of them will stand, so that you must officiate as a Spaniel yourself, which in a burning hot sun is not so pleasant.[1] I defer my sporting till after the next general action, when I hope to pick up some gunpowder. You would have been amused to see me at Fuentes after the fight was over, with a large bag under my arm into which I put all the odd articles I could find. I found myself proprietor of several bridles, amongst other things. We are about a league from Fuentes. I shall take a look at our old place; but I am afraid my teeth will chatter.

French deserters come in now and then — at least Germans in the French pay. They say they are all sick of the business, and want to get back and no wonder either, for they have not been paid for two years and you know, fighting without pay is the very devil. Very few of the French desert, the Germans on both sides make a practise of it, and continually get shot for it. A cavalry man who deserts has the money arising from the sale of his horse and accoutrements, which is a great inducement to them. Some of our dragoon horses have sold for very large prices — the French Generals all ride English horses, and wear whole boots, and pantaloons which they think very knowing. They live very well and never pay for anything. Junot stayed for some time at Lisbon, in the house of a rich merchant. He made him keep a public table for him, and when he went away, took with him a service of plate. Most of these Bucks have made immense fortunes in this way and they have always been lucky enough to make war in an enemy country, which you may rely upon is the right thing. They got their own price for everything from us, and we pay for what the French have taken. I should like to turn the tables upon them. I am sure they set us down for a parcel of fools. We are just upon the borders of Spain, and get a

[1] Hare coursing and fox-hunting were two of the favourite pastimes of Wellington and his officers in the Peninsula. The Coldstream Guards even supplied their own huntsman, Tom Crane, who had spent many years with the Fife Hunt in Scotland. Crane appeared regularly at hunts dressed in a long scarlet coat and on one occasion both he and the pack of hounds were captured by the French after chasing a fox into enemy-held territory. Both Crane and the hounds were later released by a bemused enemy. See Brett-James, *Life in Wellington's Army*, p.204. John Rous, a comrade of Mills, was a keen courser and kept a fine kennel of greyhounds as well as a large number of horses at his home in Suffolk. One of his horses, 'Quiz', won seventeen races including the 1801 St Leger.

specimen of both countries. I like the Spaniards the best of the two. They have more originality of language. Both have the same turn for stealing and take particular fancy to your small articles — it is bred with them, and they cannot get rid of it. If you happen to be in the house of a better sort of person it is just the same.

I must now conclude this epistle. I will every now and then let you hear how we are going on and do pray let me hear from you. Everything English is interesting. My best wishes and respects to all of you, and believe me, Most truly, yrs John Mills.

PS. Will you send a line to Charles and tell him the Box has arrived at Lisbon.[1]

September 4th. Rode over to Puebla. Our hut was totally destroyed. The inhabitants were delighted to see us and would insist upon our having fried bacon and wine.

September 5th. Settled the accounts of the Puebla fête.[2]

September 6th. General Graham arrived here to take command of the division. I hear he has a host of cooks and mules loaded with wine tant mieux.[3]

September 7th. Dined with Mildmay. Ciudad Rodrigo is invested but not regularly. The communication is cut off on the principal roads. The French are now assembling in force at Salamanca and the Porte de Bagnios. Half of Don Julian's predatory band are surprised and taken by the French.

September 8th. Mildmay and Crofton dined with me. We smoked and drank a good deal of wine.

September 9th. Heard of the arrival of a mail at Headquarters.

September 10th. The mail came up. Heard from G.M.

September 12th. Rode over to Headquarters at Guinaldo to a sale of Colonel Drummond's things, who died a few days ago. The wet weather has partially set in. The people of the country reckon the sun of this month is particularly unwholesome.

September 13th. A detachment of the brigade under Sullivan's command went to the village about 2 miles off to learn mining and sapping.[4]

[1] Charles Mills, 3rd son of William Mills. He joined Glynn Mills Bank, was created baronet in 1868. The title of Baron Hillingdon, of this branch of the family, is now extinct.

[2] See JM's Journal for June 4th 1811.

[3] It was generally accepted that General Sir Thomas Graham had the largest of all generals' establishments which needed no less than forty mules to carry it and around £2,000 per annum to maintain. See Ward, *Wellington's Headquarters*, p.38. Graham was noted for his splendid dinner parties and his large retinue. After the storming of Ciudad Rodrigo on January 19th 1812, Graham acquired the services of the governor's cook, Clément, who, an unwilling combatant in the fight, had hidden himself in a chimney. When British soldiers entered the place they lit a fire whereupon Clément came scrambling down. Upon hearing of the Frenchman's plight Graham offered him a position in his mess. See Brett-James, *General Graham*, p.245.

[4] This is an interesting comment by JM. Unlike the French army there was no corps of sappers and miners in the British army. All of the spadework done during the sieges in the Peninsula was done by ordinary infantrymen who loathed the work and

September 14th. Our division and I believe the others are very unhealthy. The 79th have been sent to the rear. I dined with Mildmay.

September 15th. The weather is getting settled again. Saw a comet.

September 16th. I went to a fair at Freineda. The French are going to attempt to send a convoy into Ciudad Rodrigo, which is likely to bring on a general action. The 24-pounder guns are not come up.

September 17th. The 4th Division marched through to Aldea de Ponte and adjacent places. The general opinion seems to be that there will be an affair. Mail from England. I heard from Elizabeth.

September 18th. Mail to England. Wrote to Plymouth. Rain and mud.

September 19th. In the evening we received orders to hold ourselves in readiness to march. Things look busy. The heavy guns are 10 leagues on the other side of the Coa, over which a bridge has been built.

September 20th. We are in readiness, but have not yet received orders to march. Five large howitzers that throw 24lb shot have arrived here, besides one German howitzer. The French are advancing. Soult's force has left Plasencia and marches in the direction of Porte de Bagnios, a strong pass in the occupation of the French in our front. Rain and cold. I set fire to my house.

September 21st. The Army suffers considerably from sickness. The French have reinforcements coming up amounting to 27,000 men. Amongst them are the Dutch Guards. For these four or five last nights a Comet has been visible in the north, bright with a long tail which points to the south. A mail from England. Letter from E.M.

September 22nd. The whole division is ordered to concentrate here tomorrow. The army is drawn together and is to be supplied with 3 days' provisions. Fishy.

September 23rd. The cavalry passed through to the front where provisions are likewise moving. We are in readiness to march. The Third Regiment [of Guards] marched in. Everything is in confusion; our baggage is sent on the other side of the Coa. Everything portends a battle. The Light Division has been driven in on the Salamanca road.

September 24th. Two squadrons of French cavalry passed the Agueda likewise. The convoy got in safe.[1] Previously, six hundred cavalry drove in some of ours. An officer went into Ciudad, stayed a little time and came out.

September 25th. We were ordered under arms about ten o'clock. At eleven we saw the artillery at work in the direction of Guinaldo, and our cavalry moving up. The 16th and 14th Light Dragoons charged some Polish lancers near Espeja, and routed them, killing one captain and several men, and taking one lieutenant

regarded it as 'navvies' work'. There did exist, however, the Royal Military Artificers, who might be termed the predecessors of the Royal Sappers and Miners. Their number was so few, however, as to be almost worthless. The work itself was superintended by the Royal Engineer officers and one can only assume that the intention of sending officers to a 'school' of sapping and mining was to instruct them in the very basic rudiments of the art in order that they were then able to organise their own working parties at each particular siege.

[1] The French convoy carrying provisions into Ciudad Rodrigo entered the town on September 24th 1811.

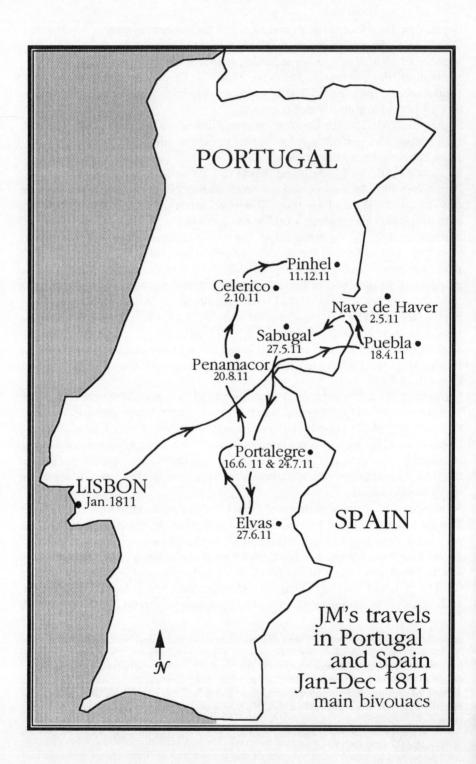

PORTUGAL

Pinhel •
11.12.11

Celerico •
2.10.11

Nave de Haver •
2.5.11

Sabugal •
27.5.11

Puebla •
18.4.11

Penamacor •
20.8.11

Portalegre •
16.6. 11 & 24.7.11

LISBON
• Jan.1811

SPAIN

Elvas •
27.6.11

N

JM's travels
in Portugal
and Spain
Jan-Dec 1811
main bivouacs

and some men prisoners.[1] I spoke to the lieutenant who said they were all, officers and men, sick of the business, and added that the Emperor ordered it and he must be obeyed. In a la tête d'un diable. The skirmishing was too distant to be discerned even with a glass. I could plainly discern the smoke of the guns and bodies moving. It is remarkable that the present scene should be so near, almost upon the ground of the action of Fuentes [de Oñoro]. We remained under arms till dark. In the evening the enemy's cavalry drove ours from Carpio. In the morning, the French advanced upon our right with a heavy body of cavalry, who took two of our guns. They were retaken by the 5th Regiment who charged the cavalry. They received the charge of the cavalry formed in a square with guns in the centre. The enemy lost I should think 100 in the day.[2]

September 26th. In the morning the 6th Division passed through. Everything is quiet in front. There are rumours of marching. Our artillery did great execution yesterday. Their cavalry exposed themselves unnecessarily to a battery of 6 guns. They then charged them and took two, which were retaken by the 5th. Lord Wellington entrenched himself before Guinaldo. The enemy did the same and we looked at each other the whole day. The French were in immense force.[3]

[1] When Wellington received news that a force of French troops amounting to about 60,000 men was approaching Ciudad Rodrigo, he was obliged to give up the blockade and move away to the south-west. As the Allied army withdrew French units made reconnaissance expeditions which resulted in the clashes on September 25th. The action described by JM took place between Espeja and Carpio where two British cavalry regiments, the 14th and 16th Light Dragoons, successfully engaged not Polish lancers but the Lancers du Berg and the 26th Chasseurs. The French lost one officer and ten men killed and five officers and 32 men taken prisoner, most of whom were wounded. British losses were just one officer and ten men wounded. As Oman points out, this was the first time that British cavalrymen had encountered lancers. See Oman, *History of the Peninsular War*, IV, 563-564. Lieutenant William Tomkinson, who was serving with the 16th Light Dragoons, thought the lance to be more of an encumbrance and added that, 'we had only one person hurt with a lance, and when retiring, they got on the ground, caught in the appointments of other men, and pulled more dragoons off their horses than anything else.' (Tomkinson, *Diary of a Cavalry Officer*, pp.115-116.)

[2] On September 25th, following the fight which took place between Cario and Espeja, an Allied force of about 1,000 infantry and 500 cavalry, supported by two batteries of artillery, clashed with a French force of some 2,500 cavalry astride the road to the north-west of the village of El Bodon. During the action the 2/5th (Northumberland) Regiment successfully charged a force of French cavalry. Charles Cocks, later to be killed at Burgos, witnessed the affair with the 16th Light Dragoons. 'The French cavalry charged....and were in possession of the guns. The 5th Regiment were lying down a little distance in the rear. The commanding officer would not allow them to get up until the enemy was close to them. At the distance of a few yards this little regiment poured a volley into the enemy and, dashing on thro' the smoke with the bayonet, charged the French cavalry, drove them back and retook the guns.' See Page (Ed), *Intelligence Officer in the Peninsula*, p.144. See also Oman, *History of the Peninsular War*, IV, 565-570. The British force at El Bodon consisted of the 11th Light Dragoons, 1st Hussars KGL, 2/5th, 1/45th, 77th, 2/83rd, 1/88th and the 94th.

[3] Throughout September 25th and 26th Wellington sat at Fuenteguinaldo in an extremely perilous position with just 15,000 men. By noon on the 26th Marmont had almost 60,000 men but was reluctant to attack. He was unaware of the golden opportunity presented to him by the absence of the greater part of Wellington's army and the

September 27th. We retreated, with our left in front, at three in the morning to the position near Villa Mayor. At three in the evening we heard firing which lasted till five. Lord Wellington retired with his force at the same time. The enemy got into Albeguaria without resistance. They tried Alfaiates but without success. We remained under arms till night. I went to bed at seven o'clock, and being very warm and comfortable in my tent, was roused at ten by an order to march immediately. I carried my tent upon my horse who was lame. It slipped off, and I was obliged to let the division pass me before I could get it on again. It constantly slipped till at last I joined the brigade and got it carried on a jackass for two dollars. After a most tedious march in the dark we arrived at Ronda. Bivouacked.

September 28th. I tumbled down under a tree and slept till six. We then pitched our tent in the rain. I went to sleep again and slept as before. Lord Wellington offered them battle on the position which they declined. Ours and the 6th Division were thrown back in reserve to support any part of the line. The French certainly had 60,000. Our army was so reduced by sickness that it did not amount to more than 35,000. Hill's Corps of 10,000 came up to Sabugal from the Alentejo. Bivouacked.

September 29th. To Gato. 5 leagues. Crossed the Coa. The French having absconded, we are marching into cantonments. The cavalry remains on the other side of the Coa on the look out. We have got off with flying colours. We have indeed ceded the country between the Agueda and Coa but it never could have been maintained if they advanced. Bivouacked.

September 30th. To Lagiosa. 3 Leagues. General Graham is here. The 5th, 6th, 7th and 8th Companies are quartered here. The is an abundance of every sort of fruit; peaches, grapes, pears, apples, figs and walnuts. It is a beautiful village in the valley of the Mondego. The river of this name rises in the mountains above. The natives are employed in thrashing their Indian corn.

October 1st. The 5th Company moved out to Val dos Ayres, the town being too full, and accommodation being wanted for sick officers passing through. I got into a large house with Mildmay and Crofton, very comfortable, each of us has a little bedroom and a dining room. The Patrone, a boy of fifteen, is a great wag here.

October 2nd. Every sort of fruit is in abundance — peaches, grapes, apples, pears, walnuts, mulberries, etc. Headquarters are at Freineda.[1] The Light Division is at Guinaldo.

bitter experiences at the hands of Wellington's 'reverse slope' tactics undoubtedly played upon his mind. While an anxious Wellington waited for his divisions to join him an equally nervous Marmont peered out and saw the usual thin line of British troops arrayed along the top of the ridge at Fuenteguinaldo. The French commander was unwilling to attack and suffer the same fate as Massena's divisions at Busaco, for example, and so did nothing and a great chance went astray.

[1] Wellington's old headquarters in the small Portuguese village of Freineda still stand today. The house in which he spent so much time is in the main 'square', opposite the church. A plaque on the building next to his house commemorates his stay there.

Val dos Ayres, near Celorico
October 2nd 1811

My Dearest Mother,

As the operations of the army for the last week have been important, the first part of this epistle must savour of Military tactics — well then to begin. The French had for some time been concentrating their force at Salamanca. They had collected there every man from the north of Spain, even as far as Catalonia. Soult who was at Plasencia, with his army, which held in check Gen. Hill's Corps, in the Alentejo, had joined them. They had besides collected there an immense convoy, which had come from France, of provisions of all sorts. Even the carriages on which they came were French. From all this, it was evident, that in the first instance at least, they would throw supplies into Ciudad Rodrigo when we invested; and to be prepared for them, it was necessary for us to concentrate our force likewise. Their army amounted to 60,000 — ours was so reduced by sickness, that it did not amount to 35,000; exclusive of Gen. Hill's Corps of 10,000, who were on their march from the Alentejo. On the 23rd, the army concentrated, having the right on Guinaldo. The 1st and 6th Divisions under the orders of Genl Graham, were on the left, upon the road to Sabugal, which it was necessary to keep open for us. On the 24th our picquets in front of Ciudad Rodrigo were driven in and the long projected convoy got safe in, without any interruption on our part. Their force was so superior that it was quite impossible to prevent it.

On the 25th they advanced towards Espeja, which place was occupied by some Dragoons of ours, the 14th and 16th. Two Squadrons of each of these regiments, aided by the light troops of Gen. Hulse's Brigade[1] routed the two regiments of German Lancers, took 1 captain, an Irishman, who would not receive quarter, besides about 100 men.[2] This took place in our front; for we were all this time in our old quarters Nave de Haver, which luckily for us was the place we were to defend; and we were the only troops in the army not bivouacked. On the right near Guinaldo, Marmont advanced a heavy column of infantry and cavalry to try and force it; he could not. Their cavalry exposed themselves for some time very absurdly to a battery of six guns, which cut them up: They then charged, and took six guns; which were retaken in the most gallant style by the 5th Foot, who charged their cavalry.[3] The remainder of the day passed in skirmishing.

[1] The light troops from Hulse's brigade of the 6th Division were from the 11th, 61st and 53rd Regiments.

[2] The Irishman in question was Chef d'Escadron O'Flyn, although Cocks, in *Intelligence Officer in the Peninsula*, p.145 calls him O'Fin. Tomkinson, in his *Diary of a Cavalry Officer*, p.115, says, 'The enemy did not wait a moment, and we drove them two miles down the wood, taking every man the infantry hit, and several besides (in all about thirty), killing ten on the spot with their commanding officer, Chef d'Escadron O'Flyn, an Irishman. O'Flyn was taken prisoner, and whether from unwillingness to go to the rear, or its being found out that he was an Irishman, he was shot by Fitzpatrick, a dragoon in the 16th, afterwards in my troop.'

[3] See also JM's Journal for September 26th 1811.

The 26th both armies entrenched themselves near Guinaldo. They looked at one another all day neither moving. The French showed themselves in very great force; on the 27th we retreated at 3 in the morning to a position near Villa Mayor. The right did the same. The right was upon Alfaiates, we were on the left, near Villa Mayor; our division still upon the Sabugal road. The enemy followed, tried to get Alfaiates but were repulsed. Our line was formed on our position, and they would not attack. We stood under arms all day, and I lay down to sleep about seven o'clock, just as I was getting comfortable, received an order to march, in a desperate cold night, and retreated — our division only — to near Sabugal, in case the enemy should attempt to get round us. We did not get in till four in the morning, when quite overcome with sleep, I fell under a tree, and slept till awoke by the rain. On the 28th the enemy retired, or as Lord Wellington expresses it, *absconded*. And here ends the account of our operations. We have got off with flying colours; for they were near double our force, and would not fight. They have indeed succeeded in relieving Ciudad, but for that purpose have been obliged to collect their force far and near; the whole army, excepting the cavalry is cantoned on this side of the Coa. The French are in Almeida.

We are in a most romantic village in the Mondego valley, equidistant between Guarda and Celorico. Mildmay, Crofton and myself, are in a most excellent house — Peaches, grapes, pears, apples, figs, walnuts, mulberries &., &., in abundance. I only hope we may remain here. We have each our separate bedroom, and one sitting room. To me it is a Palace and the only comfortable house I have been in yet.

I am sorry to say that the sick of the army is immense. The difficulty of transporting them to Coimbra, the depot, is so great, that the different towns are full of them. Few of them are dangerous cases; principally agues: but great attention is necessary.

I have not thank God, ever been better in my life than I am now and very happy at the idea of settling for the winter, this is not far from where my brother Warrior William was. He kept his secrets well, but I have discovered that during his stay in the country he never moved out of quarters: but stayed quietly at Francoza.[1] Paulet is anxiously waiting to be gazetted; some delay has occurred; but he will be in England soon.

I had a conversation with the Captain of the Lancers whom we took at Espeja. He described the disgust of the whole French army as being very great. He said, that almost all their supplies came from France, and consequently were precarious and that they were obliged to be escorted which harassed them — in short that it was a war of extermination.[2] I believe both sides are equally tired.

---

[1] Another dig at his brother William's garrison service with the 58th.

[2] The war waged by the Spanish and Portuguese partisans, or guerrillas, upon the French is, of course, well enough documented and space precludes any in-depth analysis here. Suffice to say that without the ever-present threat posed by these guerrillas Wellington's task in the Peninsula would have been a great deal more difficult. The simple matter of sending despatches required strong escorts of cavalry to ensure their safe delivery. Serious reconnaissance work was rendered extremely dangerous while piquet duty for isolated French troops was an equally unhealthy business. French atroci-

You offer me a pouch will you make me a leather one, with a leather string to it, to tie round the waist, round the inside of my clothes. Graham is the (life of the) army — all alacrity — he is on horseback from morning to night & that at sixty. He commands our division; and is a good friend to every Forlorn Guardsman. In addition to the division he is second in command. We call ourselves *unlucky* in not having anything to do this morning. Ours was the most probable point of attack, and the most important as it crossed the road to the Lines and you must observe that for our operations it is essentially necessary to prevent the enemy from getting the start of us, down that road, which of course cramps our operations. The Lancers did nothing against our cavalry — they cut them to pieces. We had but eight or ten men wounded, but most of them badly. I saw one man, who had a lance through each arm, and one through his body. He said he felt the lance enter him, and turned his horse to the left, or it would have gone through him.

On the approach of the French, the natives pack up their all, originally not considerable, but sensibly diminished by campaigning, and set off. We had crowds of them following us. They seemed in good spirits, probably from having left nothing behind them, but bare walls. They are busily employed, out of the immediate sphere of action, in making wine — the process is not delicate — a man treads the grapes, and occasionally during the operation steps out of the house, and returns with sundry particles of dust adhering to his feet, and resumes the operation. They were good enough to tell me it would be very fine drinking in a month.

Beckford and Bowles are at Lisbon — they were more fortunate than us in their voyages out. Bradshaw and Col. Fuller, two of my fellow travellers, are at Lisbon with the ague. You will hardly have patience to read this military lecture to the end. If you have; remember me most kindly to all your party, and tell Elizabeth that I shall write to her next mail — besides the impossibility of writing two letters to the same place; I am so delighted at the prospect of remaining quiet for the winter, that I cannot set down to anything. To you, who have always remained quiet, this may not appear so fascinating, but to us, who are constantly moving, at all hours, and all times, it has charms. I have bivouacked sixty nights since I have been up and I intend now, if the Beaux will let us alone to pay them off.

Adieu. John Mills.

October 3rd. Rainy day, not comfortable as the roof does not keep out water.
October 4th. Went shooting — Mildmay killed a rabbit.
October 5th. Rode to Celorico with Crofton. The weather seems to be more settled.
October 6th. Went shooting. I found some partridges in the mountains. They

ties were commonplace while guerrilla reprisals were equally regular and gruesome, giving the war in the Peninsula a savage and more barbaric side rarely engaged in by British troops, save for the sackings that followed the successful stormings of Ciudad Rodrigo, Badajoz and San Sebastian, and during the retreats from Corunna and Burgos.

were too wild and the weather too hot to do anything. I killed some quail (4),
which we found in the Indian Corn.
October 7th. Renewed my sporting. Killed 2 quails. It is intensely hot.
October 8th. A mail to England. Wrote to Ramsden, E. and Chas.

Val dos Ayres
The Valley of the Winds
Near Celorico.
October 8th 1811

My Dear Elizabeth,[1]

Here is the promised scrawl. I am afraid it will contain anything but news, for
inaction amounting almost to torpidity, generally follows grand movements.
The papers will have given you the detail of the skirmishing on the 25th and
27th. We were on the left which was not attacked, and consequently know but
little of what happened. The 5th and 21st Portuguese particularly distinguished
themselves, and indeed performed wonders. I thought for some time that the
business looked serious and I really wonder that nothing more happened, for
they can never hope for a better chance, weakened as we were by sickness. I
will venture to say that at this period we have 20,000 men in the different
hospitals. The French, masters in the terms of war, call this merely une reconnaissance. Fuentes, une reconnaissance assez vive. They have returned to their
old quarters about Salamanca, having left some few men at Almeida, merely as
a party of observation. It is reduced to ruins, though formerly a fine fortress, and
is now a picture of chaos in all its deformity.[2] Our army is cantoned on this side
of the Coa, nearer to it than it will remain for the winter; but for the two or three
remaining weeks of fine weather it would not be safe to shut up shop, for they
might come again. We expect to move soon to Viseu. Our brigade was there for
some time, during which they ingratiated themselves so much with the natives,
that they have petitioned to have us back again. It is a delightful place, abound-
ing in turkeys, and other good things, and almost the only place in Portugal that
has not had the fraternal hug of the Beaux. From the mention of turkeys in this

---

[1] Elizabeth Mills, a younger sister of JM. She married a Mr Wingfield, a master in
Chancery, as his second wife.
[2] The Portuguese fortress town of Almeida had certainly seen its fair share of
destruction during the previous year or so. On August 26th 1810, Ney's besieging batteries opened fire against the town which was garrisoned by Portuguese troops under the
command of a British officer, Lieutenant Colonel William Cox. One of the first shots to
explode in the town ignited a long trail of gunpowder, caused by a leaking powder
barrel, which led to the main powder magazine. The resulting explosion ripped the
place apart and rocked the whole area. French troops in the nearby Fort Conception
thought it was an earthquake. Nearly 500 Portuguese troops were killed and hardly a
building left with its roof. Cox was forced to surrender the place the following day. When
Brennier evacuated the place on the night of May 10th 1811 he detonated a series of
mines which caused more damage and effectively ruined the place.

honourable way you will think me a Gourmand, and in a small way I am one. Never getting large pieces of meat, we are obliged to recourse to stratagem, and disguise it with sauces. I assure you we live uncommonly well. I am here in a house with Mildmay and Crofton. We have got our little flock of sheep, and get on famously. In general I turn bachelor and live by myself. Beckford and Bowles are on their way up here. I hope they will be more fortunate than I was at first starting, which certainly did not give me a favourable idea of this most fruitful country. One day that I met with some beef which was just killed, I had nearly choked myself out of sheer voracity, not having had animal food, or anything but chocolate for four days. My fellow voyager, Bradshaw, has the ague at Lisbon.

Our good friends the Spaniards seem to be doing little or nothing but quarrel amongst themselves. They think very highly of themselves and not very highly of us. It is a common saying with them now, that Spain is like our Saviour on the Cross, between two thieves, giving France and England the honourable choice of the two. Next year will I think decide the business; their country is already conquered, and it requires more exertion to regain, than to retain. Even the Portuguese begin to hold up their heads, and tell you that the French are more afraid of them than us. They would soon be undeceived if we retired. For three hundred and sixty days in the year, a Frenchman is a better soldier than an Englishman. Their movements compared with ours are as mail coaches to dung carts.[1] In all weathers and at all times they are accustomed to march, when our men would fall sick by hundreds, and so precarious have their supplies unavoidably been for some time that at the end of a march they frequently get nothing to eat. We always drive our bullocks with us, and during the whole time, nearly three years that our regiment has been in this country, we have not been in the whole more than seven days without our allowance of bread. You will observe too, that our operations having been throughout defensive, have given us less room for manoeuvring. Another peculiar excellence of the French troops is their steadiness in manoeuvring under fire. But at fighting we beat them, and they know it. The Portuguese artillery played them a slippery trick on October 5th; they had only time to get four of their guns off, out of six and finding themselves obliged to leave two. They rode with their limbers, and left the Beaux to exert their ingenuity in getting the guns off without horses, and

---

[1] These are interesting comments by JM, acknowledging as he does the superiority of the French soldier when manoeuvring. However, as he also says, 'we beat them every time', which says much for the tactics employed by Wellington in battle. These tactics depended largely on the superior firepower of the British soldier, resulting from his linear formation as opposed to the traditional French offensive columnar formation. It does not take a mathematical genius to work out the superiority in firepower that the line has over the column, supposing those troops in line to be steady and well formed. However, it is an equation that successive French commanders appear not to have come to terms with. On those occasions when the French columns attempted to deploy into line the weight of British lead being poured into them prevented them from doing so. As with the study of the guerrilla war, space precludes a lengthy discussion of the problem. Sir Charles Oman attempted to get to grips with the line versus column issue in a chapter in his *Studies in the Napoleonic Wars*.

with only two wheels instead of four. My establishment is at present a little deranged by the absence of my valet servant who is in hospital.

I am obliged to make the cook officiate as valet, and am in considerable apprehension less he should make use of my nightcaps for pudding bags. Paulet has got a French deserter for a cook, and a very bad one he is. He tells us we have a very good dinner, consisting of seven plates — on inspection three of these plates turn out to be potatoes, cabbages and french beans. We are beginning to get supplies up from Lisbon of different small articles which we are in great want of. The demand being greater than supply, everything is very dear, particularly everything of English manufacture. Port wine is five shillings a bottle, porter the same. The rogues must make an enormous profit on the wine which is a necessary, as the vin de pays is execrable. Porter being a superfluity, they may get what they can for it. I am anxiously looking for a box which Charles has sent me. It is at Lisbon.

I suppose Francis[1] will be very great about the Winchester Prize Poems from the pen of Mr E. Sheridan. The Spanish translation is almost as good as the original. A propos to the Spaniards, Blake's army is lost; that is they may be in the West Indies, for nobody knows where they are gone to — they will not be missed.[2] Now my news is exhausted. Stir up everybody to write to me, one line is better than nothing. I forgot to tell you that when an army is cantoned it is not put into one village, and that when they fight they are not in one small field. For example, an army would be cantoned in Ringwood, Ch.Ch., Wimbourne, Poole, Romsey, Southampton, Lymington, etc, and would fight with the right on Christchurch and the left on Fordingbridge.

Remember me most kindly to everybody and believe me ever truly yours, John Mills.

October 9th. Marched to near Lazios to witness a punishment.
October 10th. Rode over to dine with Ramford. I returned at 3am.
October 11th. To Celorico. Stirling, Rose and Fremantle dined with us.
October 12th. To Celorico again.
October 13th. An English mail arrived. Letters from C and E.M.
October 14th. To Celorico. Dined with Sullivan. Wrote to Charlotte.
October 15th. To Celorico. Barnet came from the 3rd Regiment[3] to dine with us.
October 16th. Paid a visit to Raikes.

Val dos Ayres, near Celorico
October 16th 1811

My Dearest Charlotte,

The wind for some time past has served too well for England. Our latest ac-

---

[1] Francis Mills (1798-1854), 4th son of William Mills. One of the founders of the Garrick Club, he remained a bachelor and made a fine collection of pictures for the family which he bequeathed to JM.

[2] Blake's Spaniards had gone east to join the Army of Murcia and by September were engaged against Suchet close to Valencia.

[3] ie The 3rd Foot Guards.

counts from London are the 17th of September and that we reckon being very much in arrears. My meaning in this long detail is, that I am anxiously expecting to hear from you to be sure it might have been expressed in fewer words. There is no news here of any importance, except that the enemy are collecting provisions to a very considerable extent at Merida which looks like entering this country again. The season is far too advanced for them to do anything of consequence in this campaign. Merida lies upon the road to Portugal and military people have for some time been of the opinion that by this road only can an advancing army move to any purpose. Four hundred men are at work upon Almeida, to move away the rubbish and endeavour to make a field work of it - a field work means irregular fortifications surrounded by a breastwork — and to go still farther, a breastwork is formed by digging a trench and throwing up the earth to protect the men, so that to carry this explanation still farther again and to conclude it an asparagus bed is the breastwork. But a breastwork is not an asparagus bed — this must give you a clear insight into engineering as to hornworks, approaches, etc., in your own neighbourhood to whom you may apply. The noble amateurs who came out here to distinguish themselves were in considerable consternation at the skirmishing (assez vive) on the 25th and 27th.[1] Not having heard of them since I conclude they have satiated their curiosity. The Prince of Orange was unfortunate enough to lose two horses, from the eagerness of his grooms to see the fight, and from their want of discrimination in riding into the French instead of the English videttes. We are cantoned in the Vale of the Mondego, which runs between Guards and Celorico. Our regiment is in two small villages, this place and Lagiosa, where General Graham is. They are most beautiful spots and really romantically situated. The valley is narrow, surrounded by huge mountains, which form part of the Estrella. Celorico is within three miles of us, containing a variety of small articles, particularly those of a culinary nature. The communications to Coimbra and from thence to Lisbon by water will ensure us a good supply of these most necessary articles.

Gathering the Indian corn and grapes has made it an interesting scene and infused the periodical vigour into this most inactive people. The Indian corn is so productive a crop that I wonder at its never being tried in England.[2] They plant it in low places or where they can easily water it. I think it is better for horses than oats. It makes very bad bread, about as bad as rye.

Very little wine can be made in this country this year as either the French or English soldiers have burnt all their casks. Besides, they find they can make more money by selling the grapes to the soldiers. The good wine is all made near Oporto. Lamego is the chief place. The Port wine you get there is delightful, to bring it here about thirty miles; it is necessary to put spirits in. For the London market a greater quantity is necessary. As a substitute for brandy, they use agua ardente, a spirit distilled from the branches of the vine, and I believe it fully answers the purpose of brandy. If the price of wine in London bears any

[1] The actions JM refers to took place at El Bodon and Fuenteguinaldo. See his Journal for September 25th 1811.

[2] JM was ahead of his time. Maize, or Indian Corn as it was known, has recently become the main silage crop at Bisterne as winter feed for the dairy herds.

sort of proportion to the price here, there will soon be an end to three-bottle men. We pay five shillings a bottle and think it a great favour to get it but this is occasioned by the rascality of sutlers, who are allowed by Lord Wellington to make a hundred per cent profit but who generally make three hundred. The Buccillas wine which you have tasted at Bisterne is made at a place of that name in the Lines.[1] The fortifications must be against the concern and I daresay it will now become a dear wine.

Headquarters remain on the other side of the Coa at a place called Freineda, two leagues from Almeida. His Lordship is a warrior in the true sense of the word for he has never slept in a bed since he has been in the country. This is a mode I cannot say I approve of — life is too short for these pranks. At his own table he is as great a Boy as the biggest of them, but when he is angry he is a perfect tiger.[2] He makes no-one acquainted with his intentions and laughs at the idea of a Council of War — this may do with clever men.[3] The English newspapers are full of accounts of the Comet, all agreeing in the main point that it is genuine, and each writer claiming for himself no small degree of credit for the perfect use of his eyes. The Portuguese are in no small consternation about it. They are persuaded that it portends great events. Naturally superstitious to excess, it is not to be wondered at. They think us Heathens, and that we are certain of descending. I saw at Portalegre a little child with a huge powdered wig and a dress such as you Ladies wear at Court. On enquiring the meaning of this extraordinary apparition I was informed it represented an angel. Our saviour is on certain days carried through the streets, sometimes with a black coat and culottes, sometimes without any, the Virgin Mary with a black gown and white apron. They think it all very sublime, and are horrified at our not thinking so too.

[1] ie the Lines of Torres Vedras.

[2] Wellington was jovial company at the dinner table but as JM says, when angry he could be 'a perfect tiger.' Probably the most memorable — or infamous — instance of Wellington's fiery temper involved Charles Stewart, the Adjutant General, and half-brother to Lord Castlereagh, the Secretary of State. One of Stewart's duties was the interrogation of captured prisoners but one particular day one of Wellington's aides happened to be present when a group of prisoners was brought in and to save time questioned them himself and took the results straight to his commander. Stewart was so peeved by this that he refused to carry out the rest of his duties towards the prisoners. Wellington immediately sent for Stewart and found him 'full of the pretensions of this Department of his [the AG].' Wellington gave Stewart a dressing down, adding that if he would not follow orders he would be sent home. Such was the effect of Wellington's verbal broadside that Stewart was reduced to tears and apologised for his 'intemperance.' See Jennings (Ed), *The Croker Papers*, I, 346.

[3] When we refer to the army as being Wellington's army, that is precisely what it was— it was *his*, army. He was loathe to delegate and kept his commanders on a fairly tight rein. As regards so-called 'seconds-in-command', he simply did not entertain the notion. As Ward says in his definitive work, *Wellington's Headquarters*, pp.156-157, 'He [Wellington] lived in the lonely isolation which must hedge a commander of no matter how large or small a force. He confided in few and he admitted none to his counsel but such as were responsible for their advice. His reasons may be seen in his attitude to seconds-in-command, which the military authorities at home, not having altogether abandoned the council of war tradition, persisting in appointing. He would not admit their existence.'

The Army is at this moment extremely unhealthy. Celorico is at the place where all the bad cases are left that cannot get down to Coimbra and at this moment I know that they have not got medicine enough for two days' consumption and that little has been reserved by economising for three weeks. After the Battle of Talavera there was not six pounds of salts in the whole army. It will take a long time before they get a stock up but in the meantime judge of the suffering.

I am quite surprised to hear of Lord Guernsey's rash act. He cannot be idle even when we are quiet, for the cavalry are always on the advance and a subaltern of dragoons is moreover the greatest drudge in the world.

The affairs at Cadiz look ill. I am afraid there is a strong French party in the place and that it will soon fall.[1] I think Spain is already conquered and that the next campaign will show it us. They look upon us with a jealous eye and would rather submit to a French king than to be incorporated with England as Portugal is. Even the natural antipathy of the neighbouring countries will always present a cordial co-operation. Joseph has returned to Madrid; he never journeys towards his armies. We are all in consternation at the idea of the dress of the army being altered from cocked hats and coats to caps and jackets. Ye heavens, what will become of crooked legs, large heads, and still larger hinder parts?[2]

[1] JM need not have worried about the state of affairs at Cadiz. In spite of a long siege and in the face of tremendous French pressure the city remained in Allied hands and was kept well supplied by British ships. Graham's victory at Barrosa on March 5th 1811 — which saw the first capture in the Peninsula by the British army of a French 'eagle' — had eased the pressure on the place while the tenacious defenders along the coast at Tarifa played their part also. The siege of Cadiz was eventually raised on August 24th 1812 following which the Allied force there, including 5,500 British troops under General Skerrett of the 1st Foot Guards, advanced to take Seville on August 27th.

[2] At the beginning of the Peninsular War British officers wore long-tailed coats and bicorn hats worn 'fore and aft'. However, on December 24th 1811 a General Order was issued from the Horse Guards regarding the adoption of a new uniform. The coats were replaced by short-tailed jackets and the old bicorns by the false-fronted 'Belgic shako', one of the most attractive headdresses of all armies of the period, and made of strong felt. The light companies were already wearing the cylindrical 'stove-pipe' shako and it appears that instead of adopting the new 'Belgic' shako most officers wore the 'stove-pipe' version until the end of the war. In spite of the introduction of the 1812-pattern uniform the 'Belgic' shako appears to have seen limited use and was worn only by units that came out late in the war, possibly at the beginning of 1814, although some fashion-conscious officers of the Guards wore the 'Belgic' version but only because they specifically ordered them to be sent out from England. Some regiments, notably the 28th, wore the 'stove-pipe' at Waterloo in 1815. As well as these changes grey overalls were adopted instead of the existing overalls of white, or in some cases, light blue, which in turn had replaced the old white breaches and gaiters. The Coldstream and 3rd Foot Guards wore loose white trousers during the summer months and wore them at Waterloo, the 1st Foot Guards wearing grey overalls. The study of military dress at this period is a vast one, however, and one should take with a pinch of salt any hard and fast rules relating to uniform. Perhaps Robert Mercer, of the 3rd Foot Guards, summed it up best when he wrote in December 1810, 'Every person here dresses as he likes. These fancy dresses occasion much surprise and horror to the martinets who arrive from London.' (Fletcher, *Gentlemen's Sons: The Foot Guards in the Peninsula and at Waterloo, 1808-*

Paulet, I find, upon comparing notes, is alas, a rival in the charms of the fair Louise Rich. But Elizabeth having noticed, reports to the prejudice of these charms. We have agreed to defer our advances to a nearer inspection. Has the local Militia taken off any of the neighbouring belles? I am afraid that that venerable body is not very susceptible. In two years with good luck, I am in hopes of talking over these matters with you. I am sorry to hear that Harry is not quite well. I shall write to him by the next mail. I must now wind up. Remember me kindly to your aforementioned spouse, with whom I sincerely condole on the scarcity of partridges. Remember me likewise to Mr Berdmore,[1] my sisters-in-law, your little stranger,[2] and Uncle John.[3]

October 17th. Sowerby and Talbot came up, having left Bowles and Beckford behind.
October 18th. Dined at Sullivan's. Don Julian's cavalry have taken all the live cattle of Ciudad Rodrigo, and reports add the Governor of Ciudad Rodrigo.[4]

1815, p.34.) See also Chapter Three, 'Military Dress', in the above work, and also Wellington's Foot Guards, (An Osprey 'Elite' title by the same author). The new uniforms certainly caused Wellington some anxiety as it became even harder to distinguish between French and British soldiers. In a letter to Lieutenant Colonel Torrens, Military Secretary, he wrote, 'I hear that measures are in contemplation to alter the clothing, caps, &c. of the army. There is no subject of which I understand so little; and, abstractedly speaking, I think it is indifferent how a soldier is clothed, provided it is in a uniform manner; and that he is forced to keep himself clean and smart, as a soldier ought to be. But there is one thing I deprecate, and that is any imitation of the French, in any manner. It is impossible to form an idea of the inconveniences and injury which result from having anything like them, either on horseback or foot. [Captain Lutyens] and his piquet were taken in June, because the 3rd Hussars had the same caps as the French Chasseurs à Cheval and some of their hussars; and I was near to being taken on September 25th from the same cause. At a distance, or in action, colours are nothing; the profile, and shape of the man's cap, and his general appearance, are what guide us; and why should we make our people look like the French? A cocked-tailed horse is a good mark for a dragoon, if you can get a side view of him; but there is no such mark as the English helmet, and, as far as I can judge, it is the best cover a dragoon can have for his head. I mention this, because in all probability you may have something to say to these alterations; and I only beg that we may be as different as possible from the French in everything. The narrow top caps of our infantry, as opposed to their broad top caps, are a great advantage to those who are to look at long lines of posts opposed to each other.' (Despatches, Wellington to Torrens, 6th November 1811, VIII, 378-379.)
    [1] A friend of the Comptons, after whom a son was later named.
    [2] The 'little stranger' refers to the fact that Charlotte Compton was expecting a baby. See also September 14th 1812.
    [3] John Combe Compton, born in 1792, and brother of Henry Combe Compton. He became Rector of Minstead and Fellow of Merton College, Oxford.
    [4] The French garrison at Ciudad Rodrigo had a herd of cattle which was frequently sent out to graze about a mile from the ramparts of the town, accompanied by guards. Under normal siege operations this would have been impossible but as this was only a blockade Governor Renaud was able to send his cattle outside the walls with little apparent danger. On October 15th, however, Renaud was inspecting his cattle outside the walls when Julian Sanchez, the guerrilla leader, led an audacious foray against them, carrying off not only the cattle but Governor Renaud also. Renaud was replaced on

October 19th. To Celorico. Dined with Baynes.

October 20th. Sowerby and Talbot dined with us. Rain.

October 21st. Our money came up. Rode to the neighbouring villages. Rain.

October 22nd. Wrote to Harry. Rain.

October 23rd. Rode over to Celorico. Rain.

October 24th. Division field day. Beckford and Bowles came up. Rain.

October 25th. To Celorico. Rain.

October 26th. Beckford dined with us. Rain.

October 27th. Rain and wind.

October 28th. There are rumours of marching. Rain as usual.

October 29th. Wrote to E.M. and Ramsden.

October 30th. Braddyl dined with us. Rain as usual.

Val dos Ayres
October 30th 1811

My Dearest Mother,

I have given you some respite from this crabbed hand of mine, in favour of other parts of the family. I now return to you, and with the same dull narrative concomitant with a dull, rainy season; the periodical rains have begun. Fireplaces built out of windows, of stone and other rude, unfashioned materials, cemented with mud, and roofs which despise the vulgar accomplishment of keeping out rain, do not inspire the same sensations of comfort that a comfortable fireside, and the certainty of no trickling of water upon the head are accustomed to do in England. Added to this, I am afraid we are about to move and as I reckon a bird in the hand equal to two in the bush, I had rather brave all the aforesaid dangers than hazard the chance of no roof at all. Therefore, I fear the move. The Light Division which has been on the other side of the Agueda has now been obliged to fall back on this side of it, that river being fordable but in few places. Their movement must throw us farther back; we hope to go to Viseu; I am afraid we shall not.[1] The French are quiet and must now remain so, for they now cannot move even if they wished it. Both sides have now ample time to talk over the campaign, and form plans, very numerous, I assure you, for the next. Taking Badajoz, Ciudad Rodrigo and Madrid on one side, retreating to the Lines, from thence to our very nostrils in the sea, on the other — specimens of the lively and the gloomy. You see, we too are politicians. Beckford and

November 1st 1811 by General Barrie who himself had great difficulty in getting through the Allied lines into the town. See Oman, *History of the Peninsular War*, IV, 586-587. See also *Despatches*, Wellington to Lord Liverpool, 16th October 1811, VIII, 347.

[1] The Light Division had not been forced back as the result of any offensive move by Marmont. Wellington had decided that there was little prospect of any further danger from the French during the winter and so ordered his divisions into winter quarters, as did Marmont who pulled his forces back east of the Agueda. The movements of the Light Division at this time are best followed in Willoughby Verner's *History and Campaigns of the Rifle Brigade*, II, 296-297.

Bowles have joined us. The latter was taken ill upon the road but is now recovered. Public news there is none. Headquarters are at Guinaldo. The Spanish armies are lost — at least nobody knows where to find them. The common opinion seems to be that they have evaporated into population. The lying rogues publish monthly accounts of victories, which nobody believes, as there are considerable doubts of the existence of their armies. The guerrillas go on with their harassing system of warfare, and do considerable execution amongst convoys, and stragglers. The Beaux dare not even take a walk by themselves; whatever have been the fallings off from the grand cause of Spain, this minor, unacknowledged and unsupported system, has destroyed more men, and cost France more money than all their victories. However destructive it may be, it is symptomatic of decay. A great cause may dwindle, but never can flourish under a marauding plan. The business of the harvest is now over. During the rainy weather the natives sit in their houses, wrapped in large cloaks, with an earthen pan of coals in the middle of the room. We have built fireplaces in all the houses we have been in during the winter and if you ask them why they do not do the same, they acknowledge the comfort of them, wrap themselves closer in their cloaks and tell you it is not the custom — it speaks volumes of prejudice. The country we shall in all probability fall back upon has not been visited by us for some time, and speaking of it as you would of a cheese, it will last us for some time. The intermediate country between us and the French is reckoned to be very well eaten up and indeed it is. Nothing has escaped but the carcasses of the natives, and they are too thin. Between this and Oporto will last for the winter, and then we must look out for something fresh. Charles[1] would be a good devouring, hard eating soldier, if his appetite still retains its original force. The last mail brought me a letter from you of the 23rd of September. Warwickshire seems in a marrying mode.[2] I shall with all due speed write letters of congratulation. I have to thank you too for William's letter. Mock Turtle and claret make my mouth water. I hope soon to hear of his skirmishing with tigers, and taking elephants prisoners.[3] The sickness of the army I am afraid is not diminishing. They are anxious to conceal the numbers as much as possible, but we are too near Celorico, which is a general hospital, to remain in the dark. In that hospital, owing to some mismanagement, they have not now an ounce of Bark, which is the only medicine that can be given with effect.[4] In nine out of ten cases in this

[1] ie Charles Mills, JM's younger brother.

[2] Elizabeth Mills could have received news from Warwickshire from two sources; they were either from her sister, Jane, married to Charles Mills, MP for Warwick and younger brother of her husband, William, or from the Reverend Frances Mills, his younger brother and Rector of Barford.

[3] This is a reference to William Mills, JM's next younger brother. He must have exchanged out of the 2/58th on leaving Portugal and was bound for a regiment in India, since neither battalion of the 58th was serving there at this date.

[4] Sir James McGrigor, the Inspector General of Hospitals, regarded Celorico as a poor and unhealthy location for a hospital. It also had a high death rate not only amongst the patients but the staff also. When Wellington visited the hospital in December 1811 he was so appalled by what he saw that he immediately ordered the transfer of about 400 patients to the more healthy environment of the hospital at Coimbra. See Blanco, *Wellington's Surgeon General: Sir James McGrigor*, p.121. Cures for illnesses, often the ague,

country, Ague is the prevailing complaint. If beds and other comforts were to be procured generally speaking, no danger would ensue, but the want of comforts is apt to bring on low fevers. Colonel Braddyll is going out of the army immediately, tant mieux pour moi, and so are two other colonels. This is famous work. In two more years I shall expect to be Captain Mills; I shall certainly waive the captain, it sounds so vulgar. One turn in this country generally satisfies the curiosity of those who can get out, and I am afraid we shall soon lose all of that description. Paulet has been dealt very unfairly with, or he would have been in England two months ago. Colonel Smyth sent in his resignation to Lord Wellington, and upon the faith of that was allowed to go home, but instead of going out he has been bargaining for an exchange.[1] The Light Division has got a pack of hounds which go out twice a week; Lord Wellington hunts with them. They are so far from us that I have not seen them.[2] I heard of Digby Mackworth the other day. He was treated very well, and may thank his stars for his good luck. Knowing how anxious his father would be, I sent to General Hill as soon as I heard he was taken. He sent me word he had written to Sir Digby, therefore I did not. I am going to take a Frenchman who lived with Mildmay, for a cook. He deserted at Talavera and has remained with us since. In point of economy a Frenchman is infinitely superior to an Englishman as he can make a very good soup out of a mere nothing, when an Englishman requires solid beef, and as

were many and varied amongst Wellington's men. Officers took to drinking hot spiced wine from the saddle followed by a furious gallop, doses of quinine bark and opium were taken, hot stones placed on the chest and feet, buckets of cold water were poured over the sufferer's head, while the excitement of an imminent action appears to have done the trick for more than one soldier. Joseph Donaldson, of the 94th, even swallowed a pill made from a rolled-up spider's web! See Donaldson, *Recollections of the Eventful Life of a Soldier*, pp.150-151. A more scientific cure involved the extraction from Peruvian or Jesuits' Bark of cinchona from which quinine was in turn extracted. In order to make digestion easier the drug was mixed with wine. Another cure for fevers was Dr James's Powder, made from antimony and phosphate of lime which was known as the aspirin of the eighteenth century. See Blanco, *Wellington's Surgeon General*, p.39.

[1] Lieutenant Colonel George Smyth, 1st Battalion Coldstream Guards, resigned from the army on July 3rd 1811 and left for England the following day. He officially retired from the army on October 2nd 1811. See Mackinnon, *Origin and Services of the Coldstream Guards*, II, 166 & 500-501.

[2] Major General Robert Craufurd, the famous commander of the Light Division, was very fond of dogs and in a letter to his wife dated September 29th 1811 bemoaned the lack of decent dogs available for purchase. 'At this season of the year few people choose to sell them. Those who wanted to sell have done it in the spring, after the hunting season was over. Those who bought hounds in the spring have been at the expense of keeping them all summer, without any advantage from them, and certainly will not sell their pack just as the season for using it commenced. Picking up a few in one place and a few in another will probably be the worst of each pack. If a complete pack could be bought, even if they were dear, I could always sell some of them here. The sort I wish to have are beagles, or small harriers. I am determined to get the hounds in some way or other, but I do not want more than fourteen couple.' Wellington himself was a keen and very enthusiastic rider and could often be seen galloping at the head of a group of huntsmen. Indeed, George Bowles, of the Coldstream, wrote, 'He [Wellington] will certainly break his neck one day.' (Malmesbury, *A Series of Letters of the First Earl of Malmesbury*, II, 240.)

these same solids do not abound in this country it is a material point. Bowles tells me of an arrangement in the Temple family — it is very à propos. As waltzing seems all the fashion, I must add it to my other accomplishments. The Spaniards dance it very well, but in a different style with the Germans, rather more hopping. I must now wind up.

My kindest love to you all your party, and believe me. Yrs, John Mills.

October 31st. Rode over to a sale at Lagiosa.

November 1st. Taylor came over and dined with us. In the evening we heard of General Hill having made 1,000 prisoners. Orders came at night for us to march.

November 2nd. At seven the battalion marched, but was ordered back.

November 3rd. General Hill has sent a brigade to the bridge of Merida to cut off the remainder of the enemy who are dispersed. The Duc d'Aremburg and General Beaumont are prisoners — the latter commanded the cavalry at Barrosa. General Girard has escaped with the remainder of his army to the mountains. General Hill formed his force in column during the night and attacked them at Caceres, driving in the picquet with the column.[1]

November 4th. Rode out to Rotoeira with Mildmay. Wrote to Charles.

November 5th. Stirling, Stanhope and a large party dined with me.

November 6th. Bivouacked 61 nights so far, marched 174½ leagues (693 miles). Road by Lagiosa towards Celorico. Fine weather.

November 7th. A Division field day. We took up a position near Azores. The guns and light infantry in front retired and formed on the left bank of the Mondego, over the Ponte de Ladrones.

November 8th. General Hill took 1,500 prisoners. Amongst them are the Duc d'Aremburg and General Beaumont. General Girard with 600 men, most without arms, has affected his escape into Almaraz, wounded. General Hill formed his division during the night within 200 yards of the French sentries, and attacked them before they were aware of it.[2]

November 9th. The Light Division has retired from across the Agueda to Guinaldo, in consequence of that river being overflowed. The cavalry have in consequence

[1] This was Hill's action at Arroyo dos Molinos. See footnote below.

[2] On October 28th 1811 General Rowland Hill, with a force of around 10,000 British, Spanish and Portuguese troops, caught up with and surprised a small French force of 2,500 under General Girard at the small Spanish village of Arroyo dos Molinos, which hugs the Sierra de Montanchez. Hill had the foresight to cut off all three roads leading from the village the previous night and then swept into it early on the morning of the 28th. In the ensuing fight 1,300 prisoners were taken including General Bron, commanding the cavalry, the Prince d'Aremberg, colonel of the 27th Chasseurs, the chef d'état major of the 5th Corps and 30 other officers. Hill's losses amounted to just 7 killed and 64 wounded. Girard and about 400 men managed to make their perilous escape over the mountains pursued by scores of enthusiastic Spaniards who bayoneted every unlucky Frenchman they came up with. The 34th Regiment gained a unique honour at Arroyo dos Molinos, being the only regiment present to be granted it as a battle honour. By coincidence the regiment captured the drums and drum major's staff of the French 34th Regiment, trophies which can be seen today at the Border Regiment's Regimental Museum. In his despatch dated November 1st 1811, Wellington wrote that Hill, 'has done his business very handsomely.' *Despatches*, Wellington to Graham, VIII, 375.

moved too. Headquarters are still at Freineda. Dined with Sowerby.
November 10th. A large party dined with us. Adjutant General Murray broke his
collar bone, hunting with some harriers they have got at Headquarters.
November 11th. Road to Lagiosa. Cold frosty weather.
November 12th. Wrote to E.M. Five mails from England due.
November 13th. Road to Lagiosa. Met General Graham shooting.

Val dos Ayres.
November 13th 1811

My Dearest Mother,

The wind for some time past has been so unfavourable that we have now five
mails due. The latest papers we have are of the 24th of September. General Hill's
affairs must delight you all as much as it does us, he is a most excellent man,
and we are all so glad it has happened to him. Fifteen hundred prisoners have
been brought into Portalegre in the regular channel, and the guerrillas are hourly
bringing in more. General Hill's men had been very much harassed. They took
three days' provisions ready cooked with them, and for three nights never lighted
a fire, and bivouacked, of course. The nights are now so cold, and so frequently
wet that it was very severe work. We have taken some poles on which the
Eagles were carried, but unfortunately they had unscrewed and made away
with the eagles.

We are in this part of the country quite at a standstill. The French completely deceived us the other day and got a new governor and some cattle into
Ciudad Rodrigo by a masterly finesse. Salamanca is 17 leagues from Ciudad, and
none of our army is more than 12. Instead of collecting their force at Salamanca,
they picked up a hundred at one place and a hundred at another, and so formed
a convoy of five thousand men without our being aware that they were moving
a man. The Light Division which was on the other side of the Agueda is moved
back to Guinaldo. The cavalry have moved too in consequence. We are in expectation too of moving to Viseu.

Murder will out. The complaints of want of money are loud and general;
the Commissariat are enormously in debt, and have had no money for some
time. The army are three months in arrears instead of one in advance. The
natives do not admire our promissory notes, which they are obliged to present
so often before they get their money, that they frequently give it up as a bad job.
This cannot go on long. The rope now so tight, must give way in some place.
The war cannot go on without money, and unless it comes from England I am
sure it is not to be got here. Our army has been chiefly supplied from Spain; our
dollars have been paid to them, and we have ticked[1] with the Portuguese. The
French have now possession of all Spain and consequently all the coin. It may
seem all very plausible as coming from the Chancellor of the Exchequer to tell
you that we can continue the war for many years to come; either he is deceiving

[1] ie run up credit with promissory notes.

you, or he is deceiving himself. Mr Kennedy, a remarkably clever man who has for some time been at the Head of the Commissariat, has given up his situation, in consequence, it is understood, of a difference of opinion with Lord Wellington.[1] The aide-de-camp of Brigadier General Campbell took one of the French General's baggage in the affair the other day and amongst other articles four thousand five hundred dollars. They would have some difficulty in finding as much in the baggage of any of ours. Don Julian sent a box the other day to General Cole, who on opening it much to his astonishment saw a man's leg, booted and spurred. With it was a letter, in which he said that it was the leg of a Spy, which he had cut off to prevent his escape and begged to know how he would wish the remainder of his body to be disposed of. I give it you as I had it.

Lord Tweedale has got a pack of hounds at Headquarters. Colonel Murray, the Adjutant General, broke his collar bone in following the noble sport. Lord Wellington goes out regularly, and I hear they have a good sport. They have got a private theatre there too. Colonel Braddyll is going over to act Falstaff, which I hear he does inimitably. He will be a great loss to us, remarkably entertaining and clever, you must have seen the caricature of the King holding Bonaparte in his hand, this is amongst his other productions. We had a sham fight on Thursday, exerted our imaginations in fancying an enemy, and drove them gallantly with blank cartridges.[2] General Graham was very unhappy for fear we should expend all our ammunition. We are going to have another fight this week; the 5th Division is to represent the enemy.

Yeomans Walcott is going home, having got an Adjutancy in a Troop at home. Taylor is delayed, being obliged to remain some little time, to appear as evidence upon a Court Martial. I never saw a regular soldier more sick of it and considering he is an amateur, has obtained a wonderful victory over himself, or rather over his military ardour, for he seems now to have given up all idea of turning soldier. There really is such a dearth of news that I must conclude this letter sooner than usual, promising to make it up in my next.

With kindest love to all your party. Believe me, John Mills.

November 14th. Went to a plain above Linhares to a coursing match as it was called, with General Graham. There were about 60 dogs of various descriptions

[1] Sir Robert Hugh Kennedy was Wellington's Commissary General. The son of George II's physician and a Westminster scholar Kennedy was, 'a man of boundless energy and enterprise uncoupled, however, with any desire to usurp for himself or his department any powers beyond his own, yet in whose one eye there occasionally burned an ungovernable temper.' (Ward, *Wellington's Headquarters*, p.74.) Kennedy assumed his post on June 11th 1810 and remained as Commissary General until the end of the war, with just one year's interval. He was absent from the army from December 24th 1811 until September 25th 1812 and again from December 24th 1813 until March 11th 1814. According to Fortescue, *History of the British Army*, VIII, 343-344, Kennedy resigned, 'being incited thereto by the importunity of his wife, whose sister had already been the means of withdrawing from Wellington a valuable member of his staff, and no doubt had worked upon the feelings of Mrs Kennedy.'

[2] This is an interesting record of what was something akin to winter tactical training at divisional level. Blank cartridges meant merely loading muskets with a charge of powder, without the ball.

from the turnspit upwards, and as many Portuguese with springardos. We destroyed a good many hares and rabbits. Sullivan lent me his mare. The ground was too deep, from the ground springs, to ride much. Graham asked all of us to dine with him.

November 15th. Road to Lagiosa. Dined with Beckford and Bowles. The weather remarkably fine and rather a frosty air.

November 16th. A large party dined with us and sat till late in the morning.

November 17th. Road to Lagiosa. Dined with Sowerby. The Commissariat are in great confusion. There is no money to go with and very indifferent credit. The bullock cars are breaking down every day and the owners leave them to their fate rather than repair them. The owners of Commissariat mules are a year in arrears, the army three months.

November 18th. Dined with General Graham. Two Mails arrived from England. Heard from E.M.

November 19th. Mildmay got his lieutenancy. Dined with Rose.

November 20th. Dined with Phillips.

November 21st. Dined at Sowerby's.

November 22nd. Dined with Stirling. Mail from England.

November 23rd. Heard of the arrival of the stores at Celorico.

November 24th. At ten o'clock we received an order to march to the front. At twelve we marched through Sobral da Serra to Retziosa, at which place we arrived at eleven o'clock, perished with cold. I got a miserable quarter with Mildmay. 5 leagues.

November 25th. The weather is intensely cold and frosty. We marched to a village near Rismula called Aldea de Donna. Very bad quarters. 4 leagues.

November 26th. To Nave de Haver, and here we learnt that we had been made fools of for that no convoy was ever in contemplation.

November 27th. I took a walk to the hill and looked at Ciudad with my new glass.

November 28th. As one officer was to return to Val des Ayres to order up the baggage and stores, Fuller gave me the option. I set off about one o'clock not intending to go far that night, but finding Sardeira full of cavalry I was obliged to push on and did not see a single hovel for 4 leagues when I discovered Guarda nodding above. I sheltered in the only inhabited house of a village that had been destroyed by the French. I got a nap in the chimney corner. 6 leagues.

November 29th. Reached Val dos Ayres, which from the happy time I had spent there appeared like a second home. I found Crofton and Sullivan who had been left sick there. 3 leagues.

November 30th. Rode over to Celorico. I started all the baggage to Pinhel, the place where the battalion was to be quartered. December 1st. Stayed at home as the weather was so cold.

December 2nd. Rode again to Celorico and laid in a stock of hams and tongues.

December 3rd. Started with Shaw, and on our arrival at Pinhel found that Paulet had got his leave. I dined with him. A mail arrived from England.

December 4th. A large party dined with us in the form of a farewell dinner, many of whom were inebriated.

Val dos Ayres.
December 4th 1811

My Dearest Mother

I have not written to you lately owing to an unforeseen move. On the 24th of November, imagining ourselves in most perfect security and all the comparative luxury of winter quarters, an order came for us to march immediately to the front. We accordingly obeyed and halted at eleven o'clock at night. More oppressed with cold than in the most severe weather in England, we marched for two more days and found ourselves at Nave de Haver. The purpose of this move, for it was general throughout the army, was to intercept a convoy which was going into Ciudad Rodrigo. Lo and behold it was a Mare's Nest, for there was no convoy at all, and my Lord affecting to be sharp is beat.

The houses in this country in the best of times are made but for summer weather, without fireplaces; destroyed as they are by the French they are horrible in cold weather, and I cannot tell you what I have suffered from the cold. After staying three days at Nave de Haver I was sent down here to the sick whom we had left behind. I set out late, intending not to go far that day, but finding the place I had intended stopping at full of troops I was obliged to continue my journey in the dark and after wandering sixteen miles without knowing whether I was going right or wrong, the piercing cold informed me I was approaching the highest inhabited city in Europe, and to my great joy, by the pale light of the moon, descried Guarda nodding above me. It was in the right line, and in the only inhabited house in a burned village I took up my abode for the night. I did not sleep, for the house was neither long or broad enough to lie down in. The next day I came on here, and the pleasant time I had passed here made me fancy it a second home. I have been here three days and am going to start today. Our division is at Pinhel. It appears that the French have retired into the interior of Spain, having quite exhausted their part of the country. We having succeeded thanks to our appetites, are going to move too and I hear our division is going to Lamego, famous as the place where the Port wine is made, and where you drink it in its pure state, without brandy and is I am told delicious. No soldiers have ever been quartered there and the country produces everything good. It is within an easy distance of Oporto, in short, the prospect is fine. After a campaign of very long duration, more harassing than any in this country, it will be a fine time for us. Both parties are intent upon Ciudad and I have no doubt but the campaign will open with operations upon it.

Our army is very unhealthy owing to the cold and a great dearth of blankets. At Celorico the deaths for the last week have averaged fifteen a day and the number of sick five hundred. The Commissariat despond, have no money and say it is impossible to continue the war long. Lord Wellington has been putting the best face upon it by staying on the frontiers and staring starvation in the face, as Lord S. says. The humbug cannot continue long unless it rains dollars and men instead of children are born. I have just got the things Charles sent me and by the last Mail the purse and other things you sent me. Many thanks. When you write tell me the date of the latest letters you receive from me. Had I five minutes to spare I would write a congratulatory letter to the last married Uncle[1] — it must stand over till the next mail. The number of deserters has been very great of late from the French army, owing to the very great scarcity of provisions with them. The frontiers of both countries have been so exhausted during the whole of this campaign that some other theatre of war must be discovered for the next and indeed I hope the next will be more decisive. Staring an enemy in the face for a month and moving as he moves may be good generalship if the war was to continue for twenty years, but I think can but little suit means like ours. The fact is they are too strong for us. Paulet has been delayed here unavoidably, but I hope will be home as soon as this letter. He is anxious to eat his Christmas Beef at Dogmersfield,[2] but I am afraid there is no chance of it. Beckford fancies himself a good soldier. The last I saw of him was going to look at Rodrigo, purposing to go within shot of it and almost the last I saw of Braddyl, who is very miserable, was riding in the night, most bitter cold, without anything like a great coat, having lost his baggage. We have not for some time been at Headquarters, but General Graham, who is always with us, is so good a substitute that we do not regret it. He is a most delightful man, an excellent Guardsman, a gentleman without the pride and pomp of war. I told you of Don Julian having taken the Governor of Rodrigo. After he had taken him, he marched him all round the town to the no small chagrin of the troops. Will you tell Charlotte that I missed a letter from her by the last mail which I shall make a point of sending one in return for.

With kindest love to all your party, John Mills.

December 5th. Paulet was persuaded to stay another day. I dined solo at home.
December 6th. Paulet departed. I went out shooting and killed a couple of cocks and a rabbit. A mail from England arrived. E.M.
December 7th. Went shooting, killed nothing. Dined with Shaw.
December 8th. Resumed the occupation of shooting. Cold weather continues.
December 9th. The same routine of shooting, dining and sleeping till the 16th.

Pinhel
December 10th 1811

My Dear Uncle,[3]

You must I am afraid have thought me very remiss in having so long postponed my congratulations. Numerous avocations have prevented my committing them to paper, though the intelligence I have received of the intended event which promises so fair for domestic comfort was not forgotten, in spite of marches and countermarches, and all the pomp of war. That the rest of your days, and I hope they will be many, may be passed in the full enjoyment of every comfort, is the

---

[1] The Reverend Francis Mills. See December 10th 1811.

[2] Dogmersfield Park, near Fleet, Hampshire, the home of the St John Mildmays.

[3] The Reverend Francis Mills (1759-1857). 4th son of the Reverend John Mills (1712-1791), they were both successively Rectors of Barford in Warwickshire, where there are many Mills memorials.

sincerest wish of a warm heart, and an affectionate friend. If it should so happen that some small particles of common sense should fall into the heads of our rulers, and that this war so bitter a visitation upon our friends and ourselves should terminate with anything short of extermination, I shall then hope to be a witness to your happiness, and drink a Magnum to the future. You win a guinea of me — I remember well the place where the bet was made and cannot help thinking you had an eye to it at that time. I beg you will make my best regards to your spouse;[1] having been so long accustomed to call you Uncle Frank, it will be as much as I can do to prevent my calling her Aunt Frank. Things are going on but indifferently here. The army is still three months in arrears and the Commissariat without a farthing and a year in debt — so much for the Civil Department. Eighteen thousand British in the hospitals, the remainder ill fed, and grumbling is a true picture of our present state. Lord Wellington is putting the best face upon it, and stays upon the frontiers when he ought to be on the other side of the Mondego. Ciudad Rodrigo is, and has been for some time the grand object on both sides. From the preparations which I know we are making, the campaign will open with operations upon it. D'Orsenne is in force at Salamanca, and from the relative situation of both armies, which put themselves to considerable inconvenience by remaining where they are, I have no doubt but that active operations will begin the first moment the weather will permit. The rains have now set in, and will probably continue till the end of February. We are hard at work upon Almeida. Brennier succeeded so completely in blowing it up, that our utmost exertions can never make it a strong place. Our battering train is in it, and will soon be mounted upon it. Two thousand men are at work. Some think that when it is a little more advanced the Beaux will pay it a visit and ruin all our labour. We had an alarm a day or two ago, but it proved nothing. This is a horrid place on the top of a high hill; bleak as Chapel House, its being a city, and the seat of a Bishop does not raise it in our estimation, though the Portuguese think highly of it on that account. The French did not show any great veneration for the seat of piety, for they destroyed almost all the houses. I was entertained the other day by my landlord who was the priest of place, who said he would fetch me some milk as soon as he had brought in some water for my servant; the fountain too was half a mile off. There is some game about. I killed a couple of cocks three days ago. The partridges are very wild, and a very indifferent eat. Imagine a Goth of a Portuguese telling a friend of mine that woodcocks were very good for making soup.[2] Lord Wellington has got a pack of hounds at Freineda. They have had excellent sport, and killed a great many foxes. As my horse only gets a little rye straw and still less corn, I cannot take the liberty of looking at them. Lord Wellington has knocked up all his horses. I heard of Charles Bowles being in this country; as yet I have not seen him, but I hope to catch him before he leaves. Numerous amateurs have visited us, but

---

[1] Francis had married on October 26th 1811 Catherine, 2nd daughter of Sir John Mordaunt, 7th Bart. Their sons produced Mills branches at Pillerton, Warwickshire and at Bude Haven, Cornwall, which are now extinct in the male line.

[2] JM's indignation at the restriction of this bird to soup is justified, since it is one of the great delicacies of the table when roasted.

their curiosity is soon satisfied. The mail is going and I have only time to sub-scribe myself your Affectionate nephew, John Mills.

December 16th. The weather was so foggy that I found it impossible to shoot.
December 17th. Dined with Talbot. Nothing but the usual routine.
December 24th. Dined with General Graham.
December 25th. A large party dined with Rose.

Pinhel
December 25th 1811

My Dearest Mother

There is so total a dearth of everything like news that I am almost afraid of beginning a letter. If I prose you must excuse me. Things remain in the same state at the front. Neither army has made any move and we may therefore consider ourselves as not likely to move for some time. Frost has usurped the place of rain and it is fully as cold as in England. The native brutes sit wrapped up in snuff coloured cloaks over a pan of charcoal, roasting chestnuts and think us savages for building fireplaces. Were they anything but vandals they could have profited by our intercourse with them. But it has confirmed their preju-dices, made them certain that we shall all be damned and eat if possible more garlic than before. The events of the fashionable world are not lost upon us. The robbery of Mrs Perceval's diary, Mr Wellesley-Pole's perseverance and the prosperous state of the Prince Regent's uncle, have given a death blow to the speculations upon the war. In a short time some paper will have "the authority to state that the sick of the Army on the Peninsula amount to 1000," bye the bye 2000 died last month. I wish Beau Perceval would come and have a look at us here.[1] We had hoped to have wintered at Lamego, to have tasted port wine in its pure state and for something under five shillings a bottle. The riotous and burglarious conduct of one of the other divisions made it necessary to move them back and consequently we have the honour of being so much nearer our French enemies. We are tolerably well supplied with everything and at the usual exorbitant rate. You would naturally imagine that being so near Lamego we should have wine cheap; instead of French brandy they put a spirit distilled from the vine into the wine for home consumption and then modestly demand five shillings a bottle when they bring it up here. The port wine in its natural and pure state will not bear the least carriage. The whole art of making wine for the English market consists in mixing it; they have different sorts, and of different ages, and pour them from one barrel into another till they have formed the proper compound. Almost all the General Officers have their port wine out from England. At General Graham's, where I dined yesterday, we had claret, port and

---

[1] Spencer Perceval (1762-1812). He became Prime Minister in 1809 and was assas-sinated in the lobby of the House of Commons in 1812. Perceval was committed to the policy of war with France and did his best to support and maintain the war. Twenty years after Waterloo Wellington wrote to Perceval's son in appreciation of his father's efforts on his behalf. See also Oman, *History of the Peninsular War*, IV, 65-69.

other wines, all of which came from thence. Lord Wellington has always claret
and champagne at his table.[1] The Chief Magistrate of Ciudad Rodrigo dined at
Headquarters yesterday. He says the French have flour enough to last till the
end of February but are short of other things. They have been obliged to pull
down a few houses for fuel, but in other respects have not destroyed the town.
Till they leave a place they are as good guests as we are.

Lord Wellington is going to adopt a plan for procuring forage which
really looks as if he means to stay here for life. He proposes to make the natives
make hay; how far it will answer I cannot say, but if it does succeed it will be the
means of preserving a great many of our horses, who have now little else but
rye straw to eat. Lord Wellington has always hay from England. The expense is
always so great that I am really afraid to mention what it costs a ton. The cavalry
depot at Lisbon is also supplied with it. English oats too are frequently delivered
out for our horses. I prefer barley, and the animals like it better.[2] My turn will
come in about a fortnight to go to Almeida with a detachment of our men who
take it by turns to work at the fortifications.[3] The duty lasts but four days, which
is quite long enough as there is hardly a roof in the place and few of us understand the phenomena of scarps, counterscarps, and other terms nearly unintelligible to any but engineers.

Christmas Day involuntarily makes an Englishman think of roast beef and
minced pies. I am going tonight to dine with a friend of mine who gives a great
dinner upon the occasion, and with all the luxuries of the season. I give a dinner
to twelve select fashionables of New Year's Day, so you see that starvation is not

[1] Wellington kept a good table in the Peninsula although he himself admitted that
others kept better ones. The story is told of an officer who had recently come out to the
Peninsula and who, when invited to dinner by Wellington, hesitated before answering
nervously that he must decline the offer on account of having a prior engagement with
Rowland Hill. 'Go by all means,' replied Wellington, 'you will get a much better feed than
here. As you are a stranger, I will give you some useful information. Cole gives the best
dinners in the army; Hill the next best; mine are no great things; Beresford's and Picton's
are very bad indeed!' (Fraser, *The Soldiers Whom Wellington Led*, pp.120-121.)

[2] According to General Orders the correct ration of forage for all army mules and
horses was fourteen pounds of straw or hay, twelve pounds of oats or ten pounds or
barley or Indian corn. If hay brought from England was issued it was to be fourteen
pounds. Any deficiencies in straw or hay could be compensated for by an increase in the
ration of Indian corn or barley which was twelve pounds. If green forage was issued then
the ration was twenty-eight pounds. Of course, all of this depended upon there being
enough forage to begin with, which on many occasions there was not, particularly in the
winter months. The horses of the King's German Legion were considered the best in the
army, even by their British comrades. This owed much, apparently, to the fact that many
British soldiers sold their forage to buy drink whereas the Germans actually shared their
rations with their horses. For an excellent account of the relationship between horse and
soldier see Brett-James' *Life in Wellington's Army*, pp.179-194.

[3] There was then no platoon organisation in the infantry, other than in the Rifle
regiments, by which a subaltern had permanent responsibility for about a third of a
company. The captain was responsible for all aspects of his company, although he might
assign field command of a half company to his lieutenant. The ensigns, like JM, thus only
came to the fore when assigned command of a detachment for a specific task such as
siege work or on picquet duty.

in the catalogue of our misfortunes. I shall try hard but am afraid I shall not succeed in the minced pies; I have hopes of a turkey and have got a Chine.[1] When we are settled we enjoy ourselves, to make up for marching and bivouacking. You must now be tired of hearing my plans of gormandising, particularly as it will all be over when you receive this.

My best love to all your party and many more Christmases to you and to them. John Mills.

December 29th. Marched to Almeida in command of a detachment of masons to assist in repairing the works. Almeida surrendered to the French in 1810, the magazine having blown up. It is a strong place and more so from the difficulty of making approaches from the rocky ground. Brennier blew up one side of the wall on the 16th of May 1811 and made his escape with his garrison. Sir B. Spencer fired some of the French mines which were unexploded on the 6th of June when he retreated behind the Coa. The repairs which are going on there will soon put it in as good a state of defence as before. Two thousand Portuguese and British are employed on the works. I had a fracas with a native who claimed a Pointer of mine. The Town Mayor turned out the Guard who attacked our soldiers with bayonets, luckily no harm was done and the dog remained in our possession. I reported the Mayor to Lord Wellington who reprimanded him.
December 30th. Got into a tolerably comfortable house. The explosion of the arsenal and the subsequent blowing up of the town have destroyed three fourths of it. The French destroyed some of the guns by firing into them. All those that are spiked will be remounted, about seventy. Some are already remounted. The breach is made red hot and the spike is then drilled out. The guns here are of all nations. Some of the Spanish are beautifully embossed. There are three immense mortars, so large that only stones can be thrown from them.
December 31st. The snow is a foot deep. In the absence of a fireplace I am obliged to recourse to charcoal. The only well in town is filled with gunpowder which the French threw in. The inhabitants have to go for a mile for water.

[1] ie the cuts of beef along the backbone.

Chapter Three

The Great Sieges

The winter of 1811-12 was a particularly hard one. The men of both armies who had endured a hot shimmering summer were now faced with freezing snow and ice which caused the men's breeches to freeze to their legs whenever they crossed small rivers or streams. The winter months usually signalled the end of the campaign season but this winter was to be an exception. While Marmont's men huddled together around fires, blew on their hands and stamped their feet in their bleak isolated billets, Wellington's men kept warm by making fascines and gabions and other instruments of siege warfare. It was to be a busy winter. Wellington himself was not idle and while his men worked away in their camps he busied himself circulating exaggerated sick reports and false dispositions. He allowed senior officers to go home on leave and employed every ruse possible to lure the French into thinking there would be no further offensive movements from him that winter. Then, one week into the New Year, he advanced with his army against the fortress of Ciudad Rodrigo which commanded the northern corridor between Portugal and Spain. Together with the great fortress of Badajoz, which commanded the southern route, it was one of the two 'Keys of Spain' without whose possession Wellington could not hope to drive the French from Portugal. The 1st Division of the army, including the Coldstream Guards, took part in the siege operations and JM and other 'Gentlemen's Sons' shared the miseries of working in the freezing trenches, enduring 24-hour shifts during which they were exposed to harassing fire from the defenders within the town.

Ciudad Rodrigo fell to Wellington on January 19th 1812 and the following month his men trekked south to lay siege to the town's much stronger sister, Badajoz. On this occasion the Guards formed part of the covering force and were thus spared the appalling conditions in the mud-filled trenches and the horrors of the storm on April 6th. The two successful stormings — if one can call a combined total of nearly 4,000 casualties at the stormings successful — heralded perhaps the most glorious seven months of the war, culminating in the victory at Salamanca and not forgetting Hill's masterstroke at Almaraz.

But let us return to New Year's day 1812 and join JM amidst the hustle and bustle of the army encampment as Wellington's men prepare to do battle for Ciudad Rodrigo.

January 1st. Great preparations are being made for the siege of Ciudad Rodrigo.[1] The battering train is in here consisting of thirty twenty-four pounders and six eighteen-pounders, besides twenty mortars and howitzers.[2] The Engineers are preparing and sending off ammunition.

January 2nd. A hundred and fifty Spanish cars came in who volunteered to carry stores to Ciudad. Fifty thousand sand bags and quantities of entrenching tools were sent by them.

January 3rd. The Engineers got orders to proceed to the siege. All the tools were ordered to be sent off, not having any so that the work must begin quick.

January 4th. There being no tools to work with I moved off too and had proceeded to the bridge over the Coa where General Craufurd in 1810 had an affair with the enemy and lost so many men.[3] I met the battalion, who had received orders to march and went to As Navas, a miserable village where we were

[1] The town of Ciudad Rodrigo commanded the northern route between Spain and Portugal, Badajoz commanding the southern route. On the Portuguese side of the border the route was commanded by the fortress of Almeida, now effectively defunct due to extensive damage the previous year. Ciudad Rodrigo itself stands on the right bank of the Agueda river and is enclosed within strong masonry walls 32 feet high. The unusual feature of the town's defences was the double enceinte all around them, ie a double ditch divided by a strong earth and masonry bank. There was no main citadel within the town although an old Moorish castle stands high above the Agueda overlooking the old Roman bridge over the river. The town could not really be besieged from the south, owing to the river and the steep approaches to the town but to the north lay two long rounded ridges, the Greater and Lesser Tesons. It was on these that Wellington chose to position his siege guns.

[2] The standard British siege gun during the Peninsular War was the 24-pounder, an enormous gun with a barrel nine feet long. Each of these guns was capable of firing a large iron ball twenty times an hour and after each firing had to be dragged about eight feet back to its original position after recoiling. Effective firing was only of use during daylight and, unless there was a breeze, it took thirty seconds for the black smoke to clear before it could be fired again. Accuracy was vital although the method of aiming the guns was little more than a case of pointing the barrel at the target and adjusting it accordingly. Each shot was aimed at a selected spot with the intention of bringing down the wall forward into the ditch at the foot of it. This meant that not only would there be a gap in the wall but the rubble and debris would, in theory, fill up the ditch and enable the storming soldiers to approach the breach a little easier up a gentle slope.

[3] On July 24th 1810 Robert Craufurd had risked and almost lost his Light Division in an action against Ney's VI Corps. Craufurd had been in position on the right bank of the Coa River maintaining contact with the garrison of Ciudad Rodrigo. When the town fell to Ney, however, Wellington told Craufurd that he did not wish to risk anything on that side of the river and advised Craufurd to return to the left bank. His 'suggestions' were little more than that and they went unheeded by the headstrong Craufurd. But on the evening of July 22nd Wellington issued firm orders that he was to bring his division across to the left bank. Craufurd still dallied and did not begin to make preparations to withdraw until the morning of July 24th at which point he was attacked in strength by Ney who drove the Light Division helter-skelter down the rocky spurs that led down to the river itself and across the small bridge that spanned it. Craufurd lost control of the battle and it was only the superb training of his battalion commanders that allowed him to come away with the Light Division intact in spite of losses of around 350. Wellington was naturally displeased with Craufurd and the action, subsequently known as 'The Combat of the Coa', is one of the more controversial actions of the war.

packed as close as we could stow. 2 leagues.

January 5th. We are in expectation of orders to march which, however, we did not receive. The frost is intensely severe and the houses but little calculated for this sort of amusement.

January 6th. Halted.

January 7th. No orders coming to march, I walked out with my gun. The banks of the Coa are universally high and the course of this river is marked by rocks, bold and almost inaccessible. There are but few fords. The river in summer is not deep but in winter it is swelled by the mountain torrents.

January 8th. We received orders and marched through Fuentes de Oñoro to Espeja, and felt happy again at getting into a Spanish village. The difference of the two nations is very striking. The Portuguese in their houses and persons, dirty to excess and disobliging. The French have robbed them of almost everything they have had, and the little that is left they hide. The Spaniards are remarkably clean in their appearance and are fond of gaudy colours. The dress of the women is beautiful. Their houses are constantly white-washed and their floors which are of a white coloured mud are kept clean. They are very obliging and seem happy to be able to do anything for us. 4 leagues.

January 9th. Marched to Ciudad Rodrigo, 4 leagues. We had to pass two fords, one of them over the Agueda. We relieved the Light Division who had broke ground the night before, and carried a redoubt by storm in a most gallant manner, making 49 prisoners.[1] We remained shivering with cold on our ground till five o'clock. The brigade was then ordered into the trenches. I was with three companies put under the orders of Captain Ellicombe of the Engineers and posted to battery No.1. The Light Division had the night before made the first parallel, and we were to construct three batteries.[2] We marched through the trenches and then proceeded on the open ground to within three hundred yards of the town. The Engineer then marked out the ground and we set to work. The fire of shot and shell which the enemy had kept up during the day

---

[1] The Renaud redoubt on the Greater Teson, named after the town's former governor, was carried by ten companies of the Light Division under the command of Sir John Colborne of the 52nd. The storming party was led to the redoubt by Lieutenant Thomson of the Royal Engineers with men carrying ladders, fascines and axes. The fascines were thrown down and a sort of bridge formed across which the stormers scrambled over the palisades and quickly entered the work. While this was in progress another party moved round to the rear of the fort and forced the gate. The fight lasted just fifteen minutes. Only four men out of a small garrison of 50 escaped back to the town. 2 officers and 43 men were taken prisoner, 3 being killed. British casualties were just 6 dead and 3 officers and 16 men wounded. See Jones, *Journals of the Sieges Undertaken by the Allies in Spain*, pp.87-88 and also *Despatches*, Wellington to Lord Liverpool, 9th January 1812, VIII, 540-541.

[2] The divisions taking part in the siege were the 1st, 3rd, 4th and Light Divisions and each division spent twenty-four hours in the trenches. The order for duty during the siege was; the Light Division, from the 8th to the 9th January, the 12th to the 13th, 16th to 17th and for the storm on the 19th. The 1st Division, from the 9th to the 10th, 13th to 14th and 17th to 18th. The 3rd Division, from the 11th to the 12th, 15th to 16th and for the storm on the 19th. The 4th Division, from the 10th to the 11th, 14th to the 15th, and 18th to the 19th. See Fletcher, *Craufurd's Light Division*, p.179.

had then slackened, but no sooner did they hear our pickaxes than they threw a fireball which fell about twenty yards in our front and blazed for twenty minutes. During this time our men hid themselves as well as they could but unfortunately our arms were piled which they saw from the town and made a pretty good guess at our business. When the light was out they set to work again and the beasts shelled us during the night. Captain Ross of the Engineers was killed at our battery. Before daylight we had completed our work and we retired to our old ground having been twelve hours at work. The brigade lost about twenty killed and wounded. The night was intensely severe — the water froze in the mens' canteens.

January 10th. We waited on our ground till ten o'clock when we were relieved by the 4th Division. We then marched off and returned home. I went to bed at 4 o'clock and slept till 9 the next morning. There was very heavy firing in the night.

January 11th. The firing was very heavy this morning. The 1st, 3rd, 4th and Light Divisions undertake the siege, each working twenty-four hours. I walked out with my gun. The firing continued heavy.

January 12th. The batteries which our brigade threw up in the night were three for eleven eighteen-pounders each. They got great credit for their work which really was excellent. The enemy have been firing a great deal out of a four-pound swivel gun, which is mounted in a church. They fire it extremely well. There are in Ciudad Rodrigo fifteen English deserters. Two of the 88th deserted into the town.

Espeja
January 12th 1812

My Dear Mother

I have had so much to do lately that I am afraid I have been amiss in writing to you. I left Pinhel on the 29th of December to go to Almeida with a detachment of masons who were employed on the works there. I heard whilst I was there that we were likely to undertake the siege of Ciudad Rodrigo but did not give much credit to the report as the snow was a foot deep. On the 3rd the works at Almeida were stopped, all the tools being wanted for the siege. They were carried up by a hundred and fifty Spanish cars who volunteered for the occasion. On the 4th I started from Almeida on my return to Pinhel, and was much surprised to meet our brigade upon the road to As Navas, a most miserable little village about a league from Almeida. Here we stopped three days and took upon ourselves to conjecture that the siege was abandoned in consequence of the severity of the weather. On the 8th we were undeceived. We marched to this place which is a Spanish village on the frontiers, and I now come to the siege. The Light, 1st, 4th and 3rd Divisions are the only ones employed and work in the order I have put them down, for twenty-four hours at a time, moving for that time from their cantonments. The whole is under the direction of General Graham. The Light Division began on the night of the 8th and stormed a small fort on the outside of the town making 48 prisoners. They then threw up trenches at five hundred yards. On the 9th we marched from hence to relieve them and got upon the ground at twelve o'clock, having marched four leagues and forded two rivers, one of them the Agueda. At six o'clock our brigade moved up to work. We had to construct three batteries and sundry trenches; I was with three companies who were to make Battery No.1. The sun had set, and we marched along the trenches till we came to the end of them. We then stole along the open ground till we came within three hundred yards of the town, when the ground was measured out, and we set to work. The fire from the batteries had slackened as the night approached, but no sooner did they hear our pick-axes at work than they threw a fire ball which fell about 20 yards in our front and threw out such a light that they could see every button upon our coats. The ball burnt for twenty minutes during which time we lay upon our faces to hide ourselves, and they fired most gloriously. When the light was burnt out we set to work, and before daylight completed our battery, as did the others. Before the sun rose we skulked out and remained out of shot till we were relieved by the 4th Division. We then marched here and got in at four o'clock, having been thirty-four hours in the open air, with no sort of shelter, in the most biting frost, so hard that the water froze in the mens' canteens. I went to bed and to make up for lost time remained there for seventeen hours. They kept up a heavy fire upon us the whole of the time we were working, but luckily did little execution. The brigade lost but twenty men. The shells at night appeared like rockets; you see them the whole way and can judge where they will fall, and then lay flat down. Lord Wellington gives us the greatest credit for our work; without vanity, our brigade can do more work, and better, than any other division. The battering train will be mounted tonight and tomorrow we shall begin to repay them, for as yet we have not fired a shot. Tomorrow we relieve the Light Division. When I come in I shall be too tired to write much. I shall then give you an account of our second proceedings.

January 13th. Relieved the Light Division at Ciudad. Went on picquet close in to the walls at five o'clock and remained till daylight when we withdrew within the trenches and remained till eight when we marched off. Graham went with a German picquet and dislodged one of the enemy's from the convent of St Clara. We threw up trenches to within two hundred yards of the town. They kept up during the night a most incessant fire of musketry from the walls. The Coldstream lost four men, the Germans lost about 20. An officer had both his legs shot off.[1] The guns are all ready to move in. Some delay has been occasioned by two of the platforms having been blown up. The frost continues but the wind is not so

[1] On the night of January 13th the French-held fortified convent of Santa Cruz, to the north-west of the town, was successfully stormed by Thomas Graham with 300 volunteers from the King's German Legion and a single company of the 5/60th. The men crept forward in the darkness before setting about the palisades with their axes. The French opened up a heavy fire on their assailants and six men were killed and 34 wounded. The convent was carried, however, most of the garrison hurriedly retiring to the town as the stormers broke in.

cold.

January 14th. I marched home and found letters to the 30th. When we were about two miles from the town, we saw the French picquet come out and attack ours which was in the convent of St Clara. We beat them off after half an hour's skirmishing.[1] The enemy fired a great deal in the morning, aware that our guns were moving in. At night the firing continued. I did not find myself as much tired as I expected.

Espeja,
January 14th.

My Dear Mother,

I am just returned from Ciudad, not so tired as expected, and likewise have to thank you and Elizabeth for letters of the 29th of December. Last night we threw up fresh works nearer the town. I was on picquet under the walls of the town. Their fire passed close over our heads without hitting us, as luckily for us we were protected by a bank. Our men were so close at work that they fired musketry and grape during the night. A piquet of the Germans took a convent on our right most gallantly. I was on duty there from five o'clock yesterday evening till eight this morning. I got wet in my feet at first starting, which made me uncomfortable for the remainder of the night. It froze very hard; to give you an idea of it, a stream which we passed yesterday was froze sufficiently hard to bear a mule and boy on it. We lost but four men. I saw a most beautiful skirmish this morning between our picquets and the French who wanted to regain the convent, but they were beat.[2] I think the place will be ours in a week. Graham is everywhere. A more gallant or better man never lived. I believe any of us would go through fire and water for him. There is no nonsense about him. I shall bore you to death with this siege but you may easily imagine that it occupies my thoughts as much as the "Horrid Murders" do those of the editors of the newspapers.

You shall hear from me by the next mail; I shall not, I rather believe, be on duty again for the remainder of the business, if it does not last more than a

---

[1] At 11am on January 14th General Barrie launched a sortie from the town with 500 men. Barrie had cunningly chosen the hour for his attack to coincide with the precise moment at which the 4th Division was relieving the 1st Division. Whenever the division on duty in the trenches saw the relieving division approaching the guards and the working parties would withdraw to make room for them and in so doing would leave the trenches unoccupied for a short period ('a bad custom', remarked Jones in his, *Journal of the Sieges*, pp.91-92). The French saw all of this from their position on top of the tower in the cathedral and duly planned their attack to coincide. The signal was given and suddenly 500 French troops sallied out, sweeping along the trenches and filling in whole lengths of them. The convent of Santa Cruz was retaken by the French for a while until Graham restored the situation by collecting a number of workmen from the 24th and 42nd who checked the French advance, forcing them back into the town after having done widespread damage. See Oman's *History of the Peninsular War*, V, 173, and Fletcher, *Craufurd's Light Division*, p.182.

[2] See note 1 above.

week, for it is my turn to stay at home with the Colours.

Tell Harriet[1] I shall write to her by the next mail, to thank her for remembering me. I must now conclude with kindest love to all at Bisterne or elsewhere, and believe me, John Mills.

I received the Pocket Box, I thank you very much for it.

January 15th. A mail to England. Sat at home and wrote letters. Marmont, they say, is hastening down to relieve Ciudad, and is expected to be down in a week. Our battalion opened this morning and are keeping an incessant fire upon the place which is very partially returned by the garrison. Last night, the 40th Regiment stormed and took the convent of San Francisco and three pieces of artillery.[2] The picquet escaped. We are now in possession of the whole of the suburbs. The sortie made by the enemy yesterday was cowardly. We lost 28. They had 8 killed. Stanhope has his horse killed under him. Thick fog and frost.

January 16th. It is said that Marmont knew nothing of the siege on the 12th, that he was returning quietly to his old quarters at Salamanca. Our batteries continue firing, and have breached the upper part of the wall. Fog continued.

January 17th. Relieved the Light Division. The fog cleared away about 12 o'clock. I went down to the convent of San Francisco which is about a hundred yards from the walls. I had a fine view of the breaches which as yet are not large. They are at work at the breaching battery at sixty yards and another at 120. Lord Wellington, General Beresford, the Prince of Orange and staff were at the convent when we were there. We have dismounted several of the enemy's guns. They have one of ours and another burst this morning. A shell fell into our magazine, exploded and killed two men, but did not communicate to the powder. The firing was very heavy. Our men worked at night and were employed in finishing the battery at 120 yards. The brigade lost 7 men, the Germans as usual a great many.

January 18th. Before we marched off I went down again to the convent and went into the steeple, which I had neglected to do before. Our new battery had opened and was playing. They were shelling it and did great execution. Whilst I was there they threw a great many in. The largest of the two breaches had sandbags in it. "I have the honour to summons the place." (signed Wellington). "My Emperor gave me the place to defend not to surrender." (signed Barrie).[3]

---

[1] The only Mills of this name was the widow of General Scott (see August 27th 1811), but it is odd that JM did not call her 'aunt'. It may be that she had sent him some token of the General. It is also possible that this may be Harriet Somerville (see letter December 19th 1812).

[2] The convent of San Francisco was stormed on the night of January 14th by three companies of the 40th Regiment who broke into the convent with little difficulty. The capture of the convent forced Barrie into pulling those French troops still in the suburbs back inside the walls of the town.

[3] There is no actual record of this exchange of correspondence between Barrie and Wellington although a summons to surrender the town, once a practicable breach had been made, would almost certainly have followed. Under the old 'rules of war' a

The weather is not so cold as it was and I rather think it is going to break. I did not find myself as tired as before, not having been on duty the preceding night. January 19th. The firing is very heavy today. I went coursing and found three hares. In the evening at six o'clock the great guns ceased firing and afterwards we heard that Ciudad was ours. Two breaches were made about a hundred yards from each other. The largest was about fifty feet, the other fifteen wide. The 3rd Division stormed the former, the Light the latter. The Light Division was once repulsed but carried it the second time. The 3rd carried theirs at the first attempt, but on arriving at the top a mine was sprung, it is believed accidentally which blew up a great many on both sides, amongst others General Mackinnon. On their arrival at the top of the breaches both storming parties found themselves in the same predicament from a ditch having been dug, which divided the parapet and in fact insulated both breaches. A single plank was left over which the garrison retired and then removed. They do not appear to have made much resistance at either of the breaches. Our men were now in an awkward predicament. The garrison kept a heavy fire upon them till at length a way was made into the town. The scene which ensued can neither be described nor imagined. Pillage ensued. The town was on fire in several places and the morning showed the atrocities that had been committed. We were an hour and a half in carrying the town. General Craufurd was hit in the lungs, General Vandeleur, Colonel Colborne, Major Napier wounded.[1]

town was obliged to surrender once a practicable breach had been made and the garrison allowed to march out with the honours of war. If, on the other hand, a garrison chose to fight on it waived any claims to mercy once the town fell, and with practicable breaches having been made this would almost certainly have been the case. In the Peninsula, Napoleon had decreed that no garrison commander should surrender a place without it having first sustained at least one assault. Of course, this meant that once the besiegers were in possession of the place they were fully entitled to put the garrison to the sword. This change in policy almost certainly led to the shameful and disgraceful outrages that followed the successful storming of the towns in the Peninsula by Wellington's men. Curiously enough, the anger of the British soldiers was vented not upon the French defenders, who caused them so many casualties, but on the people and property of the town itself. The subject is a deep and very complex one and warrants a wider study. Fletcher's 'Taken by Storm: British Misconduct Following the Sieges in the Peninsula,' in *Military Illustrated*, No.46, goes some way to exploring the reasons behind the soldier's misconduct following each successful storming.

[1] Ciudad Rodrigo was stormed on the night on January 19th 1812. Picton's 3rd Division was ordered to attack the Greater Breach while Craufurd's Light Division would attack the Lesser Breach. A diversionary attack by Lieutenant Colonel O'Toole would be made across the Roman bridge over the Agueda at the same time. The assault by the 3rd Division, led by General Henry Mackinnon, of the Coldstream, met with stiff resistance, and heavy casualties were sustained before the 88th (Connaught Rangers) finally scrambled their way to the top of the breach to get to grips with their assailants. At the Lesser Breach the storming was somewhat easier but Robert Craufurd, leading his Light Division, was mortally wounded by a musket ball whilst standing on the glacis, cheering his men on. The town was taken and a debate raged soon afterwards as to just who entered the town first, the Light Division or the 3rd Division. The Light Division appears to have the stronger case, mainly due to the fact that the great mine which was exploded by the French in the Great Breach claimed the lives of some men of the Light Division, so quickly had they got up the Lesser Breach and along the ramparts. The storming cost

January 20th. Everyone was anxious to see the place but an order was given that one officer per company should remain at home. Those that went described the scene as dreadful. Several explosions have taken place, one of them killed some English deserters, and some Frenchmen set fire to a magazine in which they had hid themselves and were blown up. The breach was filled with bodies, in some places Frenchmen were lying wounded, in others the ruins which had been caused by the explosion were lying upon the living and the dead. Numbers of Frenchmen who had concealed themselves the night before were dragged out. 1,241 men and 49 officers were marched out. General Barrie dined with Lord Wellington. He was violent in his abuse of the Spaniards and Lord Wellington was obliged to desire him to hold his tongue.[1] Our loss in the storm appears to be about 300.[2]

January 22nd. We hear nothing of Marmont. He was to have been down by the 24th but I suppose his intentions will now be changed. Some soldiers, after they got into the town, lighted a fire in a church immediately over a magazine. The frost continues and a heavy fog with it. There are reports in circulation of us going down to Badajoz.

Espeja
January 22nd 1812

My Dearest Mother

The Gazette will have informed you of the taking of Ciudad, an event that will surprise our friends and enemies, more especially the latter who had calculated upon the subject and the result was far wide of the mark. Our batteries opened

Wellington 59 officers and 503 men whilst of the French garrison of around 1,900, some 60 officers and 1,300 other ranks were taken prisoner. 8 officers were killed and 21 wounded with 500 men killed or wounded. It was the first time that Wellington's men had taken a town by storm in the Peninsula and nobody appears to have considered issuing orders relating to the procedures to be followed afterwards. Consequently, there was some plundering and disorder but this was fairly short-lived and was nothing of the scale to be seen later at Badajoz and San Sebastian. It did, however, give the men a taste for plunder, and this contributed to the shocking aftermath at Badajoz in April 1812.

[1] There is no record of Wellington having dined with and spoken to Barrie in such a manner, although Gurwood does say that Wellington ordered Barrie to be taken away rather sharply when the former governor interrupted him whilst in conversation with Beresford shortly after the storming. Lieutenant John Gurwood, who led the forlorn hope of the 52nd into the Lesser Breach, accepted the surrender of General Barrie inside the castle within the walls of Ciudad Rodrigo, although this claim is disputed by others, in particular the men of the 88th (Connaught Rangers), whose Lieutenant Mackie claimed to have been the first into the town. See Oman's *History of the Peninsular War*, V, 589-599, for more on this dispute. Gurwood's own account can be found in Cowell's *Leaves from the Diary of an Officer of the Guards*, pp.233-238. Gurwood later edited Wellington's despatches. The castle in Ciudad Rodrigo is now one of the paradores, the state-owned chain of hotels, while Barrie's sword itself can be seen in the Royal Green Jackets Museum at Winchester.

[2] JM is some way off here. 562 casualties were sustained during the assault while the total casualty figure for the entire siege was 9 officers and 186 men killed and 70 officers and 846 men wounded.

on the 15th, a new one at 130 yards on the 18th, and on the 19th two breaches were declared practicable. One of them was about fifty feet wide, the other about fifteen. At six o'clock in the evening our batteries ceased. The 3rd Division stormed the largest, the Light Division the other. The latter were once driven back but succeeded in mounting the breach. The 3rd Division gained theirs, but when they got to the top a mine accidentally exploded and killed both friends and foe; amongst the former was General Mackinnon. The breach was so effectually cleared, that it was soon gained again. Our men found themselves in the same predicament at the top of both the breaches. General Barrie had by cutting the parapet insulated the ground immediately about it and the French retired over a single plank, which they did not forget to remove, so that our men were for some time exposed to a dreadful fire, without being able to advance.[1] At length a way was made into the town and then they had it all their own way. the enemy ran down the streets, were pursued and a great many knocked on the head. The night was so dark that our men fired upon one another; in short, the confusion was dreadful — our men were an hour and a half gaining the town. The scene of rapine that ensued, I am told beggared all description. The town was on fire in many places, every house was ransacked; in short, for the whole of the night it was given up to pillage.[2] All this time we were here. Had the assault been either the night before or the night after, it would have been our turn. I was unable to go over on the 20th; yesterday, the 21st, I went.

During the whole of the preceding day and yesterday morning, the Spaniards had been employed in burying, but the scene such as it was when I saw it, stripped of half its horrors, was beyond all imagination. The contents of the houses emptied into the streets, several of the houses on fire, and one contin-

[1] The breach in the inner wall of Ciudad Rodrigo had been retrenched on either side by two ditches, ten feet across and ten feet deep, and by two parapets thrown up behind them. Behind these parapets were two 24-pounder guns, one on either side of the breach, designed to enfilade the storming parties. These guns were loaded with grape shot and in such an enclosed space the results of a single discharge from either of these guns were appalling. The 88th actually threw down their muskets and scrambled across these cuts using their bare hands before setting about the French gunners before they could fire off a third salvo.

[2] See also footnote 3, page 102, for an explanation as to some of the causes of the disorder after the storming. The final comments on this aspect of the siege of Ciudad Rodrigo come from two famous diarists of the Light Division. Jonathan Leach, of the 95th, wrote, 'When a town is stormed, it is inevitable that excesses will be, as they ever have been, committed by the assailants, more particularly if it takes place at night. It affords a favourable opportunity for the loose and dissolute characters, which are to be found in all armies, to indulge in every diabolical propensity.' (Leach, *Rough Sketches of the Life of an Old Soldier*, p.250.) John Kincaid, also the 95th, wrote, 'A town taken by storm presents a frightful scene of outrage. The soldiers no sooner obtain possession of it, than they think themselves at liberty to do what they please. It is enough for them that there *had* been an enemy on the ramparts; and, without considering that the poor inhabitants may, nevertheless, be friends and allies, they, in the first moment of excitement, all share one common fate; and nothing but the most extraordinary exertions on the part of the officers can bring them back to a sense of their duty.' (Kincaid, *Adventures in the Rifle Brigade*, pp.56-57.)

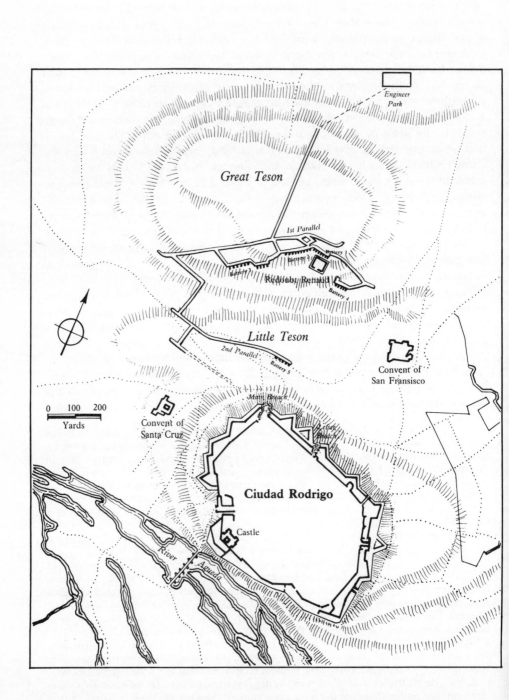

Engineer Park

Great Teson

1st Parallel

Battery 1 Battery

Battery 2

Redoubt Renaud

Battery

Little Teson

2nd Parallel

Battery 5

Convent of San Fransisco

0   100   200
Yards

Convent of Santa Cruz

Main Breach

Lesser Breach

Ciudad Rodrigo

Castle

River

Agueda

ued mass of friends and foes lying dead — caps, clothes, arms, cannon balls, ammunition, beds, chairs, wearing apparel, legs, etc. etc. filled the streets. Those who saw this scene on the morning after describe it as dreadful beyond expression. Added to all this, the houses near the breaches were knocked to pieces. A field of battle, dreadful as it is, is nothing in comparison.

On the 20th several explosions took place, from the quantity of loose powder that was about. Some English deserters who had hid themselves in a magazine set fire to it, and blew themselves up. 1,241 prisoners marched out, but amongst them were Spaniards and civilians — about three hundred are in their hospital. From what I can learn, I do not think there was much resistance made at the breaches. Our loss in a great measure arose from explosions and from their situation after they had gained the breaches; it amounts, I believe, to about 300. General Barrie dined with Lord Wellington on the 20th. Poor man, he had just finished his soup [on the 19th] when the news was brought him that we were storming, and after it was all over, some officers of the 95th sat down to the remainder of his dinner. The Summons to the town was, "I have the honour to summons the place," Wellington. "My Emperor gave me the town to defend, not to surrender," Barrie.

The 5th, a fresh division, has been brought up to repair the breach and to level our works. I rode over them yesterday; the ground was absolutely ploughed up with shells. Marmont is expected here on the 24th but nothing has been heard of him lately — he can do no good now. After all the toils of the siege are over, I find myself only worse by a trifling cold. General Craufurd is wounded in the lungs, General Vandeleur slightly. Major Napier is also hit and has lost his arm.

Our total loss in the siege is about 600. The French, when they assaulted the place, lost 4000. Their batteries were open for eight days, ours were five. Nobody seems to have the least idea of what we shall do. The general opinion is that we shall move southwards but all seem to think we shall have nothing like winter quarters. All places are very near the same to me. The frost continues, and in all probability will till it is interrupted by rain.

I saw in Ciudad yesterday three regular Barouches which no-one had thought fit to take. They really were very good and I had a great mind to have one of them. It would be very neat to have a travelling carriage.[1] On the 17th

---

[1] JM would certainly have achieved a reputation for himself had he taken one of these carriages! The sight of a Coldstream Guards officer travelling round the country in a carriage would have been noted by virtually every diarist of the age. Of course, one wonders where he would have got the horses with which to pull it! Nevertheless, the British soldier's passion for plunder knew no bounds. As soon as the victorious British stormers entered Ciudad Rodrigo they made straight for the town's wine cellars and bodegas but once drunk set about acquiring all sorts of plunder, most of which was totally useless to them. When the British troops marched out of the town at 9am the following morning the extent of this plundering became all too apparent. Wellington's men, like those of all other armies, had a liking for looting but on this occasion it appears that the British troops had gone a little too far, as this description of the Light Division on the morning of the 20th would indicate. 'There was scarcely a vestige of uniform amongst the men, some of whom were dressed in Frenchmen's coats, some in white breeches and

and 18th I went down to the convent of St Francisco, which we had taken; it was about seventy yards from the town. I saw Lord Wellington go down with Marshal Beresford, the Prince of Orange, and other celebrated characters. Therefore, I thought I might venture. There is honour amongst thieves for they did not fire upon us. The French had established shops in the town and I saw written over several of them in large characters, "Vin de Bordeaux et autres Comestibles en gros et en detail." From this specimen I suppose they lived very well; if they had any left I make no doubt but that our men made the corks fly.

I must now close my dispatch. Pray remember me kindly to all in Portman Square. John Mills.

January 23rd. The remains of General Mackinnon were buried with Military Honours by the Coldstream near the church here. His body had been buried near the breach but was moved from thence. It was dreadfully disfigured but the remains of the finest form made it impossible to mistake him.[1]

January 24th. General Craufurd, who had led the Light Division, died this morning in consequence of the wound he received in storming. The ball passed through his arm into his lungs. He was a gallant officer, and beloved by his troops. Our loss in storming was 471, and the total loss during the siege about 1,000.

January 25th. The funeral of General Craufurd took place at twelve o'clock this day, near the breach in Ciudad. Lord Wellington and his staff attended.[2] Briga-

---

huge jack-boots, some with cocked-hats and queues, most of their swords were fixed to the rifles and stuck full of hams, tongues and loaves of bread and not a few of them were carrying bird cages!' (Kincaid, *Adventures in the Rifle Brigade*, p.59.) Apparently, some of the men even had monkeys on their shoulders. Wellington was on the road also with some of his staff and such was the strange spectacle before him that he turned and asked, "Who the devil are those fellows?" The answer came back; the Light Division.

[1] Major General Henry Mackinnon, of the Coldstream, commanding the 3rd Division's columns at the storming of Ciudad Rodrigo, was killed by the great mine that was exploded by the French at the Great Breach. According to Cowell, *Leaves from the Diary of an Officer of the Guards*, p.247, he was buried in the market place of the small village of Espeja, 'and his remains were followed to the grave by his brother officers of the Guards.' Mackinnon's *Journal of the Campaign in Portugal and Spain*, published in 1812 after his death, is a remarkable work and reads more like a travelogue than a military history. In it, he describes the agriculture, geography and architecture of virtually every region and town he marched through with the Coldstream Guards. The preface ends poignantly, 'Its being published for the Benefit of Three infant Boys, who are deprived of the valuable Assistance of a Father to guide them in the Paths of Life — the Motive, therefore, that leads to the exposing to Public View so trifling a Composition, may plead an Excuse, should it be found insignificant and uninteresting.' (Mackinnon, *Journal*, pp.vi-vii). Henry Mackinnon was the uncle of the famous Daniel Mackinnon, the great joker in the Coldstream Guards and one of the defenders of Hougoumont at Waterloo on June 18th 1815. Elizabeth Longford (*Years of the Sword*, p.266.) confuses the two men and has Dan Mackinnon as being killed at Rodrigo instead of Henry Mackinnon..

[2] Robert Craufurd was buried in the Lesser Breach on January 25th 1812 in the presence of Wellington, Beresford, Castaños, the officers of the Brigade of Guards, the cavalry, the 3rd, 4th and 5th Divisions and the whole of headquarters. His loss was undoubtedly the biggest blow suffered by Wellington in the Peninsula. It is said that Craufurd was not loved by his men but when he was buried there was not a single dry

dier General Calcraft who is in advance with the dragoons reported that 3,000 infantry and 800 cavalry of the enemy's were within four leagues of Ciudad and that their support are on this side of Salamanca. They have two hundred cars with them from which it is imagined they are making a reconnaissance to ascertain whether Rodrigo is really in our hands. We were ordered to hold ourselves in readiness. Frost.

January 26th. There is a woman in this town who has but one ear. She has a small flap or lug in the usual place. I was astonished at hearing a Spanish woman singing the tune of the fairy dance, accompanying it on the lip of a kettle, and a little girl dancing, as I had so often done to the same myself. It recalled past scenes.

January 27th. It appears that the enemy's party which advanced near Ciudad on the 24th have again retired. Their object seems to have been to ascertain whether we were in possession of the town. Our works are levelled and they are now employed in making a redoubt on the ground, where the fort of San Francisco stood. Our army at this moment is very sickly. It is said that we can bring into the field but 2,700 cavalry and 30,000 infantry. The British reinforcements in the course of last year cannot amount to less than one half of this number.

January 28th. General Craufurd's effects were sold. The produce of the sale could not amount to less than 3000. There was a complete service of plate for 16. The rains appear to have set in.

January 29th. Mail day. Sat at home and wrote letters.

Espeja.
January 29th 1812.

My Dear Harry,

You will of course have participated in our joy at the capture of Ciudad. We have indeed done the Beaux. Marmont calculated that even should we attempt it, the place would stand six weeks, in which time he could assist Suchet in taking Valencia, and come back to relieve Ciudad. So completely was he in the dark, that on the 24th a strong reconnaissance came down to ascertain whether it really was in our hands, and so nicely did he manage it that from an intercepted letter (which an idiot of a Spaniard carried into the convent of San Francisco, in the suburbs of Rodrigo, which we had taken the night before but which capture my friend knew nothing) it appeared that Marmont would be before the place on the 27th. The noise of guns is not out of my ears yet. They kept up during the whole time a very heavy fire of shells, round shot, and grape. Upon the whole our loss is not great, considering that it is usual to make the first

eye amongst the six pall-bearers from the Light Division while the men of the division itself exhibited the signs of intense grief at the loss of their fiery leader during what was a most solemn and striking occasion. The most fitting and memorable tribute to Craufurd was paid by the Light Division on its return from the funeral when the men, without hesitating, plunged waist deep through an excavation filled with icy water, just as Craufurd would have ordered them to. See Fletcher's *Craufurd's Light Division*, pp.200-203, for an account of Craufurd's funeral.

parallel at eight hundred yards, and that in this instance it was a five. Lord Wellington has complimented the Guards upon their exertions. The men really deserved it, and the engineers said that they would do more in one night than any other two divisions, and it is natural they should, for they are all strong men, and accustomed to hard labour. As a proof of it, though they had fresh ground to break, for the three times that it came to their turn to work, they lost fewer men in the trenches than any other brigade, because they would cover themselves in, in one third of the time. Four divisions only were employed, which relieved each other every four and twenty hours. A proportion only of officers went into the trenches, two to a hundred men. It came to my turn twice. The first time we had to break ground for a battery; for the first hour I hardly knew what to make of it, as we were on a rising ground, and they threw a blue light which burnt in our front, and discovered our sinister intentions. Luckily, we were too near for their shells to do much execution. The second night I was on a covering party under the walls, but in a famous ditch. During the whole time we had a hard frost and but little moon. I could not see the town till 36 hours after the storm but it was then a horrid sight. Bodies were lying about in all directions, and as is always the case, stripped to the skin. The walls were terribly battered, several guns dismounted and the blood upon the gun carriages testified that our shot had told. I was really afraid of walking about; there were quantities of loose powder and loaded shells, and the town was then on fire in several places. Had the men done their duty they would have given no quarter for the garrison sprung two mines after the breach was gained.[1] The Governor, Barrie, was a shy cock — he was at his dinner when the breach was stormed and had just finished his soup — some officers of the 95th sat down to the remainder of it. When the French began to run, pillage was the order of the day. They thought no more of their enemy, but set about plundering. The drums beat, bugles sounded, to no purpose. In short, no-one knew where to go or what to do — this must always be the case in a storm at night. The first thing they seized was a large bag into which they crammed eatables, drinkables, clothes, furniture, fiddles, frying pans, in short, anything they could find. When it was full, they got into a corner and drafted the most useless. The streets when

---

[1] The ethics involved in the sacking of a town that had been defended even when practicable breaches had been made are dealt with briefly on page 102. However, Mills thoughts as to the penalties for such an action by a garrison, ie death, were echoed by Wellington himself in a letter to Canning, written in 1820. Wellington wrote, 'I believe that it has always been understood that the defenders of a fortress stormed have no claim to quarter, and the practice which prevailed during the last century of surrendering fortresses when a breach was opened, and the counterscarp blown in, was founded on this understanding. Of late years the French availed themselves of the humanity of modern warfare, and made a new regulation that a breach should stand one assault at least. The consequence of this regulation of Bonaparte's was the loss to me of the flower of my army, in the assaults on Ciudad Rodrigo and Badajoz. I should have thought myself justified in putting both garrisons to the sword, and if I had done so at the first, it is probable that I should have saved 5,000 men at the second. I mention this to show you that the practice which refuses quarter to a garrison that stands an assault is not a *useless* effusion of blood.' (Quoted in Oman, *History of the Peninsular War*, V, 260.)

I was there were filled with remnants. The quantity of caps which were lying about seemed to say they once had owners. Barrie dined with Lord Wellington the day after. He is a vulgar, impertinent fellow, and without scruple abused the Spaniards I daresay with justice, but not so did Lord Wellington who was obliged to stop him twice, and at last to desire him to hold his tongue. Barrie was for surrendering the place two days before we took it, but his engineer would not allow him.[1]

The Headquarters hounds hunt regularly, and I hear have not good sport. Graham is the crack rider. He is a famous fellow and from his conversation you would think took more delight in horses thàn in military matters. But when it comes to the point I really think he likes being under fire. He had the management of the siege and was upon the ground almost all the time. The Peer used to ride over of a morning. I saw him yesterday, he is in excellent spirits and seems delighted with his success. He said he hoped to put his foot into Badajoz yet. General Craufurd died on the 23rd; the ball passed through his lungs, carrying with it a piece of cloth, and a splinter of his ribs. I hear you have had but indifferent sport — you will I hope make up for it at the latter end of the season. I shall be quite confounded when I get back, and not know what to make. Another year and a half and I hope to set my foot on English ground. Those who have not been out of it know not the comfort of England. This wretched country is a fine contrast. I believe we are going to march down to Abrantes, not for any sanguinary purpose, but to get our clothing which has been sent there by water from Lisbon. We are about 150 miles off and from its being necessary for us to go down there you may easily imagine that the means of conveyance are not abundant. The fact is that the proprietors of mules and bullocks like most other mortals do not like to work for nothing, and therefore take themselves frequently off. In this country all the animals employed by the Commissariat are hired, at the rate of one dollar per diem including everything. Ten thousand is the compliment, but owing to desertions there is not that number left. I must now for many reasons conclude, none more imperious than want of paper.

Remember me kindly to Charlotte, and all your family. John Mills.

January 30th. The rain has so filled the Agueda that the division which is across that river cannot pass it without going some distance round. It is understood that in consequence of this, our division is prevented from moving to the rear. January 31st. General Graham has taken Barrie's cook, who I understand is excellent.[2] Rain and wind.

[1] There is no proof of this and if Barrie was acting to the letter of Napoleon's decree, stating that he should sustain at least one assault on the walls, then he would certainly not have sought to surrender before January 19th.

[2] Barrie's cook was named Clément and when the storming of Ciudad Rodrigo got underway the frightened man climbed up an unlit chimney in the house where Barrie had his headquarters. When the British troops broke into the place they immediately lit the fire and Clément was quickly flushed from his hiding place. When Graham heard of the Frenchman's plight he sent for him and offered him a position in his mess. See Brett-James, *General Graham*, p.245.

February 1st. Rain.

February 2nd. Marmont has published a manifesto in which he says that Ciudad is a place of no importance and that nothing but the cowardice of the Governor and his garrison could have put it into our hands. Headquarters returned to Freineda.

February 3rd. Ten men and an officer escaped from Ciudad on the night of the 19th.

February 4th. In consequence of the rains which have nearly insulated this place, the Portuguese have not been able to bring things to the market. Bread has risen in consequence and everything is dear in proportion.

February 5th. Some of the other divisions have moved to the rear, as well as the whole of the cavalry who must have starved if they remained in front as there is nothing but dry rotten grass for them to eat. The French have fifteen thousand men in Salamanca.

February 6th. Three French officers, deserters, came in. They report that Marmont has left Salamanca and is gone to Valladolid. Fine day.

February 7th. Heard of our intended march to Abrantes.

February 8th. Busy in preparing for our march.

February 9th. To Aldea de Ponte. I had not proceeded far when my horse was taken ill, and was obliged to be led for the remainder of the way to Abrantes, and I obliged to walk. We got bad quarters and the horses had nothing to eat. I was much alarmed by rain in the night. 4 leagues.

February 10th. To Sabugal. The morning looked like rain, a little of which came but soon subsided into a mist. The roads were dreadfully muddy and I had considerable doubts as to the arrival of my baggage as my mules were dreadfully weak and heavily laden. I was obliged to buy bread for them at a shilling a loaf. The town is much destroyed since we were last here, from the constant passing of soldiers. The castle is a beautiful building rising abruptly from the Coa. It has a tower in the manner of a bastion. 4 leagues.

February 11th. To Casteleiro, a small village amongst the mountains. The vegetation here is much more forward than at Espeja. We found plenty of green corn which we cut for our horses.[1] About a league on the right of this town is the village of Sortelha, founded by sartorius. It stands on the summit of a hill and was formerly a stronghold. Steps are cut in the rocks. 2 leagues. The men broke open the Commissary stores.

February 12th. To Caria. The road continues under the Serra d'Estrella, the summit of which is covered with snow. Several towns appear on the side of the hill. Covilha is the largest; it is the great manufactory of cloth and ranks high in point of wealth. Caria is a small dirty place — we found green corn. 2 leagues.

February 13th. To Alpedrinha — passed through the villages of Fundão and Ferra. The last league before getting in we had a tremendous hill. My baggage was very late. We dined with Rose and drank some of the wine in this place, famous throughout Portugal. It is a dirty town and has no excuse never having

[1] Green wheat or corn was used for animal fodder. No major mobile operations involving cavalry could start until the grass or corn started to grow.

been destroyed by the French. This was a very fatiguing day's march and I felt the want of a horse. 5 leagues.

February 14th. To Lardosa, a small but neat town. We found plenty of green corn but met with some obstruction from the natives who were not so easily persuaded that eating it did our beasts good. 2 leagues.

February 15th. To Castello Branco. The country is very flat. At Castello Branco we were in a large house belonging to the governor of the place who objected considerably to our cooking in his kitchen, and to prevent it put a guard there. By taking some trouble we got in. Everything is to be had in abundance but is very dear. 3 leagues.

February 16th. Halted. The promenade in the Bishop's garden was all the fashion. The guns are moving along towards Portalegre, supposed to be for the siege of Badajoz.

February 17th. To Sarnadas, a most miserable village, where with difficulty we got a miserable hole. 2 leagues.

February 18th. To Niza. Having been this road before, the vast tracts of gumcistus trees did not astonish me. We overtook some 24-pounder howitzers going up the hill above it. Beautiful weather. At Niza we got a very comfortable quarter in an Apothecary's shop. 5 leagues.

February 19th. To Govao, which is a shocking place. 5 leagues.

February 20th. To Abrantes. ½ a mile from that place we crossed the Tagus by a bridge of boats. Abrantes is situated on a high hill with commanding heights on which the Portuguese are constructing redoubts. It is sufficiently strong to resist an assault. The French headquarters were here for some time and the place is supposed to be very well inclined to that nation. There are but few fine houses in the town which is in a tolerable state of repair. The Tagus here is about a hundred yards wide. The country round is champagne. 4 leagues.

February 21st. The men were employed in fitting their new clothing.[1] Forage is to be bought but is very dear indeed. Everything is to be got here.

Abrantes
February 21st 1812

My Dearest Mother,

You will be surprised to hear of me from hence. We marched unexpectedly from Espeja; our ostensible object is to get our clothing which is here. But as Head-

[1] John Stepney Cowell records that, 'Our Division's march was directed on Abrantes, for the purpose of reclothing our fellows; with which object the clothing had been sent up to that town from Lisbon; it must be confessed, not before it was wanted, for in the *haberdashery line*, we were all a little like those troops with which Falstaff, from a delicate sense of propriety, would *not*, march through Coventry.' (Cowell, *Leaves from the Diary of an Officer of the Guards*, p.253.) This issue of clothing probably did not include new boots, for as John Lucie Blackman recorded in a letter dated March 28th 1812, the Coldstream Guards were in need of new shoes 'and other necessities'. (Blackman Letters, NAM 8807-052.) By the time of the battle of Salamanca, in July the same year, Blackman records that the Coldstream 'had marched their shoes off,' which says little for the quality of footwear in the British Army.

quarters are moving to Portalegre, and the battering train is on its way, there is little doubt but that Badajoz is to be attempted. We are this moment arrived, and as the Post is going out I have only time to write a few lines. We have had eleven days' march, and about a hundred and fifty miles. I was obliged to walk the whole of the way, as my horse is ill, and I think I am the better for it. We have been very fortunate in our weather, more so than we had a right to expect at this unusually rainy season. The whole army will move into the Alentejo, and I suppose his Lordship is going to play a great game. The difference between this and the northern part is very striking; I never wish to cross the Tagus again. There are two mails gone up to Headquarters, and I expect to have a letter from you, and I hope it will be a longer one than this, but as I really have not a moment to spare I will make up for it next time.

Phillipon, Governor of Badajoz, has let the Guadiana into the ditch.[1] You see the Guards are mentioned handsomely in the dispatch about Ciudad. Mr Gurwood, who led one of the Forlorn Hopes, is a man of good fortune, and having established his character is going to retire from the army.

February 22nd. I got leave to go to Lisbon for a few days. I propose going down by water with a party and got an order from the Commissary for two boats for that purpose. Phillipon has let the Guadiana into the ditch at Badajoz and it is said too has ruined the glacis. Some think that the preparations we are making are only with a view to drawing the enemy's attention from the southern part of Spain, others that Lord Wellington really has serious intentions on it. A large wolf which the peasants killed was brought in here.

February 23rd. Set off at six o'clock for Lisbon in a boat with Steele, Allix and Walpole. The river being rapid we made tolerable progress. Got out to breakfast at Pugnitti, where there is an old castle which stands on an island, and appears to be of ancient date. Our boatmen did not fatigue themselves much by their exertions nor did they seem to know the course of the river for they frequently ran us aground. We passed Goligoa and Santarem and got to Villarda where we determined upon remaining for the night as it was necessary for us to change our boat. We got a tolerable quarter, or rather two of them, for the party and not having any baggage with us we were obliged to sleep two in a bed. The Tagus is covered with boats conveying commissariat stores to Abrantes which is the depot when the army is in the south. The banks are flat and uninteresting. There are a few villages situated on them. In other respects there is nothing interesting. In some parts the river is very broad but shallow.

February 24th. We started in a small boat at seven o'clock. The country here is

---

[1] The governor of Badajoz, General Armand Phillipon, had dammed the river Rivellas which flowed along the eastern side of Badajoz into the Guadiana. By doing so he created an inundation or false lake which would cramp the British in their assaults on the place in April 1812. The water from the Rivellas was let into the ditch in front of the Trinidad and Santa Maria bastions, which were to be the target for the British breaching batteries. Scores of British troops drowned in the flooded ditch at the assault on April 6th 1812.

improved. The banks are more cultivated. Passed Azambuja, Villa Nova and at Villa Franca we were in time for the tide which comes up this far. Below it passed the extremity of the Lines of Torres Vedras, which come down to the water.[1] The road to Lisbon which runs close to the water is commanded by innumerable small forts, which they are still working at. This appears to be the broadest part of the Tagus; I should imagine about twelve miles. The great peculiarity of this river is its breadth till you come to the mouth of it opposite Lisbon when it is not more than half a mile. Passed Saccavem and at 5 o'clock we landed in Lisbon. We were very fortunate in our journey which by land is eighty-four miles and by water cannot be less than 100. We dined at Barnwell's Hotel. The dinner was shocking and the wine as bad. Allix and myself took very comfortable lodgings at No.14 Rua de Prior, kept by an Irish woman whose long residence in this country seemed to have obliterated all ideas of her own language. I called on Dyson and felt quite happy at seeing an old friend.

February 25th. We each had a comfortable bedroom with bed curtains, under the canopy of which I had not reposed for a year. We had too, a sitting room looking upon the Tagus. The view of the shipping and the opposite shore is beautiful. A Knight of Malta lodged in the house and we afterwards found him a very civil man. Went to Belem to look at the horses for sale and dined with Mr Stuart. In the evening we went to the Rua dos Condes, one of the three Opera Houses in this place. The others are the St Carlos and the Salitre. St Carlos is nearly as large as the Opera House in London. The Prince Regent's Box in the centre gives the house a magnificent appearance; it occupies the space of six boxes, in breadth two tiers and is hung with damask. After the Convention of Cintra, Lord Wellington and Junot dined together and in the evening went to the Opera. Junot took the Prince's Box, Lord Wellington, with some modesty, contented himself with one of the others.[2] The difference was remarked by the audience. Next to St Carlos is the Rua dos Condes, about the size of the Haymarket

[1] The Lines of Torres Vedras formed a series of fortifications, hill forts and natural obstacles which stretched across the Lisbon peninsula between the Tagus and the Atlantic. The system comprised mainly of three separate lines of fortifications. The first, to the north, ran inland from the Atlantic to the town of Torres Vedras and then to Alhandra on the Tagus. The second line ran almost parallel to the first only five miles farther south. The third line lay west of Lisbon and enclosed an area from which any re-embarkation could be made. The construction of the lines has been called one of the best kept secrets in military history and certainly Massena had little idea of their existence until he came face to face with them in October 1810. His army found the lines impossible to penetrate and while Wellington's army sat behind them, well supplied by the Royal Navy through Lisbon, the French starved until Massena was forced to retreat in March 1811.

[2] Following the battle of Vimeiro, on August 21st 1808, Wellington — then still Sir Arthur Wellesley — along with Generals Sir Hew Dalrymple and Sir Harry Burrard, had signed the notorious Convention of Cintra whereby it was agreed that the defeated French commander, Junot, and his army, would be given free passage back to France unmolested, keeping their baggage, plunder and even their arms. Furthermore, they were to be conveyed in British ships. Following the convention, signed on August 22nd, all three were recalled to England to explain to a Court of Enquiry how they had allowed the French to escape. Fortunately, Wellesley was exonerated and returned to the Peninsula in April 1809. The two other 'gentlemen' saw no further service in the Peninsula.

Theatre. The Salitre is about the same size. The chief representations there are boleros and fandangos.

February 26th. The progress of Lisbon in the last year towards Anglicism struck me very much. Every article of English luxury is to be procured here. The shops have the commodities they sell proclaimed in English as well as Portuguese — coals from Newcastle — Carboniero de Castello Novo; with the rest of the continent it must be the same, who having once been used to articles of English manufacture will afterwards buy them at any price and in spite of the prohibitions as they are cheaper in the end. Every Portuguese in Lisbon now speaks a few words of English, some of them understand it well. We dined at Mr Dermot's Hotel and got a very comfortable dinner. I had been so long removed from civilisation that I detected myself throwing a glass of water upon a carpet.

February 27th. Military is the order of the day here. All the world wears overalls and everyone calls himself a soldier. They seem here to think a battle and a siege inevitable and probably are right. The greatest exertions have been made to send artillery up to Badajoz and warlike stores are upon the road. The enemy being aware of our motions will have his choice of the course to be pursued.[1] I really feel quite delighted at being here — no noise of drums, or flourish of trumpets; no squabbling for quarters or sleeping in pig sties; a fig for orders. Here I am independent. I went with Dyson to dine with Mr Jeffreys, the British Consul, formerly Member for Poole. We are a large party and of course mixed. We sat down 23. In the evening we went to the Rua dos Condes. The easy manner of foreigners, their vivacity and good temper form a striking contrast to the phlegmatic disposition of the natives of England.

February 28th. Allix and myself had proposed going to Cintra, but as our time was so short we found we had not time to carry our scheme into execution. Our time was a good deal engaged on executing commissions. In Lisbon it is impossible to move out in the evening without a carriage on account of the immense nastiness of the natives; immense numbers of dogs who are prowling about night and day and who call no-one master are the only scavengers to this large city. When Junot was in this place he ordered them to be destroyed but the accumulation of filth rendered it necessary to countermand the order and the dogs are now as numerous as ever. The carriages (to return to them) are two-wheeled vehicles, somewhat resembling a gig with a head, drawn by two beasts, on one of whom the rider sits. The nobility, eager to imitate the English, have sometimes four wheeled machines, somewhat like a chariot but the coachman is fastened to the box by a leather strap around his body — why, I know not,

---

[1] In fact, Wellington's strategy for the siege of Badajoz involved deceiving the French into believing that his main strength still lay on the frontier at Leon. At Ciudad Rodrigo he had deliberately leaked exaggerated reports of the numbers of sick in the hospitals, senior officers were allowed home on leave and everything was done to lead the French into believing that there would be no Allied offensive operations until the spring of 1812. Similar deceptions had been employed in the wake of the storming of Ciudad Rodrigo but from February 19th onwards, Wellington's divisions began to slip away to the south towards Badajoz, leaving only a screen of cavalry behind to maintain some sort of presence. Wellington himself remained at Freineda until March 5th when he began to ride south to Elvas which was reached on March 12th.

but I never saw an English carriage. The common carriages do not stand for hire in the streets; you send for them when you want them paying five dollars the whole day, half price commencing at two o'clock. No place of public entertainment being open, we contented ourselves with going quietly to bed.

February 29th. I have not yet made any remarks upon the town itself which is situated on an inclined plane to the Tagus. There are but few fine buildings in the place. The convents are to their taste, magnificent. There is much gold plastered upon the walls and ceilings. The houses have an external appearance of magnificence not realised by the internal — excepting those houses belonging to merchants or families connected with the English. The great feature in the place is that all the trades live in the same streets. The Rua Dure is inhabited by goldsmiths. The Rua de Plata by silversmiths and so on. These two streets which run parallel to each other are the best in the town from the uniformity of the houses. The streets terminate at each end by a square. I will not say much for the contents of the above street. Two small pedlars' boxes fixed on either side of the door comprise the whole assortment. The boxes contain little else but the small chains for which this place is so celebrated. The Brazil stones are paltry. I dined with Mr Jeffrey again. After I had been about half an hour in bed, I was disturbed by the noise of many footsteps over my head. On enquiring in the morning I found that the house had been visited by the Police to ascertain whether the proper licenses had been taken out, luckily they had, but several Englishmen, proprietors of houses who had neglected to do it, were that night conveyed to prison where they remained for three days. They are obliged to send in every morning to the Intendant of Police an account of persons in the house, their association, where they came from, where they are going, whether they have a passport, or by whose leave they are there. The Police of the city is military. A number of Guard Houses are established throughout, who regularly patrol. Till very lately murders were very common, amounting sometimes to eight or ten of a night. The present system has checked them, though there are still to be found those who will do the business for a stipulated sum.

March 1st. We were engaged to dine with Mr Brown, a merchant, who has a Quinta a league from Lisbon. I did not know him till this trip. The civilities I experienced from him I shall always remember. He is the most warm hearted man I ever met with. We had an excellent dinner and a profusion of wines. We returned in the evening and went to the Rua dos Condes.

March 2nd. We were invited to a party at Mr Brown's house in Lisbon. We previously went to the Opera, from whence the miserable performance soon drove us away. We then moved to Mr Brown's where a supper was provided. Nothing material occurred. Green peas in abundance.

March 3rd. It being necessary for us to be at Abrantes, we sent Jean to Villa Franca with two mules which I had bought and a mare of Allix's and ordered a boat to be ready at twelve at night to take us up to Villa Franca. 6 leagues. We dined at Mr Dermot's, took a farewell look at the Rua dos Condes, ate some supper and got into the boat. Our party consisted of Steele, Allix and myself. We started at one in the morning.

March 4th. We all of us went to sleep and I believe the boatmen did the same though the tide ran very strong. By good luck we got to Villa Franca about seven. We got a most comfortable breakfast at an inn there, the master of which is a Frenchman, the Mrs an Englishwoman. It is the only place of the sort I ever saw in this country, and from there being no competition or other house to drive to, they charge most exorbitantly for their comforts. Having breakfasted we started for Santarem, near Azambuja. I went a little out of the way to see a place for Bull-baiting. Azambuja recalled to my mind all the misery suffered there a year before, when I lost my baggage on my road to the army. The towns through which we passed were very much improved since the departure of the French. They had new doors and floors and appeared to be comfortable. At Santarem we found the heavy brigade of German Cavalry, 1,000 strong, who had just come out from England.[1] They occupied the upper town, consequently we were obliged to proceed up a mile to the lower town. Monsieur Jean not having arrived, and having no baggage with us, we were obliged to do as well as we could. We got some eggs and wine in a shop, on which we dined and then retired to roost. 7 leagues.

March 5th. Having heard that the Brigade had moved in the direction of Estremoz we were in doubt whether it would not be best to cross over the Tagus, but on considering thought it better to proceed to Abrantes, where we arrived at 5 o'clock. We took up our quarters at the house I was in before. I got something to eat at a Casa de Pasto and retired. 9 leagues.

March 6th. Thinking it probable that we might cut in upon the Brigade at Alta de Chao, we proceeded through Longomele, a straggling village, and to our great satisfaction, found the Brigade there on the 4th day of their march from Abrantes, and the third of ours from Lisbon. Indeed, it was lucky we did find them there as the three long days marches we had made had nearly done for our animals. 10 leagues.

March 7th. Having been used in our journey to up to long distances, a march of three leagues to Fronteira seemed as nothing. I was, however, gratified by having after we got in, to ride four leagues for my watch which I had left behind. This is a very nice town and apparently has never been visited by the French. We are excellently well off for quarters.

March 8th. This being Sunday, our new Chaplain treated us with a Sermon in the church, which the priest gave up for that purpose. A number of people were collected, I really believe to ascertain whether we were pagans or not.

March 9th. Having seen some good fish in the river I made an attempt to captivate some of them but without success. Portuguese casting net.

---

[1] On January 1st 1812 the 1st and 2nd Dragoons, King's German Legion, arrived at Lisbon under the command of Major General Eberhard Bock. The two regiments formed the 2nd Brigade of the 2nd Cavalry Division and remained at Lisbon until March 12th when they marched to join Wellington's field army, arriving at Estremoz on March 23rd. See Oman, *Wellington's Army, 1809-1814*, p.359. Bock's dragoons achieved a great distinction on July 23rd 1812 when, during the pursuit of the French army following the battle of Salamanca, they caught up with the enemy's rearguard at Garcia Hernandez and broke a French infantry square and scattered another. Bock was drowned in January 1814 when his ship was wrecked whilst returning to England.

March 10th. We are about four leagues distant from Estremoz, which, as I understand, is an excellent town. There is a great deal of corn sown in this neighbourhood. I doubt whether much will survive to be reaped as in its green state our horses are very fond of it. Everything is drawing up to Badajoz and in all probability a great change is approaching. Lord Wellington's Headquarters have moved from Freineda and are today at Elvas.

March 11th. The Cortes of Spain have voted the thanks of the Spanish Nation to the troops engaged in the siege of Ciudad Rodrigo and Lord Wellington has made each man a present of a pair of shoes. Marmont and Soult are reported to be at Merida with 14,000 men, and to have levelled the works of that place. A mail to the 25th of February is arrived but as the two preceding ones are not, fears are entertained that a packet is lost.[1]

March 12th. Cold easterly wind. Generals Hill and Graham were installed as Knights of the Bath at Elvas.[2] The House of Commons has voted thanks to the army engaged in the siege of Ciudad Rodrigo.

Fronteira, 4 leagues north of Estremoz
March 12th 1812

My Dear Father,

I have to acknowledge the receipt of a letter from you, in return for which I should have scribbled a few lines sooner, but availed myself of leave of absence for a few days to Lisbon where the novelty of the scene after so long a rustication, and a multiplicity of commissions prevented my doing it. I expected to have found the brigade at Abrantes where I left them, but they had flown, and I overtook them at this place. Frank Dyson was in high spirits, and infinitely better. Lord Wellington's Headquarters were yesterday at Elvas, two leagues from Badajoz, the great point of attraction. Marmont and Soult are at Merida with fourteen thousand men and have levelled the works of that place. The army is all closed up and the battering train is ready. The speculation upon the approaching events are numerous, but must be decided ere long. It is quite impossible for Marmont to allow us quietly to take Badajoz with the force he can bring into the field, and it is improbable that Lord Wellington will move off without attempting it. Phillipon has mined the weakest parts of the town, and let the Guadiana into the ditch. The taste we had last year of this General's skill warrants the certainty of his making a good defence.[3] The place is materially

[1] Packets were the ships delivering the mail between England and Portugal.

[2] Both Graham and Hill were installed as Knight Companions of the Most Honourable Order of the Bath on March 12th 1812. A sizeable banquet was given by Wellington to mark the occasion which was attended by the General and Staff Officers of the 1st Division, the commanding officers of the Coldstream and 3rd Foot Guards, and the General and Staff Officers of the 2nd Division amongst others. The invitations to both men can be found in *Despatches*, VIII, 654-655.

[3] General the Baron Armand Phillipon was as tenacious a defender as Wellington's men could have wished to meet. He had enlisted in the Bourbon army in 1778 and by 1790 had risen to the rank of sergeant major. During the following years he saw service in Italy, Switzerland and Hanover and had served with the Grande Armée from

strengthened and the garrison consists of five thousand men. The accounts of the number the enemy can bring into the field vary considerably. We reckon upon having 50,000 infantry and 5,000 cavalry, but I should doubt our bringing quite that number to the post. A great deal will be decided early this campaign.

I had a delightful trip down the Tagus to Lisbon and was surprised to see the progress towards Anglicism in one year. Everything is now a l'anglais — old and young alike imitate, though in general but awkwardly. I dined with Mr Stuart, who says he expects to go as one of the mediators to South America, but I believe has not the least idea of it. I saw the 58th who are on duty there, and have so done ever since William left it from their total incapacity to anything else.

The Cortes of Spain have voted us thanks for taking Ciudad Rodrigo, and Lord Wellington has presented each man with a pair of shoes for his trouble, but I have not heard of anything for the officers. Honour is very unsubstantial.

The weather is still very cold. People in England used to envy the happy climate I was going to. That of Lisbon is delightful but the other parts of Portugal which I have seen, and they are now pretty numerous, are fully as cold as England and in summer as hot as India. It would perplex an English farmer to see his green wheat cut, and not for his own use when it is about ten inches high. The naturally tractable Portuguese, notwithstanding all we can say, will not believe that the small check which is thereby given to vegetation, makes it spring again with redoubled vigour, which certainly is very odd. Their crops look well but the chances of war which invert the order of things, making odds considerable that the men who sows shall not reap, have added additional indolence to the people. Providence has given them the finest soil under heaven neither requiring manure or attention.

From the deserters which come in we learn that the French troops are quite worn out. The necessity of sending strong escorts with convoys and the continual harassing of the guerrillas, give them but short periods of rest from their labours, and of course their loss is considerable in the course of the year, though I cannot help thinking that the guerillas are set too high in England. Being the only species of Spanish force which has not for some time done worse than nothing, your hopes, too sanguine, paint the actions of brigands, whose only stimulus is plunder, as heroic and are taught to believe that the exertions and determination of a very inconsiderable number of men will finally cause the extirpation of the French — never attacking except with a view to plunder, and massacring sick and wounded, disgraces a cause which is unworthy of such resorts, and looks more like the expiring glare of the lamp, than a new aura of vigour.

1805-07 and had fought at Austerlitz. He was transferred to Spain in 1808 and in fact fought at Talavera and at the siege of Cadiz. He was made a baron in 1810 and promoted to general de brigade. He had been governor of Badajoz since March 1811 and was in command at the two previous British sieges of the place in May and June 1811, both of which resulted in bloody failure for Beresford. His bold defence of Badajoz in March and April 1812 was to cause Wellington the cream of his army which was smashed on the impenetrable defences wedged into the breaches.

The Post is just going out, and I have only time to desire to be kindly remembered to all your party; I will write a long letter to my Mother by the next mail.

March 13th. Strong General Orders have been issued respecting the British troops destroying houses in different villages throughout the country and the old orders respecting cutting green corn, with the usual success. The Coldstream and Third Regiments have received the Regent's commands to have Talavera and Barrosa upon their Colours.[1]

March 14th. At twelve we received an unexpected order to march to Monforte. On our arrival we found some of the 4th Division in the town and were of course much crowded. 3 leagues.

March 15th. To Elvas. Bivouacked with four other Divisions in the olive groves between it and Fort de Lippe. Lord Wellington and Beresford were in the town and the whole of the Engineer department with their apparatus for the siege of Badajoz. I dined with Colonel Eustace. The appearance of the fires in the grove at night was beautiful. The hill appeared illuminated. 5 leagues.

March 16th. General Hill with his corps is upon the Badajoz road at Merida. General Graham has the 1st, 6th and 7th Divisions, all 9,000, two brigades of cavalry, 2,000 and two brigades of artillery, 12 pieces. This force is to be on the high road from Badajoz to Seville. We marched in columns of Divisions at 5 o'clock, descending from Elvas. The night was beautiful. The road was very broad. The battering train was on the outside of the town and the troops destined for the siege were waiting till our column had passed the Guadiana which divides Spain and Portugal, and rain welcomed our entry into Spain. The country is very level and covered with wild garlic. I saw several hares run into the column which were killed of course. We had rain till we got to Valverde near which place we bivouacked. 5 leagues.

March 17th. Our troops broke ground before Badajoz last night. We marched at 5 o'clock 2 leagues. ½ a league from Valverde we passed over the ground and through the village of Albuera. Numerous remains were still there. The hill so hardly contested is little more than a gentle rising. The great and melancholy error in the disposition of our troops on that day seems to have been in not occupying this hill which belonged to a position in front of that taken up, and which independent of that was a much better one. The battle of that day was to retrieve the error.[2] The enemy left Santa Martha with 200 infantry and 30 cavalry as our cavalry entered it. Our infantry not being at hand they made good their retreat. They had not the least idea of our advance, and had we managed well we should have caught them. Bivouacked near Santa Martha. A dreadful storm

---

[1] The Coldstream Guards were awarded the battle honours 'Talavera' and 'Barrosa' on February 12th 1812 and these were added to the Colours in 1814. The 3rd Foot Guards were likewise awarded the two battle honours at the same time which were added to their Colours also in 1814.

[2] See JM's letter to his Mother, June 27th 1811, for more on the battle of Albuera.

of rain and wind came on, which blew over our tent and wet us to the skin. 5 leagues.

March 18th. To La Para. This was a flank movement to get us under cover. The rain still continued and I had not recovered the effects of that of the last night. A hovel would have appeared a palace after what we suffered the preceding night. It is a tolerably good town. The inhabitants had never before seen English soldiers and treated us with the greatest civility. They said the French behaved very well. The state of the town and the quantity of corn growing round it were good evidence of this. They abused them of course as I have no doubt they do us when the French come. Some French cavalry had left it four days before through ignorance of our advance. 2 leagues. Rain.

La Para
March 18th 1812

My Dearest Mother,

An unexpected order that letters may be sent to England in a quarter of an hour gives me but little time to write, and as it may be some satisfaction in these important times for you to know where we are, I will say as much as I can in a few words.

The 1st, 6th and 7th Divisions, (about 10,000 men) two brigades of cavalry (2,000) and a brigade of artillery, form a corps under General Graham. Our object is to keep Drouet's corps from Badajoz, where the rest of the army broke ground last night. We advanced on the 16th from Elvas, through Valverde, Albuera, and last night at Santa Martha drove out a small advanced body of cavalry and infantry. The rain which we have had since we began our march is become serious indeed. We have as yet bivouacked, and last night the wind and rain were so tremendous that our tents were blown over, and I am still wet. We advance tomorrow in the direction of Villa France. Drouet has not got many men with him, certainly not enough to stand us, and Graham is adored by us. General Hill watches the Merida road and both our corps will eventually fall back upon the same point. The distance we now are from Portugal, and the extreme uncertainty of our movements make it probable that I shall not have another opportunity of writing for a fortnight, but you may depend upon it I shall miss none. If we had but fine weather we should do, but a bivouac with threats of rain is the devil. This is our route as yet:

14th Monforte. 3 leagues
15th Elvas. 5 leagues
16th Valverde.5 leagues
17th Santa Martha. 5 leagues
18th La Para. 2½ leagues

You see I am in a hurry. The French have not destroyed the places about here, though they have laid heavy contributions. I have had some letters from you, the last is the 3rd of March, received this day.

Our appearance here has alarmed the Beaux, who marched last night in the storm, from Almendralejo. They had but just got out of Santa Martha as we got in. We heard heavy firing last night from Badajoz, where they broke ground. They expect to take it in a month. I am glad we are not in the trenches.

Adieu. I will write the very first opportunity. Kindest love to all. J.Mills.

March 19th. We marched to Zafra at four in the morning. The French had quitted it on the night of the 17th in the midst of the rain. They had invited the belles of this place to go over to Llerena today to a grand Ball and Festival in honour of King Joseph. This is a large town and as La Para not in the smallest degree destroyed. There too, they had never seen the English. The French have turned out the inhabitants of some of the convents, but there are still six, each containing thirty nuns. The Duke de Medina Calis has a palace here, which the French have partially fortified to protect them from the guerrillas. It appears to have been merely a post for their convoys on their way to Badajoz. 3 leagues.

March 20th. The rainy season seems to have set in here in good earnest. The 6th Division marched for Llerena, where we hear that our cavalry came up with the enemy and made some few prisoners. Drouet has retired into the mountains. General Hill has taken a convoy of two hundred mules laden. The Duke de Medina Calis has great possessions in this part of Spain. He has as many towns as the King save one and was esteemed the richest subject in Europe. The present unfortunate state of Spain has left him but little. The country is pinched to the extreme by contributions. The Alcade of this town represented a few days ago to the French commander their distressed situation and told him that the inhabitants had nothing more to give but their furniture and houses. I went to one of the convents. The nuns received us most graciously. This day's halt was most welcome, the more so as the rain was incessant.

March 21st. At 6 o'clock we marched to Fuente del Maestre, a movement on our left. General Foy is said to have crossed the Tagus with two divisions of Marmont's army. Likewise, that 10,000 men are at Medellin. There is heavy firing at Badajoz, which is 7 leagues distant. We hear nothing from thence but that Lord Wellington has a touch of the ague. The rains will put a great many of our men hors de combat.[1]

[1] Heavy rain had been falling from the very first day of the siege which made life very uncomfortable for the soldiers digging in the trenches. The number of men struck down by sickness due to the rain was serious enough but the greater problem was posed to the siege operation itself. When the earth was dug from the trenches, or parallels as they were called, it was piled up in order to act as a sort of rampart to protect the working parties. The heavy rains reduced this earth to liquid mud, however, and it refused to pile up but simply ran back into the trenches. This cold slime offered little resistance to enemy musketry and shell fire and gave little or no cover to the men. On March 22nd the Guadiana was swelled so much that the pontoon bridge over the river was broken and all supplies and ammunition were stranded on the right bank. At one point Wellington even considered abandoning the siege. The following day more heavy rain fell, filling the trenches and the earth on all sides fell away, the works crumbled and the attack was suspended. It is said that these two days were perhaps the most dreadful recorded in the annals of the sieges. See Fletcher, *In Hell Before Daylight*, p.35.

March 22nd. Halted. The garrison made a sortie on the night of the 19th but were repulsed. General Picton's aide de camp was killed and Colonel Fletcher of the Engineers slightly wounded.[1] We hear that they do not throw so many shells as they did at Ciudad but that their round shot tells more.

March 23rd. Allix had a ball at his house. The ladies were not numerous but select and of quality, notwithstanding which they danced worse than any I have yet seen. The works at Badajoz are going on rapidly notwithstanding the badness of the weather. They expect to mount six batteries of six guns each tonight, to play upon the fort.[2]

March 24th. I was awoke by an unexpected order to march. Accordingly, we marched eight to Los Santos, 2 leagues, but on our arrival there found we were to go on, and went on 4 leagues to Bienvenida. We were encamped under a hill outside of the town, orders being given that no fires were to be lighted near the top of the hill. We arrived at 6 o'clock soon after General Marchant's heavy Brigade of Cavalry marched into the town. We were ordered to be in readiness to march at the shortest notice and accordingly started at ten o'clock. Our baggage was left behind. The night was uncommonly fine. The object of our march was to surprise 2,000 infantry and 300 cavalry who were at Llerena. At Villagarcia one league from thence we heard that the enemy were all in their beds at eleven o'clock. We were joined by the 6th and 7th Divisions and the cavalry. At two miles from Llerena a picquet of the enemy fired upon our skirmishers in front, who ran in upon the 7th Division. A firing commenced in which three officers of the 51st were killed by their own men.[3] As day broke we were before the town,

---

[1] At midday on March 19th Phillipon ordered a sortie to be made against the Allied trenches. Two battalions of 500 men each, with forty cavalry, marched out through the Trinidad gate under the command of General Veiland and having driven off the working parties began levelling the trenches and demolishing the works. The sortie was eventually repulsed but not before the French had caused extensive damage to the Allied trenches. The sortie cost the French 20 killed and 13 officers and 147 men wounded. British casualties were around 200. Amongst the casualties was Colonel Richard Fletcher, Wellington's Chief Engineer, who was struck in the groin by a musket ball, forcing a dollar-piece from his purse an inch into his thigh. He was confined to his tent for the next fourteen days although Wellington consulted him daily. More important was the loss to Wellington of around 200 valuable entrenching tools. These were at a premium in his army and Phillipon had offered bounties for each tool captured. See Fletcher, *In Hell Before Daylight*, pp.31-32, for an account of the sortie and the siege in general.

[2] The fort Picurina lay to the south-east of Badajoz and protected the bastions which Wellington hoped to breach. It was vital, therefore, that this fort be taken quickly. The batteries which would fire against the fort were armed with ten 24-pounders, eleven 18-pounders and seven 5½-inch howitzers.

[3] While the siege of Badajoz was in progress Graham commanded the 1st, 6th and 7th Divisions, along with Slade's and Le Marchant's cavalry, the whole forming part of the covering force during the siege. On the night of March 19th Graham led a strong force to Llerena where he hoped to surprise a French force there. Twenty-five men of the King's German Legion cavalry and some British dragoons led the way followed by Graham and Stapleton Cotton. Unfortunately, they ran into a picquet of French cavalry which lay in wait in the darkness just outside the town. In the confusion Cotton was thrown from his horse while Graham and his staff rode somewhat panicky back upon the columns following. The leading British files naturally took the horsemen to be French and opened

which it was evident the French had evacuated, notwithstanding which we
continued to manoeuvre as if there had been thirty thousand men, and gave the
enemy time to get off up the hill. Our light troops pursued them up the hill, and
were within half a mile of them, when the pursuit was stopped and this ended
the attempt at a surprise. Every inhabitant in the town declared they would
answer with their heads to have led our troops to a village where they must
have been cut off. We had marched 9 leagues and had been 13 out of 24 hours
on our legs. 9 leagues.

March 25th. Halted at Llerena which is a fine town. The enemy evacuated it on
the 18th but had returned to bring off some hospital stores in which they succeeded. The inhabitants cheered us as we marched into the town, whether
through fear, as four round shot had been fired into the town, or from the
delight of seeing us, I know not.

Los Santos, near Zafra
25th March 1812

My Dearest Charlotte,

I am afraid that of late I must have appeared very remiss. The proximity of
Lisbon to Abrantes where our brigade was for a fortnight tempted me to go
down there. I assure you the greatness of the Capital had a striking effect after
a year of rustication; everything must have an end, so had my pleasure. It has
put me in a good humour with myself, which is everything. The present is a very
anxious time with us. The 1st, 6th and 7th Divisions, two brigades of cavalry
and two brigades of artillery form a corps under Graham, and are watching the
Seville road. The enemy are not in force in Estremadura. The Comte D'Erlon/
Drouet has not more than four thousand men and with them he has fled into the
mountains. We were at Zafra on the 19th but I fancy merely went there to
frighten the Beaux. At Santa Martha on the 17th we were very nearly catching a
detachment of infantry, and a few dragoons; they had but just got out of the
town as we got in it. The French have for some time been in possession of this
country and as far as I can see or collect have not done the least harm. The
natives complain of the very heavy contributions which they levy, but all agree
in their good conduct. The state of the towns and the quantity of standing corn

---

fire, killing two staff officers and sending several others tumbling from their saddles. It
was a miracle that Graham himself was not killed or wounded. There was total confusion
in the British columns as the men panicked and fired blindly into the darkness at an
enemy that did not exist. Brett-James, in his account of the affair in his *General Graham*,
pp.246-247, adds that 'a howling pack of dogs lent throat to the disorder.' Graham was
suffering from a disorder of the eyes at this time, which was to force him to return home
for a while, and Brett-James adds that, 'on coming within five hundred yards of Llerena,
the general ordered them [his gunners] to open fire on what, in the half light, he mistook
for a column of French troops forming up for battle. That the fire was not returned
caused some surprise, until daylight revealed that the horse artillery had been pounding
away at a long brick wall!' ibid, p.247. See also Oman, *A History of the Peninsula War*, V,
230-231, and Dyneley, *Letters written on Active Service*, p.18.

speak for themselves. Hill with his corps is at Merida, watching the great road. Upon any alarm we communicate with him, or he with us, as may be requisite. Graham's and Hill's corps form the covering army. General Picton superintends the siege. He has the 3rd, 4th, 5th and Light Divisions. Thus is the whole force distributed, with the exception of the remainder of the cavalry, which is ready to act with either corps that may require it. Our works at the siege are going on prosperously. If the enemy do not raise it, we may expect to be in possession in seventeen days. At the distance we now are from Badajoz we hear very little but the report of the guns. A sortie was made on the 19th; we lost some entrenching tools. General Picton's aide-de-camp was killed and Colonel Fletcher, the Chief Engineer, slightly wounded. They fire not so many shells as they did at Ciudad, but their round shot tells more. As yet we have lost but few men; when the works get nearer, they will make it up. If Lord Wellington succeeded in taking Badajoz, a new era will be commenced, and in two months we may be in Madrid. On our march to Santa Martha we passed over the field of Albuera. The numerous bones and remnants of jackets still tell the tale and I cannot help wondering that so nefarious a military delinquent should still wear his head, and regretting that it should be in the power of a fool to throw away the lives of 6,000 men.[1] The ground he chose convicts him. He had the choice of two positions 200 yards distant from each other, chose the worst and lost his men in taking up the other after he had perceived his error. The inhabitants of some of the towns about here had not till our arrival been blessed with the sight of a British soldier's visage. They were extremely civil and looked us over from top to toe. They seemed to be very much delighted with the dress of the 42nd.[2] I congratulate myself much on being in the covering army — digging in the trenches is neither profitable or entertaining, and one sample has quite satisfied my curiosity.[3] The dreadful rains which we have enjoyed for the last week, and are likely to do for a few more, though in favour of besieging, will lop off a great many men. I would rather be in action twice a week during the time the siege lasts than work at it. Notwithstanding the important operations which are going on, we find time to amuse ourselves. We have had balls every night since we

[1] These are strong words by JM, aimed at Beresford who commanded at Albuera. JM's comments show, perhaps, the depth of feeling amongst the officers and men in Wellington's army who consider Beresford to have displayed total ineptitude during the battle which cost the lives of so many good men, in contrast to Wellington who always took the greatest care not to expose his precious army to unnecessary danger.

[2] The 42nd (The Royal Highland) Regiment wore kilts, of course. The 1st Battalion had taken part in the retreat to, and battle of, Corunna. In July 1809 the battalion had sailed for Walcheren to take part in the campaign there. The following year the 2nd Battalion of the 42nd sailed to the Peninsula and had fought at Busaco, Fuentes de Oñoro and in January 1812 at the siege of Ciudad Rodrigo.

[3] Siege work was loathed by Wellington's infantry who regarded digging as 'navvy's work.' The discomfort in hiding from the French artillery was looked upon as skulking, even though it was necessary. John Kincaid, of the 95th Rifles, likened trench work to nothing better than serving an apprenticeship as a grave-digger or a game-keeper, as he said he found ample time for both spade and rifle! See Kincaid, *Adventures in the Rifle Brigade*, p.63.

have been here. The Spaniards, though very anxious to come to them, are so afraid that the French on their return should know they favoured us with their company, that instead of an invitation we give them an order, or in other words, embargo them. There are some of high rank here but I do not think their manners are as elegant in proportion as those of the lower orders. I am quite spoiled for English rural simplicity or in other words fatfaced awkwardness. An English rustic takes his hat as if it was nailed to his head, smooths his hair with his hands, doubles the brim of his hat into the shape of a canoe, and looks anywhere but in your face. A Spaniard takes his hat off with an air, and looks you in the face. An English country girl literally drops a courtesy, and looks as if she had stole something — a Spanish girl gracefully inclines her head, and accosts you with the air of a lady, and yet the Spanish character individually so independent, is nationally dependent.

This far was written from Fuente del Maestre but an order to march has come and we are at Los Santos. I hear nothing new, therefore remember me most kindly to your spouse, and all your party.

March 26th. To Maguilla, 3 leagues. Bivouacked near a rivulet. Our cavalry have been skirmishing with the enemy who are said to be near here. Bivouacked. March 27th. The weather which hitherto has been so bad seems to have decided to be fine. We hear that the fort at Badajoz was stormed on the night of the 25th. The garrison amounting to 260 were put to the sword with the exception of 80. Our loss was about 100. The fort was stormed in two places, and by some mistake the parties fired on each other.[1] We hear that everything goes on prosperously there and that the Portuguese militia are at work. In the evening we received orders to hold ourselves in readiness to march and I was somewhat

---

[1] Fort Picurina was stormed on the night of March 25th by 500 men of the 3rd and Light Divisions under the command of Major General Kempt. The stormers were formed into three detachments; the right, consisting of 200 men under the command of Major Shaw of the 74th; the centre, consisting of 100 men under the command of Captain Powis of the 83rd; and the remainder to form on the left under Major Rudd of the 77th. Each detachment was preceded by the engineers, Holloway, Stanway and Gipps, along with six carpenters with cutting tools, six miners with crow-bars, and twelve sappers carrying hatchets, axes and ladders. See Fletcher, *In Hell Before Daylight*, pp.37-38. The attack got underway at 9pm and soon afterwards a fierce struggle began. 'The carnage became terrible, the guns of Badajoz and of the castle now opened, the guard of the trenches replied with musketry, rockets were thrown up by the besieged and the shrill sound of alarm bells, mixed with the shouts of the combatants, increased the tumult. Still the Picurina sent out streams of fire by the light of which dark figures were seen furiously struggling on the ramparts.' (Napier, *History of the War in the Peninsula and in the South of France*, IV, 107.) The fort was taken at a cost to the British of four officers and 50 men killed and 250 men wounded, out of 500 engaged. About 100 of the garrison of the fort were killed or wounded and sixty were taken prisoners, including Colonel Thierry who was in command. Many French troops had tried to escape by crossing the trestle bridge connecting with the town but it was half demolished and in the panic many of them were drowned. Only one officer and 30 men of the Hessian regiment escaped back to the town.

surprised in the morning to find myself in status quo and bivouacked.

March 28th. The 7th Division marched to Asuaga in front. We hear that Marmont is coming down with a large force and that Soult is collecting in force in Seville.[1] Bivouacked.

March 29th. The loss in taking the fort appears to have been greater than was at first imagined. The 3rd Division alone lost 300 men and 15 officers. Bivouacked.

March 29th. In expectation of moving. Bivouacked.

March 3oth. The enemy showed some cavalry in the night and the 7th Division remained under arms. They however moved off. Bivouacked.

> Maguilla
> March 30th 1812

My Dearest Mother,

I wrote to you last from La Para, and here I now am twenty leagues in Spain. We are so far from Badajoz that I can give you but little information on that matter, except that the fort has fallen with the loss on our side of 100, and of 260 French who were in it, all but 40 were bayonetted. Our two assaulting parties fired into each other which added to our loss. The breaching batteries are at work and it is thought that the place will be ours by the 6th. The enemy is employed in barricading the streets, and will make a strong resistance, and if they do it, every man of them will be put to ye sword.[2] Now for our own travels. On the 19th we marched from La Para to Zafra, a very considerable town. The French had moved out of it the day before; so little did they know of our approach that the inhabitants were all invited to go over to Llerena to a Ball in honour of King Joseph but the Beaux postponed it. We halted on the 20th. The 21st we moved to Fuente del Maestre, where we remained till the 24th. We marched from thence to Bienvenida, where we halted for five hours and started again at night to surprise 2,000 infantry and 600 cavalry at Llerena — it did not succeed. They got out of it in time and our men who had marched 9 leagues were too tired to catch them. An unfortunate accident occurred before daylight; an enemy patrol fired into the head of the column and owing to the darkness the 7th Division fired by mistake into their own men, and killed two officers and wounded another. We came here on the 26th where we have remained bivouacked ever since. The weather which at first was so bad is now fine.

Soult has collected a force from the neighbourhood of Seville and is coming down. Marmont left Salamanca on the 10th but it seems impossible that they can meet with us till Badajoz has fallen. General Hill is at Medellin, which

---

[1] While the siege wore on Soult was marching to unite with the French armies under Drouet and Darricau. As late as April 1st he was still at Seville, nine days' march away. Soult was aware of Phillipon's fine defence of Badajoz the previous year and appears to have been convinced that the town was in no immediate danger and could hold out for a while yet.

[2] See JM's Journal for January 18th, note 3, page 102, for comments on the perils and penalties risked by a garrison which chose to fight on even when practicable breaches had been made in the walls of their place of defence.

is about in line with us. We fall back tomorrow by way of Usagre, and are to be at Fuente del Maestre on the 3rd.

The French have done no sort of harm in this part of the country, of which they have had possession for more than three years. No English troops have ever been near this before. They have laid very heavy contributions upon the people, and I am glad of it, as I think they are hereabouts much in their interest. The cavalry we drove out of Llerena showed themselves this morning, in our front. The 7th Division was under arms, but they soon took themselves off as they merely came to see what we were about.

The speculations upon our future operations are various, calculating of course upon the fall of Badajoz. Our ground will soon be much enlarged as it was quite impossible before to advance into Spain, leaving Ciudad Rodrigo, and Badajoz in our rear. I should not wonder if we were to raise the siege of Cadiz but with all our late success we are now just where we were three years ago, and the French in possession of almost every fortified place in Spain, which they were not then. It would seem that the way to gain reputation is to begin by losing.

There is a mail up to the 10th of March wandering about the country after us, and for anything I know this epistle may share the same fate; being so far from Headquarters all conveyance is a matter of chance. We have scorpions and centipedes in great abundance. The sun has not been sufficiently strong to bring them out, and they remain under the stones.

We hear that the garrison does not throw so many shells at Badajoz as they did at Ciudad. A great part of the works are mined, and it is said that Lord Wellington has informed Phillipon that if he springs one he will hang him.[1] The said Governor has the gout and it is thought that the irritation of being besieged will drive in into his stomach. At all events the case is new, and I should doubt much if Sir H. Holford or any of His Majesty's Physicians had ever seen one of the sort. I should imagine it was much more likely to drive him mad.

If I do not send this immediately I am afraid it will be too late, and you will thereby lose the whole of this valuable production.

My kindest love to the whole of your party. John Mills.

March 31st. Received orders to march on the 1st. The weather which had been so favourable began to change, and we had some wind and rain.
April 1st. To Llera. The weather unpleasantly hot, the town indifferent.
April 2nd. To Usagre. 2 leagues. It was here that General Lumley with a heavy Brigade of Cavalry cut up the Polish Lancers soon after the Battle of Albuera. The enemy occupied the town with their infantry and the lancers, ignorant of our forces and enticed by some Portuguese cavalry who skirmished with them,

[1] The ditches before the breaches at Badajoz were indeed mined and were duly exploded when the town was stormed on the night of April 6th. However, it is extremely unlikely that Wellington would have considered even punishing Phillipon for doing his duty, let alone hanging him. This is just another example of the kind of rumours that pervaded the camp of the besiegers during a siege and when a storming was imminent.

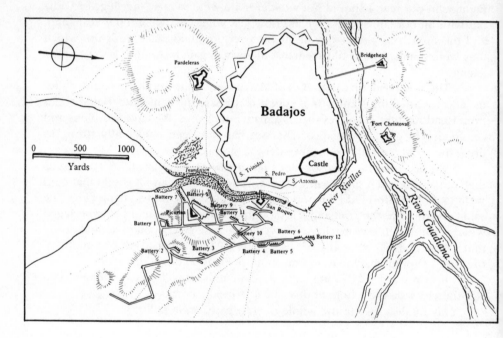

came out, and on the approach of our cavalry formed with their backs against a wall. They did not stand the charge and were cut to pieces in scrambling over the wall.[1]

April 3rd. To Los Santos, 4 leagues. A tolerable town.

April 4th. To La Para, 4 leagues. The siege seems to be going on well — three breaches are already made. Some difficulty is apprehended from the ditch which has ten feet of water in it.[2]

April 5th. Almendralejo, 3 leagues. The enemy seem to be pushing on to relieve Badajoz. Soult's corps is near us, and there has been some skirmishing.

April 6th. We marched at three in the morning to a wood near Albuera, precisely the same which the French occupied previous to that battle. At nine at night we heard a most tremendous fire of guns and small arms from Badajoz which continued till ½ past two when we were in possession of the town. Three breaches had been made, one of them 150 feet in breadth, the others smaller. At ten o'clock the Light Division were formed on the glacis in close column. On advancing to the breaches they found that the water in the ditch was so deep that it was almost impossible to pass it. The tremendous fire which was kept up from the walls added to the difficulty. They succeeded in getting some men over who stormed but were twice beat. The enemy had constructed palisades and chevaux de frise, the latter made of sharp swords. In face of such difficulties it was impracticable. They remained close under the wall attempting to get up till ½ past two, exposed to a dreadful fire of grape, small arms, gunpowder thrown on them in barrels and shells. The slaughter was tremendous — numbers were drowned in attempting to cross the ditch. In the meantime, General Picton with the 3rd Division succeeded in escalading the Castle and the town was ours. The enemy attempted to regain it, and beat General Picton out, but failed. Phillipon retired to St Christobal with his principal officers, and surrendered the next

---

[1] On May 25th 1811, nine days after the battle of Albuera, a British cavalry force under General Sir William Lumley, routed a superior French cavalry force under Latour-Maubourg. Lumley's force consisted of the 3rd Dragoon Guards, the 4th Dragoons, the 13th Light Dragoons, 9 squadrons of Madden's and Otway's Portuguese cavalry, and a small detachment of Spanish cavalry, about 2,200 sabres altogether. Lumley had withdrawn from Usagre in the face of an advance by Latour-Maubourg's ten regiments of cavalry and had taken up a position on the reverse slope of some heights on the opposite bank of a stream on which the town stands. Latour-Maubourg detached a brigade of his cavalry to march downstream and find a ford across the stream, rather than attempt to cross by the bridge. This brigade was unable to find the ford, however, but neglected to inform Latour-Maubourg, who assumed all was well and so ordered two regiments of his cavalry to cross the stream using the bridge. No sooner had they done so than Lumley launched his cavalry — as yet unseen by the French — who charged down upon their enemies with a vengeance, trapping them against the bridge which was blocked by a third French regiment. In the ensuing fight Lumley's cavalry did great execution, killing and wounding 170 Frenchmen and taking 78 prisoners. British casualties were put at just 20. Having given Latour-Maubourg a very bloody nose Lumley made a leisurely withdrawal with his prisoners. See Oman, *A History of the Peninsular War*, IV, 412-415, and Fortescue, *History of the British Army*, VIII, 218-220.

[2] See JM's letter to his Mother, February 21st 1812, for more on how Phillipon flooded the ditch at Badajoz.

morning at discretion.[1] The scene of pillage which ensued is beyond all belief, it is said that two hundred and fifty Spaniards were killed. The garrison hid themselves in the houses and were brought out by firing through the doors and windows. The British loss on this occasion amounted to 3,700 killed and wounded, besides 320 officers. The previous loss in the trenches was 1,200 making in the whole 5,220 men.[2] Lord Wellington was on a hill. He was repeatedly told that it was impossible to gain the breach, and that they were mowing

---

[1] Badajoz was taken by storm on the night on April 6th 1812. Two breaches had been made in the Trinidad and Santa Maria bastions with a third in the curtain wall between them. The breaches were to be stormed by the 4th and Light Divisions while two diversionary attacks were to be made, by Picton's 3rd Division at the castle and by Leith's 5th Division at the San Vincente bastion. The three breaches had been crammed full of chevaux-de-frise, planks of wood with row upon row of sharp sword blades protruding from them. Spikes, crows feet and all manner of evils were used to block up the breaches and the approaches to them and when the 4th and Light Divisions attacked they could find no way through. It is said that some forty separate attacks were made by them as they strove bravely to storm the breaches, but each one ended in bloody failure. Instead, Phillipon's guns blew away each successive attack, with mines and barrels of gunpowder exploding in the ditches which were crammed full of angry, despairing British and Portuguese troops. Some likened the experience to that of standing in a volcano, such was the ordeal. Indeed, the defences in the breaches proved so impassable that when the town eventually fell the troops still had difficulty in getting through even in daylight and without any French defenders firing upon them. It was the two diversionary attacks that finally won the town for Wellington. The men here scaled the walls of the castle and the San Vincente bastions, standing on each others shoulders amidst a storm of shot, shell and other combustibles. Amazingly, the men gained the ramparts and as soon as they had established themselves they entered the town and began to make for the breaches. When the French defenders here heard the bugles in their rear, both from the 3rd Division and the 5th Division, resistance crumbled and the town was won. Badajoz had been taken but at a terrible price and it was perhaps the most terrifying ordeal faced by Wellington's men in the whole of the Peninsular War. Sir William Napier, writing in his *History of the War in the Peninsula*, IV, 122-123, was at his finest when he summed up the army's achievement. 'Let it be considered that this frightful carnage took place in a space of less than a hundred yards square; that the slain died not all suddenly nor by any one manner of death, that some perished by steel, some by shot, some by water, that some were crushed and mangled by heavy weights, some trampled upon, some dashed to atoms by the fiery explosions; that for hours this destruction was endured without shrinking and the town was won at last. Let these things be considered and it must be admitted a British army bears with it an awful power.'

[2] Total British losses for the storming were 54 officers and 597 men killed, and 206 officers and 2,104 men wounded. 22 men were listed as missing. Portuguese losses were 8 officers and 147 men killed and 45 officers and 500 men wounded. The total for the storm was, therefore, 3,713 killed and wounded. Overall losses for the siege were 4,670. See Oman, *A History of the Peninsular War*, V, 594-595. Considering the small size of the area in front of the breaches and the 1,844 casualties sustained by the 4th and Light Divisions which attacked there, the sight which presented itself on the morning of April 7th must surely have been the most terrible and horrific of the whole Peninsular War. Little wonder then that Wellington was moved to tears when he inspected the breaches that morning. Wellington wrote afterwards, 'The capture of Badajoz affords as strong an instance of the gallantry of our troops as has ever been displayed. But I greatly hope that I shall never again be the instrument of putting them to such a test as that to which they were put last night.' (Quoted in Oman, ibid. V, 255.)

down our men by hundreds. He said he could not recall them till he heard from General Picton. When news was brought that he was in the castle, he said then we have gained the town. He was previously much agitated, but cool.[1] Thus ended this memorable night. The French fired a little in the streets but soon gave in. The precautions Phillipon has taken against a storm were admirable. He had insulated the breaches as at Rodrigo, but more effectively, had constructed chevaux de frise chained together and had thrown up a breastwork behind so that had we carried the breaches, the success would have been doubtful. Our men were in so large a body and so close to the walls, that almost every shot told, and the slaughter was tremendous. The attention of the enemy was so much occupied by the attack at the breaches that the escalade succeeded with mush less difficulty, though the wall was in no place less than fourteen feet. Bivouacked.

April 7th. Burying parties were employed during the whole of the day. There is a vast proportion of severely wounded. Bivouacked.

April 8th. Soult has collected a force and is coming down upon us with 23,000 men. He is at Fuente del Maestre, but it is supposed that the fall of Badajoz will induce him to turn his head.[2] We are to take up the position on Albuera, and the Coldstream is to cover the retreat across two rivers which lie between our present ground and it. I was sent to reconnoitre the fords. Bivouacked.

[1] Whilst the slaughter in the breaches was in progress an anxious Wellington watched intently from a small hillock a short distance from the main breaches. The commander-in-chief watched while the cream of his army was smashed against the breaches, nearly 1,800 of them being either killed or wounded in a space of no more than a hundred yards. Surgeon James McGrigor was with Wellington as they watched. 'At the place where we stood, we were within hearing of the voices of the assailants and of the assailed; and it was now painful to notice that the voices of our countrymen had become fainter, while the French cry of "avancez, etrillons ces anglais," became stronger. Another officer came up with a still more unfavourable report, that no progress was being made; for almost all the officers were killed, and no more left to lead on the men, of whom a great number had fallen. At this moment I cast my eyes on the countenance of Lord Wellington, lit up by the glare of the torch held by Lord March; I shall never forget it to the last moment of my existence, and I could even now sketch it. The jaw had fallen, and the face was of unusual length, while the torchlight gave his countenance a lurid aspect; but still the expression of the face was firm.' (Sir James McGrigor, *The Autobiography of Sir James McGrigor, Bt, Late Director General of the Army Medical Department*, p.273.) Just when Wellington thought he had failed an officer rode up out of the darkness with a report that Picton had taken the castle, whereupon Wellington exclaimed, 'Then the place is ours!' See Fletcher, *In Hell Before Daylight*, p.82. Picton, in fact, had been wounded in the foot and his place had been taken by Kempt. He did not, therefore, reach the top of the ramparts, as is shown in many a print of the scaling of the castle walls.

[2] A shocked Soult received the news of the fall of Badajoz on April 8th, causing him to retire at once to Llerena. By April 11th he was back at Seville. Upon hearing of the news, General Léry, Engineer in Chief to the Army of the South, wrote to General Kellerman, 'I think the capture of Badajoz a very extraordinary event; and I should be much at a loss to account for it in any manner consistent with probability.' (Quoted in Fletcher, *In Hell Before Daylight*, p.116.)

Camp at Albuera
April 8th 1812

My Dearest Mother,

You will of course have heard of the glorious result of the siege. I am sorry it is not in my power to give you the particulars. The Gazette will give you the loss, which I fear is tremendous. The ditch was filled with water and the breach was filled with Chevaux de Frise chained down, besides which there was a work at the top of it. The Light Division was twice beat at it. It was impossible to get up or on either one way or other for the heaps of dead. They were exposed for an hour to the fire of the garrison and at last got off. Lord Wellington betrayed the greatest uneasiness and was going to give orders for a retreat when word was brought that General Picton had escaladed the walls and had got into the castle. The business was then settled. From the precautions the enemy had taken we never could have carried the breach and it was from their confidence of this that the escalade succeeded. The 95th and Fusiliers are said to be destroyed and a very great proportion of officers hit. General Walker mortally wounded.[1]

We came here on the 6th to fight Soult today. He is near us now, but in consequence of the fate of Badajoz has turned his head another way. Marmont has invested Ciudad, but I fancy merely for form.[2] We have been much harassed lately. The opinion of this corps is that Graham is an old woman. I have had so high an opinion of him that I am unwilling to believe it though indeed it is the case, and that activity of body has been mistaken for activity of mind. We are in the wood the French encamped in previous to the battle.

You must see I am in a hurry, but knowing how various reports are I think you will be glad to hear. What our future operations are to be God knows — I hope never to see Portugal again and I think the enemy have acknowledged so much weakness relieving Badajoz that we may venture to go where we like, even to Madrid.

Lord Wellington's agitation during the storm was great. If Picton had not by a miracle succeeded, he was lost. A friend of mine who was with him, going down to enquire for his brother in the 95th, found him dead and stripped to the skin. He is in the greatest distress, and I must conclude this and sit with him.

With kindest love to all. John Mills.

[1] Major General George Walker led a brigade of the 5th Division in its successful attempt to escalade the San Vincente bastion. The walls here were as high as 46 feet high but in spite of this Walker's men mounted their flimsy chestnut ladders and then stood on each others' shoulders when the ladders proved too short. In a tremendous feat of bravery the British troops gained the top of the walls and scrambled over. Walker led his men, sword in hand, as they began to clear the defenders from the neighbouring bastions but between the San Juan and San Roque bastions the French 28th and 58th Regiments put up a fierce resistance and in the fighting Walker was mortally wounded when a field gun was fired close to him. Five other generals were wounded, Kempt, Harvey, Bowes, Colville and Picton.

[2] Marmont had not actually invested Ciudad Rodrigo, but he certainly did march against it, causing Wellington to march north once again when Badajoz had fallen. Marmont, in fact, retreated east into central Spain when he received news of Badajoz's fate.

Camp near Albuera
April 8th 1812

My Dear Charles,[1]

Phillipon is at breakfast with Lord Wellington and Badajoz est a nous. British soldiers have outdone their former character, and may well be proud of the name. They have shown that though beat at the breach they can escalade a bastion. I have not as yet heard much of the particulars. The breach was not practicable and Chevaux de Frise and barrels of gunpowder were put in it. The Light Division attempted to storm but in vain. They were beat back twice with enormous loss. The 3rd Division escaladed two bastions and took the town, you will have the particulars in the Gazette and will know infinitely more than I do. The town was turned inside out and sacked.[2] Soult has been moving down upon us; consequently we took up our position here on the 6th and expected to have fought him today, but I have no doubt that the news of the surrender of Badajoz has turned him back.

Marmont is affecting to invest Ciudad to draw us up there. I dread much a march to the north. We are encamped on a beautiful piece of ground; precisely the same the French occupied previous to the battle of Albuera. We expected a second day of immortality, but I do not think it will happen just at present though the day is not far off. The loss in officers has been tremendous. The 95th and Fusiliers are cut to pieces. The mail is going, therefore, adieu.

April 9th. A report is in circulation that Ballasteros availing himself of Soult's absence, has entered Seville and made havoc, destroying the magazine there.[3] Bivouacked.

[1] JM's brother Charles, the future Glynn Mills banker and baronet who seems to have handled JM's finances.

[2] The sacking of Badajoz has passed into legend and it remains one of the most shameful episodes in the history of the British Army. The British troops had endured and suffered for twenty-one days a siege of miserable proportions in terrible conditions and the victorious troops, driven to the point of madness by the fury and violence of the assaults, embarked upon an orgy of rape, drunkenness and pillage and, as Oman put it, their anger found vent 'in misconduct far surpassing that which would have followed a pitched battle where the losses had been equally great.' (Oman, *Wellington's Army, 1809-1814*, p.289.) Wellington's army was completely out of control for a full 72 hours despite efforts by him to check the outrages, including the erection of a gallows. No-one was actually hanged although the sight of the gallows in the town probably sobered up more than a few miscreants quicker than they would have otherwise have done. Napier himself wrote that, 'the tumult rather subsided than was quelled.' The accounts of the horrors of the sacking are numerous, vivid and so extensive that one suspects that having said it all about Badajoz, few were willing to add anything when San Sebastian fell in August 1813. The storming of that town was accompanied by scenes of equal horror and was made worse by a fire which completely engulfed the town. Nevertheless, eye-witnesses at San Sebastian generally limited themselves simply to likening the scenes to those at Badajoz, as if they had exhausted themselves in describing the events there. See Fletcher's *In Hell Before Daylight*, pp.97-115 for a compendium of eye-witness accounts of the sacking of Badajoz.

[3] This rumour was another false one. Soult, having been drawn out of Seville, had left the city garrisoned by a weak force under General Rignoux. Ballasteros, with a force

April 10th. In consequence of the report we moved to Nonera, 4 leagues, a wretched village near La Para.

April 11th. Halted and the report proved false.

April 12th. Moved at 5 to our old ground at Albuera. Sir S. Cotton attacked the French cavalry at Usagre and made 250 prisoners.[1] He drove them as far as Llerena where he found 1,000 infantry which obliged him to sheer off. Bivouacked.

April 13th. Encamped near Badajoz. The rain came down in torrents, which however did not prevent my going over the place. Some of the bodies still remained unburied and those that were, were so hastily done that the smell was very offensive. The town was completely gutted out, not a vestige of furniture remained. The doors and windows were drilled through with bullets. That part of the town near the breaches is a good deal destroyed by round shot. The town was not shelled out of delicacy to the Spaniards. A most wretched day. Bivouacked.

April 14th. To Campo Mayor, 3 leagues. I went over some part of the trenches, and to fort St Christobal, which Beresford breached last year, but failed in carrying. It is a strong outwork. The wall is partly of rock. Campo Mayor is a fortified place but weak. In 1810 the Spaniards took it in ten days and in March 1811 the French took it in twelve. Rather than defend it they retreated from it in May the same year, and suffered much from our cavalry on their way to Badajoz. Marmont has sent some troops into Pinhel. It is said that Castello Branco is in their possession, and that we are moving up to the north. The whole army excepting Hill's corps is moving that way. Very much crowded. Rain.

of 10,000 infantry and 800 cavalry, advanced from below Gibraltar and, by April 4th, had got to within twenty miles of Seville before turning away without doing any harm to the French other than raising the pulses of more than a few officers. On April 6th Ballasteros received news that a French force under Conroux was marching against him, forcing him to withdraw to Cadiz. As it turned out, this news was false and had probably been circulated by French spies. See Oman, *A History of the Peninsular War*, V, 274-275.

[1] On April 11th 1812, Drouet, commanding the rearguard of Soult's retreating army, was attacked at Villagarcia, just outside Llerena. Drouet evidently thought that he had only Ponsonby's light cavalry brigade in front of him whereas the heavy cavalry brigades of Slade and Le Marchant were coming up rapidly in support out of sight. When the fight began the French line, consisting of hussars, chasseurs and dragoons, was quickly and easily taken in flank by Le Marchant, forcing the French to retreat in some confusion. For once the British cavalry behaved itself and Cotton was able to control them to advantage. However, having pursued the fugitives as far as Llerena the attack was called off when the French cavalrymen finally reached their reserve infantry, numbering some 12,000. The French suffered losses of 53 killed and wounded, as well as 4 officers and 132 men taken prisoners. British casualties were just 14 killed and 2 officers and 35 men wounded. See Oman, *History of the Peninsular War*, V, 277-278.

Chapter Four

Salamanca Summer

It was a somewhat dazed and shaken British army that dragged itself, somewhat reluctantly, from the devastated town of Badajoz. The town itself had to be prized loose from the clutches of the British troops who, although exhausted after 72 hours of destruction, would probably have continued had it not been for the sobering and intimidating sight of a gallows that stood in the main square. With both of the 'Keys of Spain' in his grasp Wellington could look forward to a march on Madrid but news arrived of a threat by Marmont to Ciudad Rodrigo, won so hard in January, prompting Wellington to march north to avert this danger. Sure enough Wellington's presence in the area forced Marmont to withdraw and so began a period during which the armies of both sides marched in close proximity to each other as the lead up to the great battle at Salamanca began.

Between the taking of Badajoz and the battle of Salamanca, Hill achieved another of his great successes with the raid on the bridge of boats at Almaraz, which he destroyed in May 1812. However, this was just a curtain raiser to the main event which was to happen on July 22nd around a small, sprawling village in the middle of a typical Leon plain.

But before the battle itself took place Wellington entered Salamanca itself amidst wild celebrations by the Spanish people. There then ensued the siege of the three forts in which Marmont, by now some way to the north of the town, had left garrisons. During the siege of these forts we find JM ensconced in a house close by them with a group of other officers who were evidently intent on enjoying some sport, having taken with them their own sporting guns. The real fun started in late June, however, when the two great armies staggered into life and began a series of marches parallel with each other, the likes of which had never been seen before. The sight of the two armies marching within cannon-shot of each other must go down as one of the most remarkable sights of the war, the bands of each side trying to outdo each other. The manoeuvring came to an abrupt end on July 22nd with the battle itself which resulted in one of Wellington's greatest victories.

But let us return to April 15th 1812, and join JM at the village of Arronches where he found himself sheltering from the rain in a house with 30 other men of the 1st Battalion Coldstream Guards.

April 15th. To Arronches, a small town with a semblance of being fortified, and apparently very ancient. The 6th Division moved in before us, consequently we had but one house per company of 30 men. The rain continued.

April 16th. To Portalegre, where were also the 6th and 7th Divisions. A great fuss as there usually is here about quarters, and those we got were very indifferent.[1] Headquarters moved to Niza. Rain.

April 17th. A great fog. We halted. The French are in force near Penamacor. They have attempted to cross the Agueda, which is so swelled by the late rains that they have been unable to do it. Rain.

April 18th. A bad road and wet march to Gaffete, a small miserable village and as usual crowded. Rain.

April 19th. Halt, in consequence of the difficulty of finding cover for the troops moving along the road.

April 20th. To Niza. The first fine day we have had for some days. Headquarters are moving forward. The enemy has crossed the Coa and is attempting to throw a bridge across the Agueda, hitherto without success. 2½ leagues.

April 21st. The battalion was divided amongst four places. I went to a little village near Sarnadas called Val de Nome. The French advanced as far as Villa Velha, over the bridge at which place our sick from Castello Branco had just time to pass and to destroy the bridge when the enemy appeared on the other side. We found plenty of green forage, the more acceptable as we did not expect to find it. 5 leagues.

April 22nd. To Castello Branco, 2½ leagues. The French destroyed all they could find in this town, which was not much as the inhabitants of this and all the other places through which they passed had fled. The houses with the exception of two or three which they had burned had not suffered much. The Bishop's Palace was on fire.

April 23rd. To Escallias de Suma, 2 leagues. A Mail from England to the 1st. I got into a snug corner where I bivouacked.

April 24th. To Medellin near Pedrogão, 4½ leagues. A small place out of the high road, but not so far out but that the French have discovered it.

April 25th. By Penamacor to Mermao, 4 leagues. On our arrival there we found that we had marched by mistake for all the troops were ordered to halt in their

---

[1] The business of alloting billets was the responsibility of the Quartermaster General's department. Whenever Wellington's army was on the march a member of the said department would ride ahead to the next town along the route of the advance and would set about dividing the town into sectors, each of which would be allocated to a battalion or brigade, sometimes even a division. Having done this the sector would then be divided into streets which would be allotted to each unit. The quartermasters would then proceed to go along each of the houses in each street and would select the best houses for the commanding officers and field officers and would chalk their names upon the doors. The next best houses would be allotted to other officers, the quality of which would depend on the particular rank. For example, a captain would expect to be given better quarters than an ensign. The rest of the houses would simply have a number chalked upon the door to indicate the number of rank and file to be housed therein. One can imagine, therefore, the amount of squabbling that must have ensued between officers over the allocation of quarters and the quality of them.

cantonments. The enemy have crossed the Agueda and are marching to Salamanca. Our cavalry is this day to enter Ciudad Rodrigo and a convoy is preparing on the Douro to supply the garrison which was much distressed by their own mismanagement. On the receipt of the news of the capture of Badajoz the garrison fired a feu de joie. The French who were near thought it was the natives rising amongst the garrison. Some persons were stationed to beckon them and they advanced upon the crest of the glacis when the guns opened upon them amidst the acclamation of the multitude. Bivouacked near the river and in a swamp.

April 26th. Retrod our steps to Medellin, cursing the stupidity of our rulers. I rode out of the way through Penamacor and found our old place of abode very decently sacked.

April 27th. Halted. I went shooting with my Patrone who took all the shots away from me, and shot infamously himself. I hear we march southerly tomorrow. Indeed, we have got our route to Niza.

April 28th. The 1st and 6th Divisions are to be cantoned in the neighbourhood of Niza. The others remained in the north with Lord Wellington. We marched to Escallias de Suma where we were crammed into the town to get out of the rain. 4½ leagues.

Village near Castello Branco
28th April 1812

My Dearest Mother,

You must think me very remiss of late. We really have been so harassed of late that we are too tired to do anything when we get in. On the first of this month we marched from Maguilla on the left of Llerena, Badajoz, Portalegre, Castello Branco, Penamacor to Meimoa, from thence back again, and shall reach Niza on the 1st. We shall have marched three and twenty days in April and the weather too has been rainy. General Graham's corps will be in the neighbourhood of Niza, ready to march either north or south as circumstances may require. Lord Wellington is at Guinaldo with the divisions he had at Badajoz. Marmont is at Salamanca having entirely evacuated Portugal; during his excursion into it he did as much harm as was possible. Most of the inhabitants fled with their property into the mountains; what they left behind them was destroyed.

I wish we could transfer the seat of war to the Continent. This country is getting worse and worse every day. A war between France and Russia will afford an opening for Spain. But where is the man who can expect that she can do anything after having neglected so many opportunities. It may suit the views of interested persons to keep the idea alive, and harp upon Spanish patriotism, but where is it to be found? Certainly not amongst brigands who obey no law, and whose sole object is plunder. We received a Mail to the 14th today, and I have to acknowledge a letter from you of the same date. I am surprised you had not then heard of the fall of Picurina, ere this reaches you the whole business will have been known. I am anxious to hear what is thought of it in England.

The late rapid movements have very much weakened the army. We must have some rest or it will go to pieces. It seems more than probable that the campaign will be passed in manoeuvring to keep the places we have got. An advance into Spain is almost impracticable with any number of men, on account of supplies.

My packages from London I have just heard are arrived Lisbon. I anticipate their arrival with the army with much pleasure. I do not think I shall use much caution in opening them; but get into a corner and rummage everything. How outrageously mad everybody in England seems, it will be quite the fashion; we perhaps overlook our own follies, but I assure you we take considerable delight in hearing of the maniac-like tricks of *you English*.

I have heard nothing of or from Frank Dyson lately; he is so bad a correspondent that I shall give him up. Should you see Paulet in your rambles tell him I shall pass the same sentence upon him.

I hear very flattering accounts of Francis.[1] I am not a little gratified at the attention which those of my friends who are left have shown him, and I know it will materially assist him.

Excuse so shabby an epistle, the only excuse I can offer is a long one next time.

April 29th. Through Castello Branco to a small village in the mountains called Bemcrisa. The rest of the Division were in Castello Branco. Rain. 4 leagues.
April 30th. Val de Nome. 2 leagues. Rain.
May 1st. We marched by a circuitous route through the mountains to Villa Velha and from thence to Niza, 5 leagues in heavy rain.
May 2nd. Generals Graham and Campbell with their respective staffs take up so much room that there is a squeeze. Rain.
May 3rd. Headquarters are still at Guinaldo. Magazines are forming near Badajoz and it appears probable that we shall ultimately advance into Spain. The army having been so harassed of late must however have some rest first. Lord Wellington has recommended the officers to prepare for the ensuing campaign.
May 4th. This place, being on the high road from Lisbon, we are a good deal bored by detachments which are constantly passing through, and for which we have to make room. Rain.
May 5th. This being the first fine day for some time we had mule, pony and horse races which were numerously attended. The sport was good. Dined with General Graham whose dinners are now admirable. There is champagne and claret in abundance. He has Barrie's cook.[2]
May 6th. The racing of yesterday has driven everybody mad. Nothing but trials.
May 7th. Lord Wellington has expressed his determination to make hay in the autumn; perhaps the sun may not shine.

---

[1] JM's 4th younger brother (1793-1854), who followed him to Christ Church, Oxford.

[2] See also JM's Journal for January 31st 1812.

May 8th. Another race day notwithstanding it rained. Very good sport.

May 9th. General Graham moved unexpectedly to Portalegre. We consider ourselves safe for the present. He is supposed to have gone forward to see the state of the magazines and the works at Badajoz. Fine day.

May 10th. The 1st Battalion of the 42nd have joined the army. The few men of the 2nd Battalion will be drafted into the first and the officers return to England.[1] Detachments have arrived within these few days to a considerable amount.

May 11th. Encore races.

May 12th. The Papers from England we learned have heard of the storming of the Fort Picurina;[2] our night march to Llerena is noticed in a line and a half, so much for our labours.

May 13th. Everything remains quiet. The weather has taken a favourable turn. Should the army be in Portugal during the winter, it will be almost impossible to procure forage. We have cut great quantities of green corn and there appears to be little left. The Brigade were drawn out for the inspection of Generals Campbell and Wheatley. Our new Colours were used for the first time, bedaubed with gold, and emblazoned with the words, Lincelles, Talavera, Barrosa and Egypt, somewhat resembling the names of places written on the panels of a stage coach.

May 14th. General Hill is moving upon the bridge of Almaraz to destroy it. It is made of pontoons and has a strong tête du pont.

Niza
May 14th 1812

My Dear Charles,

We really have had so much marching that I have had no time to write to you or anybody else. I enclose you a draft for twenty pounds on Messrs Ladbroke and the second of exchange for £26 on Drummonds. I shall not touch up for any more just yet, and intend bringing myself in handsome at Christmas as I know that is the time. The fact is I have been obliged to replace two mules, which are now exorbitantly dear, and what with the rate of exchange at the army (fre-

---

[1] This was the usual procedure whenever a battalion was sent home to be replaced by its sister battalion. Wellington was loathe to send home seasoned troops and rather than do so would often form weak battalions into Provisional Battalions, or battalions of detachments as they were often called. One of the main reasons behind this move was the alarming rate of sickness amongst many battalions that came out to the Peninsula in the wake of the Walcheren fiasco of 1809. Many troops were not fully recovered even by the time they arrived in Portugal as late as two years afterwards and subsequently hundreds ended up in hospital or died without having seen much action. Wellington much preferred, therefore, to retain his seasoned troops although he had to fight hard against the wishes of the politicians at home to keep them. See Oman's *Wellington's Army, 1809-1814*, pp.187-188 for more on the Provisional Battalions.

[2] Considering the fact that Fort Picurina, the outwork at Badajoz, fell to Wellington on March 25th JM and his comrades would appear to be well behind with the newspapers, in contrast to the speed at which the mail arrived from England which appears to have taken on average eleven days to arrive in camp.

quently 6s a dollar) and the impoverished state of the country, much economy
is necessary. I really believe I am getting quite niggardly.

Well here we are and quiet, a new thing quite. The army is not in a state
to move yet. Badajoz, the bad weather and constant marches render rest absolutely necessary. I have reason to think that our next essay will be in Spain. We
are forming large magazines on the frontiers which can be for no other purpose.
It will be a new feature in this war; I shall be glad of it as I think this country will
be quite worn out in a year. In consequence of the embargo on American
vessels in the Tagus, flour has risen prodigiously, and will be still higher, as the
imports in that article are great.[1] Portugal will suffer much by being led into that
war, and will rue the day that an English army landed in her country.

The halt for a fortnight which we have now had, has I really believe made
us nearly as mad as you all seem to be. We have races almost every day. I have
established an athletic character by winning two foot races, and have rode several winning horses.[2] Graham attends, and enjoys it as much as any of us. The
old Buck gives most admirable dinners. Champagne and claret in abundance.
His personal staff amounts to eleven persons, and he always invites six or eight
others. His establishment of horses and mules is enormous. I am afraid to say
how many. The box of commodities you sent me is now I believe at Abrantes.
I shall send down for it in a day or two. The eatables arrived after the other and
are now at Lisbon. Cod's Sounds,[3] Stilton Cheese!!!

I hear that we are likely to have one more step, and I am afraid all is told.
Of course I imagine my Father will purchase for me. I cannot with decency ask
him, but as the contrary would oblige me to cut my throat, I cannot doubt it. I
have now eight before me, but one is a prisoner, ergo cannot come.[4] One more
year and then, how I shall jump when I see thy lengthened visage, most hideous
Challs.[5] That makes me think that I have heard that Robert is going to marry; I

---

[1] Although the impact of the American trade embargo was beginning to make
itself felt in the prices of the various commodities on sale to Wellington's army. he
himself was not unduly worried. 'I feel no anxiety respecting the subsistence of the army
in consequence of this measure; and I had already adopted some measures with a view
to supply the deficiencies which might be generally felt in the markets if the embargo
were to continue, which I think might be still farther improved.' Wellington went on to
add that the price of flour, 'has latterly been from 15 to 17 dollars the barrel of 196
pounds.' (*Despatches*, Wellington to Liverpool, 12th May 1812, IX, 137-140.) President
Madison was to declare the United States at war with Britain on June 18th 1812, the
justification being resistance to the Royal Navy searches of her vessels at sea.

[2] JM was to develop into a skilled amateur jockey, winning races on his own
horses at Goodwood and Newmarket. See also Epilogue.

[3] 'Cod's Sounds' was a euphemism for the old-fashioned oath, 'God's wounds'.

[4] Charles White and Thomas Bligh had joined the 2nd Battalion on promotion in
April 1812, leaving eight ensigns of the 1st Battalion Coldstream Guards senior to JM.
These were Charles Shawe, George Greville, John Talbot, George Percival, Walter Baynes,
John Stepney Cowell, Wentworth Burgess and William Stothert. Stothert had been taken
prisoner at Fuentes de Oñoro whilst Charles Shawe was about to leave, also on promo-
tion to the 2nd Battalion. See Mackinnon, *Origin and Services of the Coldstream Guards*,
II, pp.182-183.

[5] 'Challs' was a family nickname for Charles.

should think that Bob and Sally would make as odd a pair as were ever yoked. The Young Gentlemen is very ordinary certainly — I wish him success. Has anyone heard of William? The army list informs me that he has had some promotion. I suppose some of them have been devoured by the tigers or shot with arrows in storming mud walls.[1]

Francis has indebted one epistle to me — he says he does not like Ch.Ch. as much as he expected, and from his style he seems to have turned Buck. He says that a commission in the 58th is open for him. That distinguished body is now in this division, having been two years doing Lisbon duty.[2] In my days I never saw such a crew. We have just got some new Colours out. They have the names of so many places inscribed on them in letters of gold, that they look like the names of places written on the boot of Kennedy's Reading Coach. We have been reviewed this morning, and turned out 800 strong.

You will pay nothing for the nonsense this letter contains, for though I can but seldom send them free I make it a point of conscience not to make you pay for a double letter. The last accounts we had from London are of April 21st.

I have no more to say and must therefore conclude with kindest love to all friends. John Mills.

May 15th. Reports of moving are in circulation.

May 16th. I sent off two mules to Abrantes to bring up a box of commodities from England, and some corn.

May 17th. Rain and cold.

May 18th. Badajoz is getting forward and will soon be put to rights. Two thousand Spanish are coming from Cadiz to garrison it and 3,000 more are to be put into the place.

May 19th. The Headquarters remain at Guinaldo and everything is quiet.

May 20th. To my considerable consternation an order to march has arrived; as my mules were at Abrantes or on the road it was particularly unpleasant. I was obliged to remain behind. The Brigade moved to Castello de Vide. The move is in consequence of General Drouet's having moved down with a view, it is imagined, of interrupting General Hill.[3]

[1] William Mills, next younger brother to JM. He had been posted to India on leaving the 58th in Portugal. JM had seen his promotion to lieutenant in his new regiment, the 22nd Light Dragoons, and was irked by his seniority.

[2] The 2/58th Regiment joined Wellington's army in 1812 in time to take part in the battle of Salamanca on July 22nd 1812. The battalion, along with the 2/24th, later formed the 3rd Provisional Battalion as part of Barnes's brigade of the 7th Division and fought in the Pyrenees, at the battle of the Nivelle and at Orthes on February 27th 1814. The battalion returned to England at the end of the war. The 1/58th saw no action with Wellington's main field army but did see action during the operations along the east coast of Spain, notably at Castalla in April 1813.

[3] On April 24th 1812 Wellington had written to Hill instructing him to move against the bridge of boats at Almaraz. Since Marmont's pontoon bridge had been taken at Badajoz the bridge represented the only communication across the Tagus between Toledo and the Portuguese border for the French armies north and south of the river. Hill's force consisted of Howard's Brigade, the 50th, 71st, 92nd and a single company of

Niza
May 20th 1812

My Dear Father,

I have just time before I start from here to write you a few lines. The brigade has already marched on the road to Alberquerque, and I am going to follow them immediately. General Hill was to have been in Almaraz on the 16th for the purpose of destroying the French bridge of boats over the Tagus. We have not heard of his success though there can be no doubt of it. Drouet, however, for some purpose or other has moved his corps and so we move too. I am sorry for it as we were extremely well off here. We have seen the vote of thanks for Badajoz, and I am glad to see that it is well received. The word humanity which has been so happily crammed into the vote is rather a misname. We do not claim credit on that score and I have reason to think that Lord Wellington was much disappointed at the number of prisoners or at all events would have been better pleased had our men bayonetted the French in preference to the inhabitants.

I understand that his Lordship has expressed himself very openly and warmly on the scantiness of the means which Government put in his hands and says that he will never again undertake a siege, so ill-provided. He alludes amongst other things to the want of Sappers and Miners, to be had in plenty at Woolwich, of no use there, and very great here.[1]

We have now had an opportunity of speculating on the probable opera-

---

the 5/60th; Wilson's Brigade, the 28th, 34th, and one company of the 5/60th; and Ashworth's brigade, the 6th and 18th Portuguese infantry, and the 6th Caçadores. Wellington issued subsequent orders on April 30th also. (*Despatches*, Wellington to Hill, April 24th 1812 and April 30th 1812, IX, 80 & 101.)

[1] Wellington had written to Lord Liverpool on April 7th 1812 praising his men at Badajoz but complaining at length at the lack of proper siege tools and the absence of a corps of sappers and miners. 'I assure your lordship that it is quite impossible to carry fortified places by *vive force* without incurring grave loss and being exposed to the chance of failure, unless the army should be provided with a sufficient trained corps of sappers and miners. The consequences of being so unprovided with the people necessary to approach a regularly fortified place are, first, that our engineers, though well-educated and brave, have never turned their minds to the mode of conducting a regular siege, as it is useless to think of that which, in our service, it is impossible to perform. They think that they have done their duty when they have constructed a battery, with a secure communication to it, which can breach the place. Secondly, these breaches have to be carried by *vive force* at an infinite sacrifice of officers and soldiers....These great losses could be avoided, and, in my opinion, time gained in every siege, if we had properly trained people to carry it on.....It is a cruel situation for any person to be placed in, and I earnestly request your lordship to have a corps of sappers and miners formed without any loss of time.' (Wellington to Lord Liverpool, quoted in Oman's *History of the Peninsular War*, V, 255-256.) Wellington's pleas fell largely on deaf ears and although the old corps of Royal Military Artificers became the Royal Sappers and Miners on August 4th 1812, the corps was still formed too late to play any part in the disastrous siege of Burgos in September and October of that year. The new unit was present at San Sebastian, however, in July and August 1813 although even here numbers were not as great as Wellington would have wished. JM's father was MP for Coventry, 1808-12, so his comment was probably a pertinent observation on government lack of funding.

tions of the ensuing campaign. The army has since the beginning of the year been so harassed that it would seem impossible to do anything yet — at least offensively for we must always move to the flanks as they do. Magazines are forming to a considerable extent at Elvas, and at other frontier places. Ciudad Rodrigo and Badajoz are getting into a state of defence, and are each to have four months' provisions. The former a garrison of 4,000, the latter of 5,000 Spaniards. The Governor who was put into Rodrigo after the capture has been removed for consuming improvidently the provisions so far, that had Marmont been able to continue the blockade for two days longer the place must have been starved into a surrender.[1] The time for repairing completely these places, and forming the magazines, will be about sufficient to recover the army and it seems probable that the south of Spain will become the theatre of war. Some part of the army must remain in the north as long as Marmont continues at Salamanca, but as he has but 18,000 and no prospect of reinforcements, Lord Wellington would have sufficient force to keep him in check and to detach a considerable force to the south. Of course, a great deal must depend upon the temper of the Spanish Regency; unless they give us a more cordial assistance

---

[1] This was not strictly true and is, perhaps, another example of a rumour being distorted as it passed through the British camp. What had actually happened was that Carlos d'España, having been placed in command of the works at Ciudad Rodrigo, following the capture of the place by Wellington in January 1812, had neglected to carry out the necessary repairs on account of the lack of British stone masons. He also added that he had only enough supplies for twenty-three days. This, however, conflicted with Wellington's own estimates of the amount of supplies in Ciudad Rodrigo. On March 20th 1812, Wellington, in a most heated letter, full of his usual precise detail, had written to d'España saying, 'Between the 26th January and 17th February there were delivered over to the Spanish Commissary, by Mr McNair and Mr St. Remy, 50,000 pounds of biscuit, and 37,500 pounds of salt meat. There were issued from Almeida, on the 28th of February, 6,000 pounds of salt fish, and, on the 10th of March, from the same place, 10,000 pounds of biscuit, and 3,399 pounds of rice; and there were originally in the store at Ciudad Rodrigo 19,800 pounds of flour, and 1,000 pounds of biscuit. Reckoning the flour to be the same as biscuit, there would thus be in the garrison 80,800 pounds of biscuit, and 3,399 of rice. Reckoning one pound of rice equal to two pounds of biscuit, the garrison would have 87,400 pounds of that article, or for twenty-nine days, and for 43,500 pounds of salt meat or salt fish, and plenty of spirits, &c.' An obviously astonished Wellington went on to close the letter by deploring the fact that the Spanish general claimed to have only twenty-three days' supplies, saying, 'In writing this letter to your Excellency, I do not mean to make any reproach. I wish only to place upon record the facts as they have occurred, and to show to your country, and to my country, and the world, that if this important place should fall, or if I should be obliged to abandon plans important to Spain in order to go to its relief, the fault is not mine.' (*Despatches*, Wellington to General Don Carlos d'España, 20th March 1812, VIII, 668-670.) In fact, d'España, instead of keeping 3,000 men in the place, had not only put an extra 1,000 men inside but had forgotten to bring the additional supplies, given to him by Wellington. As a result, the place was in serious danger of being starved into submission when Marmont blockaded the town in April. The move forced Wellington into marching north to drive Marmont away to the east and, in effect, so began the Salamanca campaign. Ciudad Rodrigo was actually defended well by General Vives who was congratulated by Wellington when he arrived on April 26th. See also Fortescue, *History of the Army*, VIII, 392, and Oman, *History of the Peninsular War*, V, 289-296.

than they have hitherto done,[1] it is in vain to attempt to advance. What that temper was three years ago is to be seen in Wellington's correspondence — such as it has remained since — and the only hope of an amendment rests in the new members of the regency who are supposed not to be in the French interest.

We have lately had a great deal of rain but as it is in lieu of hot weather I do not grumble at it, though I had rather be broiled than run the risk of sleeping in a wet ditch. I heard from Francis a fortnight ago. I have heard of him too from Oxford, and a very good report. Some few friends of mine have had it in their power to be of use to him and speak very highly of him. I hear he is well set up in wine, and should like much to taste it which I hope to do ere long, should it please some of our elderly gentlemen to depart this life.[2] You have a much better chance of selling the commission in the 58th whilst the regiment is on service as I think there would be but few candidates for that distinguished post, if the premises[3] were to be viewed first. The officers are chiefly Irish Gentlemen with great landed property in the north, and persons of moderate fortune who have been so elegantly educated are shy of associating with them.[4] Paulet Mildmay writes me word that he has set up a curricle,[5] cut the profession of arms, and will I dare say soon enter into the marriage state. I wish him better success in that line than his sister has met with here. If I do not now conclude this I shall not be able to overtake my Gallant Crew.

Remember me most kindly to my Mother and all the family.

May 21st. I started at five with Steele and Crofton intending to proceed as far as we could on the road to Alberquerque, in which direction the brigade had marched. On our arrival at Castello de Vide we found to our great satisfaction that the brigade was to return there, Drouet's move having been a humbug. Major Currie, aide de camp to General Hill, passed through on his road to Headquarters with the intelligence of the destruction of the tete du pont and bridge of Almaraz by General Howard's Brigade on the 17th. The enemy had constructed a strong redoubt on the direct road, the taking of which would have cost time and put those in the tete du pont on their guard. The artillery was left

[1] JM was probably referring to General Cuesta's lack of co-operation at Talavera in 1809 when he failed to deliver any of the supplies and transport promised for the British army.
[2] The death or retirement of senior regimental officers in the Coldstream would have started a chain of promotions. JM might then have been promoted to a vacancy in England.
[3] ie the 58th Regiment.
[4] JM's sarcastic remarks are designed to convey a picture of rustic Ulster small-holders as the officers. Some officers were probably Irish, as the 2nd Battalion had been raised there in 1803, but most came from the half-pay list.
[5] A curricle was a light, two-wheeled carriage of great speed. Mildmay retired from the Coldstream in 1812 as a captain. He served as lieutenant in the Dogmersfield Yeomanry Cavalry, a local unit raised for internal security in north-east Hampshire in 1813. On March 12th 1813 Mildmay married Anna Maria Wyndham, daughter of the Honourable Bartholomew Bouvrie. They had four sons and three daughters.

behind and the column came by a circuitous route. An advanced work was carried and the enemy did not attempt to defend the main one. In crossing the bridge numbers were drowned as one of the boats by accident or design had got out of its place. The garrison consisted of 600 men; 250 of these were made prisoners, some few killed and many more drowned. Upon the whole it appears to be a most gallant and well executed thing.[1] The destruction of the bridge is a most essential point, as it cuts off the French communication between the north and south and obliges them to go round by the bridge of Arzobispo. 3 leagues.

May 22nd. I was quite surprised to find Castello de Vide as good a town as it is in a high state of preservation, never having been disturbed by the French. The quarters are remarkably good and clean. It is situated on a very high hill overlooked by a ridge. The ground immediately about it is in the highest state of cultivation. The old Castle from which it takes its name, overlooks the town and from it you can see eastward into Spain, and west as far as Abrantes. The weather is most insufferably hot.

May 23rd. I sat for some hours in the Castle. The heat is so oppressing that it is impossible to stir out till the evening.

May 24th. It appears improbable that we shall remain long quiet. The mysterious

[1] While Wellington prepared for the advance into Spain Hill was again detached with a small force (see also note 3 page 143), this time to attack the pontoon bridge over the Tagus at Almaraz which constituted the main French crossing point over the river west of Toledo. Also, by capturing the bridge at Almaraz, communications between Marmont and Soult, north and south of the Tagus, would be severed. The task facing Hill was a considerable one as the bridge of boats — the old stone Roman bridge had been partially destroyed — was protected on both banks of the Tagus by strong works, Fort Ragusa on the northern bank and Fort Napoleon on the southern. This fort, capable of holding 450 men, was situated on top of a hill with its front looking out over a steep bank that dropped away sharply. It was not a difficult climb for any attacking troops to negotiate, however, and entry into the fort was made slightly easier by two large scarps, rather like steps, which would bring the troops on to the ramparts of the fort. The attack on the bridge at Almaraz got underway at daylight on May 19th when the 50th and part of the 71st burst from their cover and charged up towards Fort Napoleon. Scores of British troops were struck down as they dashed forward in the open — and in daylight — but they reached the fort and flung their ladders against the scarp, the men pulling themselves on to the first of the two steps. Once accomplished, the ladders were heaved up and placed on the step in order for the men to reach the top of the ramparts and were soon engaged in hand-to-hand fighting with the defenders who were steadily driven out, back down towards the works at the river. The defenders here did not wait to meet the British but joined in the retreat across the pontoon bridge and soon afterwards the entire French force was making its way in a panic-stricken retreat towards Navalmoral. The action had lasted forty minutes and when it was over four grenadiers of the 92nd swam across to Fort Ragusa and brought back some boats which enabled the bridge of boats to be repaired. Shortly afterwards the rest of Hill's force arrived to find the action had ended in success with the French abandoning all of their works on either side of the river. These works were blown up by Hill and the bridge itself was then dragged across to the south bank and burned. Hill's raid on the bridge at Almaraz had cost him 33 killed and 144 wounded, of which 28 killed and 110 of the wounded belonged to the 50th Regiment. French losses were estimated at about 400, 259 of whom were prisoners. Hill's account to Wellington can be found in *Despatches*, Hill to Wellington, 21st May 1812, IX, 183-186.

silence kept about our future operations makes me think that something will soon be done. The enemy has of late shown so decided a weakness that we are justified in attempting anything in which our supplies will bear us out.

May 25th. We are repairing the bridge of Alcantara over the Tagus, lower down than that of Almaraz. The centre arch was sometime since blown up, and we are repairing the vacuum by means of cables on which boards will be put.[1]

May 26th. By the accession of the 1st Battalion of the 42nd, this Division is not less than 6,000 strong, which is considerably stronger than any other. The Light and 3rd are extremely weak owing to their losses at Ciudad and Badajoz.

May 27th. An English Mail arrived bringing the intelligence of Mr Perceval having been assassinated in the House of Commons.[2] We hear with regret that we are to return to our old quarters at Niza, and that the 6th Division are to occupy this place.

May 28th. To Niza. The weather which hitherto has been so intensely hot is now cold and rainy — so much for a climate which so many envy. Major Currie passed through on his way to England with despatches. Nothing like keeping John Bull on the qui vive.

---

[1] The magnificent Roman bridge across the Tagus at Alcantara, built by the Emperor Trajan, had survived for centuries until one of its arches was blown up by Wellington's army in June 1809. However, in the summer of 1812, with both Ciudad Rodrigo and Badajoz in his hands, Wellington ordered the bridge to be repaired which would reduce the route between Estremadura and Leon by one hundred miles. This, naturally, would facilitate the movement of guns and stores between Badajoz and Salamanca, the forts at the latter being Wellington's next objective. On May 24th 1812, therefore, Colonel Sturgeon, of the Royal Staff Corps, was ordered to report on the possibility of repairing the bridge. This was no easy task, as the broken arch of the bridge spanned some 100 feet wide and hung a further 140 feet above the water below. The problem was overcome by means of placing a very large, solid beam of wood at the end of each end of the broken roadway, which were then clamped to the Roman road by way of channels cut into them. These beams, once strongly secured, then acted as solid bases from which a series of eighteen cables were stretched over the gap. Eight more beams, with notches cut in them to receive the cables, were laid at right angles across the parallel ropes and lashed tight to them. The long cables were then strained taut with winches. A network of rope yarn for flooring was laid between the eight beams and planks placed upon this while a screen of tarpaulin supported on guide ropes acted as a sort of parapet. The structure was sound enough to carry not only infantry and horses but heavy artillery. Indeed, on June 20th Sir Alexander Dickson crossed the bridge with his siege artillery. The beauty of the bridge's design was that it could be rolled up in a short time if ever the enemy appeared. The completion of repairs to the bridge, added to the destruction of the French pontoon bridge at Almaraz, gave Wellington an advantage of ten to twelve marches over the French when moving troops north to south or vice versa.

[2] On the evening of May 11th 1812 Spencer Perceval, Prime Minister since 1809, was walking through the lobby of the House of Commons when a man named Bellingham walked up to him, drew a pistol and shot him through the heart. Bellingham was apparently a disgruntled businessman who had been ruined by the war and who had been knocking on the doors of various government departments in vain in search of compensation. Perceval was succeeded in his post by Lord Liverpool, former Secretary for War and the Colonies.

Castello de Vide, 3 leagues from Portalegre
May 28th 1812

My Dearest Charlotte,

It is so confounded hot I can hardly write — the very goose quill hisses. I am afraid I have not much to tell you. You know more than I do of General Hill's business, for we always look to the English papers to know what we are about; it appears to have been very well done. The usual display of gallantry; an uncommon quantity of plundering took place.[1] There was a great quantity of wine but the officers very prudently staved the casks. The point we have gained is very material. The French communication between the north and south is cut off; they must go round by Madrid.

We are repairing the bridge of Alcantara. The centre arch was blown up, and they are doing it with cables in preference to building a new arch.[2] In England you have bridges over a river every three miles.[3] In this country there are but few, and the sides and bottoms are too rocky to ford. It is therefore a very material point to be in possession of the bridges. The bye roads too in this country are in general not practicable for artillery, so in fact if a river should happen to be fordable you can only pass by the High Road. This is the case at Almaraz. A bridge of boats was some time since constructed there by the French, who built a tête de pont to defend it. It was a field work with artillery mounted at the extremity of the bridge. Hitherto we had been too weak to attempt it or indeed to turn it to any advantage if we got it, but our prospects are now so changed that we cannot well do without it. Till now I have never been sanguine as to the ultimate success of our cause; we have lost vast numbers of men at different times and gained no solid advantage. At the commencement of this year we were not as forward as we were three years ago. Of a sudden the French showed signs of weakness perfectly inexplicable. They allowed us to take Ciudad Rodrigo without a struggle. They could not be ignorant of the preparations we were making for Badajoz and yet no attempt was made to relieve it. Marmont made a paltry diversion which so effectually betrayed his weakness that it would have been far wiser for him to have remained at Salamanca. I hear they are now retiring into the interior of Spain, having levied three contributions. The first two have been paid; the towns that would not furnish the third have been burned, and I understand there are a good many. This is a measure they have frequently threatened but never put into execution, and I can hardly think they would have recourse to it had they any intention of keep-

[1] This is a curious reference. There was no plundering at Almaraz and indeed only Fort Napoleon, commanding the river-crossing, was stormed and not the town itself. Of course, there is every possibility that there may have been some wine stored in the fort, word of which may have passed along the grapevine to the rest of the army. But there are no recorded instances of any plundering there and we should not imagine that a repetition of the scenes at Ciudad Rodrigo and Badajoz took place.

[2] See JM's Journal for May 25th 1812..

[3] Both Charlotte and JM would have been thinking of the River Avon round Ringwood with its bridges and gravel fords.

ing possession. We have seen what an English army inferior in numbers can do, but I think that an inferior French will not keep its head above water. We moved on the 20th from Niza, where we had been since the 1st, towards Alberquerque in consequence of a report that Drouet/Comte D'Erlon was marching upon part of Hill's corps, and came here on the 21st as our friend had retired. We move back again today to Niza where I am afraid we shall not remain long. Some great movement is in agitation and various are the conjectures; Madrid or even an attempt to raise the siege of Cadiz are the most probable.[1]

We were extremely gay during our stay at Niza. We had races almost every day at which Graham presided. Mules and ponies were the principal operators, and showed admirable sport. Dinners closed the day, so you see we can find time to amuse ourselves.[2] You are I suppose rusticating or laying plans for a journey eight months hence[3] without fear of an order to march. I am rusticating too, but pack up my goods at ten minutes notice, and do not know or care whether I am to go north or south, to be under a roof or a hedge. There would be something very independent in all this if I had the power of commanding my notions. It has however given me a great taste, which you know I never had before, for travelling and a contempt for distance. If I was in England I could start for Russia with as much indifference to the length of the way as I could for Scotland.

The Prince of Orange distinguished himself very much at the assault of Badajoz. He was with the Light Division at the breach the whole time and displayed very great gallantry. If some of our Royal Princes had put themselves in the way of seeing something it would have been as well, but they have always been careful of their persons.[4] The appointment of General Alten to the

---

[1] No attempt was made by Wellington's main field army to assist the garrison at Cadiz. It was the former destination, Madrid, that was to be the next objective for the Allied army.

[2] When Sir Thomas Graham arrived at headquarters in 1811 to assume command of the 1st Division of the army he brought with him an enthusiasm for hunting and racing almost unmatched by any other officer in the army, despite his 63 years of age. Graham presided at several race meetings in the Peninsula and while at Cadiz would give a dinner for soldiers and Spaniards alike after each meeting. Graham is better known for his hunting exploits, however, and had first ridden to hounds as early as 1758. He was a great friend of Hugo Meynell, first Master of the Quorn, and had hunted for several years with him. See Brett-James, *General Graham*, p.21 & pp.239-240. See also the chapter 'Field Sports', in Brett-James, *Life in Wellington's Army*, pp. 195-213.

[3] As her daughter Catherine Compton (1812-1880) was born in 1812, Charlotte might have written of a recently-started pregnancy. Henry Compton (1813-1877) was the next child. Catherine went on to marry Admiral Aitchison and, on his death, Admiral of the Fleet Sir Henry Codrington.

[4] The Prince of Orange actually watched the assault on the breaches from a hillock with Wellington, Lord March and a group of other officers. Several general officers, such as Picton, Colville, Kempt, Walker and Bowes were wounded in the attack and it is highly unlikely that Wellington would have allowed the young prince to take part in the assault on the breaches. The Prince of Orange has attracted a great deal of bad press over the years, particularly by his poor showing at Quatre Bras and Waterloo where scores of good men lost their lives owing to the prince's poor judgement. Bernard Cornwell's *Sharpe's Waterloo* features an attempt on the prince's life by the fictitious hero

Light Division has given great disgust to the army; he is a German who has never done any one thing yet, and the command of that division is far the most desirous of any in this army.[1]

I believe it will be correct to tell you how the army is disposed of; Head-quarters are at Guinaldo. The 3rd, 4th, 5th and Light Divisions with some cavalry are in that part of the country. Graham's Corps viz the 1st, 6th and 7th Divisions and some cavalry are hereabouts. Hill's Corps viz the 2nd Division and a Portu-guese are at Medellin. Our brigade patronises Graham; he takes up his abode with us whenever he can, and has five or six to dinner every day.

Tell your worthy spouse to write to me and let me hear from you when-ever you can find time. When we get to Madrid I will send you a correct account of it. Remember me most kindly to all your party.

Castello de Vide
May 28th 1812

My Dearest Mother,

If a woodcock was now to take a walk with his clothes off he would find himself agreeably roasted in ten minutes. The sun appears to be perpendicular during the whole day and you would even walk at night on the shady side of the street, afraid of her rays. I have some thoughts of turning frog and sitting all day in the water. A week ago it was cold.

of the book, Richard Sharpe, who had become outraged by his conduct. Nevertheless, his bravery was never in doubt and he was wounded at Waterloo (not by Sharpe!). The Lion Mound there commemorates his part in the battle.

[1] The exploits of the Light Division when commanded by Robert Craufurd have passed into legend. During the summer of 1810 the Light Division held the line of the Coa and Agueda rivers against the continual probing of Massena's army. Craufurd brought the division to such a high pitch of training that the French never pierced his line of outposts and such was the level of communication between each post that, as Oman said, the line 'quivered at the merest touch.' The summer of 1810 is equally memorable for the controversial affairs in which the Light Division's equally controversial commander involved it, such as the notorious fight at the Coa river on July 24th 1810. In spite of his misadventures Craufurd is regarded as being the finest commander of light troops in Wellington's army and 'The Division', as it became known, became a source of much envy throughout the army. Even William Leach, of the 95th and one of Craufurd's fiercest critics, was moved to write, 'Jealousy is a demon which rears its head in all communities and societies, and, I fear, is to be found in military as well as in civil life. Amongst a certain number (I hope a few only) of malcontents in the army, the very name of "The Light Division," or the "outposts," was sufficient to turn their ration wine into vinegar, and to spoil their appetite for that day's allowance of ration beef also. In good truth, general officers were to be found, whom I could name, that bore towards us no very good will; perhaps because it was not their lot to hold so prominent a command as that of our more favoured brigadier.' (Leach, *Rough Sketches of the Life of an Old Soldier*, p.134.) Following Craufurd's death at Ciudad Rodrigo command passed for a while to Andrew Barnard. On May 3rd 1812 Charles Alten was appointed to command the Light Division and although he was a capable enough commander he was no 'Black Bob' and the division was never quite the same again, even though it did wonderful service through-out the remainder of the war.

I can give you no particulars of General Hill's business. The report is gone to Lord Wellington and you will have it all in the Gazette. It appears to have been well done, and is a most material point for us. The communication between Marmont and Soult is cut off — at least they must go round very near as far as Madrid, though these two gentlemen seem of late not much inclined to assist one another. One may cry Badajoz, the other Rodrigo, and unless they give an explanation the world will laugh at them both. We were on our second day's march from Niza in the direction of Alberquerque in consequence of Drouet's moving. The news of Hill's business turned us back and here we remain. This is one of the best towns I have been in, situated on a very high hill, the ground around it high. We can see a considerable way into Spain, Elvas and Abrantes in Portugal. The people are as civil as we can expect to find them considering the French have never been here, but what with blows and good words they will soon come round. What you will do in England when our predatory bands return I cannot think. You will be almost afraid to trust your own hands in your pockets, and should the Portuguese come with us you will see things vanish like magic. However, you will have quite time enough to prepare for us. I have just received Charles's box from England — thank you most kindly for the stockings which are just the thing. Tell my Father I am extremely obliged to him for the books which contain a great deal in a little compass, and make a valuable addition to a campaigning library. I forgot to tell him in my last letter that as soon as I can get them I will send the onion seeds. They say, that when sown in England, the seed collected there degenerates, as it is an *on dit*; I shall like to hear the success. I will send him some more wheat seeds and barley if I find any curious.

The fruit here will soon be ripe — we have cherries now. The rye harvest will commence in about a week and the wheat in about a fortnight after. I shall run away from Bisterne if I find any Gumcistus[1] in the garden — I believe it is rather esteemed a choice plant in England. Here it grows only upon the most barren tracts, and in the hot weather has a sickening smell.

I am afraid I can give you but little information as to the possible operations. We have done too much to allow us to rest long and there is so mysterious a silence at Headquarters that I cannot help thinking something important is in agitation. Our cards have played well lately, and the French have manifested so extraordinary a weakness that we may venture upon anything. I think that our time is now or never, and should not be in the least surprised at finding myself in two months at Madrid. Till this year our movements have depended upon the French. We moved as they did and halted when they did. We are now quite indifferent to their game and have it all our own way. If men enough can be sent us, as the others are used up, we shall drive them into their fortified places.

I hear nothing of Edward from any of you. Is he prosecuting his studies at Warfield? Is he grown, how is he? Promotion in our corps seems at a standstill.

---

[1] Gumcistus was one of the main shrubs of the maquis around the Mediterranean, a dark green affording good skirmishing cover for riflemen.

I hope his Lordship of Kilcoursie will be induced to prefer Hampshire to Portugal and favour us with his resignation.[1] When you cast your eyes over the army list give me credit for one place higher than I appear. Mr Stothert is enjoying the air of Verdun, and when he comes to the top of the Ensigns remains there, it being contrary to regulation that a prisoner should be promoted.[2] I have no reason to complain, for the promotion has been very rapid since I have had the honour of bearing arms.

A Captain Stothert, Adjutant to the 3rd Regiment of Guards, has published a narrative of the campaign in this country. I am told it is a miserable performance, resembling a log book, containing the precise hour in the morning that the Guards marched, and the exact period of their arriving at the end of the march, which must be very entertaining information to the world in general.[3] I keep a private diary myself, merely to mark the day. Some years hence I shall look over it with pleasure[4]. There is a town near here called Merevac, founded, according to tradition here, by the Phoenicians. These gentry we know were remarkable for their enterprise, but it seems extraordinary that they should have wandered so far inland. The spot too is by no means in the most fertile part of the country.

Hughes, formerly domestic to Mildmay and myself, is likely to find himself in a scrape. At Portsmouth before embarking he put something upon his leg to incapacitate himself from serving. He was, however, detected and will be tried for it. He was left really sick at Lisbon and has not yet joined. I am sorry for him. He is more fool than knave, perhaps both, but the former preponderating.

We hear that the French are retreating in to the interior of Spain having levied three contributions. They have burned the places that could not pay the third. The report is believed and if true could certainly look like their evacuating all on this side of the Ebro. We have just received orders to march back to our quarters at Niza. I am very sorry for it. Niza is an indifferent place. I must finish this scrawl.

Remember me most kindly to all in Portman Square and give my kindest

[1] George Frederick Augustus, Lord Kilcoursie, had been in the Peninsula with the 1st Battalion Coldstream Guards in 1810. He had returned home on leave on September 12th and does not appear to have returned to the theatre of war. Lord Kilcoursie retired from the army on March 24th 1813.

[2] Ensign William Stothert was taken prisoner of war at Fuentes de Oñoro on May 5th 1811.

[3] This is rather an illuminating remark by JM as it is a rare comment by a serving soldier upon one of the few contemporary accounts of the war. Captain William Stothert (not to be confused with Ensign William Stothert, of the Coldstream, who was taken prisoner at Fuentes de Oñoro) was Adjutant of the 3rd Foot Guards and his book was entitled *A Narrative of the Principal Events of the Campaigns of 1809, 1810 and 1811, in Spain and Portugal; interspersed with Remarks on Local Scenery and Manners, In a Series of Letters*. Published in 1812, the book is, as JM says, rather dull but has, of course, the merit of being one of the few published contemporary accounts of the campaign.

[4] One of the main sources of this volume. An entry was made for every day spent in the Peninsula in two pocket books identical in size and shape to the field message pads used in World War II. I imagine that JM would be rather amused at the thought of students of the Peninsular War mulling over his efforts in the 20th century.

love to Mrs C. Mills, the Misses Somervilles.[1] Tell Elizabeth I will thank her in form for the snuff box.[2]

May 29th. There are strong reports of us moving. General Graham has a violent inflammation in one of his eyes, and it is thought he will lose it.[3]

May 30th. It is determined that we move tomorrow. Our route is to Rondo, on the other side of Sabugal, in seven days. I am sorry to leave Niza as we had been extremely comfortable there, and being near Abrantes even very well off for the gross necessaries of life.

May 31st. The old road to Val de Nome, 5 leagues. We have so often marched this road that it quite sickens me. It is the worse stage upon the road. We turned off the high road at Villa Velha and in attempting a short cut to the village, went a league about and by a road which was all but impassable. A very hot day.

June 1st. To Castello Branco, ½ league. We found the 7th Division there, who had not received their order to march. Some Portuguese were turned out to make room for us.

June 2nd. To Solhera, 4 leagues, a miserable village not far from Alpedrinha. I bivouacked under some olive trees for preference. There is a great deal of game in this part of the country but it was too hot to go out.

June 3rd. Through Atalaia to Val de Plasagas, 2 leagues. I bivouacked as before under some chestnut trees with a small stream running close to me. I intend whilst the weather is fine to do so rather than to go into the houses, which in this part of the country are beastly.

June 4th. To Caria, 4½ leagues. A very bad road. The Estrella appeared very grand, the summit covered with snow. We hear that we are intended for Salamanca direct, where the French have left two regiments and are throwing up redoubts. Marmont with his army is at Talavera de la Reina. Deserters come in every day from Salamanca. The German Brigade was moved in with us and there being a great squeeze I pitched my tent near the water and in the midst of

[1] Mrs C Mills was JM's aunt, Jane Mills, wife of his uncle Charles who was probably staying in London as an MP. The Misses Somerville have not been identified but Harriet Somerville was close enough to the family to be staying at Bisterne for Christmas. See letter December 19th 1812.

[2] JM was a regular snuff taker. In the painting by Ferneley he is shown extending the habit to the hunting field. He later owned a prestigious gilt and enamel box which had passed from Louis XVI when Dauphin, via Marshal Saxe to the Prince Regent, who then gave it to Beau Brummel. On Brummel's social downfall he is said to have used it to pay off a creditor who tried to prevent him taking ship for France.

[3] The constant campaigning was beginning to take its toll on Graham who was suffering badly from an eye problem. 'The glare and dust, the peering through spyglasses on reconnaissance, the sleep broken by messengers arriving at all hours of the night....coupled with the nervous strain of campaigning and command and the worry over symptoms had caused a distracting spectre to dance about when he moved his right eye and to grow from the dimensions of a spider or fly to those of a tadpole.' (Brett-James, *General Graham*, p.251.) The doctors advised Graham to return home or risk losing his sight altogether. Graham duly left the army in July 1812 but thankfully recovered in time to take part in the 1813 campaign.

the finest grass I ever saw.

June 5th. In consequence of the cavalry not having received their orders, they were a day's march in our rear instead of one in advance. We halted in order to let them pass. The respite was most acceptable as we were in a most admirable place for forage. This part of the country is one of the most fertile in Portugal and is generally given up for cavalry cantonments. The French in their late inroad did but little harm. They have broke open a few doors because the inhabitants ran away and left them shut. I think it evident that their intention was to plunder and not to destroy unnecessarily as nowhere have I seen that they have destroyed the standing crops. The rye is almost ripe — in one or two places I have seen them cutting it. This year too has been so rainy that the harvest is more backward than usual.

June 6th. To Castelheiro, 2 leagues. The town was so much destroyed that there was hardly any cover for the men. I bivouacked. In the middle of the night I was woken and found that a large chestnut tree which overhung my tent and served as a kitchen was on fire. I moved the tent and in about half an hour after the tree came down on the very spot the tent had stood upon — a lucky escape.

June 7th. To Rendo. Through Sabugal, 3 leagues. The whole division assembled and bivouacked. We occupied the very same ground we did when we retired after the skirmishing on the 25th. The chestnut trees here are remarkably fine. It is a tree not common in Portugal but in particular spots. Immediately in the vicinity of Sabugal they abound. The town is in a worse situation than it was when we were here last. There is now hardly a roof in it.

June 8th. To Malhada Sorda through Villa Mayor, 4 leagues. A tiresome march and intensely hot. Lord Wellington is still at Guinaldo. Everything is ready for the advance into Spain.

June 9th. The order for us to march was countermanded.

June 10th. We marched to the woods near Puebla and bivouacked there. All is alive at the intended expedition. General Graham is to have the right column consisting of the 1st, 6th and 7th Divisions. Lord Wellington the centre with the Light and 5th and General Picton the left with the 3rd and 4th. Our force is computed at 36,000. General Hill has 13,000 in the south which will be sufficient to keep Soult in check. We went to see our old friends in Puebla who seemed delighted to see us. The French destroyed the town a great deal in their late excursion. 3 leagues. Bivouacked.

June 11th. We marched to the Agueda above Ciudad Rodrigo. The whole army moved forward today down to the river. Our corps were all encamped together and in a very bad place. Bivouacked.

June 12th. We halted on account of some delay of provisions. I rode over to Rodrigo and was happy to see the town so much recovered from the state I last saw it in. We rode round the works. Four new forts have been erected called Wellington, Castaños, Craufurd and Mackinnon. The former is finished and stands on the ground where the one we destroyed on the 19th of January did. The whole army being so near the town it was of course filled with officers. With great difficulty we succeeded in getting some ice. The day is intensely hot. Bivouacked.

June 13th. Crossed the Agueda to Tenebron, 3 leagues. All the columns moved this morning and by parallel roads. We march with our left in front[1] and as by this manner we are in the rear, we have the worst of the bargain. The villages seem destroyed. Bivouacked.

June 14th. Through Moras Verdes to the woods near Tamames, 4½ leagues. Lord Wellington and suite passed us as we began our march. The villages everywhere bear great marks of the French violence. The country is very much exhausted, bread very dear and to be got with the greatest difficulty. We caught a spy. Bivouacked.

June 15th. To some woods near Villalba de los Llanos, 2½ leagues. French picquets were about here a day or two ago. Don Julian took a prisoner, a tailor just arrived from Paris with the newest fashions who was taking a look over the bridge at Salamanca. Numerous reports are in circulation respecting the enemy. Some say they have retired, others that they are entrenched. I was on a Division picquet. Bivouacked.

Villalba de los Llanos
June 15th 1812

My Dearest Mother,

I have not time to tell you much. We are five leagues from Salamanca which place we expect to enter quietly tomorrow or the day after, Marmont having abandoned it.[2] We marched from Niza on the 31st of May and have been on the move ever since. On the 11th the whole army moved down to the Agueda, and on the 13th crossed it near Ciudad Rodrigo. The distribution of the divisions is as follows; General Graham commands the right with the 1st, 6th and 7th Divisions; Lord Wellington the centre with the Light, 5th and 4th; General Picton the left with the 3rd. The three columns move on parallel roads. Our army is about 36,000.[3] The road we have taken is by Tenebron, Tomares, Villa Alta. Of course

---

[1] The Coldstream Guards, being the senior regiment in its brigade of the 1st Division, was drawn up on the right. Marching off by the left would allow the rifle company of the 5/60th to lead, so that the riflemen could be employed as skirmishers when necessary.

[2] Marmont abandoned Salamanca on the evening of June 16th and retired north-east towards the Douro between Toro and Zamora where he had ordered Bonnet's division from the Asturias to join him along with as many of Caffarelli's troops as could be spared. A captured document gives the Army of Portugal's strength as 51,492 of which 48,396 were infantry, 3,204 cavalry, 3,393 artillery with the remainder being sappers. Marmont had 98 guns with him also although a shortage of horses meant that several pieces had to be left at Avila and Talavera. Bonnet's division numbered some 6,270 infantry. (*Despatches*, Wellington to Graham, 14th June 1812, IX, 236.)

[3] Picton's column, on the left, consisted of the 3rd Division, Pack's and Bradford's Portuguese, and Le Marchant's brigade of heavy dragoons. Graham's column, on the right, consisted of the 1st, 6th and 7th Divisions, with a single regiment of cavalry. The centre column, with Beresford, consisted of the 4th, 5th and Light Divisions, preceded by Alten's German hussars and Bock's dragoons. See Oman, *History of the Peninsular War*, V, 352. Both Picton and Graham left the army for health reasons a few weeks later. The strength of Wellington's army was just under 43,000. See Fortescue, *History of the British Army*, VIII, 460n.

we bivouac and as the weather is very fine I do not wish for a house. Tomorrow we shall be very near Salamanca, if not in it. I shall look out for the disciples of Dr Sangrado, and dare say there will be some to be found. By all accounts it is a fine place, but I should be afraid somewhat the worse for wear having been so long the Headquarters of the Army of the North. I really think we shall soon be in Madrid. The possession of Salamanca would do us but little good. The French are too weak to be able to keep possession of the whole of Spain. Never have our prospects on the Peninsula looked as well, or our army been in higher order than it is now.

Ciudad Rodrigo has improved wonderfully since I last saw it. The inhabitants who fled during the siege have returned and repaired their houses as well as they could. Shops of every sort are established, and if it were not for a few holes you see in the walls, you would hardly imagine it had so lately stood a siege. The country through which we have passed is quite a forest; immense woods and plains, no hills.

I am at this moment on picquet, and as I do not believe there is a Frenchman within twenty miles have not the least apprehension of being attacked in the night. These are busy times for us; marching in a column of fifteen thousand men is beyond description. The baggage and stores in the rear are beyond counting. We carry about ten days' biscuit and spirits with us. The bullocks walk, are cut up, boiled and devoured in two hours. I am credibly informed that the beef eats tough; in the quietest of times the beef is eat the same day it is killed. The movements of an army depend so entirely upon its supplies that unless the Commissariat is good it must either retire or be starved. We have a famous store at Ciudad even should the country give us nothing, which I am afraid will be the case. I paid a dollar today for a loaf of bread, and thought it a favour to get it.

You will perceive that this is written in a hurry — you must excuse it. We march at sunrise, get in about one or two o'clock, go to sleep for an hour, dress, dine, look at the mules, go to bed et voila tout. We have lately been so actively employed that I have not had time to write as often as I could wish. Whenever anything important is going on you may depend upon having a few lines; chit chat whenever I can find the time. I must now visit my picquet.

Therefore, with kindest love to all, wherever you may be. John Mills.

Deserters come in every day. We have caught a spy.

June 16th. We moved to a wood 2 leagues from Salamanca. Our cavalry met with the enemy's and skirmished with them for some time. We made a few prisoners. The 7th Division was much in advance of the rest of our corps. Bivouacked.
June 17th. We passed by the 7th Division and formed upon a hill opposite the town. Here we remained for some time. The 6th Division was sent round to the right of the town and the 3rd to the left. It was soon ascertained that Marmont

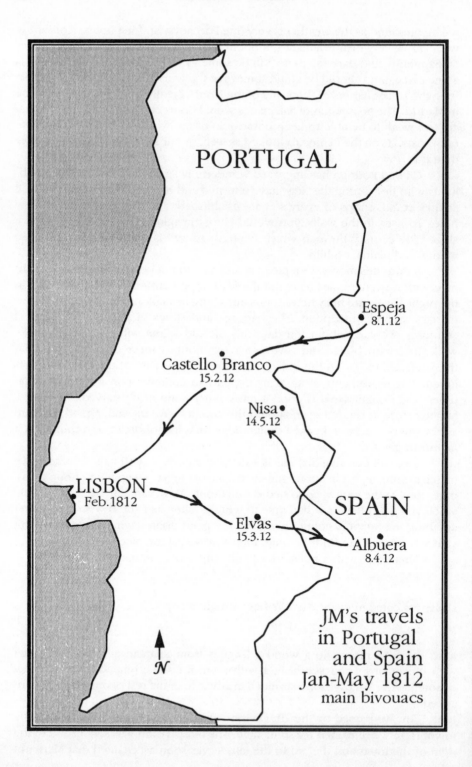

PORTUGAL

Espeja
8.1.12

Castello Branco
15.2.12

Nisa
14.5.12

LISBON
Feb.1812

SPAIN

Elvas
15.3.12

Albuera
8.4.12

JM's travels
in Portugal
and Spain
Jan-May 1812
main bivouacs

𝒩

had abandoned the town, leaving however, three small forts with men in them.[1] Our division crossed the Tormes when the 6th Division did and encamped.[2] I was of course anxious to go into the town and accordingly lost no time. The enemy kept firing from the forts but with little success. Salamanca is situated on a rising ground, the river Tormes running below. The French have destroyed a great many of the buildings but enough still remain to place the Spanish architecture high amongst European nations. The general appearance of the town, and the multitude of public buildings called Oxford to my recollection though the ruins of this University are more grand than the perfection of the other. There is something melancholy in the commencement of a ruin. The hand of time smooths in the course of time. The first state of ruin has nothing of grandeur to soften it, and draws the mind into the comparison of what it was and what it is. The principal buildings are its Churches and Monasteries. The old Cathedral Church is magnificent. The external and internal carving is beyond description fine, and in the highest state of perfection. The length of it is 354 feet, the breadth 174. There is a beautiful Sacristy. The Irish College is a fine building. Since the occupation of the Peninsula by the French the college has now been completely occupied. The Head of the college, a Dr Curtis, still remains, and though he has been fifty years resident in this country, he still speaks with an Irish accent.[3] The Anatomy school has been converted by the French into a Hospital. The square in the centre of the town is very fine — it has piazzas all round, and all the upper stories have balconies. This town, having been so long the Headquarters of the successive commanders of the Army of the North, has of course suffered much from their residence. On their departure they set fire to it in several places, but providentially it was soon put out. Bivouacked. June 18th. Our camp is about a mile and a half from the town, and as Headquarters and all the world are there, it is of course the great attraction. They keep

[1] The three forts constructed by Marmont were the San Vicente, San Gaetano and La Merced, all of which were situated above the River Tormes at the north-west angle of the town. The former was by far the strongest of the three, being constructed from the ruins of the convent of San Vicente. The fort, whose windows had been bricked up, was loopholed and connected on both sides by a wall with works, scarps, counterscarps and embrasures. Inside was a strong palisaded position. The convents and colleges that had been destroyed when the ground was cleared to make the fort provided a large amount of timber which was used for gates, drawbridges, palisades and splinter-proof shelters. The Gaetano and La Merced were also formed from ruins and were also protected by strong walls with scarps and counterscarps. Bomb-proof shelters were also constructed. See Jones, *Journal of the Sieges*, pp.158-159. These formidable forts were garrisoned by 800 French troops and between them mounted 36 guns, all but six of which were placed in the San Vicente fort.

[2] Clinton's 6th Division was ordered to lay siege to the forts at Salamanca. The division consisted of Hulse's brigade, the 1/11th, 2/53rd, 1/61st and 1 coy 5/60th; and Hinde's brigade, the 2nd, 1/32nd and 1/36th.

[3] This was Dr Patrick Curtis, Regius Professor of Astronomy and Natural History at the University of Salamanca. (See also Chapter 2 note 58 for more on Curtis). The Irish College still stands today in Salamanca and is called the Fonseca College by the locals. A fine colonnaded building, it housed the wounded following the battle of Salamanca on July 22nd 1812 and is today open to the public.

firing away from the forts, both great and small arms; occasionally a shell comes into the middle of the town. I went down to the Anatomy school where our skirmishers are firing and remained some time looking at the sport. They have hit several of our men. There was some skirmishing with the Dragoons in front. Marmont has retired with his main body to Toro, a strong position. What his meaning can be in leaving men in the forts here it is impossible to imagine. The Spaniards affect to be delighted to see us — I almost doubt whether they are in earnest.

Camp near Salamanca
18th June 1812

My Dearest Father,

The Post has been delayed to allow time for Lord Wellington's dispatches. We got within two leagues of this on the 16th. The cavalry skirmished, we had two or three officers and half a dozen men wounded. Yesterday we moved up and found that Marmont had left the place in the night, leaving the town on fire, and five hundred men in three small forts.

Our column, the right under Graham, marched upon the town, and the 6th Division occupied it. The remainder were encamped on the outside. Of course curiosity led us to see a place we had heard so much of. Headquarters and all the General Officers took quarters in it, and it was somewhat curious to see the French in possession of one part of the town, whilst we were walking about the other as if nothing had happened. The forts are too strong to take by storm; we threw up some works last night, and I suppose shall get them tomorrow. They fire at anything they see and shot Lord Wellington's orderly's horse. Marmont's cavalry made a reconnaissance yesterday and drove in our picquets. We were under arms in consequence and indeed are so now. The Light Division moved forward last night and they are now skirmishing in front. Next to Oxford and somewhat in the same style, this is the finest town I ever saw, but shockingly destroyed. The cathedral is beyond description magnificent, and the external carving beautiful. There is a very fine square with piazzas all round, and balconies to every storey.

The people are, or pretend, to be delighted to see us.[1] The nuns wave

---

[1] William Tomkinson, of the 16th Light Dragoons, wrote in his diary, 'We were received with shouts and vivas in the town. The inhabitants were out of their senses at having got rid of the French, and nearly pulled Lord Wellington off his horse. The scene in the Plaza was one of the most interesting I ever saw. The troops (6th Division) were there formed, supposed preparatory to an immediate attack. The place was filled with inhabitants, expressing their joy in the most enthusiastic manner. The women were the most violent, many coming up to Lord Wellington and embracing him. He was writing orders on his sabretache, and was interrupted three or four times by them. What with the scene caused by the joy of the people, and feelings accompanying troops in an attack on a fortress, it was half an hour of suspense and anxiety, and a scene of such interest as I never before witnessed.' (Tomkinson, *Diary of a Cavalry Officer*, p.162.) Shortly after entering the town Wellington himself wrote, 'It is impossible to describe the joy of the people of the town upon our entrance. They have now been suffering for more than

1. John Mills. Watercolour study by Sir William Hayter for his House of Commons painting.

2. Sarah Charlotte Mills. Oil painting by Sir Francis Grant RA.

3. (*Above*) Fuentes de Oñoro, May 3rd-5th 1811. This was JM's first action in the Peninsula.
4. (*Below*) 'Troops bivouacked near the village of Villa Velha, on the evening of the 19th of May 1811, showing the various occupations of an encampment.' This marvellous painting by Major Thomas St Clair gives some idea of the day to day life of Wellington's men.

5. (*Above*) The battle of Salamanca, fought on July 22nd 1812.
6. (*Right*) The interior of the castle of Burgos during Wellington's abortive siege in September and October 1812.

7. (*Above*) William Mills. Oil painting by George Romney, 1789.
8. (*Above right*) Elizabeth Mills. Oil painting by George Romney, 1789.
9. (*Right*) John Mills' Military General Service Medal, with clasps for Fuentes de Oñoro, Ciudad Rodrigo and Salamanca.

10. (*Above*) Filly, 'Kate'. Oil by J.F. Herring, 1832. Bred at Bisterne in 1829 she finished 10th in the Derby and 4th in the Oaks, 1832.

11. (*Below*) John Mills' yacht, 'Julia', winning her 11th cup at Cowes Regatta, August 7th 1828.

12. (*Above left*) Arthur Wellesley, 1st Duke of Wellington. After a painting by Goya.

13. (*Above right*) Sir Thomas Graham, Lord Lynedoch. After a painting by Sir Thomas Lawrence. According to JM, Graham was 'a friend to every forlorn Guardsman.'

14. (*Right*) John Mills, on horse, by Richard Dighton, c1840.

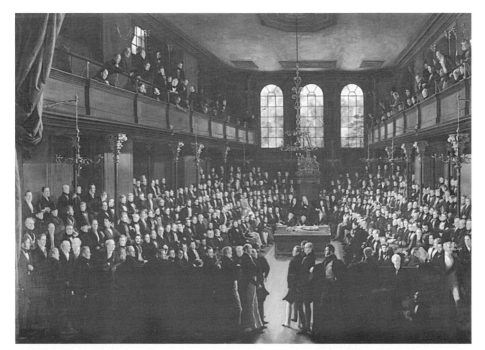

15. (*Above*) 'The House of Commons, 1833.' Painting by Sir George Hayter. JM stands on the extreme left of the picture, back row. On the right, with a sash across his white waistcoat, stands Wellington.

16. (*Below*) Detail from the same. The Duke of Richmond, of Waterloo Ball fame, stands, bottom left, with the Marquess of Anglesey behind him at his left shoulder.

17. (*Above*) John Mills, on his grey hunter, hunting with the Quorn at Quenby Hall in Leicestershire. Oil painting by John Ferneley, 1819.
18. (*Below*) Bisterne Manor, near Ringwood, Hampshire, John Mills' home.

their lily hands and throw down roses; this is the best part of the war, and we have heard and read so much of Salamanca that it seems almost classic ground. The head of the Irish College, a Dr Curtis, who has been here for fifty years, gives a bad account of Marmont. He says his soldiers should not have confidence in him or he in them. I am going into the town, and will finish this letter there. They are firing sharp from the forts.

I fear nothing more, I have been down to the forts. We are throwing up works and shall open tomorrow morning. They are firing sharp with small arms and have hit some of our men but not many. Our cavalry picquets are three leagues off on the Valladolid road, and the enemy's opposite to them.

We have taken a new tailor, just imported from Paris with new fashions.

June 19th. We threw up a battery last night, and mounted the four eighteen-pounders we brought with us. They soon battered the wall of the convent and then left off, finding, I fancy, that they could do but little good. A new battery more to the right is being constructed. Our people are beginning to find out that these said forts are stronger than they at first gave them credit for and are likely to cost a good many men.[1] The fire on both sides is incessant, but their men are so well covered it is almost impossible to hit them. We have already lost 50 or 60 men. An officer of artillery was killed this morning.[2] Several townspeople have been hit in the streets and some shots have been fired into the steeple of the Cathedral. I went down to a house out of which our men were firing. I tried but could not perceive that I did any execution. All the men but one in one of the batteries were either killed or wounded by a shell which fell in. A corporal and a private of the German rifle corps lay all day wounded without the possibility of their being carried off as they were so far advanced. Two men deserted from the forts today. They say, that the whole of Marmont's army drew lots for who were to remain and that the officer who commanded had a promise of two steps up if he held out six days and the men were to be handsomely rewarded.[3] I am

three years; during which time the French, among other acts of violence and oppression, have destroyed 13 of 25 convents, and 22 of 25 colleges, which existed in this celebrated seat of learning.' (*Despatches*, Wellington to Lord Liverpool, 18th June 1812, IX, 239.)

[1] The forts did indeed prove much more formidable than had first been thought. A week after the guns had opened fire Wellington himself wrote, 'The siege of the forts at Salamanca had not advanced with the rapidity which I expected when I addressed your Lordship last. Although, from the pains taken, and the expense incurred in their construction, and the accounts which I had received of them, I was prepared to meet with some difficulties, and provided an equipment accordingly; the difficulties are of a more formidable nature than they were represented; and the forts, three in number, each defending the other, are very strong, although not of a regular construction, and the equipment which I have provided for their attack was not sufficient; and I have been obliged to send for more, which has created some delay in the operations.' (*Despatches*, Wellington to Lord Liverpool, 25th June 1812, IX, 253.)

[2] The officer who was killed was Captain Elige, who was struck down early in the morning whilst on duty in No.2 battery.

[3] I have failed to find any real proof of the deserters' claim that officers drew lots for the honour of defending the forts. Nevertheless, the prospect of two steps' promotion must have been very tempting, particularly as the winner would know he would be

afraid we shall lose a great many men. Marmont is pushing forward his cavalry merely I suppose to feel his way. The town of Salamanca is crowded with officers who come in from the different camps to promenade. They are a great many of them very ill-looking young gentlemen.

June 20th. We heard some firing in the front, and stood to our arms. At nine we received an order to march. We manoeuvred for some time and at four took up our ground on the position. The army was drawn up there in two lines. The 1st Division was on the right and in the weakest point. The 7th Division were in front as light troops. The enemy's columns were moving down upon us, our cavalry retiring and skirmishing. At six the enemy came upon their ground, occupying a valley at the bottom and in front of our positions about a mile from us. Their main body was opposite our right. They had possession of three villages in our front. The light companies of our brigade skirmished with them till dark — our artillery played upon their cavalry, and theirs in return at ours. Quite by accident for they could not see us they got the range of our line but did no execution. At dusk the 61st were sent down to endeavour to drive them out of the villages but failed. Both armies then gave up any further contest for the night.[1] We were without either food or water, the nearest stick being a league off and the nearest stream two miles. The baggage having been sent to the rear I wrapped myself in my cloak and fell asleep. Some rain had fallen in the day, and damped my garments. Bivouacked.

June 21st. We fully expected an attack and stood to our arms an hour before daylight. After remaining for some time and seeing no disposition on either side to attack I went out in front. The enemy were very busy in their camp bringing doors and beams from the villages to use as firewood. A column apparently of about 3,000 men was coming down to them. At about twelve, some of our cavalry and a few infantry attempted to drive them off a hill on our right. After firing at each other for about two hours, both parties being nearly out of shot we gave up the thing.[2] Marmont came out with his whole staff to the hill to

---

defending a strong fort. The garrison of the forts consisted of six flank companies from the 15th, 65th, 82nd and 86th of the Line, and the 17th Leger, plus a company of artillery, some 800 men in all. See Oman, *History of the Peninsular War*, V, 361.

[1] The situation on June 20th-22nd is described by Weller as being, 'the most tantalizing of the Peninsular War for both commanders.' (Weller, *Wellington in the Peninsula*, p.209.) By June 20th Marmont had with him five of his eight divisions, some 25,000 men, while Wellington had with him his main field army, save for the 6th Division which was besieging the Salamanca forts. Wellington formed his troops up on the heights of San Christobal to the north of the town. The two armies remained within cannon shot of each other throughout June 20th and 21st and Wellington had his best chance of attacking on the afternoon of the 21st when he had a numerical superiority of 8,000 men but nothing more than some light skirmishing occurred. As he watched Marmont's force manoeuvring in front of him Wellington is quoted as saying, "Damned tempting! I have a great mind to attack 'em". (Fortescue, *History of the British Army*, VIII, p.462n.) Both sides remained where they were, however, and the battle, which at one stage looked likely, failed to materialise. Marmont again threatened to attack on the 22nd but was advised against it by Foy and Clausel.

[2] At dusk on June 21st Marmont's troops took the village of Castellanos de Morisco which lay in front of Wellington's right flank. Following this a French regiment advanced

endeavour to reconnoitre our position, but our line was thrown back behind the rising ground so that he could see little. I was within six hundred yards of him and could see all his proceedings. He was mounted on an indifferent English horse with a cocked tail. He wore a chapeau, plume, blue coat, white breeches and boots. He had a numerous staff with him and remained there for an hour. Colonel Ponsonby made an attempt to cut him off with a squadron of Dragoons but he was too sharp. The Spaniards from Salamanca brought wood and water from there for the troops gratis. The wood came I believe from the convents. Marmont's force certainly does not exceed 35,000 — ours is about 40,000 including 3,000 Spaniards under Don Carlos d'España, who are on the left of our position which extends four miles and is in two lines. Several Germans have deserted from us. The nights are cold and the days burning hot. There is nothing to keep off the sun. Bivouacked.

June 22nd. At daybreak, part of the 7th Division attacked the hill and after some hard fighting succeeded in driving the enemy off it. We lost 80 men. It was thought that this would have brought on a general action. They however made no further attempt to take it.[1] The French still continued to carry wood from the villages which now appear to be completely destroyed. Part of the 6th Division under General Clinton are in Salamanca carrying on the works against the forts. The French had a regimental parade in their camp in the evening. Bivouacked.

June 23rd. The enemy had decamped in the night, and at daybreak we could see their rearguard about two leagues off and their main body upon the hills. An unfortunate commissary who had overslept himself was caught in the village. It will be a subject of surprise to future ages that an English army superior in numbers should for three days look at an inferior French army without attacking them, that the first time since the commencement of this war that our army ever met the enemy even near upon an equality. We declined attacking them and it will hardly be credited that it is the same army, and under the same leader who

to attack Morisco itself which lay at the foot of the heights. This post was defended by the 68th Regiment which had not long been in the Peninsula. The British unit defended the place with style but at a cost of 50 men. Wellington withdrew the battalion during the night.

[1] On June 22nd Wellington ordered the 7th Division to drive the French from the heights in his front which had been occupied by Marmont on the 21st. Covered by a screen of riflemen from the King's German Legion the 51st and 68th Regiments advanced against the French while Wellington had ordered Graham to support them with the 1st and Light Divisions in the event of any stiff resistance. The heights were duly taken at a cost to the 51st of one officer and 23 men killed and wounded, while the 68th lost 8 men. The KGL suffered loses of 23. Private William Wheeler, of the 51st, took part in the attack. 'As we advanced the shot grew brisker, Sir Thomas [Graham] was in front, he wheeled his horse, and ordered us to deploy on the first division. Sir Thomas sat with his back to the enemy shading his eyes with his cocked hat, watching the companies deploy. He expressed his satisfaction at the manner we had performed the movement. As our line passed him he said, "my lads you shall give them a taste of your steel directly." We were soon within point blank distance of their line. Sir Thomas then gave the word double quick time with three cheers, and away went the enemy to the right about. We had now gained the ridge without discharging a single musket, our bugles sounded the 'halt' and 'fire'.' (Liddell Hart (Ed), *The Letters of Private Wheeler*, p.82.)

has so often attacked an enemy superior in numbers. If we are to act on the defensive why did we leave Portugal?[1] I went down to the French camp and saw all their leavings. The ground was covered with wood from the villages. Everything that could be brought out, and they could not carry off was left there. Rags, frying pans, saints. Before dusk, news came that 6,000 of the enemy's force had crossed the Tormes and were endeavouring to get in the rear of us with a view to relieving the forts. The 1st and 7th Divisions were marched immediately to the ground at Salamanca and upon the river where we had been before. Bivouacked — on picquet.

June 24th. In the morning we heard a very heavy firing on the other side of the river. It proved to be the heavy German Brigade who were checking the enemy's force. We moved across the river and were employed the whole day in taking up first one position and then another, never seeing the enemy. At length, we recrossed the river and returned to our old ground. I forgot to mention that on the 23rd the centre fort was stormed by the Light companies of the brigades of the 6th Division amounting to two hundred men. The ladders were too short and the men were unable to get out. After attempting it for some time they were beat back with the los of 130, amongst them was General Bowes who was mortally wounded and died the following day.[2] Great blame is given to General Clinton for the failure, he having reported that he would take the place. Bivouacked.

June 25th. Our baggage which left us on the 20th came up to us today, and delighted we were to get it. I went to the town. The firing from both sides had

[1] Wellington himself might be allowed to answer JM's question of why the he did not attack. 'First, it was probable he [Marmont] had advanced with an intention to attack us, and in the position which we occupied, I considered it advantageous to be attacked; and that the action would be attended by less loss on our side. Secondly; the operations against the forts of Salamanca took up the attention of some of our troops; and although I believe the superiority of numbers in the field was on our side, the superiority was not so great as to render an action decisive of the result of the campaign, in which we should sustain great loss. Thirdly; in case of failure, the passage of the Tormes would have been difficult, the enemy continuing in the possession of the forts, and commanding the bridge of Salamanca.' (*Despatches*, Wellington to Lord Liverpool, 25th June 1812, IX, 252-253.)

[2] An attempt to escalade the forts of San Gaetano and La Merced was made on the night of June 23rd by the light companies of the 1/11th, 1/32nd, 1/36th, 2/53rd and 1/61st. 'The undertaking was difficult, and the troops seemed to feel it,' wrote the historian of the sieges, Jones. (*Journal of the Sieges*, p.166.) The storming parties were hit by a heavy fire from the forts and from the guns of the San Vicente fort and it appears that very few of the stormers actually reached the walls of the forts. Out of twenty ladders the columns took with them only two were placed against the walls and it is said that so badly made were they, of green wood, that several of the ladders fell apart in the hands of the stormers as they charged forward. Six officers and 120 men were lost, amongst whom was General Barnard Bowes who, as a general officer, really had no business to be leading the attack. The brave Bowes was wounded early in the fight but had his wound seen to before returning to the fray whereupon he was hit a second time and killed. 'He was so eager for the success of the enterprise,' wrote Wellington, 'that he had gone forward with the storming party, which consisted of part of his brigade....Our loss in officers and men was likewise considerable.' (*Despatches*, Wellington to Lord Liverpool, June 25th 1812, IX, 253.) See also Oman, *History of the Peninsular War*, V, 371-372, and Fortescue, *History of the British Army*, VIII, 465.

nearly ceased, on ours from want of ammunition. Our Engineers now seem to have discovered that the forts which they imagined very weak and attacked them accordingly, are in fact very strong and will require some time to take. The rest of the army are on the position. Bivouacked.

Camp near Salamanca
25th June 1812

My Dear Father,

I wrote to you from hence on the 18th since which so many important movements have taken place that I will give you the transactions in the shape of a journal to make them at all comprehensible.

19th. The fire from the fort very hot; both musketry and guns. A good many of our men killed. We made a party and posted ourselves in a house, and fired away at the French in the fort. I do not believe I killed any.[1] Several shells fell in the town and did some damage.

20th. Marched in the morning and took up a position one league in front of Salamanca. The whole baggage of the army sent to the rear. About four o'clock saw the French columns advancing in front, and our dragoons skirmishing with them. At six they were within a mile of us. Their tirailleurs supported by guns advanced, and the light companies of our brigade skirmished with them.[2] Their round shot fell close to our line but did no damage. It was now too late for either party to attack. Their columns halted in a bottom opposite to the right of our position occupying three villages in our front. The 1st Division formed the right of the position, with the 7th in support to act as light troops. At dusk the 68th Regt. made an attempt to regain one of the villages but were driven back. Both armies then gave up any further attempt, and sat themselves down. Ours passed but an uncomfortable night. There was no wood within four miles, or water within two. Some rain had fallen in the day, and we betook ourselves to rest very hungry, and not very dry.

21st. We were under arms or rather stood to our arms before daybreak. The enemy seemed inclined to move, but however remained quiet. Things appearing peaceable I went to the front. Their columns were all opposite the right of our position, which was the weakest part. The videttes of each party were within shot, and the two armies within a mile. Of course we could see all that went on in their camp. Our line was thrown back behind the hill, so that they could see

[1] To be effective with a musket JM would have had to be about 70 yards from the fort. It is possible that some of the officers had private rifles or sporting guns with them.

[2] These consisted of no.6 company of the 5/60th, armed with the Baker rifle and dressed in green jackets, the riflemen being mostly German, and the light companies of the Coldstream and 3rd Foot Guards. They worked as a team, the riflemen picking off French officers from a good distance and falling back if necessary upon the supporting light companies with their muskets. The men would skirmish in open order, working in mutually supporting pairs and small groups, using cover and firing on their own initiative — the fire and movement of modern tactics.

nothing of it.[1] We attempted to drive them from a hill on the right, but failed. Marmont came out and looked at us, he was mounted on an indifferent English horse, and is rather a vulgar looking man. Lord Wellington was within six hundred yards of him. The Spaniards brought us some wood and water from Salamanca. The sun extremely hot.

22nd. At daybreak the 7th Division attacked the hill on the right, and drove them from it in gallant style. It was thought that it would have brought on a general action but Marmont seemed shy. Some of our Germans deserted. The French were constantly moving in and out of the villages carrying the beams of the houses and doors for firewood.

23rd. We found that they had moved off in the night to some hills two leagues to the rear. A report was brought in in the evening that 8,000 men had crossed the Tormes, and were trying to get in our rear. The 1st and 7th Divisions were moved down from the position to the river near Salamanca. At nine o'clock the main fort in Salamanca was stormed. After many attempts we were driven back, with the loss of 120 men. This was the most ill-managed business. General Clinton who had the superintendence sent but two hundred men to storm a place holding five hundred. The ladders were too short. A man cried out in English from the fort that they had better go back for it was no use to try. General Bowes mortally wounded was made prisoner, but was sent in by them. He died yesterday.

24th. We crossed the river in consequence of the enemy's force which had passed the night before, having moved. The Brigade of German cavalry kept them in check for some time. After manoeuvring all day the enemy retired, and we crossed again and returned here. The enemy are still but two leagues off. King Joseph with 3,000 is to join them tomorrow.[2]

Now the result of all this business is this; in the first place these forts are discovered to be strong places and we set about taking them as if they were weak, and have been beat having lost first and last a good many men, and having fired away all our ammunition, so that we can do nothing more at present, and moreover have all the work to begin again. In the second place, an English army of 38,000 men stood for three days on a position, looking at a French army certainly not more than 30,000, did not fight them because they would not come up to attack, and suffered them to escape. The consequence is that they will receive the impression we are not on a par. If we had attacked them we should have at all events met them on an equality. Junot had no business to leave Portugal if we were to act on the defensive.[3] Marmont has pledged himself to

[1] This was an example of Wellington's classic tactic of adopting a 'reverse slope' in order to prevent the enemy commanders seeing his main position which was consequently also protected from artillery fire. Light troops disrupted the advancing French columns by shooting their officers and as they toiled to the crest line British infantry would usually stand up in line and fire controlled volleys before counter-attacking with their bayonets. The battle of Busaco was perhaps the classic example of this tactic which was used time and time again throughout the Peninsular War and again at Waterloo.

[2] This was obviously a false rumour. Joseph did not begin to march towards Salamanca until July 21st, the day before the battle of Salamanca.

[3] JM is referring to Junot's evacuation of Portugal under the terms of the Convention of Cintra in 1808, signed after his defeat by Wellesley on August 21st 1808.

relieve the forts and I have no doubt but that he will attempt it. It is very hard work for us; our baggage is coming up to us today, and I hope to get a good dinner and bed. I will of course let no opportunity slip of letting you hear.

I have heard from my Mother as late as the 3rd at the same time from you a week earlier. I think my Uncle's death must be looked upon as a fortunate event, as the only termination of such sufferings.[1]

A French officer deserted to us last night. He says that Marmont's army at the outside is but 35,000. We see their fires from here and on the position were so close that we could see all they did. Most of the officers ride short tailed horses, wear very large cocked hats, and coats short in the waist.

We expect to move back to the position tomorrow morning. It is a dreadful place to be at. I will not starve for I intend to take a week's provisions with me. Our brigade will have a fine opportunity of distinguishing themselves if they attack us here, as we occupy the weakest point. I do not however think that they will meet us on that ground. A good many Germans have deserted from us, and but two to us.

As General Hulse was reconnoitring the fort three days ago, a man cried out to him in English, "How do you like our works?" It is said that an English artilleryman directs their guns.[2] I have already run the time of the Post going out very hard, and the paper too. Remember me most kindly to my mother and all the family.

June 26th. Some ammunition having arrived from Ciudad Rodrigo, our batteries reopened after a silence of two days. Three howitzers which had before thrown carcasses with a view to setting the convent on fire but without effect opened at four o'clock with red hot shot.[3] They set fire to different parts of the convent but it appeared as if it was as often put out. At night there was a great blaze, but it was, as it has been since proved, to a detached part. I went and had another shot at the Beaux but very few showed themselves. Bivouacked.

June 27th. The red hot shot this morning set fire to the convent in several places and the breach at the centre fort being practicable, at twelve o'clock orders were given to assault. At this moment, however, a flag of truce came in, the Governor offering to surrender the forts but the garrison to be sent to France. Lord Wellington sent word that he would allow the officers and men five minutes to retain their baggage giving them five minutes to return an answer. The time having elapsed and no answer returned the men proceeded to the assault. The

---

[1] This must be a Digby uncle on his mother's side as no brother of William Mills died at this time and it is nine months since General Scott's death.

[2] I have found no proof that an Englishman was present inside San Vincente. In the return of prisoners following the fort's eventual fall on June 27th there is no reference to any deserters or Englishmen so we must assume that it was just a rumour although in his diary for June 27th JM refers to the Englishman as being an artilleryman who had deserted at Talavera.

[3] The elevated trajectory of howitzers would allow the cannon balls, heated in special braziers, to fall inside the fort in order to start fires and often detonate stacked charges or the ammunition magazine.

white flag was then hoisted from the convent but not from the others till the breach was gained. It appears to have been a mistake as they never defended it. Thus fell into our hands these three forts, on which the French had expended an immense amount of money, had destroyed nineteen convents and public buildings, and for the last three months had employed daily four thousand persons at. I went over the convent fort which was the largest. It was immensely strong and appeared quite impossible to take. The three forts contained 800 men — 100 of whom were killed or wounded during the siege. The ditch was extremely deep and the walls were not only faced but for seven feet were of stone. The glacis was made of stones sunk to the depth of the ditch so that it was impossible to make trenches there. Marmont had pledged himself to retrieve it on the 24th; notwithstanding his promise he made no serious attempt to do it. It is difficult to imagine what his object could have been in constructing these forts. The experiment cost him 800 men.[1] Bivouacked. An English artilleryman who had deserted at Talavera was found in the fort.

June 28th. The constituted authorities of Salamanca, anxious to testify their approbation of the English, gave a Ball at the Collegio Vechio to which were invited the General Officers of the army, and the officers of the Brigade of Guards. The fête commenced at 10 o'clock in order to give the Spanish ladies time to digest their supper, thereby being more lighter on the fantastic toe. Waltzes, bolero and fandangos were danced with great spirit. Ices, cakes, liqueurs, and all sorts of refreshment were laid out in an anteroom. At twelve I retired to camp, as we were to march at three. Nothing could exceed the generosity shown to us by the Spaniards during the whole of our stay at Salamanca, so different from what was experienced at Badajoz, even at the first appearance

---

[1] The Salamanca forts finally fell on June 27th. After being bombarded with red-hot shot, which set the forts ablaze, the commander of the San Gaetano raised a white flag and offered to surrender along with La Merced provided he could have two hours in which to consult with the commander of the San Vincente fort. 'As it was obvious that these propositions were made in order to gain time till the fire in the San Vincente should be extinguished,' wrote Wellington, 'I refused to listen to any terms, unless the forts should be instantly surrendered; and having found that the commanding officer of Los Cayetanos [Gaetano], who was the first officer to surrender, was entirely dependent upon the Governor of San Vincente, and could not venture to carry into execution the capitulation which he had offered to make, I gave directions that his fort and that of La Merced might be stormed forthwith.' (*Despatches*, Wellington to Lord Liverpool, 30th June 1812, IX, 259.) After five minutes had passed, and there being no signs of the garrisons surrendering the forts, both La Merced and the San Gaetano were escaladed without any opposition. The commander of the San Vincente then sent out a flag of truce, at the same time offering to surrender the fort provided his officers could retain their baggage and the soldiers their knapsacks. By the time Wellington had considered his answer the 9th Caçadores had already entered the place and so the French marched out anyway as prisoners of war upon the said terms. See Jones' *Journal of the Sieges*, pp.157-170, for an account of the sieges of the Salamanca forts, and also Dickson's *The Dickson Manuscripts*, Chapter Four (For 1812), pp.665-672, for the work of the artillery during the operations. French losses were 3 officers and 40 men killed and 11 officers and 140 men wounded. Almost 600 unwounded men were taken prisoner. British losses were 5 officers and 94 men killed, and 29 officers and 302 men wounded. See Oman, *History of the Peninsular War*, 377.

of English troops. Whilst we were on the position they supplied us with food and water, though they had to carry both not less than three miles. They would accept too of no enumeration. Lord Wellington begged for a convent for the use of the sick. His wish was no sooner made known than linen, beds, and everything that could possibly be wanted was brought in by the inhabitants. There certainly is in this part of Spain a great desire to assist us. It arises in great measure in the novelty of the sight of English troops, none having been here since Sir John Moore's army passed through.[1] The long residence and numerous contributions which the French have levied have rendered any change of situation desirable for them. The French retired today. Bivouacked.

June 29th. Marched to a wood one mile in front of Obarda, 3 leagues. The army marches according to the following arrangements: The 3rd and 6th Divisions form the left, the 1st, 5th, 7th and Light Divisions the centre, and the 4th Division the right. The country through which we passed was a vast plain, and corn as far as the eye could see — nothing like a tree. The rye and barley are nearly ripe. All the corn about here is sown upon ridges of about six inches. Encamped with a few trees.

June 30th. To Canizal, 3 leagues. After meandering for some time by one road or another we at last hit upon the right one. The enemy are a day before hand in their retreat. We find nothing that looks like confusion, not even a broken car upon the road. The town of Canizal is celebrated in this part of the country for its wine. There are vaults underground which go down as deep as fifty feet and are filled with immense vats. The French carried off as much as they could and staved the rest. The utmost price they get for their wine here is somewhere less than a penny. Two bottles for three halfpence. The corn is forwarder here. I cut some barley and thrashed it. Excepting the few trees we encamped under I did not see any in the day's march. Bivouacked.

Canizal, 5 leagues east of Salamanca
30th June 1812

My Dear Charles,

If you do not charge the postage of this to my account I will never forgive you. I had intended to have sent the second of exchange on Drummond with that on Ladbroke's, and did not know my error till I received your letter of the 4th of June yesterday.

You will hear of the fall of the forts at Salamanca most peculiarly fortunate as they are most uncommonly strong. The masonry is beautiful, as you may imagine when I tell you that nineteen public buildings were destroyed to furnish materials. Three years labour had been expended, for the last three months of which four thousand men had been employed. In short they were as strong

---

[1] During the ill-fated Corunna campaign of 1808-09 Sir John Moore had based his headquarters at Salamanca between November 15th and December 11th 1808. It was from here that Moore began his retreat to Corunna.

as art could make them. After the unsuccessful attempt on the centre one on the
night of the 20th nothing more was done till the 26th for the best of reasons that
all the ammunition was expended. On the 26th our guns reopened, and proceeded in an attempt to make practicable the breach they had before made. (I
must here tell you that the forts were three in number, two small and one large
with a convent in it.) At the same time three howitzers opened upon the convent with red hot shot. Some parts of the building took fire, but nothing of
importance till the next morning, when the whole building was in flames. The
breach was declared practicable when a flag of truce was brought in. Lord
Wellington would not accept the terms but allowed the five minutes to surrender at discretion. The flag not being answered the assault was ordered and in
the act of storming the white flag was hoisted and the garrison surrendered. The
hot shot frightened them so much and the magazines were in such danger that
the Convent on which the others depended was not tenable. Had they not been
obliged to surrender the capture of these forts would have cost several thousand men, if taken at all. I went two or three times and fired at the tirailleurs but
could not kill any. On the 28th the French moved and on the 29th we moved
after them and are now in full cry. They are one day's march ahead of us, and
according to the best accounts intend pulling up at Toro where they have a very
strong position. But there are now so many reports current that we know not
what to believe. They are three leagues in our front at this moment. These are
anxious times for us and we are all much harassed. there is no rest in reserve I
am afraid for some time. On the 28th the Constituted Authorities of Salamanca
gave a Grand Ball to Lord Wellington to which the General Officers of the army
were invited, and the officers of the Brigade of Guards, which you may imagine
has affronted the rabble. It commenced at ten o'clock; waltzes and boleros
prevailed; ices and other simple refreshments. We departed just in time indeed
to dress ourselves and march. The people at Salamanca have shown us the
greatest attentions. A Convent was requested of them to accommodate 4,000 in
case there had been an action with the French. Not only was it immediately
given up but beds, linen, in short everything that could be wished for was sent
in for that number, by voluntary contributions. The country between this and
Salamanca is one continued sheet of corn. I am sorry to say we destroy a great
deal. You had better send this to Bisterne as they may wish to hear, and we have
really so little time now for anything that one letter is as much as I can get
through. I hope to have something important to communicate ere long. It is said
that Joseph Bonaparte has made his retreat to Paris.[1] At Zamora, Toro and
Valladolid the French have thrown up forts.

Adieu, kindest love to all. John Mills.

July 1st. We marched to a stream without a stick of timber near it, near Alaejos,
4 leagues. I did not see a tree this day's march. The whole of he country between this and Valladolid is without it. The next timber I see I shall mention it.

[1] JM was mistaken here. Joseph was still at Madrid and on July 21st began his
march north-west to try and join Marmont at Salamanca.

There is but little water too. The corn is as before, covering the whole country. They are getting in the barley. Bread is enormously dear. Hares are in abundance but the weather is too burning to go after them. When the troops get upon their ground for encamping they always kill several. The 11th Light Dragoons who are in advance, upon crossing into a village yesterday near here, found that the French had ordered two thousand rations of bread to be ready at two o'clock, which we accordingly took. They came at the time appointed and some skirmishing ensued. Four of the 11th charged 12 of their cavalry and were taken — no blood was shed. The whole army was encamped down the stream. These are extraordinary times. I do not think that the enemy will fight us till they get near Madrid. They are marching faster than us. I was upon picquet, but saw no French. Bivouacked.

July 2nd. To Medina del Campo, 3 leagues. The army was encamped near the town, and the inhabitants having never before seen Englishmen, came out in droves to see us. They also brought us wood in carts. In the evening we moved a mile further from the town. I was sorry for it, for I had found an old house in which I should have put myself. I got some young potatoes out of the garden, which the gardener did not seem to relish. Bivouacked.

July 3rd. The town of Medina del Campo was once of considerable size, but it has of late fallen into decay. It was once celebrated as the most considerable fair in Spain. Merchants came here from all parts of the world. A dispute, however, arose which put an end to it. The King claimed a duty upon all the articles entered for sale, whilst the merchants refused to pay for more than they sold. There are several convents, most of which have fallen into decay. The people seem overjoyed to see us and give Balls in honour of our arrival. The enemy has pulled up on the other side of the Douro and we have done the same on this. We heard some firing this morning in front. It proved to be Lord Wellington reconnoitring the fords, which are very deep and bad. Bivouacked.

July 4th. We moved to the other side of the town, it being supposed to be more healthy. Sir Thomas Graham is to leave us tomorrow; he has had a disorder in his eyes for some time, which growing worse obliges him to go to England. He flatters himself that he shall be able to return, but there appears to be a general break up in his constitution, and after sixty, a man suffers from a campaign in this country.[1] Some horses and saddlery belonging to his staff were sold by auction. Lord Wellington made a reconnaissance this morning — he passed the Douro with the 3rd and Light Division, and after some skirmishing crossed it.[2]

---

[1] Graham did, in fact, return to the Peninsula in 1813. See also JM's Journal for May 29th 1812.

[2] Wellington never crossed the Douro with his army. On July 3rd he advanced with the 3rd Division to the ford at Pollos and sent some riflemen of the 5/60th plunging into the water to test it. The level of the water was found to be much too high, however, and with Marmont's force strongly posted on the opposite bank he gave up any ideas he had of crossing. Marmont's force was positioned on the northern bank of the Douro with Tordesillas as his headquarters. Wellington, meanwhile, placed the 3rd Division at Pollos, guarding the ford, with the bulk of his army in and around Medina del Campo. Headquarters were established at Rueda. For the next fortnight the two armies remained in sight of each other, divided by the line of the Douro, and consequently a great deal of

Marmont's headquarters are at Tordesillas where there is a bridge over the Douro. Bivouacked.

July 5th. The weather is too hot to do anything. I discovered two rooms in a convent at the back of our encampment into which I have put myself. They are delightfully cool and form a pleasing contrast to broiling in a tent. I occupy two rooms leading into the Chapel, one of them looks like the Vestry room. Our party consists of Crofton, Bradshaw, Fremantle and myself — all having separate rooms. How completely all luxury is comparative. I fancy myself the happiest man in Europe. The convent is very much destroyed in consequence of a guerrilla having killed a Spanish renegade at the door of the Chapel. The French in consequence destroyed the convent and the nuns have taken refuge in the town.

Medina del Campo
July 5th 1812

My Dearest Mother,

You have heard from me during our late proceedings, as regularly as I could manage it. I have not been able to write as often as I would wish for in truth we have of late been so much harassed that we have had time for nothing. On the 30th I wrote to Charles from Canizal, we were then making for Toro at which place and Zamora the enemy has constructed forts. On the 1st we turned off that road and got upon that to Valladolid and on the 2nd arrived at this by way of Alaejos.

Marmont has stopped short on the other side of the Douro and we have done the same on this. That river is very deep and has but few fords. The ground too on the other side is extremely strong and would render the passage difficult. I do not, however, believe that this has anything to do with our halt. The truth is we are so far from our magazine that we must wait for supplies. The whole of the country between this and Salamanca is a vast plain, covered as far as the horizon with corn, the crops as fine as I ever saw. There is hardly a tree, and the inhabitants make use of straw instead. It is a shocking bad campaigning country at this time of year, for there being no trees there can be no shade and I assure you I am quite burnt up. I have been but one night in a house since the

fraternisation occurred as the men of both sides bathed in the streams and river in the hot July sun. Captain William Bragge, of the 3rd Dragoons, wrote, 'The French are very civil and allow us to water horses and bathe in the river; the latter experiment I have not tried although hundreds do every day.' (Cassels, (Ed), *Peninsular Portrait 1811-1814, The Letters of Captain William Bragge*, p.62.) Surgeon Charles Boutflower, of the 40th Regiment, provides us with perhaps the best summary of this astonishing period. 'In the meantime a singular mode of warfare is carried on; it is not uncommon to see five hundred of the enemy, and as many of our men, bathing together in the Douro in the most perfect good humour possible, at the same time that the cavalry of the two rival armies come down on their respective sides of the river to water, it being perfectly understood that neither party shall ever approach the river armed. Any infringement of this agreement is noticed by firing on any armed cavalry of infantry of either side.' (Boutflower, *The Journal of an Army Surgeon during the Peninsular War*, p.145.)

1st of June. We are marching in such heavy columns that it is impossible to find houses for us. But at this moment I envy not any Prince in Christendom for the sun is intense, and I have discovered two very nice rooms in a ruined convent into which I have stowed myself. It is very near the camp but the exterior appearance promised so little that no-one thought it worth while to go in. How completely all luxury is comparative. We are encamped close to the town. The inhabitants never having seen English troops before come out in droves to see us. They are uncommonly kind to us, but make us pay enormously for every-thing. Bread is six shillings for a loaf weighing three pounds, and everything else in proportion. They are just beginning the harvest here. Had we been a little later the French would have carried a great deal of it off, as it is we shall live upon it. General Graham left us yesterday on his way to England in conse-quence of a disorder in his eyes. He flatters himself that he shall be able to return. But his constitution will not stand this work which progresses hard upon a man of sixty — he is a great loss to us.

Our stay in this part of the country will materially assist Portugal. It will give it an opportunity of getting in their harvest with our assistance and in the meantime we are eating up a country, which if we did not, the French would. We shall I think get still farther into the country. Madrid is but seven days march from hence, and I really think we shall see it ere long. They say it is a very fine town. This is a very curious place. It is Moorish, and was in the days of bows and arrows, very strong. There is a square barrack capable of holding six thou-sand cavalry. The French have unroofed and otherwise destroyed it for the sake of the timber, not approving of dressing their dinners with a straw fire. We have been much more humane for we have cut down half a dozen tall poplars which were curiosities inasmuch as they were the only trees within miles. The excuse is that the men must have fires. So when we cut the barley and wheat it is because the horses must not starve. This sort of reasoning would not suit in England. Notwithstanding all this they appear at least happy to see us. Any change in their situation must be for the better. The Portuguese pass themselves for English. It seems extraordinary that the Spaniards should not know the dif-ference but I have several times been assured by them they do not. They appear to be a most incorrigibly stupid people. They are fond of dress and gaudy colours but put them on with taste. The personages you see at Masquerades as Spanish girls and noble Spaniards are not the least like what they affect.

I am afraid that another year will elapse before I join your party — it already seems an age since I was at Bisterne. If I do not make haste I shall be invalided and removed from hence to a Garrison Battalion with some other lively old chaps, to do duty at the Cape of Good Hope.[1]

Remember me most kindly to my father, sisters, and such of the mascu-line part as may happen to be at home.

---

[1] The Cape of Good Hope had been occupied by the British in 1806, Holland having been annexed by Napoleon. British command of the sea allowed garrisons to be made up of elderly or low medical category soldiers. Indeed, the 1/60th was there at this time with a significant proportion of former prisoners-of-war.

July 6th. I awoke quite surprised at once more finding myself in a house. There is a pool of water before the convent in which to my great surprise I killed two couple and a half of wild ducks.

July 7th. Confined to the house by a slight touch of the Cholera Morbis.[1] Don Julian has taken a French picquet of 20 men and having discovered three Englishmen among them they are sent to Headquarters to be hung. Our halt is occasioned by the want of supplies. They are throwing all they can into Salamanca but Ciudad Rodrigo and Almeida from whence they must come are so far off that this operation must take some time. Marmont remains in status quo. There are Balls in the town every night.

July 8th. There is a strong report of marching in consequence, it is said, of the enemy having burnt and evacuated Tordesillas and its neighbourhood. At night an order arrived to send out baggage to the rear, which however I did not comply with, luckily enough as it turned out, for it went but half a mile and returned in the morning, having been just long enough to make those that sent it uncomfortable.

July 9th. A Mail arrived here from London in fifteen days — up to the 23rd. General Picton has pushed a picquet across the Douro at Pollos. A flag of truce was sent in to request it might be withdrawn otherwise they would be obliged to use force as it was where they watered their horses. The picquet was in consequence withdrawn.[2]

July 10th. The weather continues hot. It is quite impossible to move out in the day time. The mosquitos are extremely troublesome at night.

July 11th. An intercepted letter from Marmont was brought in wherein he states that his force is insufficient to withstand us, and begging that of the Division of Caffarelli, which is supposed to be in Navarre, may be sent to his assistance. Bonnet arrived at Tordesillas on the 7th with 5,000 men. Marmont's whole force is not more than 35,000 with this reinforcement.[3] On the night of the 8th when the baggage was ordered to the rear, two signal lights were fired from the old castle into the camp and next morning a party of the enemy patrolled to a village on our left. The lights must have been fired by the Spaniards, unfortunately they were not caught.

July 12th. We marched at three o'clock to Valesende. It seems that Lord Wellington thinking the sun too hot for the men to be exposed to its effects, and there being no shade, has ordered that the men are to be put into the towns during the day and moved out at night. This day we began. We had one house per company, so small that not one third could be crammed in. The Spaniards at Salamanca were employed in removing powder and shells from the forts into the places in the town pointed out for the purpose. Instead of doing this they

---

[1] JM does not appear to draw the conclusion that if one gorges in hot weather on wild duck, shot out of season off a pool into which the convent probably drained, as he did on July 6th, a touch of dysentery is likely.

[2] See Boutflower's comment on the fraternisation on the Douro, note 67 above.

[3] JM had underestimated here. Bonnet joined Marmont at Tordesillas on July 7th. His 6,500 infantry, 100 cavalry and a light field battery brought the strength of Marmont's army up to 43,000 men with 78 guns. See Oman, *History of the Peninsular War*, V, 391.

secreted some in their houses which took fire, and ninety persons were blown up. Allix took me into his house. Others managed as they could but few got under cover. At seven the men marched and were formed for the night about ½ mile from the town to which I returned and slept.

July 13th. Started to the ground at three, at which time the men stood to their arms and remained so till four. At seven we marched back. I sat on a Brigade Court Martial on some men for passing counterfeit dollars. They make them out of buttons and they are very well executed.[1] Marched out as before.

July 14th. Retreated at 6 o'clock. The reason for these manoeuvres of ours seems to be that Lord Wellington is endeavouring to starve Marmont into attacking us. We are upon the high Madrid road, and having nothing in our front it is necessary we should be prepared. Twenty three artillery drivers were flogged for breaking open a wine vault in the house where they were quartered, the owner of which declares that they destroyed 32,000 pints of wine. There is nothing to do but sleep. The day is so completely destroyed by moving in and out.

July 15th. The Commissariat are short of money. The people of this part, indeed, universally in Spain, object to being paid in paper, so we may be masters one day, the French another. The bread must therefore be paid for, and dollars are becoming scarce. A ration of bread costs tenpence — with money. We might live long in this part of the country. The army are nearly four and the Staff five months in arrears. There are a great many Bustards about here. They are found chiefly in the vineyards and are very shy. I have heard but of one being killed. There are likewise birds they call pin-tailed grouse, the legs and head like the grouse, a single feather very fine at the tail. They appear to be more like the plover than the grouse. In consequence of some movement of the enemy's we marched at nine o'clock and encamped near Nava del Rey. Bivouacked.

July 16th. In the morning we moved into the town and were very closely packed, as three Divisions and Headquarters were in it. At six in the evening intelligence came that Marmont with his whole army had crossed the Duero. Accordingly, we were all ordered to march but owing to the quantity of troops and baggage in the town we were not clear till eleven. We passed Alejos at daylight, and arrived at Canizal, 6 leagues, at about twelve o'clock. The roads are so extremely dusty that we were almost choked. The Light and 3rd Divisions and some cavalry formed the rear and skirmished.

July 17th. The enemy entered Nava del Rey at ten o'clock. They advanced rapidly and our heavy cavalry skirmished with them and kept them in check. In the evening they formed up and everything remained quiet. They cut down a Portuguese commissary in Nava del Rey and took some stores we were obliged to leave behind. As soon as the troops were out of the town lights were exhibited from the steeple as a signal to the enemy — so much for Spanish enthusiasm. Bivouacked.

[1] This was a favourite trick amongst the more roguish elements of Wellington's army. Buttons could be easily flattened and the regimental badge upon them gave them the appearance of being coins which often fooled the more unsuspecting Spanish and Portuguese peasants.

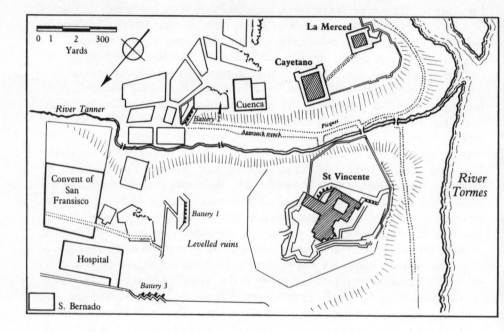

July 18th. The enemy manoeuvred a good deal in the morning, in consequence of which our division retired to Obarda but moved back in the evening to Canizal. Marmont keeps upon our flank and thereby obliges us to retire. The 4th Division came in contact with the enemy, charged them and took two hundred prisoners, amongst them a Colonel, and killed a great many. The men were so tired that they could hardly stick their bayonets into them.[1] Three men and an officer died of actual fatigue. Towards evening the enemy drew up on a height opposite to some we occupied and remained quiet. Everybody and everything is in confusion. Headquarters and I believe all the General Officers in the army are in the village, and the whole army is round about. Bivouacked.

July 19th. Everything is quiet this morning. I rode out to our videttes. The enemy occupied a range of hills, extremely strong. Our position too was formidable. They commenced cooking early, accordingly we did the same. Our artillery yesterday did a good deal of execution amongst their cavalry. The 14th charged and Captain Brotherton was run through the body but he is likely to do well.[2] A

---

[1] On the morning of July 17th Marmont crossed the Douro, forcing Wellington to retire upon Canizal to the south west. The 4th and Light Divisions, along with Anson's brigade of cavalry, under Cotton, were ordered to halt at Castrejon on July 18th whereupon they became embroiled in some skirmishing. The town of Nava del Rey, where Marmont had established his headquarters, lay to the north east of Castrejon and when Wellington was informed of this he immediately ordered the cavalry brigades of Bock, Alten and Le Marchant as well as the 5th Division to march in support of Cotton. Wellington himself arrived at Castrejon at around 7am accompanied by Beresford and his staff and had not long been on the ground before a group of French cavalry swept pass some British guns and made for the Allied commander-in-chief, forcing him and Beresford to draw their swords. The second action of the day, to which JM refers, occurred at Castrillo. Once again the Light, 4th and 5th Divisions were involved as well as Alten's cavalry. Wellington's force had drawn up on some rising ground between Castrillo, Canizal and Vallesa where it was attacked by Clausel, who commanded the French right. The attack began with a move by Carrié's brigade of dragoons, the 15th and 25th, supported by a battalion of infantry and three guns. The dragoons were driven off in style by Alten's cavalry, the 14th Light Dragoons and 1st Hussars KGL. The French suffered 158 casualties including Carrié himself who was taken prisoner along with ninety-three others. The infantry were then attacked by W. Anson's infantry brigade, the 3/27th and 1/40th, supported by the 11th and 23rd Portuguese Regiments from Stubbs's brigade. The Allied infantry set about the French with their bayonets, scattering them, whereupon Alten's dragoons got in amongst the fleeing refugees, cutting down scores and rounding up 6 officers and 240 prisoners. Allied casualties were 442 all ranks, while the French suffered at least 700 casualties. See Oman, *History of the Peninsular War*, V, 405-407, and Fortescue, *History of the British Army*, VIII, 474-476.

[2] During the action at Castrillo, Captain Thomas Brotherton, of the 14th Light Dragoons, was severely wounded when Alten's light cavalry brigade charged Carrié's dragoons. Brotherton left a most graphic account of his wounding. 'When we had crossed this stream [the Guarena] with the whole brigade, we formed and waited till the enemy had crossed also, and then we attacked him 'in succession of squadrons from the right'. The first two squadrons that charged failed to make an impression on the enemy, and were repulsed. In leading the third squadron to the charge (which was mine), I was run through the body, from the right side to the navel, about six inches. When the point of the sword came out, and as I staggered and fell, my antagonist, instead of withdrawing his sword from my body altogether, drew it up a little and then made another thrust, which went into the cavity of my chest. I was then led off the field faint and sick, and I

troop of the 11th and 12th Dragoons who were acting as support to the two guns, ran away on the approach of a party of the enemy, who cut down an officer at the guns and nearly succeeded in taking them.[1] In the evening the enemy moved part of their force to their left, in consequence of which we moved to our right and remained during the night in a plain near Valessia. Bivouacked.

July 20th. At daybreak we were formed in two lines in the plain. Soon after, the enemy were seen moving to their left. We remained as we were and offered them battle, which however they declined accepting. We were then obliged to move too. It was a fine sight to see the two armies in motion at the same time. They moved parallel to each other and at no time were more than two miles distant. They passed along a hill and we along the bottom. We described the string of the bow and consequently got ahead. It was in fact a race. Their object is to get between us and Portugal, thereby obliging us to move as they do and eventually it must end in us being obliged to quit Spain or fight. Neither side seems willing to attack though both seem to wish to fight. At one time during the march our Division came within range of the hill on which they were moving. They fired at us for some time, but without doing any harm.[2] The villages through which we passed were all deserted, the inhabitants having carried off

well remember one of my best old soldiers offering his assistance. He was wounded also, but said, "it was nothing, only a little stab in the stomach." Such however, is the mortal nature of wounds with the point (the regiment we had charged was a heavy cavalry one with straight swords), that the poor fellow, as he was leading me off the field, suddenly vomited blood, and fell down dead. I must mention that I received my wound in the act of uplifting my arm and making a cut at the head of my antagonist, on his near side. He wore a brass helmet, and the blade of my sabre broke in two on it, which left me quite at his mercy.' (Perrett (Ed), *A Hawk at War; The Peninsular War Reminiscences of General Sir Thomas Brotherton, CB*, pp.53-54.)

[1] This was the incident (see also note 1, page 177) when Wellington and Beresford were obliged to draw their swords for protection. 'On the left two squadrons, one of the 11th and 12th, were supporting two guns from Major Ross's troop. The squadrons were supporting one another, and on the advance of some of the enemy's cavalry (inferior to two squadrons), the one in front went about. Some of Marshal Beresford's staff seeing this, conceived the guns were in danger, rode up to the retiring squadron, calling "Three's about!" This of course put the other squadron about in the place of fronting the one already retiring. One person gave one word, one another, and the enemy's cavalry came up to the guns. There was no harm done, and our dragoons (the 11th) immediately advanced and drove them back.' (Tomkinson, *Diary of a Cavalry Officer*, p.181.)

[2] The parallel march by Wellington's and Marmont's armies is one of the memorable episodes of the war in the Peninsula. Throughout July 20th both armies marched parallel to each other within cannon shot but neither was prepared to face to its front and bring on a general action. John Aitchison, of the 3rd Foot Guards, wrote, 'As the enemy continued to advance on the high ground the British army moved forward by the road in a parallel direction, and for the space of three hours there was the most beautiful movements perhaps ever witnessed of two armies of 40,000 men each trying to arrive at a certain point first.' (Thompson (Ed), *An Ensign in the Peninsular War*, p.173.) Even Marmont himself recorded the amazing spectacle in his *Mémoires*, and added that he never before or after saw such a magnificent spectacle as the parallel march, of two bodies of over 40,000 men each, marching at such close quarters. Quoted in Oman, *History of the Peninsular War*, V, 412.

all the valuables they were possessed of. A squadron of the enemy's cavalry took most of the baggage of the German Hussars at Canizal. Amongst it were several women, all of whom excepting four, they sent back. The enemy, finding that we had got ahead of them, halted as we did at Ituaga, 4 leagues. I had dismounted in the morning thinking that we were going into action and by some mistake my horse did not come up to me again, and I was consequently obliged to walk. I was not very well and the heat of the sun and the depth of the sand through which we passed quite knocked me up. I believe I should have lain down, and been taken prisoner, had I not found a beast I had with me loaded with baggage on which I mounted, and thus got to the end of my journey. The want of water in this part of the country is most dreadful. The men run to the most stagnant pool of water as thick as mud, and drink it with the greatest avidity. Bivouacked.

July 21st. We marched before daylight through Moriscos, over our old position, to the ground near Salamanca upon the Tormes. I rode into the town and got some breakfast at a coffee house. Everything here is changed — the town is in a bustle, the whole of the hospitals, stores, etc. being ordered out of it, to proceed along the road to Ciudad Rodrigo. The inhabitants are frightened to death, fearing that they will have to pay for the civilities they have shown us. The square which used to be so gay, is now filled with stores on their way out of the town — such are the vicissitudes of war. I had suffered so much inconvenience from sending my baggage to the rear that I determined upon keeping it with me, and as it was all collected on the outside of the town previous to its being sent to the rear, I took mine with me to the camp, preferring to run the risk of it being taken to allowing it to go away. I had just dined when the whole army was ordered to cross the Tormes, the French having done the same. Salamanca was then open to the enemy. We took up ground near the village of Los Arapiles on some heights. A most tremendous storm of thunder, lightning and rain came on, which lasted almost all the night. I was unable to pitch my tent owing to the stoniness of the ground, so I wrapped myself in my cloak and forgetting the storm fell asleep.[1]

July 22nd. At daylight everything was quiet. About six o'clock some skirmishing took place in front, the enemy having pushed on towards us. We occupied a position in the line of which there were several heights. The French occupied one height opposite to us, so steep that it was imagined that guns could not be got up it. There was on our right the village of Arapiles and the range of hills of

[1] The eve of the battle of Salamanca is memorable for the tremendous violent storm that broke during the night. 'As fires were lit and meals cooked dark clouds began to gather overhead and as the moon began to disappear the rumble of distant thunder was heard as flashes of lightning lit up the sky as if mother nature was laying down a barrage of her own. As the troops donned greatcoats and oilskin covers for their shakos the clouds opened, a gentle trickle at first and then an almighty downpour which lasted throughout the night. Flashes of lightning illuminated the camp and at one point a bolt struck the earth in the middle of the horses of a squadron of the 5th Dragoon Guards.' (Fletcher, *Gentlemen's Sons*, p.134). The storm would later be regarded as a good omen of victory. A similar one preceded the victory at Sorauren and, of course, that at Waterloo, the most famous storm of them all.

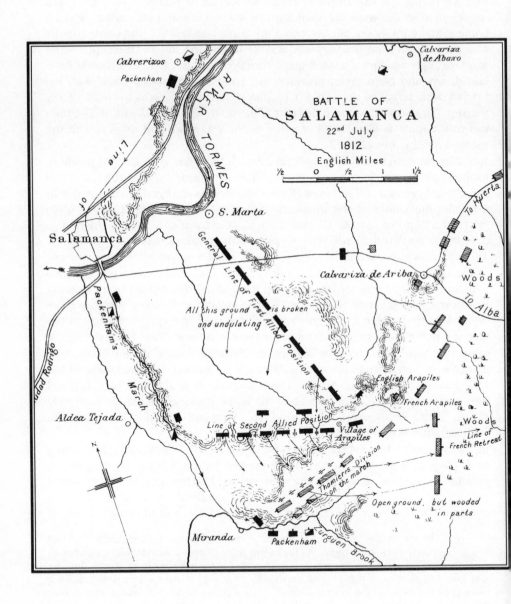

the same name running at right angles to it. At eleven o'clock the 1st Division was moved from the left of the line to the village, being ordered to attack the height the enemy occupied. They were however countermanded. Some skirmishing took place on the hills between the cavalry, which was very pretty. At three o'clock they began to fire from the height and annoyed our line a good deal. At five o'clock Lord Wellington having observed that they had detached a considerable body of troops from their left and had occupied the range of hills said, "Now they have driven me to attack them. They will not let me retreat quietly and we will show them we are not to be bullied." Everything had been prepared for a retreat, the routes had been made out, and we should have been withdrawn at dusk and in three days have been in Portugal, but the movement of the enemy upon our right made a retreat difficult. It gave Lord Wellington a fresh opportunity of gaining laurels and rescued our character from the imputations that even the most sanguine of the Spaniards were beginning to throw upon it. At five o'clock the attack commenced. The enemy had previously thrown out their skirmishers and had gained possession of the village, from whence they were driven by the light companies of the Guards. The 4th, 5th, 6th and 7th Divisions, the latter formed the second line, attacked in front and the 2nd turned their right which they did with ease. Meanwhile, the other three Divisions attacked in front and at length succeeded in gaining the hill, under a tremendous fire of artillery. General Pack's Portuguese Brigade stormed the heights, but having got nearly to the top were driven back. This was the only failure of the day. The enemy, finding themselves beaten, began to think of retreating. At this moment Marmont was wounded and he ordered a retreat. General Le Marchant's Brigade of Heavy Cavalry charged amongst them and took several pieces of cannon and made 1,500 prisoners. The retreat became general. The 1st and Light Divisions, which had been on the left, exposed only to a cannonade, moved down upon their right.[1]

[1] The battle of Salamanca was fought on July 22nd 1812 and was one of the most decisive Allied victories of the war. On the morning of July 22nd Marmont looked towards the Ciudad Rodrigo road and saw a long column of British troops marching along it which was, in fact, Wellington's baggage, and immediately gave orders for an advance in order to cut it off. As Marmont's men hurried to get in front Wellington, seeing the manoeuvre, quickly ordered a Portuguese brigade forward and soon a race developed between them and a French unit for possession of the Greater Arapil, a large box-shaped hill which stood in the middle of a vast, rolling plain. The French won the race and occupied the hill, the Portuguese settling for a smaller hill opposite called the Lesser Arapil. Wellington's route lay to the south west of the field and in their attempts to cut him off the leading French divisions, still believing they were involved in the sort of race in which they had been for the last couple of days, began to distance themselves from each other. The gap between the leading French division, that of Thomieres, and the second, Maucunes', did not go unnoticed by Wellington who, after glancing through his telescope, exclaimed, "By God! That will do!" before galloping off to the west to order Pakenham to attack with his 3rd Division. What followed was one of the most devastating attacks of the war as waves of British infantry smashed into Thomieres' division, killing him and either killing or wounding over 2,000 of his 4,500-strong division. Every single one of his guns was taken also. A series of subsequent attacks by Wellington's divisions achieved equal success, although Cole's 4th Division was hard pressed late in the fight. The 1st Division of the army, including the Guards, took little part in the battle

July 23rd. We marched at daylight and crossed the river below Alba de Tormes. The Heavy Germans who lead our Division, came up with the rear guard of the enemy, charged them in the most gallant style and broke a solid square. They took 1,500 prisoners, cavalry and infantry forming their rear guard, and one gun.[1] The country was covered with prisoners whom our men were bringing in by twos and threes and plundering. The road exhibited evident marks of the hurry of the enemy. Cars, jackasses, pigs, poultry, in short, all sorts of descriptions of things, were left upon it. Near the village of Coca our Division came sufficiently near them for our guns to play. We pursued for some time, but could not near them. They were running apparently in the greatest disorder through the corn — no order amongst them. Finding we could not get near to them and our army being much fatigued, we were obliged to halt. Accordingly, we went back about half a mile to Coca, on the outside of which we bivouacked. General Gravier, desperately wounded, was found in a small village. Marmont had his arm amputated this morning. He is wounded besides in the body, and is carried on a bier. The prisoners say they know not who commands the army now. Pigs, sheep, everything that could be found that was of course French, was appropriated accordingly. Almost all the French are dressed in great coats of different colours, white, grey, brown, etc. Their cavalry are well appointed, though their horses seem out of condition. It appears that they had not taken the chance of a retreat into their calculation. They have no provisions with them but as the harvest is upon the ground they cannot starve. Bivouacked.

July 24th. We marched at daylight having been delayed sometime waiting for the German cavalry. We passe Penaranda, the inhabitants of which came out and brought pitchers of water, a thing much wanted. They described the French as absolutely running without stopping to look. We halted at Cantaracillo, 3

---

and remained away on Wellington's left flank, although the light companies of the Coldstream and 3rd Foot Guards helped hold the village of Los Arapiles in the face of continual enemy attacks. By the end of the day Marmont had suffered some 15,000 casualties including 7,000 prisoners. Three generals were killed and four wounded as well as a further 136 officer casualties. Marmont himself was badly wounded as was Bonnet, who succeeded him, and Clausel, who took over from Bonnet. Wellington lost around 5,000 men killed and wounded. The Coldstream suffered seven men killed and Ensign Howard and twenty-two men wounded. Eighteen were listed as missing.

[1] This celebrated action took place at the village of Garcia Hernandez when four squadrons of Bock's heavy dragoons, the 1st and 2nd Dragoons KGL, caught up with the French rearguard. The French regiments, the 6th Léger and 76th Line were both two battalions' strong and totalled around 2,400 men. Upon seeing the fearsome German cavalry charging towards them the first battalion of the 76th formed square and opened fire on the leading horsemen bearing down upon them. Unfortunately for the French, one of the horses which was shot continued straight on into the square and began kicking and flaying with its legs, and in so doing created a gap into which the rest of the squadron of Germans charged. The square was destroyed in an instant although the majority of the French were taken prisoner. The 6th Léger met a similar fate when they were attacked just short of some heights which they were attempting to gain. Bock's dragoons lost 127 men out of 770 present, while the French casualties are estimated to have been around 1,100. Oman quotes Foy — commanding the rearguard — as calling the episode, 'the most dashing and successful attack made by any of Wellington's cavalry during the whole war.' (Oman, *History of the Peninsular War*, V, 480.)

leagues, the inhabitants of which fled at the approach of the French, who stripped their houses of everything. The peasants had not returned when we entered the town, but came soon after and made the most bitter lamentations at the alterations which had been made. The French are eight leagues ahead of us, and it is understood that all idea of pursuing them is given up. It would now be useless as it would be impossible to catch them.

Cantaracillo
July 24th 1812

My Dearest Father,

I have great news to communicate — Marmont is defeated with the loss of 12,000 men, and we have not done with him yet. We have taken 22 pieces of artillery, Marmont has lost an arm, seven other Generals killed or wounded, and their army dispersed.

The 4th, 5th, 6th and 7th Divisions were chiefly engaged. The 1st, 3rd and Light Divisions being on the left were but partially, but are now put in the advance in the pursuit.[1] On the 16th Marmont crossed the Tagus and we retreated in the night to Canizal. On the 21st we were close to Salamanca having been obliged to retreat whether we wished it or not, neither of us wishing to fight and Marmont wishing to get us out of Spain. The night of the 21st they were close to us as usual; it rained torrents, in short, we all began to grumble. We were so harassed that we did not care what happened, and thought Lord Wellington ought to let us fight. On the morning of the 22nd there was some skirmishing in front. They showed signs of attacking our position which was a league in rear of Salamanca. We were manoeuvred for almost all the day, and at three o'clock it seemed as if the enemy did not mean to attack. They however moved to a range of hills on our right in order to oblige us to retire. Lord Wellington than said that they should not bully him, that if they had done it quietly he intended to move off, but that he would show them that he was not to be compelled. At four o'clock the attack began. The four divisions being formed in two lines, after a great deal of hard fighting the enemy gave way. Their left was ordered to retire and their right did so without orders. They left their artillery and 3,500 prisoners and ran off just at sunset. The darkness prevented their total annihilation. The divisions who had been engaged were not able to begin the pursuit — accordingly the others did. The enemy retired through a wood and we at their heels, firing into them. At last we lost them and stopped for a few hours at Wista. Yesterday we started again at daylight. The dragoons in our front came up with them, charged and took 1,500, but we never could get up though we did our best. They were completely in disorder, nothing like marching. They were for some time running a mile in our front but we could not get to them. At two o'clock we halted. This morning we marched again here and shall I believe follow them at night. The road divides two leagues from hence;

[1] JM is wrong here. It was Pakenham's 3rd Division which executed the initial attack at Salamanca, smashing into Thomieres' division to set the battle in motion.

to Madrid and Valladolid. As yet we do not know which they have taken. The Spaniards say that they have nothing to eat, and can hardly get on. We have already taken 6,000 and every minute more are coming in. I am afraid they are too far ahead of us to do any good now.

We are delighted, as you may well imagine, at the result of our labours, which I assure you have been great. Day and night have we been marching. Our division was ordered to attack a height nearly inaccessible, before the general attack. We were, however, counter ordered and sent to the left. Colonel Pack's brigade attacked the height and were cut to pieces.[1] The darkness of the night alone saved what is left of their army. We shall still get some more for they are completely routed. They are absolutely running, have nothing to eat and do not know who commands them. We do not know as yet our loss though it is set at four thousand. Beresford shot through the body, Colonel Sir S. Cotton in the arm, General Cole body, General Leith arm broken, General Le Marchant killed.[2] Marmont is shot in the arm, amputated, likewise in the groin. Bonnet wounded, one general taken wounded, two killed, and several wounded. Their eagles are in our hands.

You will hardly be able to make out head or tail of this but I am so distressed I know not what to do. The weather is dreadfully hot, and hardly any water. At the sight of a little stagnant water we run like ducks. The whole business has been most truly lucky. Lord Wellington did not mean to fight but to retire into Portugal. Luckily for us they bullied and that brought it on. They fought very ill and seem at last to have been panic struck. Not more than half of either army were engaged. They say that Marmont ordered the retreat as soon as he was wounded; a retreat it was not for there was nothing like order. Yesterday I saw them running through cornfields and vineyards like a pack of hounds. Today they are in better order and are now five leagues ahead of us. It seems doubtful whether we shall follow them any farther or not. We have already more than six thousand prisoners. They are dispersed all over the country, and they are still bringing them in. In fact, their army is no more. Marmont is carried on a litter, and is not expected to live.

I must now go to bed, so remember me most kindly to my mother, sisters and brothers. John Mills.

[1] The three attacks by Pakenham, Leith and Le Marchant met with complete success but at about 4.30pm Wellington ordered Pack's brigade to storm the Greater Arapil. He duly advanced across the valley between the two hills with his brigade, some 2,600 strong, but did so in the face of heavy French artillery fire. By the time his men reached the Greater Arapil their ranks had been somewhat thinned and when they received a volley from the numerically superior French infantry there, they broke and fled. His brigade suffered 376 casualties during the day, mainly on the attack on the hill.

[2] A host of British commanders became casualties at Salamanca. Le Marchant was killed, while Cotton, Leith, Cole, Beresford and Victor Alten were wounded. Even Wellington himself did not come through completely unscathed as a bullet tore through his holster late in the day injuring his thigh. In the Allied army some 50 officers were killed and 235 wounded, while 846 men were killed and 3,471 wounded. A further 160 men were listed as missing, giving a total loss of 4,762. Oman, *History of the Peninsular War*, V, 599.

July 25th. The whole army halted this day to allow the stragglers which form one fourth of the army to come up. Lord Wellington in General Orders simply thanks the officers and men for their good conduct on the 22nd and then proceeds to inveigh against straggling, threatening to punish the men and bring the officers to Courts Martial. He particularly mentions the 13th, on which day more than a hundred of our men, stragglers, were picked up by the enemy in a march of twelve miles. His Lordship should recollect that men cannot march without shoes, that his army has been constantly moving for two months, and during that period harassed in an unprecedented manner and that they are four months in arrears of pay. He should not ride a willing horse to death.

July 26th. To Fuentes de Ano, 3 leagues. I never saw so many pigeons as I saw here. I killed 9 and could have killed any number had I had ammunition. That harassing practice of turning into the fields at night, recommenced here. It is absurd in as much as it keeps the men constantly on the move when they ought to be quiet.

July 27th. To Arevalo, 4 leagues. This is a very good town. The men were put into a convent, we found places in the town, out of which we were moved in the evening. I saw one of the eagles taken on the 22nd. It belonged to the 22nd Regiment, was of brass and had had a flag below, but it was torn off.[1] Some French officer of distinction died here. At every town through which we passed they have said that Marmont is dead. I have now heard it so often that I do not believe it.[2] Joseph Bonaparte, on his way to join Marmont from Madrid, was met by some of our cavalry, who made twenty-five prisoners. He had not heard of Marmont's defeat. Marmont had taken the road to Valladolid. Bivouacked.

July 28th. Not content with making us turn in and out of the towns, they make us stand to our arms for an hour before daylight, whether we march or not. I had rather march the longest march and be quiet after I come in than be thus harassed. It is said that Lord Wellington considers it healthy. Bivouacked in a pine wood near Olmedo, on the river Cueza. This is the first wood we have seen on this side of Salamanca. It is a most delightful bivouac, the river running close under us. Marmont has pulled up near Valladolid and makes a show of defending the fords of the Douro. It is impossible he can ever wait for us. Bivouacked.

[1] The haul of captured French trophies at Salamanca was quite substantial. Two eagles were captured, along with six colours and twenty guns. (*Despatches*, Wellington to Lord Bathurst, 24th July 1812, IX, 304.) Intriguingly, both Oman and Fortescue give the captured eagles as belonging to the 22nd and 101st Regiments. However, during the battle Lieutenant Pearce, of the 44th (East Essex) Regiment, took an eagle from the French 62nd Regiment of the Line which was then placed on a sergeant's halberd, the men giving three cheers at the same time. The eagle is now in the Regimental Museum at Chelmsford. I would suggest that the trophy belonging to the 101st Regiment, taken at Salamanca, was not an eagle but was, in fact, a 'Jingling Johnnie', a musical instrument which was captured by a huge sergeant of the 88th (Connaught) Rangers and carried around in triumph for the remainder of the war. No mention is made of the 88th taking the 101st's eagle at the same time.

[2] Marmont was wounded by a piece of spherical case shot when a shell from a British gun burst close to him. The piece of shell ripped his arm to shreds and broke two of his ribs. The rumour of Marmont's death appears to have been rather widespread in the British camp but he survived and lived to the age of 78, dying in 1852.

July 29th. We marched to a continuation of the same pine wood near Mogares, 4 leagues. Headquarters are at that place. They were to have been more in advance but some parties of the enemy are on this side of the Tagus. Bivouacked.

July 30th. Marched to a pine wood on the banks of the Douro, 5 miles from Valladolid. We passed through the village which the French occupied with 9,000 men last night, but had retired from during the night. None of their force was to be seen on the Douro, which the Light Division crossed. Our Division remained on this side. Marmont quitted Valladolid, leaving 300 sick. He has taken the road to Burgos. The Douro here is very rapid and the fords are bad. It is very picturesque and has more the appearance of an English river than any I have seen in this country. Bivouacked.

July 31st. I rode over to Valladolid. In the appearance of it, I was much disappointed. It is larger, but has none of the Collegiate appearance of Salamanca. In short, it is not I think to be compared with it. There is a Royal and a Bishop's Palace, neither of which have anything remarkable about them. Also a Scottish college but without Scotchmen. Instead of the square at Salamanca, there is one much larger but not regularly built and the space in the middle is occupied with stalls. None of our troops were pushed as far as this. Some of the Guerrillas took charge of the 300 sick. We were the first English officers that had ever been seen in the town, but we were welcomed by no Vivas — a universal gloom seemed spread over the town. Some of the principal families had fled with the French, those who remained were either attracted to them, or if they were not were afraid of welcoming us, lest the French should return and punish them. A great many of the shops were kept by Frenchmen who for the time being called themselves Italians, afraid that we should take them. All their money is French. In short, the town of Bregonne is not more Frenchified than Valladolid. Joseph has often described it as the only town he can completely trust. The French have here married and intermarried, and have of course created a strong interest in a residence of four years. The further we advance into Spain the more we shall see that the higher orders are more inclined to the French than to us. The lower orders would be well pleased to see the French driven out, but they will not do it. They are heartily sick of the war, hate the sight of both parties, and as to enthusiasm, never felt it. The people of England are deceived, are gulled. They are told of spirit that does not exist and of armies which are not to be found. All sorts of French produce is to be purchased here. Claret, vin de Grace, etc, but money is hardly to be got. Dollars as a favour at 6s 6d. Marmont is at Arandom on the Burgos road. Bivouacked.

August 1st. We marched to a convent under the town of Portillia, 2 leagues, into which the whole Brigade was put. The officers took up their abode in a garden under cover of vines. I got into the gardener's house. Lord Wellington, with the 3rd and 7th Divisions, is trying to cut off Joseph Bonaparte somewhere in the neighbourhood of Arevalo. Turned out as usual.

August 2nd. No orders for marching having arrived, we congratulated ourselves in a day's half. In the evening, however, an order which we ought to have had in the morning arrived and we marched at dusk to a pine grove near the village of Cogeces. Bivouacked.

Portillia, four leagues south of Valladolid
August 2nd 1812

My Dearest Mother,

The victory of the 22nd has given us an opportunity of seeing Valladolid, and I think we shall ere long visit Madrid. The gazette will give you a much better account of the battle than I can do; besides, I have forgotten a great deal of what I then saw. The night before the action the rain came down in torrents, and the lightning showed us the visages of our enemies. You will think I am exaggerating when I tell you that some liquor or rather rum caught fire in pouring it from one canteen into another. I wrapped myself up in my cloak and slept soundly. I was so tired I could have slept in a river. For some time on the 22nd it appeared as if the enemy would have attacked us, which Lord Wellington wished. They however declined, as we were very advantageously posted. In the evening they moved so that our retreat would have been difficult and in fact they obliged us to attack them. Lord Wellington was certainly much tied up. He repeatedly said he longed to attack them; as it was I think he allowed himself to be forced to attack. Nothing could exceed the gallantry of our troops. In their advance they were exposed to a most tremendous fire of artillery. The French stood well at first, but they were overpowered. Most of their General Officers were obliged to leave the field and the order for a retreat was given too late for it to be executed. Our part of the line had a fine view of the business. We were out of reach of their musketry but the round shot made us now and then take our eyes off from the contending parties. The severe part of the action lasted about an hour and a half. I saw our line advance, and occasionally could see through the smoke the contests in the different places, but there was so much noise and such confusion that it was quite impossible to make anything clearly out. I had not the most distant conception but that it was a small body on both sides fighting hard for some ground that both wanted. Our division was first in the pursuit. We were for some time at their heels, but they desisted from firing, and the wood was so thick we could not see them, so we lost them. We crossed the Tormes at Alba de Tormes, and at Coca came so near them, that both they and we were running.

Our army was fairly knocked up and we halted. We afterwards followed them by way of Fuentes de Ano, Arevalo, Olmedo, and halted on the 30th on the Tagus, two leagues from Valladolid. Our army has been so incessantly harassed since the beginning of June that it is now fairly knocked up. We are going on for five months in arrears of pay, the men have no shoes; in short, unless the present system is altered the Hospitals will be crowded. We are daily losing men and if we stand still for a week the seeds of sickness long since sown will show themselves. This is always the case after hard work.

Lord Wellington has adopted lately a new plan; he puts the men during the day into the towns to get them out of the sun. In the evening he moves them into an open field, where they remain for the night and at daybreak they are again marched into the town so that we are never quiet. God knows we have had marching enough by day and night and have not grumbled, but added to all this to be unnecessarily and experimentally harassed is heartbreaking. There is one consolation, that he will soon have no men left to play these tricks with. Himself and the General Officers not feeling them, are not as well aware of them as we are. They always take care to find a good house. We are à la fresco.

We are moving now in the direction of Madrid. King Joseph is not far from here with twelve thousand men. He had come from Madrid intending to join Marmont but we have cut him off from him and Lord Wellington is endeavouring to take him with the 3rd and 7th Divisions. Marmont is said to be dead. He had his arm amputated the day after the action and is, besides, hit in the side. He was carried on a bier and borne by six men. It is more than probable that the heat of the weather and the anxiety of his mind has been the cause of his death. It seems likely that Lord Wellington will go to Madrid, leaving Marmont's army to itself. It is so cut up that it will be unable to do anything for sometime. We have no chance of rest for some time come what may. I have lost my servant and a horse he was on. He was ill and following my baggage, but I believe mistook his road. I have reason to think he is dead.

I am sorry to say I hear of no promotion. I wish I could persuade some of them to go out. Beckford is ill at Salamanca; he was not with us the 22nd. General Le Marchant, who was killed on that day, died in the arms of his son, who was acting as aide-de-camp to him, a dreadful situation.[1]

Give my kindest love to my Father, Brothers, sisters, cousins, etc.

August 3rd. Halted. It is ascertained that Marmont has retired to Burgos. The French soldiers are singing and capering fancying they are going to France. Joseph has retired from Segovia to Madrid, having it is said destroyed the former place and left his artillery behind him.[2] Bivouacked.

---

[1] General Gaspard Le Marchant had commanded a brigade of cavalry at Salamanca consisting of the 3rd Dragoons, 4th Dragoons and the 5th Dragoon Guards. The brigade was launched into the attack against Maucune's and Brennier's divisions following the initial onslaughts by Pakenham and Leith. Le Marchant's dragoons smashed five battalions of enemy infantry in an orgy of destruction. As Le Marchant pursued the battered survivors into woods to the south east of the battlefield he was shot through the spine by a French sergeant major. Le Marchant's son, Carey, was with him on the battlefield but was not present when his father was shot. 'Clowes [who commanded the 3rd Dragoons] came up, and, having sent for a litter to carry the body, turned sadly back up the hill. The first officer he met was Carey, hatless and in bounding spirits, full of news of the slaughter of Thomieres' division. He was looking for his father, and Clowes, 'too much affected to communicate the news to him myself,' was about to refer him to the Assistant Adjutant-General, Lieutenant Colonel Elley, when Carey saw the stretcher being carried off by two dragoons. He took one look at that so familiar face now carrying the haggard shade of death, and threw himself upon the body in an agony of grief.' (Thoumine, *A Scientific Soldier: A Life of General Le Marchant, 1766-1812*, p.195.) The loss of Le Marchant, a brilliant cavalry commander, was probably the greatest loss to Wellington after that of Robert Craufurd, commander of the Light Division who was killed at Ciudad Rodrigo. In the absence of Henry Paget, Le Marchant was Wellington's best cavalry commander. Salamanca was his first major action of the war.

[2] King Joseph received the news of the battle of Salamanca during the night of July 24th-25th at Blasco Sancho, close to Avila. He immediately issued orders for a retreat by the way he had just come, from Madrid. Shortly after reaching the Guadarrama Pass,

August 4th. Not liking my ground, I pitched my tent under some fine pine trees and close above the river. The number of sick in the army is now enormous. The late hard work has sown the seeds of a great deal of future sickness. A fortnight's pay has been issued to the army who are now paid to the 10th of April. Bivouacked.

August 5th. General Clinton is to remain in this part of the country with the 6th Division and one regiment from the other Divisions, making a force of about eight thousand men. He is to watch Marmont. The remainder of the army will move in the direction of Madrid. Bivouacked.

August 6th. We marched at daylight to a pine wood near the village of Remondo, 1½ leagues. I walked out with my gun and had some sport. Salamanca is filled with sick and wounded officers — not less than seven hundred. I killed here two birds of the grouse species. They are not uncommon in this part of Spain. They fly about, seldom resting upon the ground. The plumage is grey, yellowish about the head, the breast black. The meat of the breast is in layers of black and white, similar to the black cock.[1] A flock of about two hundred geese were discovered in the village. They were bought in half an hour at 4 shillings a piece. Bivouacked.

August 7th. Marched to a wood near a small mill called Molino de Terneroso — a very hard bivouac.

August 8th. To Los Huerjos through Carbonero, 2 leagues. The peasants here wear leather jackets, the women a most extraordinary sort of cap, one of which I bought from curiosity. Petticoats too seem in fashion. From our ground we could see Segovia, distant about five miles and the Sierra of Guadarrama running majestically near it. The ground for some distance near here is intersected by ravines of an extraordinary depth. I killed a stork and gave it away not thinking it eatable. The inhabitants both in Spain and Portugal have a great veneration for these birds — it is sacrilege to kill them, and is punished with the greatest severity. They build on and frequent the churches. I do not remember ever to have seen them on any other building — probably their veneration arises from thence, but it ceases when they see them in the fields when they kill them immediately. Several General Orders have been issued against killing them. Bivouac.

August 9th. We marched to the Royal Park of Rio Frio, leaving Segovia on our left. The 1st, 4th, 5th and Light Divisions were quartered in this park. It is of a very considerable extent, walled and well wooded. All the lodges were destroyed. The Palace was built about fifty years ago for the Queen Dowager — it was never completely finished. It is an immense square building. The ground floor seems to have been destined for the servants. The Courtyard is magnificent, a colonnade running all round. The grand staircase is remarkably fine and is supported with large solid granite pillars. The rooms on the upper floor enter

however, he turned towards Segovia, which was reached towards the end of July. He departed Segovia on August 1st.

[1] JM is very precise here in his description, from which the bird can be clearly identified as the now-infrequent Black-bellied Sandgrouse, not the more frequently seen pink variety.

into one another with folding doors, and the communication goes all round through the infinity of rooms and a corridor connected the private doors to each. The Palace, never having been inhabited or furnished, did not of course appear to advantage. The frame work is magnificent and the entrance particularly striking. I rode over to see Segovia, a town of the same class as Salamanca. The houses of individuals appear much finer than either at that place or Valladolid. The Cathedral and tower are the only public buildings. At the latter place the keeper shows the room where Gil Blas was confined. He desires you to observe the heights of the window which Gil Blas complains of.[1] There is a fine old aqueduct, extremely airy. In other respects, Segovia has but little worth seeing. The inhabitants receive us just as coolly as they did at the other towns. I have had a very hot ride of a league and a half and back and returned with a head ache. Bivouacked.

August 10th. Otero de Herreros, 1½ leagues. The Light Division marched at the same time with us and the baggage of both clashed. I was on the baggage guard and had a great deal of difficulty in getting ours along. This duty prevented my going over to see the San Ildefonso about two leagues from Rio Frio. The Palace and gardens I hear are beyond description. Everything is in the highest order. A guard of one hundred men under the command of an adjutant has always been quartered in the Palace. Lord Wellington and suite were in it two days ago. King Charles used to be there a great deal for hunting. The old gardener abused Godoy and the Queen. The former he said was extremely ugly. Joseph has been there but twice, and then but for a day at a time. I regret not having been there, but I hope I shall yet have an opportunity. Bivouacked.

5th Remondo, 2 leagues
7th Molino de Temoroso, 3½
8th Los Huerjos (through Carbonero), 4½
9th Rio Frio (Segovia on the left), 2
10th Otero de Huerreros, 1½

Otero de Huerreros
August 10th 1812

My Dear Father,

The last time I wrote was on the 2nd from the convent near Portillia, enjoying myself with the idea of a halt. I had just sent a letter to my Mother when we were ordered to march to a pine wood near Cogeces where we remained till the 6th since which we have marched as above. The mail goes tomorrow, and as we shall in all probability march before daylight I shall sit up an hour later than

[1] Gil Blas was an adventurer in the tradition of Robin Hood. His origins are French. Jakob Ludwig Felix Mendelssohn-Bartholdy the composer, more commonly known as Felix Mendelssohn (3.2.1809-4.11.1847), wrote an overture dedicated to the legend of Gil Blas. Mendelssohn travelled to France frequently from an early age when he would have undoubtedly have encountered the stories.

usual to give you an account of our proceedings.

We appear to be bound for Madrid from which place the peasants say that Joseph has retired. We are four leagues from the Guadarrama Pass; our advanced dragoons are already beyond it. I believe it is very strong and would have cost us a great many men had they been able to defend it. But as that is not the case Madrid is ours.

General Clinton remains on the Douro with six thousand men. Castaños is ordered to join him with his army consisting of about fourteen thousand. The united force will watch Marmont and check him if they can do it, should they find him coming down. He is thought to be at Burgos but on Lord Wellington's moving to Madrid is likely enough to move down.[1] Our force is very considerably diminished from sickness and our situation now is such, and so important is every hour, that no time can be given to recover. No less than seven officers of this regiment went sick to the rear in one day. Thank God and my stars I have not felt anything amiss yet.

We are now coming into the interesting part of the country, are upon the King's High Road and have league stones to mark the distances. At Rio Frio we were encamped in a Royal Park belonging to the Queen Dowager. There is a most enormous Palace built about fifty years ago but never inhabited. It is a square building of about two hundred feet to a front. You drive in (I did not) under colonnades. The ground floor seems to have been destined for the servants. The upper floor is laid out in rooms opening into each other with folding doors. You may imagine the extent when I tell you the front and the communication went all round, the stables, and other buildings in proportion. The hundreds of windows had all of them plate glass. The palace appears never to have been inhabited. The park is of considerable extent and walled but though this is the finest thing I ever saw, I missed seeing a much finer by going to see Segovia — one thing is that I could not see both; I mean the King's Palace at St Ildefonso. Should anything prevent us marching at daylight I shall ride over to see it. I hear that it is finer than Versailles, the gardens beautiful and superb water works. I will not tell you what I hear of it for I hope to see it. If I do not you shall hear what others say of it. Lord Wellington moved out of it today.

Segovia is of the same class of towns with Salamanca and Valladolid. It has a fine cathedral but no other public buildings. The houses of individuals are

[1] Following Marmont's wounding at Salamanca the French army was placed under Clausel who withdrew the army north-east towards Burgos and Vittoria. Wellington entered Madrid on August 12th and although Clausel, whose army was still in a state of some shock following its mauling at Salamanca, chose not to advance against him, he did despatch Foy in order to rescue the French garrisons at Zamora, Toro and Astorga. Toro was successfully evacuated on August 17th but before Foy reached Astorga he received information that the garrison had surrendered on August 18th. He subsequently marched to Zamora and after having successfully brought off the garrison and its stores he returned to rejoin the main body of Clausel's army at Tordesillas. The evacuation of the garrisons at Toro and Zamora did not worry Wellington, however. On August 23rd, he wrote to his brother Henry, 'I hope the French will carry off the garrisons of Zamora and Astorga, as well as that of Toro. Anything is better than that I should have to attack and carry those places.' (*Despatches*, Wellington to Sir Henry Wellesley, 23rd August 1812, IX, 374.)

finer than in either of the other towns. The man who shows the tower, shows you likewise the room where Gil Blas was confined. He desires you to observe the window, which Gil Blas complains of being so high. I really met a party returning from thence who believed in the reality of the character. There is an old aqueduct, extremely curious, and that is all that is to be seen. It is full of as much apathy and unconcern on the part of the inhabitants as in other places. We are now marching parallel to the Sierra and shall do till we come to the Guadarrama. When we have passed that the Escorial and Madrid will keep us on the tiptoe of expectation.

Our progress now becomes entertaining. There is something else to see, some pleasure for our trouble. The whole of the country I have seen since I left Salamanca is alike fertile. The corn is now all collected round the villages and towns. It is first trod out with mules drawing a sledge which has sharp stones fixed, and projecting at the bottom; it is by this process reduced to chaff. They then separate the corn by sifting it, but as all this is done upon the grass or hard ground the grain is foul. They have no detached farm houses and the corn is all collected in heaps together; the scene is very pretty. They are slow about it. I have seen them work for a month past and they do not appear to have got any under cover yet.

General Maitland is said to have landed in Catalonia from Sicily. If well conducted it will be a powerful diversion in our favour, but it will require a great deal of skill. The object I imagine is to make Suchet move upon him, which will leave Hill to deal with Soult, and ultimately raise the siege of Cadiz.[1] Our affairs are much altered within six months. I little thought on the 22nd that we should now be so near Madrid. Much as you may be disposed to praise our exertions I think you will now see to the bottom of this Spanish patriotism; they are no more likely to stir than the dead. They have not the most distant intention of so doing, though the lower orders would be well pleased to see the French out and us after them. The 3,000 Spaniards under Don Carlos d'España who have been with the army for six months, and Castaños's army keep up the juggle; you will still send out arms and clothing which will still continue to be sold, and Spanish patriotism will be credited, till they cut our throats or show some mark of disapprobation too decided to be mistaken.

I should have acknowledged sooner the receipt of a letter from you of

[1] General Frederick Maitland (not to be confused with Peregrine Maitland who commanded the 1st Foot Guards at Waterloo) landed at Alicante on August 7th 1812 with a force of some 6,638 troops. These consisted of the 20th Light Dragoons, 167; 1/10th, 935; 1/58th, 871; 1/81st, 1,274; 4th Line KGL, 750; 6th Line KGL, 750; Royal Artillery, 177; Marine Artillery, 30; Royal Engineers, 47; Staff Corps, 14, plus detachments of Roll's, Dillon's and Cantabrians, 1,238. (Fortescue, *History of the British Army*, VIII, 556.) This force had sailed from Sicily where Lord William Bentinck, having been appointed Envoy Extraordinary and Commander-in-Chief in Naples, commanded. This British force was supposed to act in conjunction with Spanish forces in order to create a diversion on the eastern coast of Spain. The operations here did not form one of the more glorious episodes of the campaign in the Peninsula. Soult gave up the siege of Cadiz on August 24th, which released some 5,500 British troops under Colonel Skerrett who took Seville three days later before marching north to join Wellington's main field army.

the 16th of July. Many thanks to you for your kind expressions with regard to my promotion. I am not very sanguine as to the probability of an opportunity occurring soon. All those who have been able have already left us, those who remain being chiefly soldiers by necessity; we cannot hope that the promotion will continue as rapidly as it has been. There is one person (Greville) who does not purchase, but he is too far from me to give me any chance of profiting by him. Bradshaw is about to leave us.

11th August. I wrote the preceding part of this letter last night. We marched at three this morning to St Raphael. I have remained behind a few minutes to direct this letter. I shall not now have an opportunity of seeing St Ildefonso which I regret exceedingly. We march now an hour before daylight to avoid as much as possible the heat of the day.

With kindest love to my Mother and all your party. John Mills.

Chapter Five

Madrid

Following Wellington's rout of Marmont at Salamanca he had to make up his mind whether to march on towards Vittoria and the Pyrenees or to turn southeast towards the Spanish capital, Madrid. With hindsight, it is rather tempting to consider what might have been had he chose the former course. The French were in total disarray and even given the French reinforcements in the area a thrust by Wellington towards Vittoria, a year before it eventually came, may have shortened the war considerably. But that is all open to debate. In the event, Wellington chose the politically sound move and marched on Madrid. His army entered the city on August 12th amidst more wild celebrations which, as JM noted, no doubt resembled those that greeted Joseph on occasions. JM, in fact, is very cynical throughout his letters regarding the Spanish people, and not without reason perhaps. We find signals being given to the French once the British had vacated a town and we know that the Spanish people themselves regarded the British and French troops as being similar in one aspect, that both took what they wanted. The only difference was that Wellington's men paid (usually) for their supplies whereas the French simply helped themselves.

JM's stay in Madrid appears to have been largely an enjoyable one as it gave him the opportunity to see the great museums and palaces the city had to offer such as the Prado and the Escorial. In fact, the park at Philip II's great palace is where the Coldstream encamped during the army's stay at Madrid and it is where we find JM at the start of this chapter.

August 11th. We marched to the Park of the Escorial near Guadarrama, 4½ leagues. Near Otera we came upon the Royal road to Madrid. It is a magnificent pave, the only thing like a public road that I have yet seen in the Peninsula. About two leagues from Otera we began to ascend the Sierra at the celebrated pass of Guadarrama, defensible with 5,000 men against millions. The road is cut diagonally. The mountains are magnificent and covered with pine wood. At the top of the hill is a pillar marking the boundary between Old and New Castile, with the following inscription:

Ferdinandus Santus Pater Patua,
Nam Intrique Castella,
Montibus Superatis,
Fecit.

Below the view is magnificent. We entered the Park of the Escorial by a lodge, distant a league and a half from the Palace.

August 12th. An unexpected halt gave me the power of riding over to the Escorial. It was built by Philip the 2nd in commemoration of the Battle of St Quintin, gained by the intercession of St Lawrence. The said St was fried upon a gridiron, and in remembrance of his sufferings the Escorial is built in the shape of a gridiron. The Saint stands over the doors with one in his hand, and others are disposed of in different parts of the building.[1] The approach from Madrid is extremely bad. A few ragged poplars stand on each side of the road and on the way to the Palace are different buildings belonging to the Court and inhabited by different persons attendant on the Royal Family. There is no carriage entrance within the Palace. The cathedral is very heavy but has an air of grandeur about it. The Mausoleum of the Kings and Queens of Spain is beautiful. There is a descent of several feet by a marble staircase. The mausoleum is an octagon built entirely of marble and illuminated in the centre by a massive brass lamp. The sides are fitted with niches, into which urns are put. There are in the whole twenty-six, but fourteen of which are filled — 7 Kings and 7 Queens. The ashes of Charles 5th are here. There is one something similar at Genoa, belonging to the Medici family. There is no gilding on it, which is more correct.[2] A great part

---

[1] The imposing Escorial Palace was built by Philip II to commemorate his victory over the French at the battle of San Quentin in Flanders on August 10th 1557. The palace was built by the architect, Juan de Herrera, under the supervision of Philip himself, and has 1,200 doors, 2,600 windows and took 1,500 workmen some 21 years to complete. The battle of San Quentin was fought on St Lawrence's Day which is why Philip decided to build the palace to recall the saint's martyrdom. He was martyred over a gridiron so the palace was built to reflect this fact and measures 206m x 161m and 676m x 528m.

[2] The Royal Pantheon, or Pantéon de los Reyes, was begun in 1617 in the reign of Philip III. The chapel lies exactly beneath the high altar of the church in the Escorial. Cut into its eight sides are niches into which have been placed sarcophagi containing the remains of Spanish monarchs. With the exception of Philip V and Ferdinand VI all Spanish monarchs, dating back to the Emperor Charles V, are buried here. Each of the sarcophagi is made of dark grey marble decorated with brass letters. The chapel can still be visited today and is a truly imposing and solemn place.

of the building is occupied by the convent, such was the bigotry of the times. The Battle of St Quintin is painted on the ceiling of the staircase and in one of the courts are different bad paintings. There were some fine ones but Joseph has removed them. The battles of the Moors and Spanish are painted on the walls of a gallery. The Royal Apartments are stripped of every article of furniture. The fine tapestry pictures have been removed but the rooms are extremely low, small, bad and very few in number. I was shown a small closet with a private door wherein Godoy and the Queen used to sleep.[1] In the convent there is a fine library. The books, however, have all been removed. Joseph has been here but twice, and then only for a night. Upon the whole, I was much disappointed with the Palace. It is a heavy mass of building, ill laid out. The convent and cathedral occupy a great portion of it. The town is immediately at the back of it, and takes off from the effect. The Park is of an immense extent. The trees are not fine and most of them Pollarded. I am sorry to say that through the laziness of our men in lighting their fires, the Park was on fire in several places. The grass being so burnt up catches immediately, nor is there any possibility of stopping the fire — it meets with a road and stops itself. Immediately behind the Palace runs the Sierra de Guadarrama, the scenery of which is beautiful, none of it is desert and bleak. The Park is covered with pines and on the whole it is grand. The front view is wooded, the trees standing too thick and by no means fine. In some places there are enclosures, in short there is nothing about it which indicates a park. The whole thing is heavy and ill laid out, and the fame of the Escorial can only have been raised by Monks pleased to see so great a sacrifice made to their pageantry. I heard that there was a Summer House in the garden, extremely well worth seeing — accordingly I went there. Tired to death of heavy buildings, I was glad to have seen what I had but not for words would I have again gone through it. The Summer House is in fact a villa, built for the leisure hours of the Queen. The approach is through a kitchen garden. The house is on the outside neat, but has no pretensions to anything more. But ye Gods on entering, I thought I was in enchanted ground. The rooms were all small, excepting the dining room — 36 feet by 13. The ceilings were round and painted in the most exquisite manner, after the Arabesque. I have seen on a screen, an attempt at something of the sort, but this beggars all. In fact, it is that species of light ornamental painting done by the fine artists. It is all upon oil cloth. The passages and staircases are of different sorts of marbles, beautifully executed. The ceilings above stairs are of the same sort as those below. The floors are of different woods inlaid. The furniture had all been taken out. The

[1] The Prince of the Peace was the name given to Manuel Godoy, y Alvarez de Faria (1767-1851). Godoy, the son of a poor nobleman, was a soldier in the Company of Life Guards when he struck up a relationship with Queen Marie Luisa. As a consequence he rose to power and was able to take control of the politics of the country, mainly through the indolence of the king and as a result of the Queen's immoral favours. His corrupt dealings enabled the French to enter Spain in 1808 but in March of that year the people, not unnaturally distressed by the French presence, rioted and sacked Godoy's palace. He was despised by the people and when they discovered him skulking in a cupboard they set about him and it was only the intervention of Ferdinand VII, who had assumed the throne in the wake of Charles IV's abdication, that saved him from death.

silks with which the walls were hung were removed. I never was so much
struck with anything. It was exquisite and complete paradise. I returned to camp
dissatisfied with the Palace but raving about the villa.

August 13th. We marched at daylight to Ponte de Ralamar, 4 leagues. Lord Wellington entered Madrid yesterday amidst the shouts and acclamations of the
people, I think rather incautiously displayed, for should Joseph return he will
work them for it.[1] On the 11th our advanced posts were at Rosas, a league in
front of this, and 2½ from Madrid. Joseph's cavalry had retired and our picquets
were posted. They however showed themselves again, and Colonel D'Urban's
Brigade of Portuguese Cavalry (which had been dismounted some time since
and had just been remounted) were drawn up to charge. On the advance of the
enemy they were panic struck, went to the right about, charged through the
Brigade of Heavy Germans, and rode in amongst the Brigade of Horse Artillery.
The enemy, seeing the confusion, rode at the Germans, some of whom had the
bits out of the horses mouths, and cut them up. They took three guns which
being unable to carry them off they destroyed. They took the Colonel of the
Germans and Captain Dyneley of the Horse Artillery. The loss of the Germans
was 100. This fine Brigade, which has of late so much distinguished itself, came
out from England eleven hundred strong, and are now reduced to three hundred.[2] Bivouacked.

August 14th. We marched to Madrid, 2½ leagues, and encamped in a public

[1] William Wheeler, of the 51st, wrote, 'Our division marched right in front, and as
our regiment is on the right of the division we were the first regiment that entered
Madrid. I never before witnessed such a scene. At the distance of five miles from the
gates we were met by the inhabitants, each had brought out something, viz. laurel,
flowers, bread, wine, grapes, lemonade, aquedente, tobacco, sweetmeats, etc. etc. etc.
The load represented a moving forest, from the multitude of people carrying boughs.'
(Liddell Hart (Ed), *The Letters of Private Wheeler, 1809-1828.* p.90.) Wellington himself
wrote, 'It is impossible to describe the joy manifested by the inhabitants of Madrid upon
our arrival; and I hope that the prevalence of the same sentiments of detestation of the
French yoke, and of a strong desire to secure the independence of their country, which
first induced them to set the example of resistance to the usurper, will induce them again
to make exertions in the cause of their country, which being more wisely directed, will
be more efficacious than those formerly made.' *Despatches*, Wellington to Lord Bathurst,
13th June 1812, IX, 355.

[2] During Wellington's advance on Madrid, part of his vanguard got itself into a
sharp fight at Majalahonda on August 11th. D'Urban's brigade of Portuguese cavalry, the
1st, 11th and 12th Dragoons, were within seven miles of Madrid and so wrote to Wellington
to ask whether or not he should press on and enter the capital. While he waited for the
reply he threw his men into the village of Majalahonda where his men took the opportunity
of having a rest after the last few days manoeuvring in the hot sun. At about 4pm,
however, a large number of French cavalry were seen approaching. These consisted of
the 19th and 22nd Dragoons, Palombini's Italian *Dragons de Napoléon*, and the 1st
Westphalian Lancers, under General Treillard, as well as Reiset's brigade of dragoons, the
13th and 18th, some 2,000 men in all. In spite of being outnumbered three to one,
D'Urban resolved to stand and fight and after sending for help from the German brigade
of heavy dragoons, just three quarters of a mile in their rear. The Portuguese advanced in
a determined fashion but when they were just a few yards from the French they turned
about and bolted, leaving D'Urban and several other officers stranded, and forcing them
to cut their way out. The cavalry were pursued for a mile by the French who also overran

walk near the great entrance at the gate of San Vincente. We passed the Royal Palace of the Prado, much destroyed. It is an exceeding bad house and was only used as a sort of Post House between Madrid and the Escorial. The Park wall is forty miles round. We were delayed some time before coming upon our ground as we had to pass through the Casa de Campo of Joseph and his pheasants were to be driven in. I took this opportunity of going through the house. The collection of pictures is extremely select. It was Joseph's favourite residence and is fitted up with the greatest taste. I could not help lamenting that Lord Wellington's scruples prevented his taking any of the affects belonging to Joseph from respect to Ferdinand, considering them as his property. I found out a small house on the banks of the river with baths before it. I was so anxious to see the town that the moment I was at liberty I went in. The hurry of seeing the capital made me so anxious to see everything that in fact I saw nothing but the shops and streets, and I stared like a countryman just come up to London for the first time. The entrances are for a mile lines with double rows of trees. The gates are in fact arches with superb iron gates, and superb fountains with different devices at all of them. The first coup d'aeil is very striking — the Palace is at the principal entrance and gives an imposing air to the town. The streets are broad and very clean, so much the reverse of Lisbon. There are an immense number of fine houses and the shops are like those in London. At the extremity of the town

and captured three guns, commanded by Captain Dyneley who was captured along with fourteen of his men. (See Dyneley, *Letters written on Active Service*, pp.42-43.) A party of forty German dragoons, who were out on a scouting mission, joined the fray but were badly cut up also after putting up a gallant fight. When D'Urban reached the village of Las Rosas, where the brigade of German dragoons were resting, he found them hastily mounting their horses and in the rush many of them rode out to face the French wearing just their shirts and some wearing forage caps. Some of them even rode bareback as there had hardly been time to saddle up. The Germans fought virtually alone as most of the Portuguese showed little stomach for the fight. A fierce struggle ensued during which the Germans were forced back upon Las Rosas but by this time the 1st Light Battalion of the KGL, which had also been resting in the village, came forward and opened fire on the French, forcing them to withdraw and bringing the desperate business to a close. Nearly 200 Allied cavalry were lost, mainly Portuguese who had 33 officers and men killed, 52 wounded and a further 23 listed as missing. French losses were roughly the same. Wellington called it, 'a devil of an affair.' (*Despatches*, Wellington to Cotton, 13th August 1812, IX, 351.) In his despatch to Lord Bathurst, written the same day, a somewhat disappointed Wellington wrote, 'I have reason to believe, both from the manner in which the enemy came on to the attack of the Portuguese troops, and from other circumstances, that they had been informed that we had none but Portuguese dragoons in front, and that there were no troops in the neighbourhood to support them. The occurrences of the 22nd July [Salamanca] had induced me to hope that the Portuguese dragoons would have conducted themselves better, or I should not have placed them at the outposts of the army. But every day's experience shows that no reliance can be placed on cavalry which is not in a perfect state of discipline, and of which the men do not feel a perfect confidence in their officers. I shall therefore not place them again at the outposts, or in situations in which by their misconduct they can influence the safety of other troops.' (*Despatches*, Wellington to Lord Bathurst, 13th August 1812, IX, 354.) See also Oman's account, *History of the Peninsular War*, V, 508-513. D'Urban's own rather short account appears in his *The Peninsular Journal of Major General Sir Benjamin D'Urban, 1808-1817*, pp.282-283. There is also a good account in Beamish's *History of the King's German Legion*, II, pp.89-95.

is the Prado, a public walk where the people assemble in the evening. It is about a mile in length, overshadowed by large trees and numerous fountains in it. Here are to be seen the young and old, the fair and the ugly, who come to enjoy the cool of the evening. Beyond the Prado is the bon Retiro, formerly the Palace, but since converted into a citadel and fortified. It was to have been stormed this day but to the surprise of everyone, the Governor surrendered and the garrison marched out with the honours of war to be sent as prisoners to England. I had the curiosity to see them march out. They were most of them drunk. They were as fine a body of men as I ever saw, all of them in new clothing and loaded with all sorts of things. Some danced and sang, abused their officers, some tore their hair with rage. The Spaniards who were looking on were not sparing of abuse. The French gave them as good in return and said they were glad they were prisoners. Thus without having broke ground we got possession of the place, of seventeen hundred men, and most enormous stores — clothing, arms, ammunition, etc., besides 30 pieces of artillery. Their surrendering is quite unaccountable.[1] The Governor was afraid of being shot, and sneaked out first. Some of the 3rd Division, who took possession, began plundering, and the officers were put under arrest, and are to be brought to a Court Martial. I got a most excellent dinner at a hotel — claret, vin de grase, etc. In the evening the houses were all illuminated. The inhabitants seem delighted to see us — they call us their deliverers. I never thought the Spaniards in earnest before but they really seem overjoyed. During the day, tapestry, silks, curtains, etc., are hung out of the windows. The whole town seems mad. Groups of English officers and Guerrillas, parading up and down the streets dressed in the most grotesque manner. Whenever Lord Wellington appears he is followed by an immense crowd eager to get a glimpse of him. Don Carlos d'España, in the absence of Castaños acts, as Commander in Chief. He has issued a proclamation confiscating the property of all those who had left Madrid with the French. I went to the play — the actors were but indifferent. There are two Houses in the town. Some of the principal actors have left Madrid with the French. I returned home at night, so astonished at what I had seen, and surprised at finding myself in Madrid that I could hardly believe but that I was dreaming.

August 15th. I resolved to dedicate this day to sights. The Palace is an enormous

[1] The fort at the Retiro, the Fort of La China, was defended by 68 officers and 1,982 men under the command of Lafon Blaniac, governor of the province of La Mancha. The outworks of the fort, a series of loop-holed walls and *flèches*, were taken by detachments of the 3rd and 7th Divisions on the night of August 13th. The following day Lafon Blaniac surrendered the fort to Wellington, much to the annoyance of his men who thought they could hold out for some time. Any defence would have been totally futile, however. There was a severe shortage of water in the fort, which had no strategic importance, and any loss of life on the part of the British would probably have led to large-scale slaughter of the French defenders. As well as the garrison a further 6 officers and 429 men surrendered in the hospital outside the Retiro. 9,000 barrels of gunpowder, 189 guns and 20,000 other arms were taken in the fort along with the eagles of the 51st Line and 13th Legér. (*Despatches*, Wellington to Lord Bathurst, 15th August 1812, IX, 359.) Oman claims that the second eagle belonged to the 12th Legér. *History of the Peninsular War*, V, 517.

building, though it is hardly finished.[1] It is a beautiful building and has a magnificent appearance. The suite of rooms are princely and filled with the choicest pictures which have been taken from all parts of Spain. All those which were at the Escorial are here, amongst others the Madonna with the fish. The ceilings are all painted. The person who showed me the rooms knew nothing about the matter and as there was no catalogue I had to lament it the more. The State Room is about 150 feet long, fitted up with bronzes and glasses. Amongst the pictures are the Prometheus, and the St George and the Dragon by Rubens. The collection is supposed to be one of the finest in the world and the grandeur of the rooms is well suited to them. Lord Wellington resides in the Palace and occupies the apartments of Joseph. The stables and offices are upon the same scale. The Palace of the Prince of Peace[2] is near the Palace and has a fine collection of paintings. The Quartermaster General occupied the apartments and they were not to be seen. The Academy contains a collection of paintings, natural curiosities and specimens of sculptures. The paintings are not numerous, but the collection, for a small one, is thought to be perfect. There are several by Morello, a Spanish painter of great celebrity, whose works are held in such estimation that by a decree of the Cortes they are prohibited from being exported. Amongst many others are, The Judgement of Paris, Diana at the Bath, Graces, Bacchanals, Apollo and Daphne, (all by Rubens), Transfiguration by Raphael, Titian Venus, with a portrait of himself. The museum of natural curiosities is extremely well arranged. Amongst the curiosities are a cup of a solid topaz, and a lump of gold weighing 16 pounds. There were some rooms filled with busts, etc. Spain has of late been drained of the best pictures from all the minor collections. The authorities of Madrid have made a present to Bonaparte of a collection of paintings. Joseph has done the same, but the collection at the Academy has remained untouched and that at the Palace has been increased. The streets exhibit the same gay appearance — crowds of people come down and see our tents. They seem much astonished at our furniture.

In the evening a grand ball was given to Lord Wellington. One third of the officers of each regiment were invited and all the officers of the Guards. Three thousand persons were there, of course a great squeeze. There were a great number of pretty women, very elegantly dressed and with a profusion of diamonds. The Spanish women of a morning wear long veils which they put on to perfection. In the evening they dress as they do in England. I think their figures in general remarkably good. Lord Wellington came in the State carriage drawn by six mules, the harness of crimson velvet. When he entered the room the people crowded from all quarters to see him. Waltzes, boleros, country dances and figures were danced. There was ice, wine, refreshments, etc. The rooms were so full and hot that I went away earlier than I should otherwise

[1] The Royal Palace, or Palacio Real, was begun in the 18th century. It stands on the site of the former Moorish fortress or Alcazar which was rebuilt by Emperor Charles V and destroyed by fire in 1734. Some of the state apartments, such as those of Charles III, were only completed in 1788 and so may have appeared to be 'only just finished' as JM says here.
[2] ie Manuel Godoy.

have done.[1]

August 16th. Joseph has retired from Aranjuez, having destroyed the bridge over the Tagus. His advance is eight leagues from Madrid. Notwithstanding the joy testified by the Spaniards, I do not hear of their making any exertions, nor do I think they will. I cannot help being surprised at the unreserved manner in which they welcome us. The return of the French is at all events not improbable and they will then pay for it. Several persons who were in the French interests have left. The Governor and other persons in office are in our interest. They accepted the places in order to be of use to their country. The contributions that have been raised have been so extremely heavy that the inhabitants are reduced to a state of the greatest want. The lower orders are actually starving. Bread and all other necessaries of life have been at an enormous price and Madrid is solely a town subsisting by the residence of the Court. It has no great manufactories. The streets are very wide and there are a vast number of good houses. All the small articles of English manufacture are to be procured here. The hotels are remarkably good but crowded. The illuminations having lasted three days are now discontinued. The streets lose much of the gaiety of their appearance as the tapestry and silks are taken from their windows. I think the Spaniards remarkably happy in the furniture of their Palaces. It is as handsome as can be made and more substantially so than ours. Clocks are a great article of furniture with them — in the Palace there could not have been less than 300 of different kinds, some of them made in London. The weather is most intensely hot. The only way I have of keeping myself cool is by bathing twice a day in the baths opposite my house and by drinking quantities of iced lemonade which they make here to perfection. The Prado was this evening quite deserted, the whole population having gone to see Joseph's Casa del Campo, a great treat as nobody had before been admitted within the walls. A band played there.

August 17th. It was with no small regret that I heard that we were to leave Madrid before the Escorial tomorrow. Marmont is at Valladolid, and General Clinton has retired to Olmedo. I went early into the town and remained there the whole day determined to have as much fun as I could. I drove about in a one-horse chaise, the Hackney coach of Madrid. My friend the driver was more surprised than pleased at the pace. Senor Cavallero as they always call us here, puts me in mind of Gil Blas. It is a more courteous expression than Senor Official as the Portuguese call us. The Post between this and Badajoz is re-established for the first time, the communication with that place now being open. The merchants here will cash bills upon England, a convincing proof of their confidence in our remaining. I left Madrid to return to my house, with great regret — I had spent a happy time there.

[1] The Brigade of Guards was usually kept fairly close to Wellington's headquarters and as such its officers were often to be found in large numbers at any function given by the local dignitaries. Being the 'Gentlemen's Sons' the officers of the Guards were equally at home on the ballroom floor as on the battlefield. One of JM's comrades, Captain George Bowles, wrote home saying that there were so many people present that he was almost 'squeezed to death.' See The Earl of Malmesbury, *A Series of Letters of the First Earl of Malmesbury*, II, 306-307.

Madrid
August 17th 1812

Well off for titles:

Don FERNANDO POR LA GRACIA DE DIOS, REY DE CASTILLA, de Leon, de Aragon, de las dos Sicilias, de Jerusalem, de Navarra, de Granada, de Toledo, de Valencia, de Galicia, de Mallorca, de Sevilla, de Cerdeña, de Cordoba, de Córcega, de Murcia, de Jaen, de los Algarbes, de Algercira, de Gibraltar, de las Islas de Canaria, de las Indias, Orientales y Occidentales, Islas y Tierra-firme del mar Océano, Archduque de Austria, Duque de Borgoña, de Brabante y Milan, Conde de Abspurg, Flandes, Tirol y Barcelona, Señor de Vizcaya y de Molina, &c.

My Dearest Mother,

I must begin this letter in time or I shall forget half I have to tell you and as I have seen many curious things within these few days I should be sorry for it. I am now in the suburbs of the town of Madrid, the troops bivouacked on the outside. The owner of my house is an old servant of King Ferdinand and makes me a present of this paper, which he says he carefully hid during the presence of the French.

I wrote to my Father on the 11th previous to marching. We passed over the Sierra de Guadarrama by the pass of that name, and encamped in the park of the Escorial. The pass is extremely strong and if defended it would not have been possible for us to force it. As it was probable we should halt the next day I deferred going into the Escorial; though we were within the walls of the park we were five miles from it and we had a tedious march. A most unfortunate event happened in the evening five leagues in front of us. Some of the enemy's cavalry advanced upon ours at the village of Rosas. Ours consisted of a brigade of Portuguese and the Heavy Germans who have behaved so gallantly of late. We charged in line; the Portuguese went to the right about, rode through the Germans, and knocked over three of the guns belonging to the Royal Artillery. The French cavalry seeing the confusion, charged, took three guns and killed a good many of the Germans, who though deserted stood their ground in the finest style. They destroyed the carriages of the guns which they spiked and left. They took Captain Dyneley, whom you have seen at Christchurch,[1] also the Colonel of the Germans. Everything had been going on so prosperously that this reverse threw a gloom over our splendid prospects. It was wrong to put the Portuguese cavalry in front; they are but newly raised regiments and moreover they differ most essentially from their infantry inasmuch as they never were known to stand a charge.[2]

Lord Wellington entered Madrid on the 12th amidst shouts of the people, who were almost mad with joy. Joseph left a garrison in the Retiro, formerly the Palace but now converted into a fort. I rode over to see the Escorial — it is

[1] There was a Horse Artillery barracks at Christchurch, Dorset, about five miles to the south of Bisterne.

[2] See JM's Journal for August 13th.

situated in a park of immense extent. At the back of the Palace runs the Sierra de Guadarrama. the situation is extremely fine, though the trees about it are pollarded which has a bad effect. This Palace was built by Philip the 2nd in commemoration of the battle of St Quintin, which was gained by the intercession of St Lawrence to whom the whole building is dedicated. The said Saint was, for maintaining certain religious opinions, cruelly broiled upon a gridiron. Therefore, the building is in the shape of a gridiron. The statue of the Saint stands upon one, and representations of this article of kitchen furniture are scattered profusely throughout the building. The pile is of immense size; it has within it twenty squares. The cathedral and Convent are in the very heart of it and it is so arranged that there is not a good room throughout the building. The Mausoleum of the Kings and Queens of Spain is of marble and the stones are four in each and face of an octagon.

The pictures, tapestry, etc. have been removed to Madrid by Joseph, who never inhabited the Escorial. It is a lonely place and the Guerrillas infested the neighbourhood.

I had got upon my horse to ride back when I was desired to go to a villa in the garden; I was tired to death of corridors, quadrangles, etc., with the simplicity of princes, and the duplicity of monks — in short, I was much disappointed, as I had expected to see the finest place in the world, and found a huge ill-planned mass. The exterior of the villa resembles very much an English one, such as you see six miles from London. The interior was simple. It stood in a garden, and there was a little pool with golden fish. You can form no idea of the interior; it was enchantment. The ceilings were vaulted and painted in the Arabesque style, but more beautiful than you can imagine — it was on oil cloth.

Each room was done on a different pattern. The passages and staircase were of marble, different sorts inlaid. The doors and floors of different woods inlaid. I was with a person who had travelled over the whole continent, had resided in Italy where this sort of thing is not uncommon, and who is an excellent judge of pictures. He said he had no conception that that style of painting could be carried to the height, that it must have been done by some eminent painter, whom the command of a King alone, could make descend to that style. There was an admirable dining room and about eight other small rooms on each floor. If I live to be as old as Methuselah I shall never forget it and shall always connect the idea of the villa at the Escorial and fairy land. Excuse my raving but I am mad about it. I am sorry to say that we burned a great part of the park. Everything now is so dried up that the least spark catches fire, nor is it possible to extinguish it till it dies a natural death by meeting with a road or a wall. At this season of the year it happens not infrequently that the whole country round a camp is on fire. I have arrived so nearly at the end of my legitimate paper that I must conclude without giving you an account of Madrid, or make you pay double for it. As I have no doubt but that you will like to hear some account of this celebrated city I shall go on. Lord Wellington I before told you, entered it on the 12th. Our division did not come up till the 14th, and is bivouacked close to the town under the tress of a public walk. I have got into a small house. I must begin by prefacing that a person who for three months has been incessantly marching and living under tress, (if he could be lucky to find them), who has been worried and harassed till he is almost mad, is naturally inclined to look at the bright side of a town, to think it rich because he sees all sorts of shops, which he has not seen since he left Lisbon, and to think the women pretty because they are not so sunburnt as to conceal their features. I will however give you a true account.

The different entrances are nearly the same, double rows of trees for a quarter of a mile upon the roads and magnificent arches under which you pass, for they can hardly be called gates as the town is not walled. There are several entrances, all equally fine, no houses nodding over your head but all upon the grand scale — no buildings that would be better away, which give an idea either of a want of power to command, or wealth to purchase. An Englishman is forcibly struck with the grandeur of the appearance before he sets his foot in the town. There are magnificent fountains at the gates; Neptunes in cars, the waters foaming from the mouths of the horses and other devices. The streets are broad and long, the houses of the Nobility magnificent. The principal streets have piazzas under which are shops of all sorts. I will now proceed to give you an account of the wonders, beginning with the Bon Retiro, a large fort, formerly the Palace, but of late years it has been converted into a citadel. Joseph, on his departure, left a garrison consisting of seventeen hundred men in it. On the 13th it was summoned and invested. On the 14th it surrendered without having fired a shot, or our having thrown up a single work. I can account for it in no other manner than that the Governor was bought. The garrison obtained no other terms than they would have done if a breach was practicable, and without the loss of a man we obtained sole possession of Madrid, eighty pieces of cannon, stores of all sorts complete to an extraordinary amount, and clothing for 50,000 men. I went to see the garrison march out — it was a curious sight. The Governor sneaked out, being afraid he should be shot by his men. The soldiers were picked men and as fine as I ever saw. Most were drunk, some danced, some cried and tore their hair and abused their officers. All abused the Spaniards and I heard nothing of the sort applied to us. On the contrary, every man said something, some asked for the road to London, others said they had much rather be prisoners than remain in Spain. In short, such a scene you cannot imagine. They of course helped themselves handsomely to their own stores, each man having on his back as much as he could carry.

Before I go any further I must tell you that the reception we have met with has been cordial to a degree. The town has been illuminated for three nights. The houses are all decorated with tapestry, silks with the family arms; velvet embroidered curtains are hung out of all the balconies. The grandee and the peasant seem alike to show their zeal. The men and women (particularly the latter) hug us in the streets and call us their preservers. Wherever we go, "Viva los Inglesas" resounds.

Now though there might be humbug in all this some very material points are gained. First, one would have thought that the fear of the return of the French would have made them cautious, as they would certainly smart if they did. Second and thirdly, it shows clearly that they detest the Yoke, for the French have been established here four years, have considered it as their capital, have carried on a form of Government and must have had sufficient time to form interests. And yet Madrid on the first opportunity shows the most decided aversion and openly gives us the most unequivocal proofs of their sentiments. I never have been sanguine with respect to the Spaniards. They once made an attempt to recover their King; it was feeble, failed and they thought they had done their duty and enough, since which a few guerrillas and an army which now and then appears have been magnified into great exertions. They thought we had the worst of it. The late successes have made them think once more of their situation. They see the English army victorious and enter their capital, they think the tables are turned and I think they will once more make an attempt. If they do I think I shall see you ere long; our army is flushed with success and would take a good deal of beating. By proclamation the estates of all those persons who have gone off with the French are confiscated. Amongst the number are some of the noblesse.

The Royal Palace, a modern building, stands at the entrance of the town from Segovia. It is enormously large, and the finest building I ever saw. The suites of rooms are fitted with pictures, and the furniture beyond description brilliant. You know I am no judge of paintings, and the person who showed me knew nearly as little. They are entirely selected from the best Masters — all those from the Escorial have been brought here. Amongst others the Madonna with the fish. There are a vast quantity of rooms entirely filled. I understand that so large a collection of fine pictures exists but in Paris. Lord Wellington lives in the Palace but does not touch the pictures, considering them the property of Ferdinand. The Academy is a collection of pictures, natural curiosities and sculpture. From the following specimen you will see that it is worth seeing; Judgement of Paris, Rubens, Diana at the Bath, the Graces, Bacchanals, Apollo and Daphne, Atalanta Coracci; Transfiguration, Raphael, The Sharpers, The Titian Venus with a portrait of himself, in short, there are none but by Masters of the greatest celebrity. The collection is not as large but more complete than at the Palace. There are about fifteen rooms filled with curious specimens, amongst other things a drinking cup of solid topaz, and a lump of gold weighing sixteen pounds. There are several rooms filled with sculpture. The country house belonging to Joseph is just opposite where we are encamped; there are some extremely fine pictures in it.

The palace of Godoy, Prince of Peace, is now inhabited by the Quartermaster General and is not to be seen. The collection there is very fine. I think the furniture of the Spanish Palaces far superior to ours. The ceilings are all painted. There are in the palace and Academy several pictures by Murillo, a Spanish painter whose works are thought so highly of that they are prohibited from being exported.[1]

On the 15th the Supreme Authorities gave a Ball to Lord Wellington, the invitations the same as at Salamanca. There were about three thousand persons present. The rooms as you may imagine were large. The women were dressed

[1] JM was to inherit some pictures, attributed doubtfully to Murillo (1618-1682), from his brother, Francis, the art connoisseur and who left his collection to JM.

precisely as at a Ball in England. A great many diamonds. In the morning the Spanish women wear large veils which they put on most gracefully, indeed, it would be worth while for the English ladies to learn of them, excepting that I see no difference in the dress. In the evening they are dressed as you are. They waltz extremely well. They dance figure dances and country dances — the former they excel in I think. They move their arms most gracefully. You will begin to think I am likely to fall in love with them. I could do such a thing to be sure as I think there are a great number of pretty women here. But I am in one respect too much of an Englishman to be pleased easily for they consume a great deal of garlic. In other respects they are delightful and you may meet with those who do not use that same vegetable. There is a naivety about them that is very pleasing and none of the reserve so peculiar to Englishwomen. Entering their capital as we have done with flying colours, and our enemy flying before us, you may imagine is a great advantage. They make much of us and all mortals you know are tickled by flattery.

They have two opera houses open but neither singers nor dancers or actors of any celebrity. The best singer has taken her departure with the French. They dance the bolero and fandango well. The latter the Spaniards are peculiarly fond of and dance in the streets.

An Englishman talks of the fine appearance of London of the streets, etc. A foreigner is I believe generally disappointed. He sees no handsome entrance, no fine streets and no public walks. The Turnpike at Hyde Park Corner, Portland Place, and the Mall do not appear extraordinary to him, as every town of importance in Spain can show better specimens of each. The Parade here is one of the finest public walks in Europe. It is filled of an evening with well dressed people, and much as is thought of Kensington Gardens on a Sunday, a greater number of persons are collected here every evening, and the walk is not mentioned in the same day.

Joseph appears to be an inoffensive man, heartily tired of his kingdom and retained only by the positive order of Bonaparte. He has raised a considerable contribution throughout the country but has paid regularly for everything. The Spaniards speak well of him but abuse Sebastiani and other Generals who have acquired vast wealth by plunder.[1] They consider all their misfortune brought on by Godoy (the Prince of Peace) and the Queen. I have now told you all I know of Madrid, and I am sorry to say we leave it tomorrow with the 4th and 5th Divisions for the Escorial where we are to be cantoned.

Lord Wellington remains here, as do the 3rd and 7th Divisions. You may imagine that we do not like the thought of leaving it, however, we are thankful for seeing as much as we have done. Our future operations must now depend

[1] Napoleon's younger brother, Joseph, had assumed the Spanish throne somewhat reluctantly from Marshal Murat in 1808. He assumed the position of commander-in-chief in Spain in May 1812 but lacked his brother's genius for war. 'Uncle Joe', as the Spaniards called him, was never really liked by them but one suspects there was a good deal of grudging respect for him. He showed a great deal of good sense on an administrative level whilst in Spain and was never the ruthless sort of despot that one might have expected from a king forced upon an unwilling population.

upon the enemy. Marmont is endeavouring to rally his broken army but the most important force they have is the army of Drouet and Suchet.[1] A month will now decide a great deal and if as the Bayonne papers give us to suspect, they have met with reverses in the north, I think it not impossible but they may give up the contest in the Peninsula. I really hope that it will not be very long ere we meet, and if the severity of our service is trebled I shall still not grumble, if, I think it will in the smallest degree accelerate our return to England.

As this is quite a pamphlet in size, will you send it to Charlotte? I will by the next mail write to thank her for her letter of the 23rd of July which I have just received. I am glad to hear so good an account of all of her family.

Lord Wellington drives in the state coach with six mules, always accompanied by two or three of the prettiest. Beckford is still at Salamanca from ill health. Agues and fevers the common diseases of this country have obliged no less than nine officers of this regiment to leave us. I must now conclude. Give my kindest love to my Father, Sisters and all others who may be with you.

August 18. We marched to the Ponte de Ratamar, 2½ leagues, and bivouacked. I went round to the park as I knew there were some deer there. I saw three but could not get a shot at them.

August 19th. To the Escorial. Two Brigades of our Division were put into the Palace. The 5th Division were in some other buildings. I bivouacked in the Park.

August 20th. The 7th Division marched in this morning. There are now here the 1st, 4th, 5th and 7th Divisions, besides two Brigades of Portuguese. The town is like a barrack. I go into parade and get out again as fast as I can. My bivouac is quite retired and I am not in the least annoyed by the troops. I walked to the Casa del Campo, and admired and envied it. Bivouacked.

August 21st. There was to have been a masquerade at Madrid on the 19th. Don Carlos d'España ordered it to be put off on the grounds of it being a French amusement and pernicious to the morals of the people. The real reason I understand was that Lord Wellington proposed attending it, and it was thought that someone in the French interest might take advantage of so favourable an opportunity of terminating his Lordship's existence, though he himself had no such apprehensions. Bonnet has assumed the command of Marmont's army during the indisposition of the latter. He has moved to Valladolid with 15,000 men and our cavalry has been driven across the Douro. The 5th Division marched from here to reinforce General Clinton who has retired upon Olmedo. Bivouacked.

August 22nd. The merchants of Madrid have advanced 300,000 dollars to be repaid in thirty days, which will make an issue of a fortnight's pay to the army.

[1] The French army, now commanded by Clausel in Marmont's absence, had retreated to Burgos. Clausel's men, in spite of being numerically superior to Wellington's, were still suffering from the shock of their rout at Salamanca. Drouet had joined Soult who abandoned the siege of Cadiz on August 25th 1812 and together they retired east towards Valencia. Suchet, meanwhile, could never really be ignored by Wellington but, as he spent the Peninsular War embroiled in operations along the eastern coast of Spain, he was never really a threat.

Joseph has retired from Aranjuez on the road to Valencia, having broken the bridge over the Tagus. His Spaniards are deserting fast and the army is ill-supplied. Bivouacked.

August 23rd. Captain Dyneley of the Horse Artillery, who was taken prisoner at Rosas on the 11th, has made his escape. He took advantage of a mutiny in which a regiment of German cavalry was obliged to charge some infantry, and walked off. The French General behaved very well to him, and gave him fifty dollars, having been plundered of his own. He supped with the general the night of the affair, and got champagne and every luxury.[1] He says that there are a vast number of persons in the French interest who have left Madrid and are following the army. At night the carriages form square and the troops encamp round them. The distress from want of money and provisions is very great. Bivouacked.

August 24th. General Maitland has landed in Catalonia with 10,000 men from Cadiz. If well managed it will form a powerful diversion in our favour.[2] As three officers per regiment are allowed to go to Madrid, Allix, Bradshaw and myself applied for leave and agreed to start early tomorrow.

August 25th. We started at three o'clock and got to the Golden Fountain at Madrid by eight. I breakfasted and attempted to lie down but was assailed by such hosts of bugs, notwithstanding the bedsteads were of iron, that I was obliged to get up again. We found that we had unfortunately missed a Ball given last night at the Palace by Lord Wellington. I went over the Palace again, principally with a view of seeing a picture of Joseph's wife and two children by David, a pleasing painting. I measured the State Room about 93 feet by 34 which is not very correct proportion. In the evening I walked on the Prado which was not very full. Two English officers astonished the people in a tandem. The Play in the evening was taken from an English afterpiece, miserable as usual. They have now put a sentry behind the scenes to prevent persons from going through. Therefore, I never intend going near the House again. Bivouacked.

August 26th. A Bull fight was to have taken place today, but was postponed in consequence of Lord Wellington's intention of going to Toledo, which he too has postponed. There is something extremely pleasant in the dress of the Spanish women. They wear chiefly black gowns, the sleeves and the bodices of different colours. They walk extremely well. I had not money enough to buy Lopez's maps which are published here. They are in 102 sheets and cost bound up to 25 dollars — at Salamanca they asked 30.[3] The stores which were in the

[1] Dyneley's letters were published in *Proceedings of the Royal Artillery Institution*, Vol.23, 1896, under the heading 'Letters written by Lieut.-General Thomas Dyneley, CB, RA, while on active service between the years 1806 and 1815,' and were edited by Colonel F.A. Whinyates, RHA. In 1984 they were published by Ken Trotman in a single volume. His own very graphic account of his capture can be read on pages 42-43. On pages 50-51 of the same book he recounts the story of his escape along with another British prisoner, Bombadier Morgan, who had been taken along with Dyneley at Majalahonda.

[2] See also JM's letter to his father, August 10th 1812.

[3] A good map of Spain and Portugal was, of course, an essential part of every officer's campaign equipment. The best and most widely used maps were those printed

Retiro have been so plundered that but little remain. It was intended to have
served some of them out to the army. Major Pierrepont is just come from Salamanca where he has been employed in taking a plan of the fields of battle.[1] He
found a French officer lying wounded five days after the action, not having
during that time tasted anything. Several wounded persons were found who
had lain even longer than that. The corn was standing and it was not possible to
find them all. Few if any were buried and the stench was quite pestilential —
such are the horrors of war. Don Carlos has issued orders for forming eight
regiments of Madrid Militia, each regiment consisting of 800, besides which
there is to be a regiment of cavalry. I am glad to see anything like a stir amongst
them, though I should not think that the Militia would be very capital. The
weather is so systematically hot that I am obliged to have recourse to quantities
of iced lemonade which they make here extremely well.

August 27th. The bugs have tormented me so much during my stay here that I
shall be glad to get into my own bed again. I started at six o'clock and returned
home at eleven, well pleased with my journey, but not sorry to return.

August 28th. An order has come out in consequence of some officers of the 1st
Division having spread a report that the Division is ill-quartered at the Escorial.
Whoever spread the report is, if found out, to be put under arrest — a specimen
of liberty. The foraging parties were fired upon by the Spaniards and two or
three Portuguese hit. These fellows and the Germans plunder to a great extent.

by López and Faden. The famous 'Lopez' map of Spain had been published by Don
Tomás López from 1765 onwards, each sheet covering a single province. William Napier
paid twenty guineas for his copy. See Bruce (Ed), *The Life of Sir William Napier*, I, 109.
The atlas of López's maps had been published in England by William Faden and was the
most popular map amongst British officers serving in the Peninsula. It had to be pasted
upon canvas before being used and when joined together its four sheets were said to be
able to fill 'a moderate sized room'. See Warre, *Letters from the Peninsula, 1808-1812*,
p.116. Four sheets of the map, used by John Burgoyne in the Peninsula, and still contained
in their slip case, are in the possession of the Royal Engineers Museum, Brompton. Sir
John Moore carried Faden's map with him during the Corunna campaign. See Ward's
Wellington's Headquarters, pp.103-106 for more detail on the maps of the age.

[1] Major C.A. Pierrepont was a former captain in the 20th Regiment before being
appointed Deputy Assistant Quartermaster General in April 1811. He was promoted to
major on the Permanent Staff and Assistant Quartermaster General in July 1811. Pierrepont,
who was later killed in the attack on the hornwork at Burgos on September 19th 1812,
was one of a group of officers, mainly from the Staff Corps, who were employed in
sketching the battlefields and the country while the war was actually in progress. By the
end of 1810 Portugal had been surveyed by these officers on a scale of four miles to the
inch. The results of these officers' labours, and those of a Captain Mitchell, who lived in
Spain and Portugal to complete them after the war had ended, can be seen in James
Wyld's monumental *Atlas containing principal battles, sieges and affairs of the Peninsular
War*, published in London in 1841. Wellington's reliance on the maps of Faden and López
was somewhat eased as a result of the labours of these officers. The French commanders,
on the other hand, suffered from a lack of detailed knowledge of the ground. They could
not and dare not send out their own officers to carry out similar surveys of the land as a
result of the activities of the guerrillas. It was dangerous enough sending despatches
back and forth without risking officers' lives sketching the land. The important subject of
military topography demands a study in itself. See also Ward's *Wellington's Headquarters*,
pp.108-114.

They form themselves into parties of twenty or thirty and scour the country round for two leagues. I have no doubt but that they were on this occasion committing some such depredations on the pretence of getting forage. Bivouacked.

August 29th. An order for us to march tomorrow to Guadarrama on our road to Arevalo arrived. I should have liked to have remained here a little longer, though I dare say I shall not be long in finding another tree as good as the one I have got.

Escorial
August 29th 1812

My Dear Elizabeth,

I am bound to write you a letter in return for a very long one I received from you after your return from Breamore.[1] At the same time I am afraid you will lose your eyesight in deciphering the numerous pamphlets I have lately written. The division marches tomorrow on its way to Arevalo, where General Clinton is with a corps of observation. Bonnet has assumed the command of Marmont's army and is I believe trying to advance upon Salamanca. I believe that Headquarters will remain at Madrid and that no others but ourselves will move. I am sorry to leave this place as it is near Madrid, to which place I have made a trip for three days, again admired its wonders and lamented the fall of a nation once so great. The stately mien of both men and women gives the appearance of an independence which you do not see amongst even the higher orders in England. The dress of the women is extremely becoming. The long veil which comes over the shoulders behind will make me remember them should I see again in England a lady in a habit and a thing called a veil tied on to a black hat.[2] They wear black petticoats, the body and sleeves of some other colour and as they pique themselves on walking well are very particular about their shoes. Though I am in love with their dress and manners I have as yet not lost my heart; that is, I have it still and can call it my own, though I have had some narrow escapes. But as you might be prejudiced against a Spanish sister-in-law I shall not dwell upon the black hair, piercing eyes and elegant form. I suppose you would be curious to know more. When we have driven the French across the Pyrenees and you see me with one arm cut off in the interesting part, neither too high to be a stump, or too low to look vulgar, I will take a walk to this place when I shall get my forty pounds per annum.[3]

The Papers to the 6th have reached us, containing the flying reports of the 22nd. I am sorry they are so exaggerated, as you will have been disappointed. An officer whom I saw the other day tells me that going over the ground five days after, he found a French officer wounded, who had been lying there all the time, without having tasted water. Others were found after that

---

[1] Breamore, Hampshire, is twelve miles north of Bisterne. Elizabeth had probably been visiting the Hulse family at Breamore House.

[2] JM is describing riding dress as still worn by ladies riding side saddle.

[3] JM is referring here to the £40 disability pension.

time. None of the bodies had been buried and the air was quite pestilential. If Russia does anything, the event of that will be of the utmost importance. Joseph has got into Valencia, where I suppose he will remain till he can look about him a little. I hear of no news from the south excepting that there is an idea that the siege of Cadiz will be raised — it is merely an idea I believe.[1]

The different French corps seem to be at sixes and sevens, and not to have recovered their astonishment. Headquarters remain at Madrid. Lord Wellington has borrowed three hundred thousand dollars of the good people of Madrid, to be repaid in thirty days — should his Lordship move they will begin to quake. I think their liberality ill-judged, for should the tables turn Joseph will know where to borrow money. The numerous tribes of verse makers, and caricaturists, will have reason to lament their wit, as the French, though good judges, may not exactly admire them. In short, with one act or another they will find themselves awkwardly situated.

Lord Wellington gave a ball at the palace on the 24th, extremely well regulated and the natives highly delighted. There was to have been a masquerade in the town but the Governor countermanded it on the grounds of it being a French amusement. The fact of the matter was that he was afraid someone in the French interest might take advantage of so favourable an opportunity for assassinating his Lordship, though he himself had no such fears, nor is he troubled with any of the sort, for the day that the Retiro surrendered he walked up and down with the Governor close to the place, trying to persuade him to give in, which he did not then succeed in doing. I am afraid he will be hit some day or other, as no-one runs greater risks; as yet he has never been touched.[2] Lady Wellington would be jealous if she were to hear of his proceedings. I never saw him in his carriage without two or three ladies.[3] His audience room is crowded

[1] The siege of Cadiz was raised on August 25th 1812.

[2] Wellington was never one to delegate responsibility while in the field and this extended to the battlefield. He was often in the thick of the fighting and had the uncanny knack of being in the right place at the right time during moments of crisis. At Waterloo, for example, he appeared at the scenes of crises on more than one occasion and during the final attack of Napoleon's Old Guard he appears to have assumed command of Maitland's Foot Guards. 'The finger of Providence was upon me', he later said when asked about his remarkable survival during the battle. He did not come through the Peninsular War totally unscathed, however, and was struck by a bullet on more than one occasion. At Orthes he was hit by a ball which drove the hilt of his sword into his hip, causing some bleeding and laying him low for a few days. On July 27th 1809, on the morning of the first day of the battle of Talavera, he narrowly avoided capture whilst carrying out a reconnaissance from the top of the Casa de Salinas. A Sorauren, on July 28th 1813, he just managed to evade the clutches of some French dragoons who entered the village at one end as he galloped off out of the other after dashing off a despatch to Murray. Wellington had similar close shaves at Castrejon, on July 18th 1812, and at Quatre Bras, two days before Waterloo, when he and his horse, Copenhagen, were forced to leap into a square of the 92nd Highlanders with French cavalry in hot pursuit.

[3] Wellington was indeed a great favourite with the ladies. Whilst in Paris at the end of the war he was frequently seen in the company of such beauties as the Duchess of Duras, Juliette de Récamier and Madame de Staël. Foremost amongst Wellington's female 'friends' was the Italian opera singer, Guiseppina Grassini, who was frequently

in the morning with persons bringing petitions and though I have two or three times passed the room I never saw any male petitioners, and I am informed that the prayers of the fairest are always sooner attended to than those of the others. But perhaps it is all fancy. I was very much struck with a thing which I have seen in Lisbon and other places, but never to the extent it is practised in Madrid. Innumerable women and children are seen in the streets selling water at half-penny a glass. The persons who buy it are of the lower orders; in no place have I ever seen so many fountains, to which one would think they might apply — such is the laziness of the people.

We have heard of General Maitland having landed in Catalonia with 10,000 men from Sicily, and the communication with him is open. This reinforcement will be very seasonable as I am afraid we cannot look upon any great numbers from England. There are now 13,000 British in the different hospitals, and this campaign has put a great many hors de combat. I should think the utmost force that Lord Wellington would bring into the field independent of General Hill would be 23,000.[1]

You must give my kindest love to my father, Mother and the rest of the family. John Mills.

seen on Wellington's arm. It is rumoured that he moved his headquarters in the Peninsula on more than one occasion at the prospect of attractive female company but moved it again when the information proved incorrect. In Brussels, during the Waterloo campaign, Wellington outraged certain sections of society by his behaviour. 'The Duke of Wellington has not improved the *morality* of our society, as he has given several things and makes a point of asking all the ladies of loose character.' (Anglesey (Ed), *The Capel Letters*, p.102.) Perhaps it is not surprising that his own marriage to the unhappy Kitty Pakenham was a sad affair.

[1] This is a most accurate estimate by JM. When Wellington left Madrid on August 31st, bound for Arevalo, he had sent ahead of him the 1st, 5th and 7th Divisions, Pack's and Bradford's Portuguese brigades, and Bock's and Ponsonby's cavalry, altogether numbering 23,000 men. See Weller, *Wellington in the Peninsula*, p.234. Although this is not the total number of troops Wellington could muster it is, nevertheless, the exact number with which Wellington began his march north-east towards Burgos.

Chapter Six

Débâcle at Burgos

After an enjoyable two weeks' stay at Madrid JM marched north-east to Burgos to lay siege to the town. The experienced stormers of the 4th, 3rd and Light Divisions, the heroes of Badajoz, were to take no part in the operation but remained behind and thus it was that Burgos, the last resting place of the legendary Spanish hero, El Cid, was not to go the way of Ciudad Rodrigo and Badajoz. This is no reflection upon the conduct of the Foot Guards and, indeed, Wellington later singled them out for praise. But the whole operation was flawed from the start, something which Wellington later recognised was his own fault. The siege material was in short supply, sappers and miners were, once again, non existent, and, worse still, there was a woeful lack of adequate siege guns.

The castle of Burgos itself was by no means as tough as the former two citadels to fall into Wellington's hands but its situation, perched as it was upon a high hill and having three lines of defences, made the place a very awkward customer. This, coupled with the fact that the castle was stoutly defended by a determined garrison and its resourceful commander, Dubreton, was to ensure that the castle of Burgos remained free of Wellington's clutches. The failure to take the place resulted in one of the worst disasters of the war, the retreat to Portugal, but first we must join JM on the road through the Guadarrama Pass on the road to Burgos itself.

August 30th. Marched to Guadarrama, 2 leagues, and bivouacked. The Governor and garrison of Guadalajara, amounting to 700, passed through here two days ago on their way to England. They surrendered to the Spaniards after the fall of Madrid. We hear that Castaños who had been so long besieging Astorga had at length got possession of it by capitulation, but that on the following day a French force appeared and has been obliged to leave the place.[1]

August 31st. Marched to Villacastin, 5 leagues, and got under cover. The Guadarrama pass is better coming from than going to Madrid. The troops passing to and fro have been careless in lighting their fires and in consequence the whole hill is burnt.

September 1st. Instead of getting up at daylight to shoot, I got up to march to St Chidrian, 3 leagues, where we got under cover. The country about here puts me a good deal in mind of Portugal, hilly and rocky. The rocks in some places are most curiously placed, large fragments standing on each other. They look as if the lightest touch would throw them down.

September 2nd. Marched to Arevalo, 4 leagues. The road from Madrid and Valladolid meet here. We found the 5th and 6th Divisions in the town and we were consequently very much crowded. By great good luck I got into a house with Allix. General Wheatley died today at the Escorial of an intermitting fever.[2]

September 3rd. Headquarters came in today from St Chidrian and the Divisions were moved out and bivouacked to make room for them. There is more confusion and fuss about quarters with these gentry than with the whole army besides. I remained, and by these means got a day's halt. It appears that Soult has issued a proclamation on evacuating Andalusia wherein he states his confidence in the Spaniards and leaves the defence of that part of the country to them. It is also believed that the siege of Cadiz has been raised. Castaños having heard that Foy was advancing rapidly upon him to raise the siege of Astorga, sent away all his heavy guns in the night, continuing his operations as if nothing had happened. The French surrendered the next day and they had just time to get the prisoners out and retire when Foy made his appearance. Sir Howard Douglas who has for some time been in Galicia on a species of Military Diplomacy is arrived here from thence. He represents the Spaniards as being very active but fears that our late brilliant successes have made them jealous of us. There are a vast number of Guerrillas in the north who will harass the French a good deal.

September 4th. Marched to a wood near Olmedo, 5 leagues. The general opinion seems to be that we are going to drive the French from Valladolid as far

[1] The garrison of Guadalajara surrendered to the guerrilla leader, Don Juan-Martin Diaz, El Empecinado, on August 15th. Commanded by General de Prieux, it consisted of some 900 men of the Royal-Étranger and Royal-Irlandais, two regiments of foreigners in French service. Astorga capitulated to Castaños on August 18th, with the relieving force under Foy just thirty-six hours away.

[2] Major General William Wheatley actually died at the Escorial Palace on September 1st 1812. He had commanded a brigade with distinction at Barrosa and commanded a brigade of the 1st Division at Salamanca until his death. His letters appeared in Vol. LVIII, 1919, of *The United Services Magazine*, under the title, 'Letters from the Front, 1812,' edited by G.E. Hubbard.

north as we can get them and to return to Madrid to meet Soult who will be moving upon it. He is by far the best General the French have in the Peninsula, though he made a trip at Oporto in 1809.[1] The deserters who have come in say that on the appearance of our columns, three guns are to be fired as signals to the different posts to retire. The siege of Cadiz is certainly raised. Bivouac wet and cold.

September 5th. We marched to Hornillos, 1½ leagues. This is a small village where the people either had or pretended to have fevers — it is a common trick on the approach of troops to get into bed and swear they have an infectious fever, hoping that no-one on hearing it will go into the house. A Mail from England brought us the Gazette of the battle of Salamanca and of the Marquisate conferred on Lord Wellington. He does not shine in his dispatches. They are so confusedly written that I defy anyone not present to make head or tail of them — he does not make the most of his business. We also hear that a Brigade of Guards, three Squadrons of the Horse Guards and three of the Blues are coming out. The forage of this country will not keep their tails in condition.[2] The Division bivouacked two miles farther on. I got into a house which was lucky as it rained.

                                                             Hornillos, near Olmedo
                                                             September 5th 1812

My Dear Charlotte,

We have just heard of the news of the victory being received in England and of the Marquisate bestowed upon Lord Wellington. I assure you that he is very proud of it and seems highly delighted.[3]

On the 29th the 1st, 5th, 6th and 7th Divisions started from the Escorial on an expedition against Marmont's army commanded by Bonnet. We hear this

[1] Marshal Nicholas Soult was surprised by Wellesley at Oporto on May 12th 1809. Having deployed his forces facing west in anticipation of an attack from that direction, he was shocked when news reached him of Wellesley's audacious crossing of the river right beneath his very nose. When first informed that parties of red-jacketed soldiers were seen on the French-held side of the river Soult merely suggested that they were Swiss, who also wore red, whereas they were, in fact, British troops of the 3rd Foot. Once the river had been crossed and a bridgehead established, more British came over and the town was as good as won. That evening Wellesley sat down to a dinner that had been prepared for Soult at the marshal's former headquarters. Following this successful operation Soult was forced to retreat from Portugal.

[2] The Brigade of Guards was, in fact, only the 1st Battalion 1st Foot Guards who arrived at Corunna on October 1st. The battalion joined Wellington's field army on October 24th and the following month the 3rd Battalion 1st Foot Guards, which had been marching up from Seville with Skerrett, joined the army also. Together, the two battalions formed the 1st Brigade of Guards. JM's jab at the Household Cavalry was not without foundation. These dandies, the cavalry equivalent of the Foot Guards, arrived in the Peninsula looking immaculate but almost immediately discarded their combs and brushes as being unnecessary items. Needless to say the appearance of these inexperienced troops changed quite dramatically over the coming months.

[3] Wellington became a marquess on August 18th 1812.

morning that he has retired from Valladolid towards Burgos to which place I have no doubt but that we shall follow him though the rogues will hardly dare to meet us again. The 3rd and Light Divisions are left as a garrison in Madrid and they have had the best of it, for we have had some rain and are likely to have more. The Marquis is just gone through to the front to reconnoitre.

Sir Howard Douglas[1] has come from Galicia where he has been for some time in the capacity of Military Diplomatist. He says that the Guerrillas there are very active, but thinks the Spaniards jealous of our late successes. It is like them, and I daresay is true. Soult has published a Proclamation on leaving Andalusia wherein he commits the care of that province to the Spaniards and at the same time withdraws from Cadiz. Thus the labours of three years are abandoned.

Affairs here look well, and if men can be spared from England we may do a great deal before Christmas. It is a busy time for us, but as there is a fair prospect of success we shall not grumble as we used to do about marching and countermarching in Portugal all about nothing.

I took a trip from the Escorial to Madrid, but was obliged to leave it before a grand Bull-fight which took place there in honour of Lord Wellington. I hear it was a magnificent sight. The fighters were on horseback and suffered no injury, though their horses were killed. I wrote so long an account of Madrid to my Mother that I shall not bore you by repeating it. The inhabitants were alarmed when they heard that Lord Wellington was leaving it, but their fears subsided on finding that two divisions were to remain, and on his telling them he should soon return. Joseph took great care of his princely self and never looked behind him till he got safe into Saragossa. He is not much of a soldier. In an intercepted letter he talks of disconcerting English phlegm and the slowness of our movements; he found us however too quick for him once. I really pity him — he has had a restless reign and would willingly give up his Kingdom and all it contains but his brother will not hear of it. He is quite a harmless man, the Spaniards say addicted to spirituous liquors — of this they have a great aversion. I never saw a Spaniard drunk, and when they see our soldiers in that state they lift up their hands. The above mentioned Prince was formerly a limb of the law.[2] I see many of the officers of the Artillery here, whom we used to see at Christchurch. The Miss Walcotts come always into my head upon these occasions.[3] They will be glad to hear of Captain Dyneley's escape for if I mistake not he was the Prince of Beaux. Mr Swabey has hitherto escaped me, but I dare say that he will turn up some day.[4]

Beckford has been very ill at Ciudad Rodrigo. He is obliged much against

[1] Sir Howard Douglas Bart. (1776-1861) British general and diplomat who was later Governor of New Brunswick, Commissioner of the Ionian Isles and MP.

[2] This 'limb of the law' reference is to Joseph Bonaparte who studied for the bar at Marseilles.

[3] The sisters of Yeomans Walcott, of the Royal Horse Artillery. See JM's letter, August 20th 1811.

[4] The diaries of Lieutenant William Swabey, Royal Artillery, were published in Woolwich in 1895, entitled, Diary of Campaigns in the Peninsula for the Years 1811, 12, and 13, and were edited by Colonel F.A. Whinyates.

his inclination to go to England for the recovery of his health.[1] Salamanca was so crowded with sick and wounded officers after the action that it was with the greatest difficulty they could get medical assistance. Some of our officers were obliged to sell their watches and other things to buy bread.

We are much amused at hearing that the Life Guards and Blues are coming out here. It will take a double allowance of corn to keep even their tails in condition, and I am afraid they will use the flat of their swords thinking they have to deal with a mob.[2]

The French Imperial Guards are not as fine, but I think their dress handsomer. They wear the old Roman helmet with horse hair hanging down. The dress of their infantry is very unbecoming. They wear coats very small and cut away.

We shall soon have a great deal upon our hands; Soult will no doubt make a push for Madrid and though General Hill will follow him he will not be strong enough to fight and, until we have disposed of the gentry before us, we cannot leave them as they would annoy our rear. Our game is in good hands and our men would face any number with confidence. Castanos, hearing that Foy was advancing rapidly upon him sent all his heavy guns away in the night. The garrison, knowing nothing of the matter, surrendered the next day and he had just time to get his prisoners out and his army on the march when Foy appeared. This was doing well.[3]

The letters you mention having written to me did not come both to hand. The one directed to me 'Spain' has not reached me. You must have taken me for some notorious character such as the leader of a forlorn hope. The one that did reach me came much sooner than those by the Regular Mail.

I must now conclude with desiring my respects to your honoured spouse, who will I hope let me hear what sport he has had in Dorsetshire this year — I hope better than last.[4]

Remember me kindly to the rest of your family. John Mills

September 6th. We marched to a wood on the right bank of the Douro, 5 leagues. This was a long and tedious day from four in the morning till five in the evening.

[1] Ensign Francis Love Beckford left the 1st Battalion Coldstream Guards on October 4th to return home on sick leave. He then spent the whole of 1813 in England on recruiting duties and resigned from the army on December 29th 1813. See Mackinnon, *Origin and Services of the Coldstream Guards*, II, 510.

[2] JM appears never to pass up the opportunity of poking fun at the Household Cavalry! After having joked earlier about the appearance of the cavalrymen he chooses to mock their role in the Peninsula. The Household Cavalry had seen no overseas service at all during the Napoleonic Wars but had remained at home where it had been used as a police force. The cavalry was used to put down riots and mutinies, the standard method being beating the miscreants with the flat of their swords.

[3] See JM's Journal for August 30th 1812.

[4] Henry Combe Compton's mother, Catherine Richards, was the heiress to the Mapperton and Winterborne Whitchurch estate in Dorset. Partridge shooting was the September sport.

At Boecillo the 1st, 5th and 7th Divisions were formed behind the hill. The enemy did not appear to have the smallest idea of our approach. The cavalry went forward and crossed the river without opposition. By the river side they took five men who were foraging. They advanced skirmishing and took a few prisoners. The three divisions crossed the river and advanced to within a mile of the village of Cisterniga where the enemy showed symptoms of resistance. They had constructed a fort on the left and their men were very advantageously posted on some hills and strong ground. Their videttes and ours were close to one another. I was glad to see my old friends and all the show of war. The 1st Division was ordered to attack the hills, to be supported by the 5th who had not come up, and before they did the enemy moved off, the greatest part of his force not leaving sufficient to make it worth our while to attack. We should on our way up there have been very much exposed to their guns which were on a commanding situation. At four o'clock they fired three guns as signals without shot so the deserters said true. At five o'clock things remained quiet and we moved off and bivouacked in a fir wood in our rear. The enemy appear to wish to gain time to get their sick, stores, etc., out of Valladolid. They do not seem to have had the slightest idea of our near approach. It seems strange that Lord Wellington did not push on — I much doubt whether they would have defended the village. At all events we could have forced it, and obliged them to hurry out of Valladolid which is not more than two miles from the village. They were employed during the whole night in getting their stores out of the town and carried off an immense quantity of corn and provisions in cars.

September 7th. At eight o'clock we marched to Cisterniga which the enemy had evacuated in the morning. We here saw an encampment of theirs for one regiment, the completest thing possible. The kitchens were arranged in a line, one for each company, and likewise stands for the arms of brick, neatly whitewashed. The huts were made of straw, there being nothing but fir wood near. The whole was the neatest thing of the sort I ever saw. After halting for half an hour in the village, we moved forward and came down (leaving Valladolid on our left) to the river Pisuerga, which is here broad and deep. The enemy were upon the opposite side; their columns halted for some time as if to have a good look at us, and then moved off with the greatest deliberation. They had destroyed the bridge and there is but one ford near here and that a very bad one. Nevertheless, it appeared as if we might have cut them off as the nearest road to Burgos is on this side of the river and we were much surprised that an order arrived to halt and bivouac on the ground we occupied. The inhabitants of Valladolid showed rather more joy this time than when we were last here. They may feel more confident now as our troops are in the town which was not the case last time. However, they are certainly very much in the French interests.

September 8th. The news of General Hulse's death arrived from Arevalo. It is extraordinary that General Wheatley and himself began their acquaintance at school which continued during the remainder of their lives. They entered the Guards at the same time and obtained their rank together. They were appointed the one to the first and the other to the second Brigade of Guards, the object of their ambitions, though neither lived to receive the intelligence. They were taken ill within a few days and died of typhus fever. In General Hulse the service has lost a most valuable officer. He was the man of greatest promise in this army and had he lived he would have risen to greatness. His Brigade had voted him a sword for his gallant conduct at the Battle of Salamanca, a testimony never before conferred upon any officer in this country. His loss will be severely felt.[1] It appears that Santocildes with his army is moving upon the enemy's rear and that we are waiting till he has accomplished it.[2] The reports of the enemy's strength vary much. They certainly do not seem to have more than eighteen thousand — ours is rather under that. They are going off to Burgos. The town was illuminated at night and every usual demonstration of joy exhibited. I did not go out to see it as I was persuaded it was not sincere.

Valladolid
September 8th 1812

My Dear Father,

We pursued our march from Madrid through Arevalo and on the 6th came to the village of Boecilla, two leagues from Valladolid where we found that the enemy had not the least suspicion of our approach. The cavalry crossed the difficult fords of the Douro without opposition and took some foragers, and had a small affair — some skirmishing ensued. The fords are so bad that the three divisions (1st, 5th and 6th, the 7th being a day's march in the rear) were some time crossing. We moved on to within a league of Valladolid and about a mile from Cisterniga. Here the enemy had thrown up a work and drawn his men up upon some very advantageous ground. The 1st Division was ordered to attack, supported by the 5th. We waited half an hour for that division which was longer fording the river than it ought to have been. In the meantime the enemy had withdrawn part of his force and as they seemed inclined to go off quietly Lord Wellington thought it better to let them go.

Yesterday morning they abandoned Cisterniga, into which we marched and found they had left Valladolid crossing the river Pisuerga, having destroyed the bridge. We moved down to the river which is not fordable for infantry and

[1] Both Wheatley and Hulse did indeed die on the same day, September 7th 1812. William Wheatley had been commissioned in the 1st Foot Guards on June 23rd 1790, while Richard Hulse had been commissioned in the Coldstream Guards on March 24th of the same year. Their deaths were recorded in a despatch from Wellington to the Duke of York, regarding the command of the two Brigade of Guards. (*Despatches*, Wellington to The Duke of York, 7th September 1812, IX, 399–401.)

[2] Wellington was exasperated by the conduct of Santoclides between September 12th and 16th. On September 12th he wrote to his brother, Henry, saying, 'Santoclides has been six days marching. He was yesterday within three leagues of us, and knew it last night, but he has this morning moved to Valladolid, eight leagues from us, and unless I halt two days for him, he will not join us for four or five days. Then, out of 30,000 men that they feed in Galicia, he has only brought 11,000 infantry and 350 cavalry to join us.' (Despatches, Wellington to Henry Wellesley, 12th September 1812, IX, 422.) Santoclides did not join Wellington's army until September 16th and the pressure on Clausel's retreating army was eased slightly.

looked at them. They seemed to know our predicament and took themselves off with imaginable coolness. We halted there and have not marched on today though we expect it tomorrow. It is quite impossible to judge of the Marquis's intentions. On the 6th he might have got upon them or at all events might have hurried them out of Valladolid. They were employed during the whole night in conveying stores out, which would have fallen into our hands, and even yesterday we could by running for it have cut off their retreat by Burgos, as the nearest road is on this side of the river. However, today's halt has given them a start which we cannot make up. Their force looks to be about twenty thousand; ours, with the 7th Division which is come up is about the same including cavalry. Santoclides, with some of his precious Spaniards, will be here tomorrow. The sight of the enemy again puts us all upon the alert. It is now some time since we had that pleasure.

Soult I fancy is certainly moving upon Madrid where we have left three divisions. His, Suchet's and Drouet's force united will make up fifty thousand, and if King Joseph can join him twenty more.[1] The raising the siege of Cadiz and abandoning Andalusia has given them a formidable force. They will now begin and manoeuvre us. We have had it all our own way since Salamanca and I am afraid it will prove that they are more frightened than hurt. The Marquis has the full confidence of his army and knows better than to get into a scrape. There will be a great deal of manoeuvring on both sides, and it will be the object of neither to risk a battle.

You will be extremely sorry to hear by the last accounts there are no hopes of General Hulse's life. He was seized about ten days ago with a fever and has been progressively worse ever since. When the last account came from Arevalo he had violent convulsions and twitchings, the almost certain forerunners of death. His loss as an individual will be nothing in comparison to that of an officer. There is no-one in this army that stands as high in the estimation of everyone. He had just had a sword voted to him by his brigade for his gallant conduct at Salamanca, which has been done to no-one before. General Wheatley died at the Escorial on the 1st; it is somewhat remarkable that they both entered the Guards together, were the greatest friends, rose to rank together, and Wheatley died of the same fever with precisely the same symptoms as Hulse. It is more extraordinary that by the last mail, Wheatley was appointed to the 1st and Hulse to the 2nd Brigade of Guards, the object of ambition of both. I have got thus far and find that the mail is either going or gone, and if I do not send it as it is I shall be too late. I will make up for it next mail.

September 9th. We halted for another day. News arrived of Colonel Skerrett's having entered Seville with his Division. The enemy defended themselves for some time in the street. A considerable quantity of stores has fallen into our

---

[1] The junction of the various French armies did not come about until October 1812, by which time Wellington's army was retreating to Portugal via Salamanca following his abortive siege of Burgos.

hands.[1] Our light dragoons have had some skirmishing in the front today and were driven back.

September 10th. To Trigueros, 4 leagues. The Division was delayed some time by the others crossing the river. The ford is deep but the bottom good and hard. The inhabitants were much delighted at seeing English troops for the first time. I was much pleased during my stay at the gardener's house near Valladolid to see their method of watering gardens. They have a large wheel round which are fastened earthen pots which throw up the water. The wheel is worked by mules and asses. The water runs off by one principal stream and is diverted to the different beds by one man. Everything is watered twice in the day. It is absolutely necessary in this hot climate, but I think it takes off from the flavour and makes them soft. We are getting into the vine country. Nothing now is to be seen but great tracts of vineyards. I gathered the first ripe grape today, much later than in Portugal last year. The cellars for the wine are built on the outside of the town and are hollowed out of the rocks. Some rain.

September 11th. To Villamuriel, 3½ leagues. The Division bivouacked near Dunnas, but the town was so crowded with General Officers that I went a league further and got in just in time to miss some very heavy rain. The inhabitants had suffered much from the French who carried off even their beds. They moved out from hence yesterday evening.

September 12th. We marched to the ground near Magaz where we bivouacked, 1 league. It seems that the slowness of our movements is in consequence of the backwardness of the Spaniards who are instead of advancing in the enemy's rear are retiring. We left Palencia on our left. It is a city and appears a good town but I could not go into it. Soon after we got upon our ground we had some rain which continued during the evening and night. The men had not a tree near them and were soaked with rain. The French are retiring slowly and our dragoons skirmish with them every day. Bivouacked.

September 13th. Marched to Torquemada, 2 leagues. Headquarters were in this place which is very much destroyed. The French have only the merit of putting a finishing stroke to it as the Spaniards did it themselves four years ago at the time of the Battle of Rio Seco.[2] Rain.

September 14th. To Quintana del Puente, 2 leagues. This place is most admirably destroyed but like the last, of four years standing. I never saw a town in Portugal so ruined. Schuster the messenger arrived in fourteen days from London by way of Corunna with dispatches. The French go off very leisurely —

[1] The siege of Cadiz had been abandoned by Soult on August 25th 1812 after two and a half years. The following day Skerrett attacked Seville. During the fighting the grenadier companies of the 1st Foot Guards and some Spanish troops stormed the gate of the suburb of Triana, driving the enemy before them. The French force consisted of some eight battalions of infantry and two regiments of cavalry but when the Guards burst in on their positions they were soon sent retreating towards Cordoba, leaving behind them their baggage, accumulated plunder and 200 prisoners.

[2] The battle of Medina del Rio Seco was fought on July 14th 1808 between 21,900 Spaniards, under Cuesta and Blake, and the 14,000-strong French army under Marshal Bessieres. The battle resulted in complete victory for the French who suffered just 500 casualties against 3,000 Spanish.

their rear guard never moves till they see the head of our columns. They then fire three guns as signals which are answered by three from the rear. General Clinton thought he had discovered that the bridge here was mined and loaded. They accordingly dug but no powder was discovered. More rain and no prospect of being able to get the troops under cover.

Quintana del Puente, 10 leagues from Burgos,
September 14th 1812

My Dear Charlotte,

A letter I received yesterday from my Mother informed me of the happy event in your family and I assure you that I am most truly rejoiced at it, though I believe it took none of us unawares.[1]

The straggling letter from you has at length arrived having made a tour to Greenwoods where the postage was paid, which was the reason of its not proceeding directly upon its travels.

The victory at Salamanca seems to have made as great an impression in England as could have been expected. To our cause it is of the most essential importance. It has opened the way into the heart of Spain and made our enemies quake. We cannot get them to look at us, do all we can. They are now retreating a day's march ahead of us with an army numerically superior. The guerrillas are close at them and annoy their stragglers. We think that Castaños is between us and Burgos, and if he is worth a rush he will make them stop till we can get up to them but he is a slippery chap and his men not great warriors. They have the opportunity and it is not our fault if they chose to be idle. At Burgos they have a very strong fort and great magazines, it being the only depot between Bayonne and Valladolid. We are prepared with everything to take it and have got with us grates for heating shot, which will set fire to their premises and astonish them not a little. Poor Hulse died at Arevalo on the 8th of typhus fever. His loss will be deeply felt as an individual and an officer. It is hard that one who had upon so many occasions distinguished himself should be carried off in that way. He would one day or other been a great man. It would have been comparative happiness had he died in the field. He was attended during the latter part of his illness by a surgeon of ours in whom he had the greatest confidence, but he came too late to be of any assistance.[2]

An English brigade under Colonel Skerrett has entered Seville after some

[1] The 'happy event' referred to by JM was the birth of Charlotte's eldest daughter, Catherine (1812-80), who was to marry first Admiral Aitchison and, on his death, Admiral of the Fleet Sir Henry Codrington. John Combe Compton, their first child, had died earlier in 1812.

[2] The 1st Battalion Coldstream Guards had two Assistant Surgeons serving at the time of Hulse's death. They were Thomas Rose and Edward Nixon. The battalion Surgeon, Charles Coombe, was, ironically, on sick leave in England at the time so it is likely that Hulse was attended by one of the two Assistant Surgeons. Thomas Rose became the battalion's Surgeon in July the following year.

opposition. Ballasteros has some Spaniards there and has the chief command. Lord Wellington said the other day that he was afraid he would think he might do anything with English troops and accordingly despatched an aide-de-camp with orders for him. The possession of Seville is very important apart from its being so considerable a town, for it connects the communication between the upper part of the country and Cadiz. Seville is as large as Madrid and is, I understand, a most beautiful town. There is great indignation amongst the inhabitants of this part of the country at the murder of Nisquinez, a guerrilla chief, by a French servant. He was the terror of this part of the country, that is he killed a great number of straggling Frenchmen. If you believe the accounts of the country people he has killed many thousands. I believe he was an active man. The guerrillas say they will not have Ferdinand the 7th for their King but will choose one of their own. They are right to keep the thing up for should affairs become quiet these gentry would be out of employment and could never turn their hands to anything like honest employment. Jack Early would be a good recruit.[1]

The weather is now so bad that campaigning is more than a joke. We are never under cover even of a shrub for this country is not favoured with anything bigger than a vine. The rain comes down in torrents. Headquarters and the staff are always snug in houses, and do not care about the weather and you must know that our Noble Marquis is not gifted with much feeling — ambition hardens the heart. He only regards the comforts of his men as far as it is actually necessary to his purposes; all have their faults and this is his.[2]

Our cavalry skirmish every day with the French rearguard who are not in a hurry to go off. It seems that the Spaniards who are in their rear are retiring without attempting to impede them, so that for all the good they do they might as well be in Portugal. However, they have promised to be in the way tomorrow.

We are much disappointed at Lord Wellington's dispatch; he has made as little of it as was possible and a story well told is you know half the battle. His Lordship may fight but hang me if he can write. He had a fine opportunity for a flourish in the turn which the charge of many cavalry gave to the day but he merely mentions the charge unadorned by comments.[3] In cases like these, simplicity loses its effect. The private letters are amusing. One man writes that had

[1] Jack Early was the Bisterne partridge poacher. See JM's letter, September 3rd 1811.

[2] This was, and still is, the perennial complaint of soldiers, ie, that the General and Staff Officers always got the best quarters whilst the soldiers doing the real fighting found themselves out in the open or in squalid quarters. See JM's Journal, April 16th 1812, regarding the billeting procedures in Wellington's army.

[3] JM is referring to Wellington's despatch to Lord Bathurst informing him of the victory at Salamanca. (*Despatches*, Wellington to Lord Bathurst, 24th July 1812, IX, 299-307.) It was, of course, virtually impossible for Wellington to submit anything more than a basic outline of each of his great victories and his Salamanca despatch was no different. His account of the actual fighting takes up four of the eight pages and when referring to Le Marchant's devastating charge he writes, 'The cavalry under Lieut. General Sir Stapleton Cotton made a most gallant and successful charge against a body of the enemy's infantry, which they overthrew and cut to pieces. In this charge Major General Le Marchant was

the hills been made of red hot iron our troops would have gained them — it would be hot work. But the most beautiful thing is an account of a woman who is stated to have found her husband amongst the heaps of dead — she did no such thing; the husband was a sorry sneak, and she was walking about the streets of Salamanca looking at the illuminations the night after. This amiable woman has since been married.[1] The accounts of the ci devant Miss Nolan are truly good. What an absolute Hottentot the man must be, deformed I dare say. It is a sad precedent, for no young lady will now despair. I daresay the remaining virgins will look well towards the west as the men seem to be simplest there. I would as soon have married a hun. I must now begin the conclusion. I will write to your rib by the next mail. Kindest love to all at Manor House.[2]

September 15th. Marched to Villodrigo, 2 leagues. Castanos arrived at Head-

killed at the head of his brigade; and I have to regret the loss of a most able officer.' Given the dramatic circumstances of Le Marchant's charge one has to say that Wellington's despatch does not do it justice. On the other hand, regarding the Foot Guards, Wellington does actually draw Bathurst's attention to their light companies, under Lieutenant Colonel Alexander Woodford, which held the village of Los Arapiles against repeated enemy attacks. Given the fact that only the light companies of the Foot Guards were involved in the actual fighting JM cannot complain about the credit given to his own regiment. However, he is not the only one to draw our attention to the lack of credit given in Wellington's despatches. For example, during the French sortie from Bayonne, on April 14th 1814, Hinüber's King's German Legion suffered 328 casualties in driving the French from St Etienne but received not a single mention in Wellington's despatch, something which caused much resentment amongst the Legion's officers. On April 24th 1814 John Rous, of the Coldstream, wrote, 'We are much disappointed at the way in which Lord Wellington mentioned the passage of the Adour by the 1st Division, and the taking of St Etienne....He does not mention the German Legion once.' (Fletcher (Ed), *A Guards Officer in the Peninsula*, p.117.) Hinüber actually wrote a letter of complaint to Wellington but was given short shrift by Pakenham, the Adjutant General, in reply. Colborne's successful action at Waterloo during the repulse of the Imperial Guard was another such act that went unmentioned by Wellington.

[1] According to the *Regulations and Orders for the Army, 1811*, wives were allowed to accompany their husbands overseas at the rate of six per company. The manner in which this was decided usually led to very emotional scenes as each wife stepped forward to draw from a hat a ticket, upon which was written either 'to go' or 'not to go'. Naturally, the successful wives were overjoyed, in spite of the hardships that were to come. On the other hand, those left behind — the majority — faced an uncertain future with bleak prospects. George Gleig, author of *The Subaltern*, left a most touching account of such a scene as his regiment, the 85th, prepared to embark for the Peninsula in 1813. 'When Mary unrolled the slip of paper, and read upon it the fatal words, "To be left," she looked as if Heaven itself were incapable of adding one additional pang to her misery. Holding it with both hands, at the full stretch of her arms from her face, she gazed upon it for some minutes without speaking a word, though the rapid succession of colour and deadly paleness upon her cheeks, told how severe was the struggle which was going on within; till at length, completely overpowered by her own sensations, she crushed it between her palms, and fell senseless into the arms of another woman.' Gleig, *The Subaltern*, pp.14-15. If one of the wives lost her husband in battle she normally married one of his comrades in order to retain her official status.

[2] This was the official name of the Compton home at Minstead, still occupied by a descendant. Until 1792 the manors of Bisterne and Minstead had been linked together since Saxon times.

quarters and brings word that his men will be up tomorrow. Rain.

September 16th. Marched to Villazopeque, 2 leagues. The French picquets were about half a league in front and their columns showed no disposition to move off. There was some skirmishing without loss on either side. At last our cavalry supported by some infantry drove in their outposts and the main body retired a little way. Their horses are in a wretched condition which ought not to be as we find quantities of corn wherever they have been. They have destroyed all the villages in this part of the country and have killed some of the inhabitants. What the poor creatures are to do I know not as the harvest is just in and they have destroyed it all. Castaños's long expected army arrived today consisting of about twenty thousand men. They are in general, soldierly-looking men and tolerably clothed. They have about four hundred cavalry which are bad. I saw one troop of hussars which looked well, and his artillery looks well appointed. Santocildes commands them, Castaños being the Captain General over the northern armies. The enemy remained at night on some strong ground in front. Lord Wellington had issued orders stating it to be his intention to attack them in the morning should they remain in the position they occupy.

September 17th. The troops were under arms before daylight and the column soon after moved. The enemy moved from their position on seeing the head of the 1st Division which was sent to turn their left. The road ran between two high ridges of hills, on both of which our troops advanced. The enemy retired skirmishing along the side of the ridge on their left and seemed desirous only of letting their main body get off. The cavalry too skirmished and with but little loss on both sides. It was a long day as we advanced slowly and halted frequently. Late in the evening we stopped at Burial, 4 leagues, and bivouacked in some very indifferent ground. Rain and very cold.

September 18th. We moved to within half a league of Burgos and after remaining a long time under our arms and trying forty men and three women by Court Martial for stealing onions, we bivouacked in a strong field and one of the coldest winds I ever felt. We were near the works which consist of an unfinished work, a strong redoubt and the Castle. The latter appears to be tremendously strong — ditch within ditch and palisaded. They have thrown stones within the tower of the castle and have made it solid so that shot cannot hurt it. They have several guns on it. They were driven out of the town and there was a great deal of firing with musketry on both sides. They command a great part of the town and fire at people in the streets.[1] Rain.

September 19th. We moved in the morning by a circuitous route to avoid the fire

[1] The castle of Burgos occupied the summit of an oblong conical hill and was enclosed within a triple line of defence, except on one side. The outer line of defence, often referred to as the 3rd line, consisted of the original wall of the castle which had been strengthened by an earthen shot-proof parapet. The second line of defence was of a similar construction which in turn was well palisaded. The inner line of defence surrounded the old castle keep. Each of these defensive lines was protected in turn by a ditch while the keep had been developed into a strong casemate called the Napoleon Battery. Also, inside the first or inner line of defence stood the church of La Blanca. The main strength of the castle of Burgos lay in the natural formation of the ground. It stood upon a hill with steep sides to the south, which made it almost impossible to attack,

of the forts to the other side of the town for the pleasurable purpose of working. Major Cocks with the Light companies of the Highland Brigade supported by General Pack's Portuguese Brigade took possession of the unfinished work without French opposition. They retired into the redoubt and kept up a heavy fire at our men. At eight o'clock the redoubt was ordered to be stormed. The 42nd, as the strongest regiment in the Division, was selected for the purpose, supported by the Light companies of the Highland Brigade and General Pack's Portuguese Brigade. At eight o'clock they advanced to storm but the Portuguese who thought to raise their spirits by it began to shout at two hundred yards distance and thereby drew the enemy's fire upon them. The 42nd advanced gallantly and planted their ladders which proved to be too short and after persisting for some time they were beat back. They returned again and with Major Cocks with his Light Infantry companies got in first, his men scrambling over without ladders. The French then gave way and after some little time the fort was ours. The loss was about 250. We made 70 prisoners and bayonetted a great many. There were 500 in the place, the remainder of whom made their escape by the covered way into the Castle.[1] The working parties then began and dug some trenches and suffered but little during the night.

September 20th. The works continue. They find it difficult to throw their shells into the trenches, as we are working so near them. They fire a great deal and do not do much execution. They are not sparing of their ammunition. The garrison is said to consist of two thousand men. The Governor is a General of Division who volunteered his service.[2] I rode into the town. Some parts of it are unsafe as the Castle commands many of the streets. It appears to be a very old town, the

while to the north the castle was protected by a hill of similar height upon which stood the hornwork of St Michael with a ravine separating the two. The scarp at the front of the hornwork was some 25 feet high while the rear of the place was protected by a strong palisade. The French garrison consisted of 2,000 men with nine heavy guns, eleven field pieces and six mortars or howitzers. See Whitworth Porter, *History of the Corps of Royal Engineers*, I, 319, and Jones, *Journal of the Sieges*, pp.186-187.

[1] The hornwork of St Michael was stormed on the night of September 19th. 150 men of the 1/42nd were detailed to open fire on the defenders lining the ramparts while the storming parties, consisting of Pack's Portuguese, were preceded by a party of the 42nd, under Lieutenant Pitts, Royal Engineers, carrying ladders. While this main attack was being delivered a third party, consisting of the light companies of Stirling's brigade of the 1st Division (the 1/42nd, 1/24th and 1/79th), under Major Charles Cocks, would move round to the rear of the work in order to force an entry there. The attack got underway at 8pm but ran into difficulties soon after when the Portuguese refused to mount the ladders. The attack was, therefore, beaten back with great loss. Fortunately, Cocks' party, at the rear of the hornwork, managed to break in after a desperate fight during which scores of his men were struck down. However, the work was taken, mainly through the efforts of Cocks himself, but at a cost of 420 men killed, wounded and missing. The French suffered losses of 198, of which 60 were taken prisoners. Seven guns were taken by Cocks' also. See Page (ed), *Intelligence Officer*, pp.193-195, Fortescue, *History of the Army*, VIII, 574-575, Jones, *Journal of the Sieges*, pp.190-191, and Oman, *History of the Peninsular War*, VI, 26-28. Oman gives the covering party of the 42nd as 300, whereas Fortescue and Jones put the number at 150.

[2] The governor of Burgos was General Dubreton, a general of brigade. Oman describes him as, 'one of the most resourceful and enterprising officers whom the British

streets narrow. It appeared to have been a good deal knocked about as the French had destroyed a vast quantity of stores and had pillaged some of the houses. The inhabitants looked sulky and Frenchified, as it never could till lately have entered into their imagination that an English army would have entered the town.

September 21st. At twelve I went into the trenches and remained there till six. They fired at us on going in and coming out, as in this place it is quite exposed. The moon is at the full and the nights are as bright as day. We worked at a communication and a one-gun battery. The news of today is that Caffarelli has joined Clausel with 7,000 men and the enemy have pushed on their advanced posts 1 league[1]. The covering party is very much exposed and have lost a good many men today. General Hulse's horses etc., were sold today.

Camp near Burgos
September 21st 1812

My Dear Father,

The mail is going immediately, but I cannot let it go without letting you have a line. On the 17th the enemy made dispositions as if to fight us near Villazopeque. Ten thousand Spaniards under Castaños joined us the day before and Lord Wellington in orders stated it was to be his intention to attack. At daylight the columns were in motion, but they moved off and some skirmishing ended the bravado of both sides. On the 18th the army encamped near this. The enemy were driven out of the town and the garrison only remained in the works. On the 19th we moved to our present ground of encampment by a circuitous route to avoid their fire, and it was then determined that the 1st Division and General Pack's brigade of Portuguese should have the glory of taking the place. I must now tell you what sort of place it is. There is a castle separate from the town, situated on a high hill, and fortified most beautifully, ditch within ditch, and palisaded without end. It commands most of the streets so that though there are some troops in the town to prevent a sally, it is not safe to move out. Besides the castle there is a fort on the hill which it was absolutely necessary we should get possession of before we could attack the castle. It is very strong but the palisades not quite finished all round. On the evening we came here (the 19th) it

army ever encountered. He earned at Burgos a reputation even more brilliant than that which Phillipon acquired at Badajoz.' (Oman, *History of the Peninsular War*, VI, 23.) However, there is no evidence to suggest he volunteered his services. Following the restoration of the Bourbons Dubreton held the rank of Lieutenant General and whilst commanding in Strasburg had an opportunity of paying military honours with that garrison to the Duke of Wellington who was then on an inspection of the frontiers.

[1] This French reinforcement to the Army of Portugal consisted of about 7,000 conscripts. Nevertheless, Wellington was quite confident of being able to take Burgos before the French force was strong enough to interfere with his operations. Furthermore, he was hoping that Sir Home Popham, operating inland from the northern coast, might harass the French and prevent any large force from the Army of Portugal from marching upon Burgos. (*Despatches*, Wellington to Lord Bathurst, 21st September 1812, IX, 443.)

was resolved that this work should be stormed, and the lot fell upon the 42nd Regiment, and the Portuguese brigade. At eight o'clock these worthies advanced. The Portuguese, to raise their courage, cheered at 200 paces and thereby drew the fire upon the party. The first attempt failed, the ladders being too short. The second succeeded thanks to the native courage of Englishmen, not to the support of our allies who behaved themselves in a most dastardly manner. Our loss was severe, amounting, I hear, to six hundred in killed and wounded. We made seventy prisoners and bayonetted a great many. They had 500 men in it, the rest of them escaped by the covered way into the Castle. Having thus gained the first object the trenches were begun, and we have been hard at work ever since. I was at work last night, and shall go on again tomorrow. They have not hit a great many in the trenches as we are now almost too close for anything but musketry. Their guns annoy us chiefly in going in and coming out. The moon favours them as the nights are nearly as light as day, but upon the whole we have as yet been fortunate. The castle will prove very formidable and will take some time yet. They have a garrison of two thousand, commanded by a General of Division, who volunteered his services upon the occasion. I hear his name is Rey.[1] The news of today is that Caffarelli with 7,000 men has joined Clausel's (late Marmont's) army, which had retired upon the Vittoria road about eight leagues from hence and that in consequence of the reinforcements their advanced guard had today advanced a league. Should he come down upon us I have no doubt that we shall leave our Spaniards to take care of our works, and advance in front of this to fight if they will meet us. I much doubt whether anything would tempt them to do this.

I am so occupied with thinking of our works here, that I am afraid this will prove somewhat unintelligible. The rascally Portuguese work very ill, consequently are more exposed and get more frequently hit than our men. I hope that their conduct will be fully exposed and that no more will be said of their distinguished conduct which few have had discrimination enough to find out. The victory of Salamanca appears to have had a greater effect in other quarters than we could possibly have expected. It will encourage the Russians and at all events show them that the French are not invincible. The more I see of English troops the more I am convinced that nothing can withstand them. The more hazardous the project the better they do it.

The Quartermaster General of this division, Major Pierrepont, was killed in storming the fort. I was talking with him three hours before and he mentioned a very narrow escape he had had two days before, a spent ball having hit him in the right breast without hurting him. It is extraordinary enough that he was killed by a ball which entered that very place.[2]

Bradshaw resigns and goes home as soon as this is over; he will be a

---

[1] JM is mistaken here. The governor of Burgos was in fact Dubreton. General Rey commanded the garrison at San Sebastian during the siege there between July and September 1813.

[2] Major C.A. Pierrepont had been one of the officers employed by the Staff Corps in sketching the battlefields in the Peninsula and the country itself while the war was still in progress. (See JM's Journal August 26th 1812, for more on Pierrepont).

great loss to us. I must send this off now — it goes in Lord Wellington's private bag, no public mail being made up.

My kindest love to my Mother, and all at Bisterne. John Mills.

September 22nd. The works go on well; we have increased the fire and our musketry and in some degree silenced theirs. They fired from behind some oxen which graze on the outside of the Castle and our Riflemen were obliged to shoot them which otherwise would not have been fair. The 5th and 7th Divisions have advanced and the enemy retired again eight leagues up the Vittoria road. At twelve at night an attempt was made to storm the outer works of the castle. The Portuguese were to have attacked it in the flank, whilst four hundred men from this Division escaladed the wall in front. A party of 130 of the Brigade of Guards led the way with the ladders. The enemy opened a tremendous fire, on which the Germans filed off to the right and the Scotch followed them. Our men got the ladders up with some difficulty under a heavy fire from the top of the wall, but were unable to get to the top. Hall of the 3rd Regiment [3rd Foot Guards] who mounted first was knocked down. Frazer tried and was shot in the knee. During the whole of this time they kept up a constant fire from the top of the wall and threw down bags of gunpowder and large stones. At last, having been twenty-five minutes in the ditch and not seeing anything of the other parties they retired having lost half their numbers in killed and wounded. 3 officers were wounded. The Portuguese failed in their attempts. Thus ended the attack which was almost madness to attempt.[1]

September 23rd. Lord Wellington sent in a flag of truce for the purpose of getting our wounded and dead. A cessation of operations was agreed upon for three hours. They brought the wounded up in stretchers half way up the hill, and lent our men the stretchers to carry them on, which were returned in like manner. They had treated our wounded in the kindest manner, giving them soup and things to eat and dressing their wounds. The body of Major Laurie

---

[1] The first assault on the castle of Burgos was made at midnight on September 22nd. The stormers, some 400 in all, were drawn from the 1st Division, their object being the outer line of defence at the western front of the castle. The wall here was between 23 to 25 feet high but it was unflanked and the stormers would not have to brave the sort of fire that their comrades experienced at Ciudad Rodrigo and Badajoz. Also, a sunken road, in which the stormers formed up, took them to within sixty yards of the ditch, thus giving more protection. While this attack was delivered a Portuguese battalion would assault the southern side of the castle walls at a position which was defended by just a small guard. The attack was a dismal failure which saw the Portuguese turn back as soon as the French guards opened fire on them. The stormers of the 1st Division were left to do the job on their own but their numbers were far too few for the task. They charged forward through a withering fire and those who reached the tops of the ladders were either bayonetted or shot down by the French defenders who also threw down scores of combustibles, grenades and other explosives into the ranks of the British troops. After about fifteen minutes the attackers withdrew, leaving behind 158 of their number killed and wounded. The French suffered losses of just 9 killed and 13 wounded. See Fortescue, *History of the British Army*, VIII, 576-577, Oman, *History of the Peninsular War*, VI, 29-30, and Jones, *Journal of the Sieges*, 192-194, for accounts of the attack.

who commanded the party was found and was the only one that was stripped.[1] For an hour after the truce was at an end they did not fire a shot. They seemed confident about holding out the place till they were relieved which they looked upon as certain. At six at night I went to the trenches and continued till one. The moon did not rise till late which made it much more pleasant. The party was at work finishing a battery. I had but two of my party hit though they threw several shells into the very place they were at work. It appears we are undertaking this siege without sufficient means of any sort. There are but two regular engineers employed. We have but eighteen hundred round shot and everything else in proportion. They have discovered that one of the batteries is enfiladed as well as a communication. A party broke ground near the suburbs. It is to be carried on by sap, and the outer wall is to be blown in.

September 24th. Our batteries were to have opened this morning consisting of 3 eighteens and 2 howitzers to throw red hot shot into the convent, but the enemy had in the night mounted two fresh guns which enfiladed ours and it was necessary to make some alterations which will prevent their opening as soon as was expected. They seem to have slackened their fire, particularly during the night. I rode again into Burgos for the purpose of looking at the Cathedral, a perfect specimen of Florid Gothic. The steeples are particularly light and elegant. The interior is ornamented by some admirable carving in the highest state of perfection. The chapels were richly ornamented and finer than any I have seen. Upon the whole it stands next to Salamanca.[2] I saw a group of Muleteers anxiously watching the proceedings of a large clock, and as it was nearly two o'clock I waited to see the result. Over the clock was the figure of a man dressed in red with large mustachios with a book in his hand. He struck the

[1] Major Laurie, of the 1/79th, commanded the British troops during the attack on September 22nd. In a letter to Lord Liverpool dated November 23rd 1812, printed in Despatches, IX, 573-574, Wellington was critical of Laurie's conduct during the attack, writing, 'the troops ought to have carried the exterior line by escalade on the 22nd of September, and if they had we had means sufficient to take the place. They did not take the line because [Major Laurie], the field officer who commanded, did that which is too common in our army. He paid no attention to his orders, notwithstanding the pains I took in writing them, and in reading and explaining them to him twice over. He made none of the dispositions ordered; and instead of regulating the attack as he ought, he rushed on as if he had been the leader of a forlorn hope, and fell, together with many of those who went with him. He had my instructions in his pocket; and as the French got possession of his body, and were made acquainted with the plan, the attack could never be repeated. When he fell, nobody having received orders what to do, nobody could give any to the troops. I was in the trenches, however, and ordered them to withdraw.' Wellington's orders for the attack on the exterior line of the castle of Burgos can be found in Despatches, 22nd September, IX, 447-448. No doubt Laurie, had he survived, would purposely have got himself killed soon afterwards anyway, as this appears to have been the norm for any officer who incurred Wellington's wrath, such as Bevan, following the Brennier's escape from Almeida, and Sturgeon, after he fouled up the postal system in the spring of 1814.

[2] The cathedral at Burgos is the third largest in Spain. It was begun in 1221 by Ferdinand III and parts were still being added as late as the 16th century. The bones of the legendary Spanish hero, El Cid, and his wife Ximena, lie beneath the massive columns in the transept.

hour with it on a bell, each time making a hideous grimace which pleased the audience wonderfully.[1] They fired three shells over the town at some mules but in general they are very quiet, only now and then firing musketry into the town. An officer of the 42nd was killed in the trenches this morning, and another dangerously wounded in carrying him off. An officer of the 42nd had his leg carried off by a shell. We are sapping and shall mine and blow up the wall that was attempted the other night and the report is, that our guns will not open till this is accomplished.

September 25th. One howitzer opened today but without effect — the wheel broke. The sapping goes on but slowly as they have but few who can work at it. The Engineers give a shilling a piece for all the large French shot that are brought and sixpence for the smaller. The men go out to look for them and stand watching the places where they hit, running the chance of being hit for the chance of getting a shilling or two. We are very well supplied here with the gross necessaries of life. Butter, bread, vegetables, country wine, etc. There is no claret to be got in Burgos now, as the Spaniards when they entered the town destroyed almost everything. The usual price of it is three and sixpence per bottle.

September 26th. The siege of this place promises fair to rival that of Troy in duration. Every day shows the deficiency of our means, the strength of the place, and the ingenuity of the garrison — in the refinements of war they far exceed us. We are stubbornly brave, they are gallant in spirit, but in all inventions and devices we must be content to copy, and the experience costs us dear. An acting Engineer was killed, an artillery officer wounded.[2] The sap goes on well. They are so near that the garrison roll down live shells and throw hand grenades. We keep up a heavy fire of musketry which keeps their heads under. The 6th Division have a working party near the river, not connected with our works. I believe the object is to make a place for musketry.

September 27th. We are making a zig-zag to go close down to the wall for the purpose of putting musketry in. Our fire at the embrasures keeps theirs down. The working party at night broke ground at twenty yards from the wall.

Camp before Burgos,
September 27th 1812

My Dearest Mother,

A messenger is going with dispatches by way of Corunna and I have been offered his assistance in conveying a letter which will if it has luck reach you long before the Mail. I wrote by the last Mail to my Father giving an account of the operations of the siege performed by this division, commencing on the 19th. Since writing to him an attempt was made on the 22nd to take part of the works

---

[1] This is probably the Papamoscas, or Flycatcher Clock. Built in the 16th Century the clock stands high above the beginning of the cathedral nave. A jack opens its mouth on the striking of each hour and was — and still is — a very popular sight.

[2] The acting engineer officer was probably Captain Kenny, of the 9th Regiment and Assistant Engineer, who was killed while placing a gabion in the trenches.

by storm. Four hundred men of the division were selected for this; 130 of the Guards, the Germans and Scotch Brigade making up the rest of the number. At twelve at night they sallied forth and were received at about fifty yards from the wall by a most tremendous fire. The Germans faced about, the Scotch followed and our men went on. They were some time in getting the ladders up, and when it was done they knocked them and the men down. For five and twenty minutes they continued their attempt, the French, firing from the wall they were attempting to get, and throwing down bags of gunpowder, and large stones. Lord Wellington then ordered a retreat, and half the party was left killed or wounded in the ditch. Frazer of the Coldstream is badly wounded in the knee. Hall of the 3rd in the head slightly. Talbot got safe off. The thing was badly managed; the Portuguese were to have made an attack to our right and have engaged the attention of the enemy but their leader was wounded and they went off. The Germans and Scotch went nobody knows where. They lost a few men but they did not do their duty. It seems madness to have thought of taking it by storm. The wall was full thirty feet high, and strong palisades at the top of it. The next morning a flag of truce was sent in and it was agreed that operations should cease for three hours. They had taken our wounded into the fort, had dressed their wounds, and given them as much soup as they could eat. They brought them half way in bearers and were then met by our men, who not having bearers to carry them in, borrowed theirs, and afterwards returned them with all due form. Major Laurie of the 79th who commanded the party was found dead.

We have now so many officers doing duty that our turn to go into the trenches does not come very often. I have been in twice and escaped unhurt, though once covered with dirt from a shell which burst near. Our means are very inadequate, to the undertaking and we are obliged to mine with the intention of blowing up the wall that was attempted the other night, not having the ammunition to batter. They have got it so near the work that the French roll down shells upon them. You may imagine our means are not complete when I tell you that Lord Wellington offers a reward of sixpence for the French shot, and the men are fools enough to stand in a place where the shots come over that are fired in the distance, watching where they fall, running the risk of being shot for the chance of sixpence.[1] Our batteries, such as they are, are ready to open, but they wait till the mine is sprung.

Clausel advanced on the 21st but has since retired. The 5th and 7th Divisions have moved forward and they say that the French have taken up a strong position near Pancorvo. They cannot, however, by any manoeuvre make us abandon this. Soult manoeuvring upon Madrid would be their only chance and he is not attempting anything of the sort; in time we must have it but as our

---

[1] There appears to be little evidence to support JM's claim that Wellington offered rewards for enemy shot brought into the British artillery park. However, as he was short of ammunition (for example, see *Despatches*, Wellington to Popham, 26th September, IX, 450) he may well have made it known that such rewards were on offer. Phillipon, the governor of Badajoz, had offered bounties for any captured British entrenching tools, so the practice was by no means unusual.

means are deficient it will be some days yet. The moon has hitherto been as bright as day during the whole night and they could see all our motions. She has now turned over a new leaf and we work in darkness.

The town of Burgos is very old, very dirty and the streets very narrow. The only thing worth seeing in it is the cathedral, a beautiful specimen of the Florid Gothic. It has four spires which look so light from the way in which they are carved, that you would think you might blow them over. The interior is beautifully carved and in the highest state of preservation. I saw groups of muleteers staring at a clock with their mouths open; their curiosity attracted mine and I joined their party. The clock was about to strike two and the ceremony was performed by the figure of a man who was leaning out of a window, dressed in red with an immense pair of mustachios. He had a book in his hand and struck the bell of the clock with it, making at the same time most hideous grimaces. The discerning audience testified their approbation by grimaces if possible superior to those of the figure. This clock is famous throughout this part of the country where it is regarded as a prodigy.

We are very well supplied here with the gross necessaries of life. The luxuries such as tea, sugar, etc., are very dear, moist sugar 2s 4d per pound, and I have some thoughts of leaving it off as all who have so done from sometimes not being able to buy any for a week together, assure me that tea is better without it. Claret is sold at 3s 6d a bottle but there is none left and we drink the country wine which is little better than vinegar and much worse than small beer, at 2s. Dollars cost 6s and to be had as a favour. I have heard of 8s being asked.

We are encamped just out of reach of shot but have the pleasure of hearing all the noise, to which I am now so accustomed that unless I listen for the purpose I do not hear it. I do not mean to say that I am deaf, but I am inattentive to it.

I expect to be at Bisterne by the first of September next and hope to find a room ready for me. If not I can bivouac under the plane tree, though I had rather be under cover.[1] I have parted with the servant I brought with me from England. He got idle and drunken and would have died had he remained much longer. It was better for me and not worse for him that we parted. Sir Henry Sullivan has just joined us from England. He will return again immediately as Hulse's death gives him his company, for which he had offered to others a great deal of money.[2]

The 1st Battalion of the 1st Regiment of Guards has landed at Corunna and is on its way to join us. I do not envy them their march and I am afraid I shall myself have a long one to perform soon, being in dread of being sent

[1] The plane tree at Bisterne still stands today and John Mills would have observed it daily from the Bisterne dining room. Its girth makes it the second largest in England.

[2] Captain Sir Henry Sullivan, Bart, was on sick leave in England for most of 1812. He had returned to the Peninsula only to discover that Major General Richard Hulse's death gave him his lieutenant colonelcy. Sullivan subsequently returned to England on promotion to the 2nd Battalion Coldstream Guards. He rejoined the 1st Battalion in March 1814 but was killed during the French sortie from Bayonne on April 14th of that year. A fine portrait of Sir Henry, by Edridge, exists and is featured in Fletcher and Poulter's *Gentlemen's Sons*.

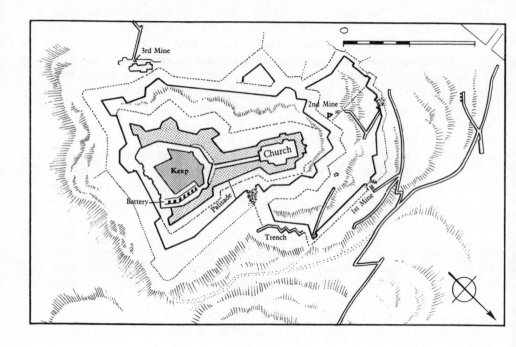

upon detachment to Lisbon — look at the map, but I hope not.[1] Bradshaw resigns, and quits the profession of arms as soon as this siege is over. He complains of the slowness of the proceedings as I shall do in his case. I am afraid Frazer will lose his leg. The ball is in the knee joint and cannot be extracted.

The latest papers we have are of the 1st of September. A packet goes twice a week from Corunna but I believe the Mails still go by way of Lisbon. Lord Wellington's dispatches go by the former.

There is a report, but not confirmed, that Massena[2] has arrived at Bayonne with 7,000 men. The French on retiring from this thought they were bound for France. If we could once get them out of Spain they would never get them back again. They would all desert, so mortal is their antipathy to this place.

I must conclude with my kindest love to all of you and beg leave to return thanks for the favour of numerous congratulatory epistles.

September 28th. The mining goes on but slowly and as our chief hopes depend upon it, we think the siege doubtful. I went into the trenches at six in the evening and remained till twelve. We broke fresh ground nearer than on the preceding night but though they kept up a very heavy fire of musketry with occasional rounds of grape they did not hit a man. They threw two fireballs, one of which fell about ten yards from me and burned for twenty minutes. I wonder much that they do not throw more as during the time they are burning it is impossible for me to work.

September 29th. A number of people were collected on the hill at two o'clock to see the mine explode. The ceremony did not take place. Lord Wellington and suite rode too near the Castle and were fired at, one shell fell near. Our working party at six broke ground again, but the garrison kept up so hot a fire that after losing a good many men they were withdrawn. At twelve o'clock the mine

[1] The 1st Battalion 1st Foot Guards arrived at Corunna on September 26th 1812 and began its march to join Wellington's army four days later. The battalion eventually joined up with the main army at Torquemada on October 24th during the retreat from Burgos. Unfortunately, the first few months of service in the Peninsula proved to be a real trial for the 1st Brigade of Guards, consisting of the newly-arrived 1st Battalion 1st Foot Guards and the 3rd Battalion 1st Foot Guards which had come up from Cadiz via Seville. The brigade had not long been in winter quarters at Viseu when it was hit by an outbreak of fever. During the first seven months of 1813 the brigade lost no less than 800 dead. Wellington subsequently ordered the brigade to march to the healthier climate of Oporto where the number of men dying through sickness began to drop. Nevertheless, at the end of March the 1st and 3rd Battalions 1st Foot Guards could only muster 355 and 430 fit men respectively. It would not be until June 24th 1813 that the brigade was strong enough to rejoin the main army in time for the operations that would see Wellington's army over the Pyrenees and into France. (Fletcher, *Gentlemen's Sons*, pp.150-151.)

[2] Massena had been sent to Bayonne as a replacement for Marmont by the French Minister of War, Henri Clarke, on the latter's own initiative, Napoleon being well on his way to Moscow. As it turned out Massena never returned to Spain but, exhausted by years of campaigning, declared himself unfit to face the rigours of yet another campaign. Napoleon, incidentally, had appointed Reille to replace the wounded Marmont but by the time the order filtered through to Spain the Army of Portugal was already being commanded by Souham.

exploded. The noise it made was very inconsiderable, so that it was scarcely heard by those in the trenches — it was a rumbling noise. It had the desired effect and made a very tolerable breach. A party of the 6th Division were awaiting the explosion to storm. Some confusion arose and a sergeant and six men only got up. Of course, they were soon beat down and the thing failed. The officer who commanded the party has been called upon for the reason of the failure in writing.[1]

September 30th. Our howitzers opened today upon the breach, which is practicable though not very good. They fired with very great precision. The French were very hard at work endeavouring to cut off the communication between the breach and the other parts. At nine there was a heavy fire, so much so that I was persuaded they were storming. It turned out to be the garrison firing upon our men who were throwing up a battery at fifty yards. Captain Bouverie of the *Medusa* is arrived with dispatches from Sir Home Popham who has again been unsuccessful upon the coast.[2] As a diversion it may be expedient to employ a Naval man but he should be much limited. Sir H. has first and last lost many a good man besides all his field artillery.

October 1st. A new battery was erected last night to bear upon the breach for

---

[1] A gallery had been started on September 25th and by the 29th had been excavated to a length of sixty feet. A charge consisting of twelve barrels of powder totalling 1,808lbs was placed beneath the outer wall and was exploded at midnight on the 29th. The resulting explosion was fairly unspectacular but it did bring down a section of the wall which was then stormed by a party of 300 men who were preceded by a 'forlorn hope' of an officer and twenty men. Unfortunately, there was no engineer officer available to lead the way as all four Royal Engineer officers present during the siege were wounded or sick. It was the first time in the war that a breach had been assaulted without the aid of such an officer. As a result a sergeant and four of his men reached the top of the breach, only to be knocked down, three of them being wounded. The officer with the main storming party completely lost his way and led his men to a part of the wall which was still intact and soon afterwards retired altogether without having even reached the breach. 29 British casualties were sustained during the abortive attack. I cannot find any evidence to suggest that Wellington asked the officer in command for an explanation of his failure to deliver an assault on the breach, although this is not to say that Wellington did not do so.

[2] Sir Home Popham had been making several attacks on French-held places along the northern coast of Spain throughout the summer. The attacks had met with a small degree of success and had certainly kept the French forces under Caffarelli busy and prevented him from detaching any troops to join the Army of Portugal in front of Wellington. The commander-in-chief duly replied to Popham on October 2nd, saying, 'The great object for me is that you should draw the attention of the enemy, by your operations, from those which we are carrying on on this side.' (*Despatches*, Wellington to Popham, 2nd October 1812, IX, 464-465.) By this time, however, Wellington must have known that the capture of Burgos was beyond him and he says as much in the same despatch. 'I am very much afraid that I shall not take this castle. It is very strong, well garrisoned, and well provided with ammunition; and I have not been able to get on as I ought. I have, however, got a mine under one of the works, which I hope will enable me to carry the exterior line; and when that shall be carried I hope that I shall get on better. But time is wearing apace, and Soult is moving from the south; and I should not be surprised if I were obliged to discontinue this operation in order to collect the army.' And yet Wellington was to continue this miserable siege for almost another three weeks, which cost the lives of many good men.

three guns, which were drawn down during the night from one of the others. They opened in the morning and fired two or three rounds when they found they were commanded by two that the enemy had mounted during the night. They fired so much that our artillery men were driven out. I went up on the hill at four o'clock. They had not dismounted any, the distance being too near for round shot. They threw a vast number of shells and with the greatest accuracy, almost every one falling in the battery. Lord Wellington seems to have got into a scrape — his means are most perfectly inadequate and he has already lost 1,000 men. To shift the blame upon others he complains they do not work well. In short, during the whole of this campaign from the tone of his orders, it would appear that the conduct of the army had been mad.[44] The few words he said after the Battle of Salamanca had more censure than praise. This is not the way to conciliate an army.

[44] On October 5th he wrote to Beresford saying, 'I do not know what to say of this damned place.' (*Despatches*, Wellington to Beresford, 5th October 1812, IX, 471.) But if he was understandably frustrated by the efforts of his army to take the castle he really had only himself to blame. Burgoyne, of the engineers, complained about the insufficient numbers of the storming parties, while others thought Wellington had simply overstretched himself. Captain George Bowles, of the Coldstream and a comrade of JM, wrote on October 11th 1812, 'This is one of the longest jobs the noble Marquis has had in hand for some time, and much as I *revere* him, I must say that in this case he has shown rather more of a quality nearly allied to obstinacy than is to be wished. The fact is that he was repeatedly told by those whom he consulted previous to commencing operations, his means (three eighteen-pounders, four howitzers) were totally insufficient, which has since proved unfortunately to be the case.' (Malmesbury, *Letters of the First Earl of Malmesbury*, II, 315-316.) By the time Wellington had reached Ciudad Rodrigo at the end of the retreat from Burgos he could at least own up to the fact that it was, after all, his fault, and said as much in a letter to Lord Liverpool. 'The fault of which I was guilty in the expedition to Burgos was, not that I undertook the operation with inadequate means, but that I took there the most inexperienced instead of the best troops. I left at Madrid the 3rd, 4th and Light Divisions, who had been with myself always before; and I brought with me that were good the 1st Division and they were inexperienced.' He went on, 'I see that a disposition already exists to blame the Government for the failure of the siege of Burgos. The Government had nothing to say to the siege. It was entirely my own fault.' (*Despatches*, Wellington to Lord Liverpool, 23rd November 1812, IX, 573-574.) The decision to employ the 1st Division at Burgos was indeed his own, and, perhaps with hindsight, was the wrong one given the fine record of the 3rd, 4th and Light Divisions at the sieges of Ciudad Rodrigo and Badajoz. But surely by intimation he still appears to shift the blame upon the 1st Division, referring to it as inexperienced and insinuating that it was not up to the job, despite his undenied praise of the conduct of the Guards during the siege. And regarding the inadequate means, which he denies earlier in the despatch, he contradicts himself in the same by saying that the stormers should have taken the outer line on September 22nd, 'had we means sufficient to take the place,' and goes on to blame the Field Officer, Major Laurie, for the failure. (See also JM's Journal for September 23rd). The causes of the failure are discussed in Oman's *History of the Peninsular War*, VI, 49-51, Fortescue's *History of the British Army*, VIII, 583-586 and in Jones' *Journal of the Sieges*, pp.215 and pp.247-262. The sieges were perhaps the most unsatisfactory episode in Wellington's campaign in the Peninsula, marked by a deficiency of men, matériel and skilled engineers. A lack of all these things conspired to make the siege of Burgos one of the low points of the war.

October 2nd. The enemy's fire yesterday destroyed one eighteen-pounder and damaged the carriage of another — the latter can be repaired. Lord Wellington persisted in making a battery close to the other. In the course of the night it was completed. Luckily the guns were not put in it as they shelled it in the same manner they had done the other. There is an idea that the siege will be turned into a blockade. There was a little skirmishing in front.

October 3rd. At one a.m. I went into the trenches and remained till six. We finished the embrasure of a four howitzer battery. We have now about eight times as many batteries as guns. A great deal of rain fell during the night and the trenches were full of mud.

October 4th. Lord Wellington has given out orders wherein he tells the two Divisions engaged in the siege that unless they work better they will not obtain the same credit that other Divisions have done, at the same time excepting the conduct of the Brigade of Guards which has been as exemplary here as all other places. Our guns re-opened in the morning upon the old breach which at two o'clock appeared to be very practicable. It was then determined that the outer wall should be stormed at daylight, the other attempts at night having failed. The 24th Regiment supported by two hundred men of the Division were to go up the old breach. The signal for the attack was to be the explosion of the mine. The 6th Division were to mount the breach which the mine was to make. At four o'clock the hill was covered with spectators. I took post in front of the breach and about half a mile from it. At half past five the mine exploded and made an excellent breach. The troops rushed forward from the place where they were concealed. A Grenadier officer of the 24th led that regiment in the most gallant style. He was first on the breach but when near the top appeared to find great difficulty in getting up, the ground slipping from under his feet. Just at this moment about ten Frenchmen appeared; they seemed quite confounded and not to know what was going on. Two or three ran to the old breach, one fired close to the officer but missed him, the men then peered over and the French ran off as fast as they could into the fort. The 24th advanced and hid themselves behind a pile of shot from whence they commenced firing. Thus far the French seemed taken quite unawares. The explosion of the mine and the storming were so instantaneous that they had not time to do anything before the men were in and then it was too late. The 6th Division got in at their breach without any sort of difficulty. The French now opened a most tremendous fire from every part of their works — musketry, shells, round shot and grape. Every musket and gun seemed to be at work. Our men returned the fire, and as it was getting dusk the sight was truly magnificent. As it got dark the fire slackened.[1]

---

[1] The first breach in the outer wall at Burgos had been made by the mine exploded on the night of September 29th. The mine which was exploded on October 4th, also beneath the first or outer line of defence, consisted of some 1,080lbs of gunpowder and when this was detonated nearly 100 feet of the rampart was sent twisting and turning into the air by the explosion which killed several French defenders at the same time. Then, through the clouds of dust came Captain Hedderwick leading the 2/24th which had been divided into two halves, the first, under Lieutenant Holmes and the second under Lieutenant Fraser. Each storming party was to attack a separate breach which was

I reckon myself fortunate in having had so good an opportunity of seeing it —
it is a chance if ever I may have another. As soon as it was dark the working
commenced, and in the course of the night a trench was dug parallel to the
breach, to afford cover to the men. At twelve o'clock the garrison made a sally
but were repulsed. At first they drove our men back, but the tables were soon
turned. It was accompanied by a very heavy firing and loud and repeated cheers.
October 5th. It is thought that a hundred will cover yesterday's loss. The men
are well covered, and an incessant fire of musketry is kept up on both sides. It
is said that the French officers could not get their men on in the sortie. The
enemy is manoeuvring in our front with a view to drawing us off. We are now
too far engaged to be drawn off. Colonel Jones of the Engineers, an able officer,
was wounded yesterday. He was to give Lord Wellington the signal that the
mine was ready and for that purpose got out of the trenches and stood in the
open, and was of course immediately hit.[1] At five o'clock our musketry slackened from want of ammunition. The garrison made a very spirited sortie with a
view to regaining what they had lost. Our men were taken by surprise and
driven from the breach. For some time the French had possession of the whole
wall excepting a small space at each end. After destroying all our work and
carrying off the tools, they retired. Our loss is from two to three hundred. Clitheroe
was wounded whilst leading his men up the breach.[2]
October 6th. It would seem impossible to maintain ourselves where we are as

done in style at cost of 68 killed and wounded. See Porter's *History of the Corps of Royal
Engineers*, I, 324, and *Despatches*, Wellington to Lord Bathurst, 5th October 1812, IX,
472-473.

[1] Lieutenant Colonel John Jones, of the Royal Engineers, was wounded while
giving the signal for the assault to begin after setting off the mine. Apparently, Jones
raised his hat in the air from his position in the trenches but it was not seen. He tried
repeatedly to give the signal but without success until he was forced to step into the
open, whereupon he naturally attracted the attention of a few French marksmen who
opened fire on him. The first shots missed but soon enough Jones was hit, apparently in
the ankle, which caused him to fall. He managed to regain the safety of the British
trench, however, and the mine was duly exploded. According to Porter, Wellington
blamed Jones for needlessly exposing himself to enemy fire and as a consequence he
received no mention in Wellington's despatch. See Porter, *History of the Corps of Royal
Engineers*, I, 324-325. Jones subsequently wrote the standard work on Wellington's sieges
in the Peninsula, *Journal of the Sieges Undertaken by the Allies in Spain in the Years 181
and 1812*, London 1814.

[2] In his journal for October 5th 1812, Lieutenant Colonel John Burgoyne, of the
Royal Engineers, wrote, 'At 5pm the enemy made a sortie from their covert way (which
they had cut out along the counterscarp a few days before), and by the gateway at the
end of their palisaded line, and rushing down got possession of the first breach, commenced firing, while parties destroyed our lodgement within and removed the tools. The
parapet on our left of the breach, which had been turned against them, our men maintained, and at one period the enemy were on one side of the lodgement, and ours on the
other, with only the parapet between them. Major Arnot, the field officer commanding,
and Captain Clitheroe, of the Guards, jumped on the parapet, and endeavoured to get
our men to make a charge over it and attack the enemy who were in the breach in the
rear. They were both wounded, being only followed by a few men; they were picked off
from the second line.' (Quoted in Porter, *History of the Corps of Royal Engineers*, I, 326.)
Clitheroe was a Captain in the 3rd Foot Guards.

we cannot put men in front of our working party and whenever they choose to sortie they can destroy all our works. It rained incessantly the whole day and it would seem that the rainy season has set in. The covering party is now to be found by entire regiments to furnish 450 men to be relieved every twelve hours. Our party marched off at seven but the rains had made the trenches so bad, that the party did not get to the breach till ten o'clock. I was sent with twenty men as an advance party to give alarm on a sortie. My post was under the pile of shot;[1] on any appearance of a sortie I was to advance, charge, and keep them off till the tools could be got away or in other words to be a dead man for the sake of a few pickaxes. On taking my post I discovered that our firing parties fired just over my head and several times hit the shot I was under. I sent several times to order them to level higher but I confess I was very glad on being withdrawn at daylight. Had a sortie been made I should have been between two fires, and between one and the other stood but a bad chance. The enemy threw a vast number of fireballs during the night for the double purpose of seeing where we were, and setting the gabions on fire. The distance is now so very short that a great many men are lost and almost killed every day.

October 7th.[2] It rained incessantly during the day and night. They dismounted another eighteen pounder this morning so that there is now but one left and yet the siege is continued though the chance of success must be very remote. At three in the morning the garrison made another sortie. They advanced under favour of a very heavy rain and got up to the breach without being perceived, and drove our men from every part of the wall. The Germans were on the covering party. After some time the Germans succeeded in regaining the wall after a most obstinate defensive, being so closely engaged that they knocked each other about with their butt ends. Major Cocks, of the 79th, the Field Officer in the trenches, was killed at the beginning of the business. His loss is irreparable. He was of the greatest promise and during the three years he had been in the country had greatly distinguished himself.[3] Every officer present was either

[1] This shot pile appears in the majority of the contemporary maps of Burgos and lies between the 2nd and 3rd line of defences at the north-western angle of the town.

[2] I would suggest that JM made this entry in his diary very early on the morning of October 8th and certainly after the French sortie, made at 3am on the 8th, during which Charles Cocks was killed. The weather was so appalling that JM, on duty, was probably waiting for a convenient moment in which to write up his diary for October 7th. Following the sortie he included his account of it in his entry for the 7th and when he made his entry for October 8th he mentions 'the business of last night', when he actually means that morning.

[3] Charles Cocks was shot dead by a French soldier as he rallied the working parties during the French sortie. The following morning Wellington walked into General Frederick Ponsonby's room and said simply, "Cocks is dead," and walked out. His death was a severe blow to Wellington who thought very highly of him and is said to have wept at his funeral, one of only three recorded instances of the great man giving way to his feelings, the other occasions being the aftermaths of Badajoz and Waterloo. Wellington said that, `had Cocks outlived these campaigns, which from the way he exposed himself was morally impossible, he would have become one of the first generals in England.' (Fortescue, *History of the British Army*, VIII, 580.) In his despatch to Lord Bathurst Wellington wrote, `I consider his loss as one of the greatest importance to this

killed or wounded, and the loss in men is about a hundred and fifty. They levelled all our works and buried some of the sappers alive. Two officers and 50 men were in my post behind the shot. They [the French] got into their rear — the officers were killed and hardly a man escaped. I cannot help thinking myself very fortunate in having escaped.

October 8th. The disasters of last night have depressed everyone. We are just where we were three days ago and whenever the garrison chooses the sortie they can drive us out. The weather too conspires against us, and our resources so inadequate at first, and since so much reduced, give us no hopes of success — it must end in a blockade. The French stole out so quietly last night that they came upon the trench before the men at work had the least idea of their approach. The first intimation was finding the earth shovelled down upon their heads. One of the sappers finding it impossible to escape allowed himself to be buried, and came out when they retired. Another followed his example but was struck twice with a pick-axe, at which he said he would be damned if he stood that and ran off. The man who was buried said that a French officer of Engineers who stood over his men directing them, was shot. The rain continues.

October 9th. We fired red hot shot at the convent but with no success. They have dismounted our only sound eighteen pounder, and a howitzer, and knocked one of the batteries to pieces. It is almost impossible for us to keep a gun at work more than an hour. They fire with such accuracy that they are sure of dismounting. At seven in the evening the Coldstream again went on covering party. I remained in the upper part of the works. The men were put close up to the wall and the new breach. At about eight the garrison attempted a sortie. They no sooner showed themselves than they were driven back by our men in the most gallant style. Buckeridge was killed as well as some men.[1] Our parties maintained themselves during the whole of the night. We had two sentries on our side of the sally port. They opened it once and our men fired down. They think they hit a good many men as there was a great cry. This covering party is become quite a perilous service, we are so near that many men must be hit.

October 10th. The conduct of the Guards last night is the general topic of conversation here and is universally praised. A drum major deserted from the fort yesterday. Two others from the party were shot in the attempt. The drum major says that many would desert but that they are too strictly watched. He says they have lost 500 men, and that there is a fever in the place. The rain which is incessant has made the trenches almost impassable.

October 11th. General Paget arrived from England this morning to act as second in command in the room of Sir Thomas Graham.[2] The round shot is entirely

army and to His Majesty's service.' (*Despatches*, 11th October 1812, IX, 483.) After the death of Cocks Wellington's heart was not in the siege and it is probably one of the reasons that persuaded him to abandon the operation.

[1] In Jones' *Journal of the Sieges*, p.205, he records that, 'The garrison attempted in the night to work at the new breach, but were several times driven in by the judicious conduct of Ensign Buckeridge of the Coldstream Guards, who was unfortunately killed in performing that service.'

[2] Sir Edward Paget, a brave man who had lost an arm at Oporto in 1809, arrived in Spain to take command of the 1st Division of the army. As to the position of second-

expended and 'Thunder' the only eighteen-pounder, 'Nelson' being in the mud and 'Lightning' ditched.[1] Rain.

October 12th. The rain is quite incessant. We are trying to accomplish the remainder of our work by mining. The French have countermined, but are much alarmed by our mines. The whole of their force is bivouacked. Their sick and wounded were in the fort but our hot shot forced them to move and they share the rain with the others. They are very ill off for wood and are obliged to burn their palisades. Our cavalry dove in the enemy's outpost this morning which had advanced.

October 13th. The mine now runs forty yards — fifty will bring it under the enemy and then it will explode. The enemy attacked our outposts this morning and Colonel Ponsonby was wounded in the thigh. We had one man killed and three wounded this morning going near the town for wood.

October 14th. His Lordship has been strongly advised to give up all the idea of taking the place but he is still obstinate. I believe he is determined to wait for the mines which may perhaps frighten them into a surrender.

October 15th. Our regiment formed the covering party and I went on at half past one in the morning and remained on till five. My post was to observe the gate of the Castle and I had forty men. At twelve o'clock our batteries made another attempt but they no sooner opened than twelve guns were brought to bear upon our three. In half an hour the battery was knocked to pieces and the men driven from the guns. I take this to be our last dying speech. They throw during the day a vast number of shells and as the day was dark I could see them in the air which I never remember to have done before. The splinters came back into their own works and troubled us as though under cover we were not more than twenty yards from the Castle wall. A man sitting round the fire was hit. Two Frenchmen jumped out from behind a bank and shot two sentries who were posted in advance. Upon this two officers went out to see whether there was any better place to post them and whilst looking another Frenchman jumped out from the same place, levelled and pulled at them but luckily his piece missed fire. The French army advanced a little, but did not drive in our outposts. Rain in the evening.

October 16th. Sir Edward Paget was to have seen our Brigade out this morning

in-command of the army, well, there never really was one in the British army in the Peninsula and Wellington refused to believe that such a position even existed. In a letter to Beresford at the end of the retreat from Burgos he said, 'I have always felt the inutility and inconvenience of the office of second in command. It has a great and high sounding title, without duties or responsibility of any description; at the same time that it gives pretensions, the assertion of which are, and I believe you know I found them in one instance to be very inconvenient. Every officer in an army should have some duty to perform, for which he is responsible; and I understand a general officer commanding a division or larger body of troops to be in this situation. The second in command has none that any body can define; excepting to give opinions for which he is in no manner responsible.' (*Despatches*, Wellington to Beresford, 2nd December 1812, IX, 592.) See also Ward's *Wellington's Headquarters*, pp.156-157. The question of Paget's acting as second-in-command was soon made academic for he was unfortunately captured by a French patrol on November 17th during the retreat from Burgos.

[1] These were the names given to the only three heavy British siege guns at Burgos. 'Nelson' was so named because it had only one trunnion.

but the rain prevented it. The enemy made a reconnaissance in front and it is thought that Massena was present.[1] Some movement has been made by our troops and the 6th Division had orders to hold themselves in readiness. There was but little firing either upon the fort or us during the day.

October 17th. Notwithstanding a rainy morning, Sir Edward Paget inspected us. Our battery opened early and the embrasures having been altered it was enabled to play for the greatest part of the day. The 3rd Regiment was on covering party at night and a mine exploded that was intended to blow up some palisades. It succeeded but ill, and the men were unable to force their way through. Two officers were wounded and about twelve men.

October 18th. The Coldstream formed the covering party in the morning. Harvey was killed whilst visiting his party. The battery continued firing upon the breach and succeeded in making it very good. At three o'clock it was communicated to us that the place was to be stormed at 4 o'clock. The signal was the explosion of the mine, on which a flag was to be held up on the hill. The mine exploded — the explosion was attended with so little noise that though we were anxiously expecting it, we could hear no noise. The earth shook a little, we looked to the hill and saw the flag. The 300 Germans stormed the breach and got well up it. They then attempted the third line, by a place in the wall which was broken down. It ended in their being beat out of the whole with the loss of 7 officers and a great many men. Our party was to escalade the wall in front. Burgess ran forward with 30 men, Walpole and myself followed with fifty each and ladders. Burgess got up without much difficulty, Walpole and myself followed. The place we stood on was a ledge in the wall about three feet from the top. A most tremendous fire opened upon us from every part which took us in front and rear. They poured down fresh men and ours kept falling down into the ditch, dragging and knocking down others. We were so close that they fairly put their muskets into our faces, and we pulled one of their men through an embrasure. Burgess was killed and Walpole severely wounded. We had hardly any men left on the top and at last we gave way. How we got over the palisades I know not. They increased their fire as we retreated, and we came off with the loss of more than half our party and all the badly wounded were left in the ditch. Burgess behaved nobly — he was the first up the ladder and waved his hat on the top. I found him lying there wounded. He begged me to get my men up and in the act of speaking a stone hit him, he fell on the ledge and was shot dead. The time we were on the wall was not more than six minutes. The fire was tremendous, shot, shells, grape, musketry, large stones, hand grenades and every missile weapon was used against us. I reckon my escape particularly fortunate. A party of sixty men attempted to escalade on our right. They were met by a very superior force and were immediately driven back but with very little loss. The mine destroyed a small church on the right. Colonel Brown[2] with some Portuguese got possession of it. It completes our possession of the whole of the first

---

[1] Massena was not present at Burgos and had not even entered Spain at the time. See JM's letter to his Mother, September 27th 1812, note 2, page 235.

[2] Colonel Gustavus Brown, 5/60th Royal Americans, commanded the 5th Portuguese Caçadores after a distinguished career in the West Indies.

line which was before incomplete. The failure of this is to be ascribed entirely to
our want of men. Had we but double the number we could have maintained
ourselves but they dropped off so fast and none coming to supply their place,
we failed from sheer weakness. Crofton was slightly wounded in the arm whilst
waiting with the support. Walpole had his arm shattered with a grape shot,
which struck him likewise in the side, but the shot most providentially glanced,
striking and tearing Ninon de l'Enclos, which he happened to have in a side
pocket at the time, otherwise it must have killed him. Thus finished this trying
day.[1] I was slightly wounded in the arm by a stone, but not the least hurt.

October 19th. In the storm of yesterday we had 60 of the 130 killed or wounded.
A great number never got up and many were pushed down without being
wounded. The Germans lost seven out of nine officers — the men in the same
proportion as ourselves. Notwithstanding the failure we are still going on. They
attempted in the night to regain the church but were after some sharp work
driven back. We began to mine from near the church. A party of French came
out, took one miner who was on the outside, and shut the others into the mine.
They were rescued from their perilous situation by a party of Caçadores. Lord
Wellington expressed himself perfectly satisfied with our attempt, and the impossibility of remaining any longer than we did.[2]

October 20th. Our Division marched at daylight to the strong position in front of
Burgos leaving the 58th and some Portuguese to live in the trenches till our
return. The French army appeared on a range of hills opposite. In the evening
some cavalry and three divisions of infantry moved into the plain below us,

---

[1] The last assault on the castle of Burgos got underway at 4.30pm on October
18th. As soon as the mine beneath the San Roman Church was exploded Colonel Brown's
detachment of Spaniards and Portuguese would rush forward to occupy its ruins. At the
same time 200 men of the Foot Guards would pass through the breach in the first line of
defence before attempting to escalade the second line opposite. While this was in progress
a further 200 men of the King's German Legion would assault the more easterly breach in
the second line. As soon as the mine was detonated the Germans dashed forward and
managed to gain the breach in the outer line of defences. After this, however, they found
their progress checked by a galling fire from within the second line and although some
of them made it as far as the parapet of the third, or inner, line they were gradually forced
back having suffered 82 casualties out of the 300 engaged. The Guards, meanwhile, had
passed through the breach in the first line before rushing forward with their ladders to
escalade the second line. The ladders were placed against the wall and the men rushed
to the top in the face of a heavy firing from the defenders within the defences behind the
wall. The men of the Coldstream and 3rd Guards remained on top of the ramparts for
some ten minutes or so but in spite of gaining a fairly long section of it they could not
hold on to their hard-won gains and they too were forced back having suffered remarkable similar casualties to the Germans; 85 out of 300 engaged.

[2] The Coldstream lost 60 killed and wounded during the assault including four
officers; Captain Edward Harvey and Ensign Wentworth Burgess, both killed, and Captains George Crofton and John Walpole, wounded. The 3rd Foot Guards suffered 25
casualties and the King's German Legion 75. In his despatch to Lord Bathurst Wellington
wrote, 'It is impossible to represent in adequate terms my sense of the conduct of the
Guards and German Legion upon this occasion; and I am quite satisfied, that if it had
been possible to maintain the posts which they had gained with so much gallantry, those
troops would have maintained them.' (*Despatches*, Wellington to Lord Bathurst, 26th
October 1812, IX, 512.)

apparently with the intention of attacking us in the morning. The 5th Division on our flank moved down to attack them. They stood their ground so long that I thought we were in for a good thing. Our artillery fired upon them, they went to the right about and we returned to our old ground. General Souham commands in the room of Clausel. Caffarelli has joined with 5,000 of the Imperial Guard. The remainder are either conscripts or the debris of Marmont's army. Their cavalry are remarkably good, some of them just joined. The 7th Division and some Spanish had a brush on the right and both behaved very well according to what I can collect. The enemy have about 35,000 infantry and 5,000 cavalry. We have about 14,000 infantry and 1,300 cavalry — the Spaniards nearly the same.[1] Bivouacked.

October 21st. Everything was quiet in the morning. The men were ordered to hut. At two the baggage was ordered to retreat. In the evening preparations were made for a retreat. At dusk we stole off quietly and what is most extraordinary, at the very same moment the French did the same. We halted for some time at Villa Irin. I went with Colonel Macdonald into a house to warm ourselves as it was a cold night. We found General Alava and General Longa, the celebrated partisan. We talked with them for half an hour. They then returned to their beds and their place was most ably supplied by some guerrilla servants to the above mentioned chieftains. We were hungry and desired them to get us some supper. They knocked the Patrone about, who immediately produced some bread, wine and salad. They furnished us with some boiled beef of their own, and some eggs destined for the breakfast of their masters. Fortified by our good cheer we sallied forth, prepared for the dangers of the night. Our Division was ordered by way of expedition to pass through the town and over the bridge of Burgos, on which two of the Castle guns bore and about a hundred yards from it. The moon shone clear. Luckily we got over without the loss of a man. They did not see us which was almost a miracle. We marched all night and halted for a short time during the morning then moved again and halted at Celada del Camino.

[1] Wellington's own estimates as to the relative strengths of the French and Spaniards can be found in *Despatches*, Wellington to Lord Bathurst, 28th October 1812, IX, 519-520. 'They [the French] are certainly in very great strength. The Army of Portugal have received a reinforcement of 10,000 men (including cavalry) from France, and I have reason to believe that there are two divisions of infantry now with this army, belonging to the Army of the North. The cavalry of the Army of the North is certainly with the Army of Portugal, and they have at least 5,000 good cavalry. I do not think that I am sufficiently strong to contend with this army thus reinforced. I have here only four weak divisions of British and Portuguese troops, and three very weak brigades of cavalry. There are with this army 12,000 Spanish troops of the army of Galicia, including 600 cavalry, and the cavalry under Don Julian Sanchez.....By accounts from Lieut. General Sir R. Hill to the 26th instant, I find that the enemy had approached the Tagus with their left, and had moved their right upon Cuença. He does not state the force they have with them, but I should imagine not less than 50,000 men; and, as far as I can judge, there are not less than 40,000 now opposed to this army. Both armies are infinitely superior to ours in cavalry and artillery, as well as in total numbers.'

Chapter Seven

Retreat to Portugal

On October 22nd 1812 JM found himself slipping away from beneath the walls of the castle of Burgos as Wellington ended what he later called, 'the worst scrape I ever was in.' The castle had remained out of his grasp following a miserable month-long operation that cost the British over 2,000 casualties. It was the one great failure of Wellington's campaign in the Peninsula and was one that was to become worse as the old drink- and supply-related problems that had beset Sir John Moore's army during the retreat to Corunna surfaced once again. The retreat began amidst much disappointment but gave little hint of the hardships that were to come. The real problems began when the army wandered into Torquemada, one of the main towns in this wine-producing region. The town's cellars were stacked to the ceilings with barrels of newly-made wine which were quickly staved open by the British troops. Men tumbled into the huge barrels in their frenzied efforts to fill their bellies while others, paralytic after their exertions, lay in the gutters with streams of wine dribbling from their open mouths. The pursuing French troops harassed the British rear-guard wherever and whenever possible but at such places as Torquemada they simply rode in and rounded up the stragglers who were, for the most part, too drunk to realise what was happening.

Wellington's retreating army began to arrive at Salamanca on November 8th where it was met by Hill's force. But the ordeal was by no means over for Wellington and indeed the leg of the retreat to Ciudad Rodrigo between November 15th and 20th was the worst of all as the men struggled through a sea of mud in the pouring rain, the majority of them marching on empty stomachs, the commissariat having long since broken down. During the retreat Sir Edward Paget, who had only recently arrived in the Peninsula to assume the post of Wellington's second-in-command, was taken prisoner by a French patrol. Wellington's tattered army finally began to arrive and concentrate at Ciudad Rodrigo on November 20th and it would have been very small comfort for Wellington if he could have known that his great future adversary, Napoleon, would have to suffer a far worse retreat than his own following his stay at Moscow.

JM's own experience of the retreat would appear to be rather better than most. However, there was little to eat and, like many others, he chose to ignore Wellington's orders regarding plunder and acquired more than a few fat pigs along the way. It is at this point that JM begins to feel rather embittered at the war and his posting to England comes as a more than welcome relief. Certainly, his sojourn in Lisbon in December 1812 must have seemed like paradise when he reflected upon the miseries of life in the trenches before Burgos and the retreat from there, which is where we find him on October 22nd.

October 22nd. The retreat of an English army is always attended with great complaint. Twenty-two wounded men were left at Burgos under the charge of a surgeon. The Commissariat were obliged to destroy a great quantity of stores, not having the means of transport. The scene was as usual — numbers were left behind drunk. The hornwork was blown up and the guns dragged out and buried before our troops in the trenches. I could have cried on passing Burgos to think that the result of all our labours should have ended in a retreat and the bones of so many brave fellows should have been left there to bleach the cursed soil.[1]

October 23rd. In the morning we were surprised to find the French cavalry at our heels. They attacked ours with so much spirit that ours retreated in great confusion and had it not been for the gallantry of the Light German Brigade under Colonel Halkett, who formed square and kept them off, they would have been entirely destroyed.[2] It is extraordinary that our cavalry with the very great

[1] Wellington gave orders to abandon the siege of Burgos on October 21st. The wheels of the guns and the wagons were muffled with straw so as to be able to pass through the town in secret. The men themselves were ordered to march with trailed arms but with the moon shining brightly it would have been very easy for the French to detect shako plates and arms. Fortunately, the move appears to have been completed in secret, the 1st and 7th Divisions crossing the bridge over the Arlanzon in the town without any trouble. Only when some Spanish cavalry panicked and crossed the bridge at a gallop were the French aroused, at which they opened fire on their retreating enemies. French troops, under Maucune, entered Burgos at around 10am on the 23rd to congratulate Dubreton and his men. The 22nd marked the first day of the retreat but as JM points out even then the men had begun to get drunk and the Commissariat to run into problems.

[2] On October 23rd the French light cavalry of Curto's division caught up with and engaged the British rearguard at a bridge over the tributary of the Arlanzon at Venta del Pozo, near the village of Villodrigo. The British rearguard here consisted of Anson's light cavalry brigade, Bock's German dragoons and two battalions of KGL infantry under Colin Halkett with a battery of horse artillery in support. Anson's cavalry brigade had been hard pressed by the French until it came in sight of the bridge, on the other side of which were drawn up Bock's dragoons with Bull's artillery. At this the French squadrons halted while further French reserves came up. The French commanders, Souham and Caffarelli were now on the scene and ordered no slacking in the pursuit of the British rearguard. With nearly 6,000 cavalry at his disposal Souham had every right to believe that he could drive away the British and while several squadrons began to pick their way across by way of a ford to the right other squadrons made their way across the bridge. This move offered Anson a chance to repeat Lumley's victory at Usagre by charging the French before they had time to form up on the British-held side of the river but by a stroke of bad luck Anson's brigade formed up in front of Bull's guns, thus masking them from the French who were now crossing the river in large numbers. Furthermore when Anson's cavalry finally moved out of the way the gunners fired much too high and the French formed up unhindered. Bock's German dragoons, the 1st and 2nd KGL Dragoons, were first to charge, both regiments engaging the French in a fierce fight while Anson's brigade came up behind them. Oman called the ensuing struggle, 'one of the most furious cavalry melées ever seen,' (Oman, *History of the Peninsular War*, VI, 74,) as the cavalry of both sides became inextricably mixed. Eventually the British were forced back and it was only Halkett's KGL infantry that intervened, bringing the French to a halt and allowing both Bock and Anson to reform their men. The French followed the British rearguard at a distance but did not interfere throughout the rest of the day. Casualties were 230 on the British side and somewhere in the region of 300 on the French.

superiority of horses on their side, can do nothing with them. We had a long and tiresome march of seven leagues and got upon our ground close to Torquemada after dark. The whole of this is grape country. The wine had just been made and deposited in large vaults in the vineyards — they were soon found out. The men fetched it away in the camp kettles and many were so drunk that they could not move from the place. Two were drowned in the vats. The disorder was not confined to the vaults; the town was completely sacked. The houses were destroyed for firewood and the Commissariat doors were plundered and riot, such as never was seen before, prevailed.[1]

DESIGNATED TO LORD WELLINGTON

Praise when not deserved is worse than censure. It has in this sense been frequently bestowed on the Hero of these campaigns. It is therefore necessary to examine into facts to discover his errors and separate the praise bestowed on his faults from the applause on his merits. His first appearance on the stage was at Vimeiro. That he had but little to do in the ignominious treaty which followed the victory is the general opinion, so general indeed that the censure so liberally bestowed on his coadjutors touched him not and in the opinion of ye world he stands acquitted. On his return to Portugal as Commander of the forces, he found the French in possession of all beyond the Douro. To strike the decisive blow he marched direct upon Oporto and by a masterly manoeuvre crossed that river in the face of the enemy and drove them from the town. Whatever subsequent praise he has obtained this achievement will ever rank his highest and it may be said with truth of the extraordinary boldness of the measure. If he outlives the next campaign, which he has a fair chance of doing, this Farrago[2] will call to mind much that he would otherwise forget, and as it is Sacred to Nonsense let none who do not sacrifice to her open it.[3]

---

[1] Upon arrival at Torquemada the British troops found the place, and the outlying villages, full of newly-made wine. The town was the centre of the wine district and the cellars were stacked to the ceilings with barrels which were quickly staved in. The troops outdid many of their former antics by getting drunk in a remarkably short space of time and, indeed, Napier claimed that twelve thousand men at one time were in a state of helpless inebriety. Private William Wheeler, of the 51st, wrote, 'from Burgos to Salamanca is chiefly a wine country and as there had been a good harvest, and the new wine was in tanks particularly about Valladolid the soldiers ran mad. I remember seeing a soldier fully accoutered with his knapsack on in a large tank, he had either fell in or had been pushed in by his comrades, there he lay dead. I saw a Dragoon fire his pistol into a large vat containing several thousands of gallons, in a few minutes we were up to our knees in wine and fighting like tigers for it.' (Liddell Hart (Ed), *The Letters of Private Wheeler, 1809-1828*, p.106.) Hundreds of British soldiers were still lying drunk when the French entered the town the following day.

[2] A farrago was a medley.

[3] This is a curious little piece from JM, still obviously sour after the recent experience at Burgos. One imagines that this was written during a quiet moment in a bivouac somewhere along the road from Burgos. Once again JM's disillusionment with Wellington and the war is rather transparent and the reference to 'praise when not deserved' is a veiled criticism of some of Wellington's achievements in the Peninsula.

October 24th. The men were in such a state in the morning that it was impossible to do anything with them. There was scarce a sober man in the army — how they got through the day's march I know not. Officers of every regiment and a strong rearguard were left behind to force the men on. I had eight mules to put them on, but could with difficulty keep them on. 500 stragglers were taken this day. We halted and bivouacked near Duenas, 4 leagues, having passed the River Carrion. The enemy came close up, but we did not allow them to cross the river. The 1st Btn of the 1st Guards joined us from Corunna, twelve hundred strong and very fine men but very young soldiers. Their inexperience amused us much.[1]
October 25th. In the morning the enemy closed up his columns, seemingly with the intention of forcing the river. One of the bridges was mined but before it was completed the enemy advanced some infantry hidden amongst their cavalry and the mine was sprung — it failed. They came over the bridge and took 60 of the miners belonging to the 1st Division. It was particularly hard upon them as they were all that remains of the Burgos miners.[2] Towards evening they made an attempt to cross the river under a heavy fire of artillery. The 5th Division lost 550 men. The Spaniards ran away at the first but Alava, Lord Wellington's Spanish secretary, led them on most gallantly and they drove them into the river with very great loss. We moved to support, but it was all over and we returned and bivouacked.[3]
October 26th. To Cabezon, 3 leagues. The bridge over the Pisuerga is commanded by very high ground on which we posted some artillery and likewise commenced mining. In the course of the night they patrolled up to the barricade and some shots were exchanged. Our parson was taken the other day in a village near Duenas. The French occupied the other bank, and extended towards Valladolid to which place a Division was sent, the bridge having been previously mined.

[1] The 1st Battalion 1st Foot Guards had arrived at Corunna on October 1st 1812. JM's observations on the soldiers as being very young and inexperienced are very pertinent as hundreds of them would soon be struck down with sickness. See also Chapter Two, note 1, page 61, for more on the 1st Foot Guards and their problem with sickness.
[2] The Royal Sappers and Miners was formed on August 4th 1812, too late for any of its personnel to take part in the siege of Burgos. See Whitworth Porter, *History of the Royal Corps of Engineers*, II, p.141. The miners referred to by JM were probably men of the Royal Military Artificers, the new corps' predecessors.
[3] October 25th 1812 was a bad day for Wellington. Several bridges were blown up in the wake of his retreating army. However, the bridge over the Carrion at Palencia was taken by Souham before it could be mined. The bridge over the Pisuerga at Tariego was partially destroyed but the French managed to cross by way of the arch which had not been damaged and some 40 men of the working party were taken prisoner. The bridge at Villa Muriel, on the other hand, had been destroyed but part of Maucune's division crossed the Carrion by way of a ford and advanced against the Spanish troops in position there. These gave way and the French went on to take the village of Villa Muriel itself, forcing Wellington to send the 5th Division against them. The French were subsequently driven from the village by the British but only after the latter had suffered around 500 casualties. Wellington's friend and Spanish liaison officer, General Miguel de Alava, was badly wounded whilst trying to rally the fleeing Spaniards. There are confused and somewhat conflicting accounts of these actions in Oman, *History of the Peninsular War*, VI, 77-82, and Fortescue, *History of the British Army*, VIII, 602-603.

October 27th. About eleven o'clock Lord Wellington sent in a flag of truce to request that some women who had been taken on the 24th might be returned. Taking advantage of this moment they brought up some Horse Artillery and as soon as the flag was withdrawn commenced firing with the intention of driving us from the heights. Ours so commanded them that they were soon obliged to retire. General Souham sent sixteen women in with a message to Lord Wellington assuring him that he was reconnoitring when the flag came in, that the artillery was brought up without his knowledge, and that he was extremely sorry for it and hoped no harm had been done. I saw their General afterwards riding with an escort of Gendarmes. Their camp was so close to us that we could see all their motions. The women said they behaved very civilly to them. October 28th. Things remained the same. They made another attack to drive us from the heights and with similar success. I was ordered to proceed on detachment to Lisbon and I lost no time in obeying the order. I got as far as Valladolid, 2 leagues, and bidding adieu to the delights of bivouacs, wet and dry, took up my abode for the night at my former quarter in the garden, the Patrone seeming delighted to see me.

Cabezon, near Valladolid,
October 28th 1812

My Dear Charles,

There is a tide in human affairs and at present it runs strong against us. It is heartbreaking to think of the change. On the 21st we moved out of the trenches and found the rest of the army in position in front of it. In the evening they showed a force in the plain and we moved down to attack and allowed us to come close up when they moved off. To the surprise of everyone we retreated at dusk on the 22nd and what is more extraordinary the enemy did the same. We marched over the bridge of Burgos, the moon shining clear and only about a hundred yards from the castle. Fortunately they did not discover us. I could have cried on looking up at the scene of all our labours and at the thought of leaving so many gallant men unburied and uselessly sacrificed. On the 25th we stopped at Duennas, and the 5th Division lost 500 men. Our retreat had been irregular; we were closely pressed by superior numbers and our men weak from constant rain and fatigue — an English army cannot retreat. They took vast numbers of stragglers. On the 26th we retreated here where we are strongly posted in front of the bridge which we have mined. The Pisuerga is scarce fordable and the only thing we can do if forced is to retire on the other side of the Douro and defend it. I am so out of spirits with the whole thing that I am not sorry at being about to start on detachment to Lisbon, where I expect to remain five months. I have now but three above me and have great prospects of promotion, so that I calculate upon not joining the army again.[1] I have been in this

---

[1] The ensigns above JM were George Percival, Walter Baynes and John Stepney Cowell. It is interesting that as well as those of JM, the letters and memoirs of both Percival and Cowell exist today. Percival's are with the National Army Museum, London. Cowell's were published as *Leaves from the Diary of an Officer of the Guards*, in 1854.

country now some time, have been absent but eight days from my regiment, have seen a great deal and suffered something, and I confess look forward with pleasure to a little tranquillity. I am only afraid of the expense, as Lisbon is the most extravagant place in Europe. I must however do the best I can and live quietly. Let all my letters be directed to Lisbon; it will cause my friends to pay postage but it will ensure my getting them. I shall be a month on my journey down.

We have left 150 wounded behind us and many of those we have carried on have died. Our party lost on the 19th one half in our attacks in killed and wounded. They had knocked and pushed down every man. Burgess was killed and Walpole so severely wounded that there is a great chance of not getting over it.[1] I think I am in luck. Now some consolation is that Lord Wellington has expressed himself in the most flattering terms. What is to become of our affairs here? Our army consists of 14,000 British and Portuguese and as many Spaniards. The French have 35,000.[2] The Marquis has ruined his character, has lost 2,000 men in the siege, wasted two months of the most precious time and brought a most formidable army upon him. He has exposed his troops to five weeks constant rain and brought on a great deal of sickness. Soult threatens Madrid with an immense army; Hill has an inferior and motley crew. In short, I think it all stands on the hazard of a die. If my things are not sent, let them go to Lisbon. I send you enclosed drafts to the amount of £76 12s which acknowledge by return of post. They will more than cover any drafts.

The French have pressed us closely every day. Our cavalry have suffered as they are outnumbered. The rivers that we have passed have befriended us much as we have been able to retard them by blowing up the bridges. On one occasion we were taken in — the mine failed. The miners returned to it and were made prisoners. They made an attempt yesterday to drive us from the bridge and brought up some guns. The ground above it is so commanding that they were however soon dismissed. They made another attempt this morning and with similar success.

I am going to start this evening and therefore am in no little hurry. I will write more fully by the next mail. At present it is as much as I can do to get ready.

October 29th. I intended starting at my leisure, by seeing troops marching by the town thought it high time to get off. I was proceeding with my baggage through the town when I was met by a vast crowd of persons rushing through the streets, screaming violently. It was some time before I could find anyone

---

[1] This was the attack on Burgos on October 18th 1812.

[2] JM was not too wide of the mark here. In a despatch to Charles Stuart, Wellington put his own numbers at, '20,000 British and Portuguese. Amongst the British are all the foreign troops in the army; and I have not 1,500 English cavalry and only 24 pieces of artillery.' *Despatches*, Wellington to Charles Stuart, 31st October 1812, IX, 524. In a similar despatch to the Earl of Bathurst ,Wellington estimated the number of Spanish troops with his army at 12,000 while the French army immediately opposed to him was put at not less than 40,000. (*Despatches*, Wellington to Bathurst, 28th October 1812, IX, 519-520.)

sufficiently collected to inform me the reason. At last I was told that the French had crossed the river, entered the town, and were coming down the streets. I sent my baggage off at a trot. The things kept tumbling off every moment and at last succeeded in getting safe out. The whole scene was most capital. Everyone swore they had seen French Dragoons in long grey cloaks and I believe after all that not a Frenchman was there. I passed our columns at Puente del Duero, where they were to be bivouacked for the night and as all the bridges were blown after they had passed, the progress of the French must be stopped for some time at least. I proceeded 4 leagues to La Seca where I found a vast number of wounded and sick who had been sent off to make the best of their way to Salamanca. Some of them had not been dressed since the 24th and most had not had rations for two days. About twelve o'clock my servant woke me and said that the town was in uproar and the French expected in every moment. I got up and found as he said. The wounded were crawling off as well as they could and the people were wringing their hands. Having got my baggage loaded I requested the Patrone to show me the road to Medina del Campo. In going through the market place he attempted to run off. I drew my sword and he accompanied me to Medina, 8 leagues.

October 30th. I had great difficulty in getting into a house. At last I got the window open and found a party of guerrillas there. I had not been in bed long when another alarm reached me. This was rather too much and I determined to wait till daylight. I ventured to hint to the guerrillas that being mounted and thirty in number, they might stop and have a look at the enemy, but they said their horses were young and that they must make the best of their way to the mountains. It rained during the whole of my journey to Tresons, 4 leagues, where I got into a comfortable house taking rank a lieutenant colonel.

October 31st. Having had a long march I determined to halt and rest my animals. Numbers of wounded came in during the day and many of them told me they were actually starving, having had nothing to eat for three days. The people here were very much alarmed hearing that some French Dragoons were prowling the country.

November 1st. I got to Petuga, 5 leagues. The whole country between this and the Douro, 15 leagues, is an open plain without a tree and almost entirely planted with vines. I observed the people of the town to be very melancholy and hardly able to lift up their heads. They told me that a party of sick and wounded had passed through the day before and being nearly starved had plundered the town, and taken from them all they had.

November 2nd. To Salamanca, 4 leagues. I had some difficulty in getting a quarter and found here as elsewhere that the Spaniards began to think that the difference between the plundering of a French and an English army was not so great as they had expected. I found a great many Guardsmen here sick. The hospitals were sending all their sick to Ciudad Rodrigo to clear the place in case of a retreat. I observed a great many officers here. Some had remained since the 22nd of July. There were wounded of all sorts and in almost every different part of the body. A great many appeared in boisterous health, particularly the Portuguese. A General Hospital always abound with skulkers who object to doing regimental duty. Frazer came in today, having performed a journey of 40 leagues from Burgos and looking very ill.[1]

November 3rd. They seem very much alarmed about the French here. The moving of the sick to the rear confirms their fears. I went to visit the forts. We have completely destroyed them. The surgeons have told Frazer that he must lose his leg. He seems wonderfully composed. The Parson of our Division was taken on the 24th and not having been returned yet I suppose they mean to keep him.

Salamanca
November 3rd 1812

My Dearest Father,

You will be surprised to hear that I am here but without the army, though I think they will soon be here. I am so far on my way to Lisbon where I am to take charge of sick and stores and expect to remain there about four months, and I think the chances of promotion are so great that I hope to start from thence for the happy land. During the time I have been in the country I have been absent but eight days and I confess I look upon my present duty as a lucky escape from a great deal of hard duty. Our want of success at Burgos and the subsequent retreat will cause a great deal of dissatisfaction in England. I think it has turned the tide of affairs here and Spain I think is lost. If ever a man ruined himself the Marquis has done it; for the last two months he has acted like a madman. The reputation he has acquired will not bear him out — such is the opinion here.[2] After our unsuccessful attempt on the 19th the works were still carried on. On the 21st we moved forward two leagues to a very strong position in front of Burgos, where we found the French army opposite to us. In the evening their movements obliged us to move down the hill and they avoided our attack. On the evening of the 22nd we retreated and improbable as it may appear, the

[1] Captain Charles Mackenzie Frazer had been wounded in the leg at Burgos on September 12th 1812.

[2] Wellington referred to Burgos as 'the worst scrape I ever was in', in a *Despatch* to Charles Stuart, Wellington to Stuart, 31st October 1812, IX, 524. Coming on top of such a successful year, which had seen the capture of both Ciudad Rodrigo and Badajoz, as well as the great victory at Salamanca, not to mention Almaraz, JM was probably right in thinking that the British public would feel disenchanted by the failure at Burgos. 1810 had been a hard year for Wellington who was plagued by calls for a return home. 1811 had seen a turn in the army's fortunes whereas 1812, up until Burgos, had been a series of glorious victories. JM's own opinion of Wellington is probably due as much to the miseries of the retreat from Burgos as to the actual failure of the operation. This is not, however, the first piece of criticism levelled at him for JM was never one to be blinded by the Peer's reputation. He disapproved of the wording of Wellington's despatches on a number of occasions as can be seen throughout this volume, and was particularly critical of the despatch carrying the news of Fuentes de Oñoro. This is, perhaps, another indication of JM's boredom with the war in general. What had started out as a great adventure had become rather tedious and the bitter experience at Burgos and the subsequent retreat had disillusioned him. Nevertheless, his opinion of Wellington has remained a constant and honest one throughout his letters and journals.

French retreated too, till finding our motions out they advanced again. Our retreat was attended with great disorder. The cavalry behaved most infamously and were saved from annihilation by the extreme good conduct of a German brigade of infantry.[1] They bivouacked the whole army one night close to some large wine vaults; the consequence was that the whole of them were drunk and in the march of that day we lost 500 prisoners. On the 24th we pulled up at Duenas and lost 500 men, 100 of whom were left behind wounded. At Cabezon we pulled up on the 26th and with the Pisuerga in our front, the bridges of which we destroyed, we maintained ourselves till the 29th when the enemy's movements obliged us to abandon that river and retire across the Douro, the bridges of which we likewise destroyed and thus I believe things remain now. The French have about 35,000 infantry and 5,000 very good cavalry. We have 23,000 infantry and 3,500 cavalry, but about half of this force is Spanish so that we cannot look with much confidence to any action. Hill is I believe still at Madrid.

I left the army on the 29th as they crossed the Douro, having primarily had to make my escape at the gallop out of Valladolid as there was an alarm that the French were in the town. Such a scene of confusion I never saw — men, women and children scampering in every direction. I got to Valdestillas that evening. In the middle of the night I was awoke by my servant who told me the French were close to the town; I made a very precipitate retreat from thence. I found the whole country in alarm till I got here, but I did not mind them, having determined not to be made a fool of again. I found all the wounded had orders to move out from hence and some alarm still prevailing, in consequence of some dragoons having slipped across the river. I shall halt here for two days longer, principally to assist poor Frazer, who is to lose his leg tomorrow. The sufferings he has undergone during the journey from Burgos have been so great that it will be a happy termination to them. The scenes I have witnessed during my journey here are beyond all belief. All the sick and wounded were ordered off to make the best of their way here. I saw a great many who had literally nothing to eat for three days. Many died and some I saw unable to move, their wounds not dressed for four days, and nothing in the world to eat. You would suppose that the Spaniards would assist them — quite the contrary. They find that there is in fact but little difference between the depredations of a French and English army and they are quite tired of us. I never saw anything more different than the reception we meet with now, and what it was three months ago. I really have no hopes now, and it is really difficult to say whether they are culpable for not making exertions. They are plundered by both parties and a change is not worth the exertion.

Our past labours have brought me very near my promotion. I have but three above me now, Percival, Baynes and Cowell. Frazer will of course leave and there is every chance of two or three more doing the same. I cannot help being sanguine about it, though I think I have grounds for building castles.

[1] This was the action at Venta del Pozo. See JM's diary, October 23rd 1812.

I am sorry for the dissolution of parliament, though it was so near its natural dissolution that it must have been expected. You know so well the trouble and expense attending an election, that I am sure you will feel happy at not running the risk for so short a time.[1]

If the continuation of the Ministry depends upon us, I think it will be cut short. We have a great proportion of luck which has eked out our slender means wonderfully. The tide has ebbed and it will require more men than you can send out to set things right, for the hard work of this campaign has sent a great many to the other world and sewn the seeds of fever which will show itself when we halt, which the weather will in a short time compel us to do.

The deaths here have for some time averaged twenty-six a day, at Ciudad Rodrigo more, as they have had a fever in the hospital; a hole is soon made in a large force at this rate. You shall hear of me from time to time as I proceed upon this long journey, but as I have now bid adieu to the terrors of war, I am afraid my productions will not be interesting. With the kindest love to all.

November 4th. Having seen some of the principal cities in Spain since I was here before, I am of the opinion that this is the finest, making allowances for the destructions committed by the French. The Cathedral of Burgos is the only one that can be compared to this and the square is unrivalled. That of Madrid is nothing to it, and the latter has no Cathedral.

November 5th. Frazer lost his leg today and is doing very well. I propose starting tomorrow having halted here as long as I can manage. I have a long journey before me but mean to take my time and hurry neither man nor beast. Headquarters remain at Merida and the army occupies the line of the Douro. The French are repairing the bridge of Tordesillas and command our side of the water so much that we cannot molest them.[2] They are likewise repairing the forts at Toro which we destroyed after taking.

November 6th. To Calcada de Don Diego, 4 leagues. The woods between this and Rodrigo feed a great many pigs. My servants stormed a flock and brought

---

[1] This is a reference to William Mills, JM's father, MP for Coventry, who had decided not to stand for a further term.

[2] The bridge over the Douro at Tordesillas was defended by a battalion of Brunswick Oels, half a company of which occupied an old medieval tower on the south bank of the river as an outlying picquet. The rest of the battalion was positioned a few hundred yards behind the tower. The bridge itself had been damaged when its main arch was blown up by a mine. On the morning of October 29th a unit of the French 6th Léger, under Captain Guingret, approached the bridge but after seeing the condition of it saw there was little chance of crossing it. However, Guingret immediately called for volunteers to swim across and drive off the Brunswickers on the opposite bank. No less than 11 officers and 44 men volunteered, each man stripping off before plunging into the cold, icy waters of the Douro, their arms and accoutrements being placed upon a hastily constructed raft which they floated across with them. Once across the daring French troops, to all intents and purposes naked, charged forward and drove the astonished Brunswickers from the tower. The rest of the battalion of Brunswickers did little better but withdrew at the first appearance of the French. Having driven off the defenders Foy's

off a very nice roaster much against the consent of the proprietor.[1] I met with Digby on his way up to the army. He dined with me and envied my journey. I could not return the compliment though mine was the longest.

November 7th. To four houses by the roadside, 4 leagues. This day's march was likewise successful for we espied a nice flock of pigs without a guardian. We charged and took prisoner a nice porker of about sixty pounds. The road is covered with sick. The bullock drivers run away with their beasts and leave the poor wretches to bivouac. I took a purveyor into my house whose mules had run away with almost all his baggage. I had some difficulty in procuring a bed for him. The Patrone made the best of his way to bed as soon as we started talking about it and claimed he was a sick man occupying the only bed he had. I begged my friend out of it and the purveyor had the benefit of having it ready warmed for him.

November 8th. It rained and I halted on that account, sooner than I should otherwise have done so at St Martin del Rio, 3 leagues. The only recommendation this house had was plenty of goats milk.

November 9th. To Ciudad Rodrigo, 5 leagues. I got an indifferent quarter in the suburbs which are given up to British troops, the town to the Spaniards. The

---

sappers came forward and began to establish a communication by way of ropes with the opposite bank. The episode was one of the boldest acts of the war. Wellington was naturally annoyed by the affair and wrote, 'I had sent orders to the regiment of Brunswick Oels to take post in its [the bridge's] ruins in such a manner as to prevent the enemy from repairing the bridge. I had the mortification, however, of learning, on the night of the 29th, that this regiment had been obliged to abandon its post.' (*Despatches*, Wellington to Lord Bathurst, 31st October 1812, IX, 525.) Fortescue, in his *History of the British Army*, VIII, 605, passed his own judgement on the Brunswickers. 'This battalion was not trusted by the British, owing to the number of deserters that passed over to the enemy from its ranks; and beyond question, if one of the Hanoverian battalions had been at Tordesillas in their stead, the event would have been very different.'

[1] Plundering was an offence usually punishable by death, although JM appears to have flouted Wellington's orders with effrontery on this day and over the next few. 'A nice roaster' probably went down well enough with JM, a Guards officer, and his servants, but one wonders how the rest of the men viewed this, given the number of miscreants who, following similar acts, were left dangling from the gallows in the wake of the Judge Advocate. One suspects that this is an indication of the depths to which the levels of discipline had sunk during the retreat from Burgos. However, given the breakdown in the Commissariat one can forgive such acts as being necessary for survival, although it was not a view shared by the Commander-in-Chief. Indeed, Fortescue, in his *History of the British Army*, VIII, 617, writes, 'Large herds of swine belonging to the peasants were wandering in the woods, and upon them the men wreaked their ill-feeling, as much from mischief as from hunger; firing so heavily that Wellington thought that the enemy had made an attack, and so recklessly that two British dragoons were wounded...Wellington hanged two of the swine-slayers but to no purpose.' Rifleman Edward Costello recalled an attack upon some Spanish supply wagons. 'The temptation to our hungry maws could not be resisted; leaving our fires, and getting up to the cars, screened by the darkness of the night, we managed to get a portion both of biscuit and aguardiente; but the Spanish guard, discovering our fellows, commenced firing on them; this was quickly returned, and several, I believe, were shot; indeed, the firing continued all night, which alarmed the chief part of our army.' (Brett-James, (Ed), *Edward Costello: The Peninsular and Waterloo Campaigns*, pp.113-114.)

breach which had been some time since repaired has fallen down owing to the heavy rains and is now nearly in the same state that it was when we entered it. The Spaniards seem particularly jealous of English officers and will not even allow them to walk upon the ramparts. They are also particularly quick in putting the English soldiers into the guard. This is really too good a joke. By a letter today from Salamanca I find that Headquarters are there. It will not be long I think before they get farther down.

November 10th. The Spaniards are constructing four new forts on the commanding points we worked upon during the siege, and which, if well finished, will particularly strengthen the place. On looking over it, it does not appear as strong as we gave it credit for. The wall is extremely weak in many places and might be easily escaladed in twenty different points. The necessity of throwing out redoubts shows the weakness of the place, besides rendering a much larger garrison necessary. To pass away the day I played pools at billiards with some Spanish officers and though I did not win one, lost but ninepence.

November 11th. Having refreshed my party by a day's halt, Greville, who happened to be going the same road, started with me and we proceeded to Ituero, 3 leagues. On the road we charged some pigs, the drivers of which took to their heels with much noise but they were too large to be portable. We must feed ourselves before we leave the Frontiers as we shall see nothing of the sort afterwards.

November 12th. To Aldea de Ponte, 4 leagues. The first town in Portugal. Before quitting Spain we stormed a pig. The owner followed us some way and at length took post behind a well, cried out to us, and knowing his distance held up his fist. At Albergueria we carried off some hay and then got into Portugal. Fare thee well, Spain — I have seen a great deal, suffered a great deal, and taken a great deal. On the whole I am quits with you. The people are the finest in the world but enervated by a bad government. They have all an air of individual, manly independence, but as a body are useless and helpless. Adieu — thy sister country, bastard in language and manners, has only the advantage of being nearer England. Portugal, the most contemptible of lands I will not spare thee. I will thump thy people and take whatever I can find. England, wouldst thou but see the land thou art fighting for, the ground on which thy people's bones are bleaching, thou wouldst curse the ambition of thy rulers. I had to thrash some domestics before I could establish myself in my quarters. The Patrone was Captain More, or Head Country Gentleman of the place — a cunning fellow, as far as words went, but knew to a tittle what he was obliged to furnish officers with, and stuck most religiously to the letter of the law. He told me that the Portuguese Dragoons who had behaved so ill near Madrid were dismounted and sent to do garrison duty in Almeida.

November 13th. To Sabugal, 4 leagues. It quite makes me ill to travel this road again. I thought that I had taken leave of it forever. The town which I have seven times passed through and each time proved more destroyed has now not more than half a dozen inhabitable houses in it. The inhabitants are a most miserable rascally set.

November 14th. We halted this day it being a commissariat station. Our marches

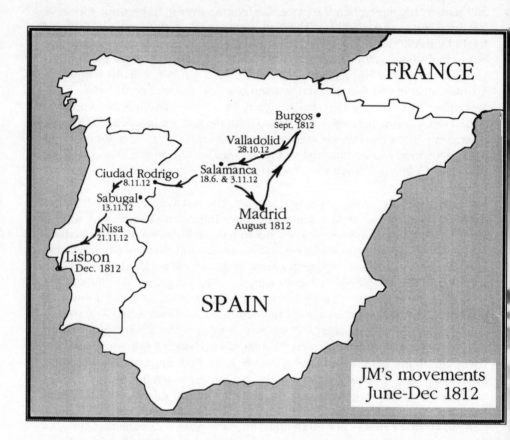

FRANCE

Burgos ●
Sept. 1812

Valladolid
28.10.12

Ciudad Rodrigo
8.11.12

Salamanca
18.6. & 3.11.12

Sabugal ●
13.11.12

Madrid
August 1812

● Nisa
21.11.12

Lisbon
Dec. 1812

SPAIN

JM's movements
June–Dec 1812

are but short, and my steed is looking better than it did when I started. We touch up these gentry very handsomely, but they will not hear of an officer of the line exceeding his allowance. There is an English commandant here, as detachments are frequently passing through. Being resident here must be some little worse than being buried alive. Sixty French prisoners and five officers came in. They were taken in the Retiro and were at that time sick. They complained much of the length of the march, and the approborious epithets bestowed upon them by the natives. They said that the Spaniards received them at Madrid with the same demonstration of joy that they showed to us. November 15th. To Caria, 4 leagues. We did not take the direct road to Castello Branco but preferred the more circuitous, as being better and having it to ourselves. Accordingly we got into the two best houses in the town. On our road we picked up a goat in milk — some recompense for a favourite one I lost in Spain. The ignorance of all in the rear as to what is going on in front is really deplorable. A Portuguese officer who came into Sabugal before I left it said that Lord Wellington and all his staff had been taken prisoners but that he had been rescued after three hours hard fighting. Such stories are very prevalent in the rear. General Hill left Madrid and joined Lord Wellington at Salamanca on the 8th.[1] We are losing our laurels by inches. It would have been better had we not gained them, as the people seeing us so often advance and retreat have no confidence in us. Rainy day.

November 16th. The master of the house who had been absent the day before made his appearance before I started. He was a young man, and the most gentlemanlike Portuguese I had ever met. The leagues are extremely long here and it was late before we got to Fundão where the people were very anxious about news. We of course humbugged them, as I found they were the more civil in proportion to the news they received.

November 17th. We went up the Siva by a most mountainous road and were, during the greatest part of the time, enveloped by clouds. The scenery is beautiful, the mountains are covered with chestnut trees and the ravines which are very numerous are planted with vines. Each mountain stream has a mill; in short, I know of nothing in Portugal more beautiful. Rain coming on, we stopped sooner than we otherwise should at 2 leagues.

November 18th. To Castello Branco, 3 leagues. It looked as wretched and dirty as ever. Our army is retreating from Salamanca and of course the game is up. They have had very rainy weather and have lost a great many men.

November 19th. To Sarnadas, 2½ leagues. I got a very tolerable quarter in the Curate's house which is now the only tolerable one.

November 20th. The rain detained me till the middle of the day when I started for the small villages in the mountains near Villa Velha. My entrance was somewhat unpropitious as a large coach dog which had followed me from Castello

---

[1] The armies of both Wellington and Hill finally concentrated at Salamanca on November 8th. This brought the strength of Wellington's army up to 52,000 British and Portuguese and 16,000 Spaniards. There were 3,500 cavalry as well as 108 guns. Wellington's position at Salamanca extended from San Christobal to the north, across the Tormes and on to Alba de Tormes, on the right. The 1st Division of the army, including the two brigades of Guards, were positioned directly in front of Salamanca itself.

Branco made an assault upon a pig which halloed most lustily thereon. The peasants immediately turned out en masse armed with old guns, pitchforks, and other savage weapons. The mountaineers are here, as well as elsewhere, a wild, lawless crew and as I prevented them from killing the dog I thought they might chance to slay me. They were very sulky, and not at all disposed to accommodate me with a quarter. I helped myself to the best I could find which was most wretched.

November 21st. To Niza, 3 leagues. I thought the passing again over Villa Velha would have made me ill. It reminded me of past labours and the recollection of even the most unpleasant events is sweet. I got a very good quarter and dined with an officer of the 48th.

November 22nd. We halted and I went out coursing and found neither hare nor other four-legged animal. General Paget is taken prisoner.[1] It appears that the retreat from Salamanca to Ciudad Rodrigo has been attended with more disasters than that of Sir John Moore.[2] Sir E. commanded the centre column and perceiving an interval in the two divisions rode back to rectify it. Some French Dragoons concealed amongst some trees dashed out and took him off. What a sad reverse we have had in a short time.

[1] See JM's letter to his Father, December 11th 1812.

[2] The retreat to Corunna in the winter of 1808-09, culminating in the battle there on January 16th, was one of the great disasters of the Peninsular War. Indeed, the battle cost the British commander, Sir John Moore, his life when he was killed towards the close of the action. The retreat was attended by a great deal of disorder, sparked off mainly by the inability of the Commissariat to supply the men which, combined with the terrible winter weather, made for a harrowing experience for all those concerned. The retreat from Burgos was accompanied by similar terrible scenes, particularly the section of the retreat from Salamanca to Ciudad Rodrigo, between November 15th to 20th. During this particular leg of the retreat the heavens opened to such an extent that the roads were turned into rivers of liquid mud. At Corunna, the roads were slushy, icy quagmires that sucked the shoes from the men's feet. The roads to Ciudad Rodrigo were equally bad, swampy morasses into which hundreds of men stumbled, never to recover. The pursuing French had no need to attack, they simply rounded up the stragglers in their hundreds. 600 were taken on November 16th alone. Once again rations were in short supply, the men became dispirited and angry and the usual scenes of pillage and disorder resulted. In one of the better accounts of the retreat William Grattan, of the 88th (Connaught Rangers), described the poor state of the rations; 'The rations arrived alive (I mean the meat), as usual after midnight, but no kettles reached us for an hour after the poor famished brutes had been knocked on the head. Each man obtained his portion of the quivering flesh, but before any fires could be re-lighted, the order for march arrived, and the men received their meat dripping with water, but little, if anything, warmer than when it was delivered over to them by the butcher. The soldiers drenched with wet, greatly fatigued, nearly naked, and more than half asleep, were obliged either to throw away the meat, or put it with their biscuit into their knapsacks, which from constant use, without any means of cleaning them, more resembled a beggarman's wallet than any part of the appointments of a soldier. In a short time the wet meat completely destroyed the bread, which became perfect paste, and the blood which oozed from the undressed beef, little better than carrion, gave so bad a taste to the bread that many could not eat it. Those who did were in general attacked with violent pains in their bowels, and the want of salt brought on dysentery.' (Grattan, *Adventures with the Connaught Rangers, 1809-1814*, pp.293-294.) The accounts of the ghastly retreat are lurid and numerous, one of

Lisbon
December 11th 1812

My Dearest Father,

As you know that I was on my road to Lisbon, I hope you have not been uneasy at my not writing. The journey was long and tedious. I have however to console myself with having escaped some very hard work for such was the retreat from Salamanca to Ciudad Rodrigo. My friends tell me that Sir John Moore's retreat was a joke to it. The army is now in cantonments where it will in all probability remain for some time. The marquis will have time to ruminate on his errors and recruit his now small army. The events of the campaign appear to them a dream and I can now hardly bring myself to believe that I have seen Burgos. The losses in this campaign have been so great that people at home must begin to open their eyes or they will be bankrupt in men and money. I was sorry to hear that William had been getting into a scrape. His refusal to obey orders was absurd, the more so as it changed a good case into a bad one, for at a mess table the Commanding Officer is upon a par with the others, and any assumption of authority there is always looked upon with the greatest jealousy. I know that had the Colonel of my own regiment used the words imputed to Major Fraser, not an officer would have been found to sit at table with him. He has been very lucky in getting out of it and it will be a severe warning for the future. The provocation was so great that considerable allowance must be made.[1]

I wrote to Sir James Bland Burgess on the death of his son, fearing he might have seen it in the Gazette, or that an official letter from the Adjutant would communicate the intelligence to him.[2] It was impossible to get his body out, the fire being so heavy, and as we marched the next morning I had not an opportunity of sending in a flag of truce. It is better that his family should not know this, as they might be uneasy. He was a noble fellow and deserved a better fate. The only thing during the whole business that struck me at all was

the reasons for this being that so many of the officers and men who left their letters and journals to posterity were forced to endure it, unlike that at Corunna where, although equally terrible, the eye-witnesses are far fewer. Wellington was naturally — if somewhat unfairly given the nature of the conditions — furious at the behaviour of his men and made no bones about it. His anger was subsequently directed at his officers, however, and his notorious Memorandum, which sparked off so much indignation throughout the army is dealt with on page 264, note 1.

[1] This is a reference to his brother, William, serving with the 22nd Light Dragoons in the Madras Presidency. It appears that he had refused to leave the Mess when ordered to do so by a Major Fraser, who seems to have given William grounds for offence. Quarrels were not unusual in India in view of the consumption of too much wine in a hot climate. Duels, though illegal, could ensue. The reference is not easy to understand because although Fraser is described as his 'commanding officer' there was no officer called Fraser in the 22nd Light Dragoons. William may have been on detachment in a mixed mess, as the 22nd Light Dragoons left Madras for the Java expedition in 1811 and stayed a year, serving with distinction under Raffles.

[2] Ensign Wentworth Noel Burgess, the son of Sir James Bland Burgess, was killed during the attack on the Castle of Burgos on October 18th. See JM's Diary, October 18th 1812.

seeing his body. His conduct had been so extraordinarily gallant and he was so universally liked, that I could have cried. The errors committed at Burgos lost us Spain. The impossibility of our again gaining it must now be evident even to the most sanguine. The Spaniards too will be averse to any future attempts as those towns which welcomed and assisted us will pay too dearly for their enthusiasm to run any further risk. With the Battle of Salamanca to back us we complained that the Spaniards were lukewarm, but what should we find them again?

I am badly lodged here, but on the whole get on very well. I find this place more Anglified every time I see it. Men, women and children ape us, and most of them clumsily.

As I am now tolerably proficient in the language I find myself quite at home. The first thing I shall do when I get to England will be to set about languages, for really the misery and nonentity of neither knowing what is said or being able to speak is beyond description. As an instance, a friend of mine is very much in love with a very pretty woman, but unfortunately, neither he nor she understand one another, and he has begged me to act as interpreter. Now the chances are that I fall in love with her myself, or at all events not interpret accurately.

Our credit is getting bad here, the Commissariat not being able to take up their bills; dollars are at five and tenpence, which is much higher than when the French were expected here. The fact is that the expense of the war is beyond our means and the murder will out one day, for the money that is independent of the actual expenditure, is enormous. Every horse brought from England costs forty pounds for his passage, and the number sent out is very considerable; in the Artillery alone, the actual loss is estimated at a hundred per month.

Compton tells me that you have exchanged some land in Avon for the little fields near Bisterne. It will be a great advantage in point of game, and indeed on every consideration. I hope to find Bisterne very much improved and the trees somewhat higher.[1]

Sir Edward Paget is sent to Bayonne. He was taken in the high road in the interval between two divisions. He was so angry that for some time he refused to tell who he was. The French say he is très triste et très fier and I dare say he is; not one of his aides would go in to him which has brought great discredit upon them; I think they ought not to have deserted him when he was in need of them. He was a most excellent man and would have made a good officer. He had served for a short time in the beginning of the war in this country and with a good deal of credit.[2] But war as it is and war as it used to be are two such different things; that what was a good general would now be a bad one. Service

---

[1] This would be with the farmers on the south side of the estate. For nearly 100 years successive Mills rationalised detached outlying farms or fields by exchanges with their neighbours, the principal one being with the Morants on the north side in the 1860s. The reference to the trees being somewhat higher alludes to a planting programme started by William Mills which was subsequently taken much further by JM, his son, grandson and great-grandson, all called John Mills.

[2] General Edward Paget was captured by a 3-man French patrol on November 17th. Paget was riding back to the leading brigade of the 7th Division to try to order it

is the only thing for an officer or soldier and it is a matter of surprise how we used to get off on expeditions as well as we did. We now see that it is only by imitating the French that we can get on at all, and we have still a great deal to learn, particularly the art of retreating, which we are children at, and which they do inimitably. The retreat from Burgos did not cost less than six thousand men, when we ought not to have lost five hundred;[1] in short, this campaign has been more instructive than all the others put together, but we have paid so dearly for the lesson that it would have been better not to have learnt it. 5,000 men have left Sicily to reinforce General Maitland on the coast of Catalonia; our retreat must however change the whole plan. That army will not be missed, as during the whole time they have done nothing and as Lord Wellington says have always been thinking of the best way to get back to their ships. The Americans frighten our ships of war here, most of them being manned by English sailors, and carrying as many men as we do.[2] I must now conclude with my best and kindest love to my Mother and all your party.

Lisbon
December 19th 1812

My Dearest Mother,

I have received a long letter from you of the 29th full of congratulations in having changed the scene to Lisbon. I am very comfortable, forget the soldier and enjoy myself. I dine somewhere or other every day thanks to my friends. I can now communicate but little military news. Everyone seems disheartened at the conclusion of the campaign. For the first time during the period of my being in this country I perceive that the Gazette returns are incorrect and that to a very considerable extent. I have from the first complained of the humbug practised upon the people of England but the low deception of false returns proves the badness of our case. Lord Wellington talks with confidence of an active campaign the beginning of the year; it may be so, and if Russia gains her point the French will evacuate Spain, but I have seen enough to know that the English can never drive them out. And now after a most severe campaign, successful as

to close up with the rear brigade of the 5th Division. He was riding alone, save for his Spanish servant, and when the three Frenchmen, from Vinot's light cavalry, swept out from their lair at the corner of a wood, he was easily taken. Paget had just one arm, the other having been lost at the crossing of the Douro at Oporto in May 1809. He had not long returned to the Peninsula, having been sent there in order to assume the post of Wellington's second-in-command.

[1] When the divisional returns were completed on November 29th 1812 they showed a startling 4,921 men missing since October 29th and this did not include the number of men killed and wounded in the various actions and those sick in hospital. Oman estimates the number of casualties due to actions as being around 1,200 which, added to the 4,921 missing, is a sad testament to the British army during the retreat. See Oman, *History of the Peninsular War*, VI, 154-155, for more on these figures.

[2] The redoubtable American frigates had plenty of seamen of their own from the ports along the east coast of America, but they also drew on British sailors who were only too glad to escape the harsh discipline of the Royal Navy.

far as the courage of soldiers could make it, the army, naked, without hay, and
reduced by sickness, is told that they have conducted themselves so ill, that
they have brought all the evils upon themselves. Is this fair? What encourage-
ment has a man to do his duty?[1]

In the novelty of anything like a civilised life I endeavour to forget the
past; at least the toils of it. When I do look back on the campaign it appears as
a dream. I would not have missed it, as I have seen a great deal, and under
circumstances that no-one ever lived before or can again.

I have received a most flattering and kind letter from Sir J. Burgess in
answer to the one I wrote to him communicating the death of his son. He seems
to feel the loss severely.

---

[1] JM is referring here to Wellington's infamous Memorandum of November 28th,
addressed to 'Officers Commanding Divisions and Brigades.' In it, Wellington took to
task his officers for allowing their men to get out of control during the retreat from
Burgos. In the course of a full three pages, Wellington criticised his officers for their lack
of effort, pointing out that, 'the army under my command has fallen off in this respect [ie
fit for service] in the late campaign to a greater degree than any army with which I have
ever served, of which I have ever read....It must be obvious however to every officer, that
from the moment the troops commenced their retreat from the neighbourhood on the
one hand, and from Madrid on the other, the officers lost all command over their men.
Irregularities and outrages of all descriptions were committed with impunity, and losses
have been sustained which ought never to have occurred....We must look therefore for
the existing evils....I have no hesitation in attributing these evils to the habitual inatten-
tion of the Officers of the regiments to their duty.' (*Despatches*, 28th November 1812, IX,
582-585.) Wellington went on to point out the failure of his officers to see to their mens'
welfare, the lack of care in the issuing of provisions, forage, ammunition, etc. He even
compared his officers unfavourably with their French counterparts. The Memorandum
took no account of the terrible conditions endured by the army during the final days of
the retreat and naturally infuriated those regiments which had at least maintained some
sort of order. Virtually all of Wellington's officers regarded it as an affront and, in fact, so
enraged were they that many of them sent it to the newspapers in England where it was
instantly published, prompting a wave of resentment throughout the whole army. Even
Wellington's close friends thought the order to be unjust and, as Fortescue, the historian
of the British Army, wrote later, 'in so far as it denied that the Army had suffered extraordinary privations and comprehended every corps in one sweeping damnatory sentence,
undoubtedly it was so.' (Fortescue, *History of the British Army*, VIII, 621.) The epithets
given to the private soldiers are many and are the more famous of all Wellington's
sobriquets and yet on this occasion he turned on his officers, laying the blame for the
disgraceful conduct during the retreat to Burgos squarely on their shoulders. JM obviously considered this criticism unfair and possibly had grounds for complaint, given the
breakdown of the Commissariat, for example, which forced men to turn to plundering in
order to exist, there being no other food supplies with the army at certain times during
the retreat. The officers also suffered, many of them surviving for days on just a meagre
supply of nuts. As we have seen with JM, the officers, too, turned to illegal methods in
order to survive. For many of them it was simply a matter of life or death and in such
circumstances how was an officer to control his men when all they wished to do was to
live? Drink was another matter, of course, but even here, some men, such as Edward
Costello of the 95th, were convinced they would have died had it not been for the wine
they drank. See Brett-James (Ed), *Edward Costello, The Peninsular and Waterloo Campaigns*, p.114 See also Fortescue, *History of the British Army*, VIII, 621-623, and Oman,
History of the Peninsular War, VI, 156-161, for more analysis.

Digby Mackworth has been here nearly a month.[1] He seems a foolish fellow; he made an assault on the heart of a Portuguese lady by sending her a print of the Hottentot Venus at which she very naturally was not much entertained. The society of the natives here is not good. All the principal people have followed the Royal Family to Brazil. Their parties are very dull to those who do not play. Lasquenet[2] is the great game, and so fond are they of it that they will play all night. The love of gambling is not confined to higher orders. The beggars in the streets have each their pack of cards. The English form a very considerable society here. Sir Charles Stuart keeps an open house and delightful it is. In short, Lisbon is a place where an Englishman is fully justified in living with his countrymen as the society of the inhabitants is now indifferent, and their only object to ape us. I have not as yet been able to visit Cintra and other beauties in the environs of this place. The truth is I have had so much rambling that I am glad of an opportunity of remaining quiet, but I shall not quit this without making the usual tour of the environs. My letters from the army speak with great satisfaction of the comfort of winter quarters. Their rest is however somewhat disturbed by a march of twelve miles twice a week to keep them in practise, though one would have thought they could not forget the way to march.

Lord Wellington is gone to Cadiz to get some of the refractory spirits to rights; it seems that his appointment as Generalissimo of the Spanish Armies has caused a good deal of dissatisfaction amongst some of the Spanish generals who look with jealousy on any innovation. It may too be necessary for him to persuade them we have lost nothing, which, I think, he will be some time doing.[3]

I left a commission with a friend of mine to enquire after young Ward. The Division he is in was and still is far from ours, and the communications very irregular, but I will write again today upon the subject and you shall hear from me when I get an answer. The regiment, however, has not had anything to do since Badajoz. Detachments arrive here from England almost every day. Shirley

[1] Digby Mackworth had been exchanged for a French officer having been taken prisoner in June 1811. See JM's letter August 6th 1811.

[2] Lasquenet was a card game of German origin.

[3] Wellington had been appointed Generalissimo by the Spanish Cortes in a letter dated November 18th 1812. 'I have the honour of receiving your Excellency's letter of the 18th of November, in which you have enclosed the copy of the decree of the Cortes, by which I have been appointed to command in chief the Spanish armies.' (*Despatches*, Wellington to Don Josef de Carvajal, 4th December 1812, IX, 604.) In the same despatch he laid out his conditions for acceptance of the position which included the control of promotions and appointments, the right to dismiss any officers not doing their duty, the application of State resources as he saw fit, and the appointment to his headquarters of a Spanish chief-of-staff to whom all military reports from the various regions of Spain would be sent. He left for Cadiz on December 12th, arriving there some eleven days later. The main purpose of his visit was the re-organisation of the Spanish army and to ascertain for himself the state of affairs there, following on from the conditions set out in his letter of December 4th. Wellington returned to the army on January 25th 1813 having considered his mission to Cadiz to have been a successful one. See Oman, *History of the Peninsular War*, VI, 194-213, for an in-depth account of Wellington's dealings with the Spanish Cortes and the Portuguese Regency.

brought out a hundred men of ours but has lost 50 and the remainder are all sick. He landed at Corunna and had of course to make a long march. He was fortunate in not being taken, being for some time in ignorance of the retreat. Mr Jeffrey, of Poole, is Consul here. Mrs Jeffrey means to give a good dance to which I am invited. They are a good sort of vulgar people, and are of some consequence here, he fancying the situation of Consul very little inferior to that of ambassador. George Digby[1] is here and takes convoy to England. I have not had an opportunity of introducing myself to him, and I think he has sailed this morning. He carries home Sir Stapleton Cotton and suite as well as the Portuguese Ambassador, a tolerable crowd. The Opera is extremely good — Bertinotti is first singer — the ballets I cannot say much for. What think you of their converting Macbeth into a dance? I think Mrs Siddon would be astonished to hear of Lady Macbeth performing a pirouette. The music of the orchestra is infinitely superior to that in London and I think the House finer. Tell Harriet Somerville if she is with you that I hear sad accounts of her cruelty.

My kindest love to all your party, and wishing you all a Happy Christmas. Believe me, Ever Affectionately Yours,

---

[1] A cousin of JM's on his mother's side.

Chapter Eight

Holland

JM spent the winter of 1812-13 in comfortable quarters at Lisbon in charge of the battalion's stores and the sick. In February 1813 he sailed home to England on leave. He was never to return to the Peninsula but remained instead with the 2nd Battalion in England until November 24th 1813 when he sailed for Holland as part of a detachment of six companies of the battalion under the command of Lieutenant Colonel Lucius Frederick Adams. The expedition to Holland followed Dutch appeals to England for assistance in the wake of their rising against the occupying forces of Napoleon. The British Government responded with a force of 6,000 troops under Sir Thomas Graham. The object of the campaign, other than that of encouraging the Dutch people, was the capture of the port of Antwerp and the fleet which lay at anchor in its harbour.

The campaign was a less than glorious affair. The Allied commander, Bülow, who was present at Breda with a small force of Prussians, advanced halfway to Antwerp before retiring in the face of an apparent threat from a French force under General Macdonald. This forced Graham into cantonments close to Bergen-op-Zoom which quickly became the objective of the British commander. As JM played no part in this latter operation we need not dwell upon it, other than to say that when Graham attacked it on the night of March 8th 1814 the assault was repulsed at a cost to the British of 2,500 men.

JM himself returned to England in February 1814 having been struck down with illness, probably pneumonia. He spent the remainder of that year recovering but such were the effects of his illness that he was forced to resign from the army on August 31st 1814.

In spite of the glorious record of the 1st Battalion Coldstream Guards in the Peninsula, it could be argued that the greater glory was won by the 2nd Battalion which went on to fight at Waterloo on June 18th 1815. By a twist of fate, the six companies of the 2nd Battalion Coldstream Guards marched into Antwerp at the conclusion of the campaign in March 1814 and remained there for the next four months. In August 1814 they marched to Brussels where they were joined the following month by the remaining four companies which had sailed from England on August 27th. The battalion remained at Brussels until March 1815. This meant, of course, that when a certain French emperor made good his escape from Elba in February 1815 and marched on the Belgian capital four months later, the 2nd Battalion Coldstream Guards was perfectly placed to take a hand in his final downfall at Waterloo. Had not JM been taken ill in Holland he would have remained with the battalion and fought at Waterloo where he would have found himself one of the defenders of Hougoumont.

Hague
Tuesday, December 7th 1813

My Dear Charles,

I wrote to you yesterday from on board the Dictator at anchor in Scheveling roads. Here I am at least in an excellent house with Jack Talbot,[1] the master of which will not hear of our eating anywhere else but in his house, which is as good a one as a gentleman need wish for. We were carried in Dutch fishing boats from the ships to Scheveling, where the surf is so high that it is quite impossible to avoid getting wet. From the boats we were carried ashore in waggons. From thence to this place is about two miles, the road straight and paved, an avenue of trees. The reception we met with was as warm as the Dutch are capable of giving. They made a considerable noise, but if that was not as loud as I expected, it was fully recompensed by their kind treatment. The soldiers all think themselves gentlemen and walk about arm in arm with very respectable people. In short, we have it all our own way and excepting 200 Marines we are the only military, the others not having yet arrived. The Prince of Orange was received with great acclamations and they seem delighted to have him back again. They speak of Bonaparte in great detestation and according to their account he has extorted from them all they have. I think they are even now in a fright lest he should regain the country, which he vows he will do, and take vengeance on them.

The town is quite beautiful and I saw it to great advantage as last night there was a grand illumination in honour of the Hereditary Prince[2] whose birthday it was. The streets are well paved and the houses remarkable clean, both inside and out, in fact they are just what you see in Dutch pictures. Their taste is formal and everything is on the small scale. The weather is so extremely cold that I have not been able to see as much of the town as I could wish. We move from hence tomorrow or the day after, in which direction I know not, but probably to Gorkum, to which the Crown Prince[3] is advancing. There is there a garrison of 4,000 men but it seems doubtful whether they will defend it. Another report was that we were to go to Helder. I think we shall have a good deal to do; I hope it may be over quickly. You may conceive the ignorance in which

---

[1] John or 'Jack' Talbot had served with the 1st Battalion Coldstream Guards in the Peninsula between October 1811 and December 1812 before returning home on promotion to join the 2nd Battalion.

[2] This is presumably a reference to the Prince of Orange, the young Dutch prince who had served on Wellington's staff in the Peninsula. He was wounded at Waterloo. The Lion Mound on the battlefield commemorates his part in the battle.

[3] This may be a reference to Crown Prince Bernadotte of Sweden (1763-1844) who had served with distinction under Napoleon and was created a marshal of France. However, Napoleon dismissed him from the army following the battle of Wagram in 1809. The following year he became Crown Prince of Sweden and three years later, following Napoleon's seizure of Swedish Pomerania, he found himself fighting on the opposite side of his old master as commander of the Army of the North in Germany. He became King Charles XIV in 1818. He took part in the initial stages of the Dutch campaign before invading Holstein.

Bonaparte keeps his subjects when I tell you that till within this fortnight, the Dutch were in perfect ignorance of all that has passed in Spain. The defeats too at Leipzig[1] were magnified into victories, and anyone that ventured to hesitate in his belief was immediately confined.

The exchange is against England. A pound note is worth 9 guilders; a guinea 12s and 8d. A guilder is about 1s 8d. I cannot admire the women. They are large and fat without any shape, their dress not becoming. Grimaldi's hat[2] is a joke to the machines they wear on their heads. They wear wooden shoes, and the noise they made last night waltzing in the streets was something louder than a dray cart.

I have proposed sending a letter to Bisterne by this mail, but I find I shall not have time. If you can get a franc you may well send this.
Believe me, Ever truly yours,
John Mills.

Maes Sluys
Monday December 13th 1813

My Dearest Mother,

My letter to Charles would inform you of our having reached the Hague on Monday last, and I am sorry to say that we left it on Saturday, reached Delft yesterday, and proceeded here today to be ready for ulterior operations. Willemstadt and Breda have surrendered, the Russians and Prussians have moved from Rotterdam to Goericheim, or as it is pronounced Gorkum, and will begin to bombard it today. Their army is in high order excepting a great want of shoes. I imagine that we shall, on the arrival of the other troops from England, co-operate with them in the reduction of Antwerp, Bergen-op-Zoom and the other Dutch places. We were entirely well off at the Hague, and made much of. The inhabitants everywhere give us free quarters, and are civil to a degree. The soldiers say they wish to remain here all their lives, for they get as much as they like to eat and drink for nothing. In fact, as yet it is anything but campaigning, as you may imagine when I tell you that I march in a post coach. I cannot say that I am a great admirer of the country. There is nothing like a hill and but very few trees. The towns are quite beautiful; their houses exceedingly clean, and the exterior ornamented in different ways. At the Hague there is little to be seen; the houses are very fine but the French have levied so many contributions that the inhabitants are too poor to live in them.

The conscription for the Garde d'Honneur was so severe, that all the noblesse have been obliged to serve as privates, it not being allowed to provide

---

[1] On October 16th-19th 1813 the Allied armies of Russia, Prussia and Austria had inflicted a crushing defeat on Napoleon at Leipzig. This gruelling battle, often called the Battle of the Nations, resulted in losses of 60,000 men on both sides.

[2] Grimaldi was the great clown of the age. He once said of Daniel Mackinnon, the great joker of the Coldstream Guards, 'he had only to don the motley and he would completely eclipse me.'

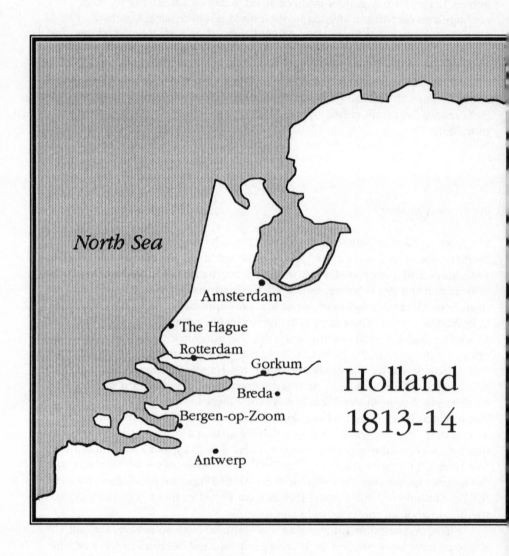

a substitute, and there is not a family that has not either a brother or a son now serving with the French army. I went on Friday with a party to Leyden, where they had not seen any of our troops. The town was in an uproar and five hundred people followed us through the streets. The college there is not worth seeing, but we were fortunate enough to meet with the Principal, a very excellent man, who showed us everything worth seeing, amongst other things a magnificent collection of paintings.

The Cossack you saw in London was very superior to any that I have yet seen. They never sleep in a house, and I saw some at the Hague encamped in a stable yard. Both friends and enemies dislike them, for they take whatever they choose. They swear that on their entry into France they will destroy man, woman and child, and that they will first pillage Paris and then burn it, for nothing could persuade them but that the French burned Moscow.[1] There are some Bosnian Cossacks, who use bows and arrows, and are quite naked.

The weather is very cold, and if the frost continues the rivers will be frozen up. We find here French productions of all sorts. I am no judge of lace or cambric but they say it is very fine. China too in abundance, but the Dutch say ours is better, and my landlord produced yesterday some common white plates of English manufacture, which he said were very curious.

Before the revolution commenced Count Hoggendorf, who organised it, went to the chief Magistrate at the Hague and told him that he feared a disturbance would take place, begging him to demand 10,000 men of the Emperor, which was done. The Emperor said that so far from sparing that number he could not command 2,000. This was just what Mr Hoggendorf wanted to ascertain, and the orange flag was immediately hoisted.

As yet we have no balls, but they say they will begin immediately. There was a very indifferent French play at the Hague, ill-attended out of compliment to us. They frequently pretend not to understand French to show their aversion to the Nation; even the children speak it. My kindest love to all at Bisterne, and believe me, my Dearest Mother. Ever affectly yours,
John Mills.

Ouds Capel
December 31st 1813.

My Dearest Mother,

The Post is so irregular in this country that I never know when to write, but you may get this some time another, and will hear that I am alive and well.

We have been constantly moving since we left the Hague; more I believe from not knowing what to do than anything else. We appear to have no sort of plan. Antwerp and Bergen-op-Zoom are so strong that they are quite out of the

[1] Napoleon entered Moscow on September 14th 1812 to find the city evacuated by its inhabitants. The city was set alight by the Muscovites themselves in an attempt to deprive Napoleon of his greatest prize. The Cossacks to whom JM refers evidently believed that the French had burned the city themselves.

question. Our army consists of six thousand,[1] and very ineffective, either old men or boys. In our regiment there are several men who were in this country twenty years ago.[2] I am afraid the period of our stay here will be longer than we at first imagined. We find out that we are not meant as a Guard to the Prince of Orange as we are told.

I regret much that the scene of our operations is likely to be in Brabant, where there is hardly anything worth seeing, except we get to Brussels. It is here beyond anything *triste*, to say nothing of the cold. We are quartered in farmhouses, and find that their civility is fast evaporating. More than one half of the people are against the Prince, and those that are for him think they have done quite enough when they put orange ribbons in their hats. They are making no exertions whatever; I cannot conceive a more inactive people.

This part of the country swarms with Cossacks; the inhabitants are in great fear of them. They seize everything they want, and they say, eat a quarter of beef per day. I wish they were farther off, for the property even of allies is not sacred. We are now taking the outpost duty, but I suppose shall soon be relieved by some other regiment. A curious mistake has been made by the Bank; a quantity of gold has been coined in England, of Dutch and Hanoverian currency. Unfortunately, the Hanoverian money has been sent here and the Dutch to Hanover. The soldiers are very angry at it.

There is an abundance of travellers in Holland but I have hardly seen any of them. I met with Mr S. Stanhope who was going to Greece via the Hague. Something like Lord Bathurst's instructions to a party of Guards were left behind at Harwich. They were to go from Scheveling to the Hague, but should they be cut off from thence, they were to march upon Amsterdam. Ringrose has suffered excessively from the rheumatism since he has been here, and I am afraid that I shall be obliged to send him home if he does not get much better.[3]

We have strong reports of the preliminaries of peace being signed. They come from the French. Every day presents fresh obstacles to this desirable event. Napoleon still holds his head high, and the demands of the Allies must increase with their successes. Holland must now be given up. We hear that the new conscription in France goes on ill; he has been obliged to make use of his Douanniers[4] as regular troops. Five thousand of these, together with conscripts are now at Rozendaal about nine miles in our front. We should attack them with pleasure but they will not stand. They are in near a large wood to which they betake themselves on any alarm. Marshal Macdonald has within the last few days been into Antwerp. He was mistaken for Bülow and we of course thought he was coming to drive us into the sea. I have as yet received but one letter from

[1] Graham's force consisted of the Guards brigade (detachments, 1st, Coldstream and 3rd Foot Guards), Skerrett's brigade (2/37th, 44th, 55th, 2/69th, Veteran Batt.), Mackenzie's brigade (2/35th, det. 52nd, 73rd, det.3/95th), and Gibbs's brigade (2/25th, 33rd, 54th and 3/56th). Fortescue, *History of the British Army*, X, 4.

[2] JM is referring to the Coldstream Guards having landed at Bergen-op-Zoom on April 1st 1793, some twenty years before, to take part in a two-year campaign, equally miserable.

[3] Ringrose was presumably JM's civilian servant.

[4] The Douanniers were Customs officials.

England, and that from Charles, whereby I judge that some must have miscarried. Mine may have experienced the same fate therefore don't fancy I am dead if you do not hear from me, especially as I endeavour to keep out the vapours by the use of tobacco and Geneva.[1] The last article is not expensive, about five shillings a gallon.

My kindest love to all at Bisterne and believe me, Ever affectionately yours, John Mills.

Steenbergen
January 17th 1814

My Dearest Mother,

I assure you I have not had an opportunity of writing to England for the last ten days or I should have let you hear how we are going on. We get neither letters or papers from England. I have as yet received but two, one from Francis and another from Charles. I got leave to be absent from the regiment from the 4th to the 9th and went by Rotterdam to the Hague, intending to go on to Amsterdam, but found the roads in so bad a state from the snow, that it would have taken up too much of my time to have proceeded. I was much delighted with the Hague. All the Dutch families of consequence were assembled there, and it began to wear the apparatus of a Court. I was presented to the Prince at his levée, and dined with him afterwards. He is almost too condescending for a Prince. I was much disappointed in Rotterdam; the canals are magnificent but the town is very much like the east end of London, and the hurry and bustle which now prevails there makes the resemblance much greater. The disagreeable part of the tour was the being obliged to return so soon. On my joining I found the army on the point of moving and as the dispatches will inform you we moved up the Anvers with General Bülow's corps, 17,000 strong, and after a skirmish with an advanced post returned, or rather retreated as Marshal Macdonald was advancing upon us with a strong corps. The trip though short was very severe, more so than any we have seen in Spain. The frost was so intense that even my wardrobe was frozen, and our marches were generally in the night. The Coldstream were fortunate in being left two days to watch Bergen-op-Zoom by which we escaped some of the hardships. It is difficult to imagine what the object of going up could be. The weather precluded the possibility of besieging, had we had force enough, which we had not by one half.

We are given to understand that we shall remain quiet for a month, and tourists are setting off for various places. My turn will not I am afraid come round again, but I shall be very well contented with remaining quietly here, where we are well housed and in a very tolerable part of the country.

The Crown Prince has for some time been expected down in this part of the country but it seems he still stays in the north and very great doubts are entertained as to the propriety of his conduct. The Prussians are particularly

---

[1] Geneva was another name for gin, and was a corruption of the word 'juniper'.

violent, and openly charge him with having spoiled the campaign. Both Bülow's corps and ourselves are completely locked up till he comes down to us.

Lady Castlereagh arrived at the Hague whilst I was there; I heard of her playing sixpenny whist for preference, which is now to be the preferred game. His lordship, it is said, is about to return, the conference having been broken up. We have had a great many deserters come in, chiefly Dutch and Germans. They say that vast numbers are only waiting for an opportunity of coming over. The Dutch commandant of Anvers came over when we were before it with the keys of the sluice gates, which he says he was desired to open if we attacked it. There would be but little chance of drowning in this weather. It is said that a General of Division was killed in the affair before the town, but the Prussians got his coat, the Germans his boots, and a Scotchman his watch, and when thus stripped it was impossible to tell his rank.

I hope this may reach you before the rivers freeze up, which I am afraid will soon take place, as there is no probability of a thaw. Remember me most kindly to all friends, and believe me, My Dearest Mother, Ever affectionately yours, John Mills.

Epilogue

John Mills and his Successors

After 20 years of Napoleonic exclusion from the Continent many wealthy British families wanted to travel. In due course JM's next brother, Francis (1793-1854), followed his interest in the arts to France and Italy and, dying a bachelor, left his fine collection to the family.

JM had found that army travel in Portugal, Spain and Holland had sufficed him for the rest of his life. His father lived until 1820 to manage Bisterne so JM was free to develop his social contacts in London's highest society. Captain Gronow, 1st Foot Guards, now the Grenadier Guards, who returned to London from southern France with his battalion in 1814 writes, 'The dandies of society were Beau Brummell....the Duke of Argyle, the Lords Worcester, Alvanley and Foley, Henry Pierrepoint, John Mills, Bradshaw....They were great favourites of White's Club, in St James's Street, where, in the famous bay window, they mustered in force.' He adds, 'At the present time one can hardly conceive the importance which was attached getting admission to Almack's, the seventh heaven of the fashionable world. Of the 300 officers of the Foot Guards, not more than half-a-dozen were honoured with vouchers of admission to this exclusive temple of the beau monde.' He goes on to say later, 'a number of gentlemen, remarkable for their eccentricities of dress and manners, were the lions of the day both in London and Paris. For example, we had such men as Brummell, Pierrepoint, John Mills, Meyler, Bradshaw and others, who seemed to think that the principal object of their existence ought to be that of obtaining notoriety by their dress.' It is interesting to note that Bradshaw, mentioned on both occasions, had been JM's brother ensign travelling forward to join the Coldstream in April 1811.

JM clearly approved of Brummell's taste, for Gronow writes of Brummell's Chapel Street house, 'The furniture was in excellent taste, and the library contained the best works of every period and of every country. His canes, his snuff-boxes, his Sèvres china, were exquisite.' JM, after he inherited Bisterne in 1820, created a Regency library at Bisterne, equipped with just such a collection of books. He owned a tortoiseshell cane banded in gold, bought the gold enamel snuff-box, which the Prince Regent had given Brummell, after the latter's disgrace and exile, and owned a great dinner set of turquoise Sèvres. One wonders whether much of this came from the sale of the Beau's effects.

Although Regency dandies might seem social butterflies in town, they were to be seen in the first flight in Leicestershire when the fox-hunting season opened. A fine portrait exists of JM by John Ferneley, painted in 1819 and exhibited in the Summer Exhibition of that year. He is shown, a small neat figure in his red coat on a great, dappled grey hunter. He is coolly taking snuff while in the background hounds are moving off from Quenby Hall in Leicestershire to draw Billesdon Coplow, and others urgently mount. The ensign riding 'Docktail' through Portugal and Spain had become the hard man to hounds.

After William Mills, his father, died in 1820, his mother wrote to JM regretting the fast company with expensive tastes he was keeping. The Prince Regent was now the Sovereign, the hectic London pace had begun to pall on a man in his thirties and JM began to concentrate on Bisterne and his country interests.

The first of these was riding on the flat. He himself rode his own horses to win two magnificent silver gilt cups, on 'Gossoon' at Goodwood in 1824, and on 'Squirrel' at the Lambton meeting in 1825, when the cup was filled with 135 guineas. He started breeding his own racehorses at Bisterne, where the racing 'plates' of the filly 'Kate', bred there in 1829, hang. She won four sweepstakes at Newmarket in 1832, but JM was not to achieve that half of his ambition, 'to win the Derby and marry the prettiest heiress in London.' 'Kate' ran 10th in the 1832 Derby and was favourite in the Oaks but finished 4th. The heiress will be judged in due course.

Summers at this period must have been intensely busy, for JM raced his crack yacht, 'Julia' as a member of the Royal Yacht Club. An oil painting of the Cowes Regatta of August 7th 1828 shows the 'Julia', 42 tons, winning her 11th cup. She is cutting fine past the guard vessel, heeling over in strong weather to show that she was undecked like a fishing boat. Yachts began to be decked in 1832, when the Club was elevated to the Squadron.

However, behind JM's sporting ventures, which must have kept a good many people employed, there was a grim agricultural depression, usual after the end of a great war, when British farmers were no longer essential to the supply of food. The agricultural mechanisation was further affecting rural labour and encouraging Luddite tendencies. In the winter of 1830 a rider, who called himself 'Lord Hunt', started leading a large and growing mob through Sussex towards Hampshire. They started by burning the new threshing machines but soon began to set fire to properties in general. When JM and other Ringwood magistrates heard that the mob was marching south from Salisbury and was attacking West Park, near Fordingbridge, they called out at night all principal landowners with their farmers and staff and the shopkeepers of Ringwood, Christchurch and Lyndhurst in aid of the civil power. Lord Malmesbury and his brothers from Hum Court joined JM and his brother-in-law, Henry Compton, at Ringwood. JM, a Justice of the Peace, but more importantly the only local man of influence with practical military experience, was the natural leader in the emergency. Moving off at 6.30am next day this improvised mounted force met the armed mob, who had been driven off from West Park with casualties by volleys fired by the household, guests and the gamekeeper, just north of Fordingbridge. There, JM's motley band charged and dispersed the mob, and the wretched labourers, who had been misled by 'Hunt', made off. 'Hunt' and three other ringleaders were tried and hanged at Winchester.

Since there was no effective police force, telegraph or railway, and the nearest cavalry at Dorchester and infantry at Portsmouth, the Lord Lieutenant of

Hampshire, the Duke of Wellington, established and fitted out five troops of Yeomanry in the New Forest area. He later reviewed them in the Forest; on disbandment five years later, John Mills took home the green and gold guidon of the 'Vale of Avon' troop, in which he had served.

On the political scene events were moving towards a crisis and in 1831 JM was elected as the Whig MP for Rochester, serving until 1834. According to family tradition he was one of a small group of Whigs, thought sound by their commitment as landowners, who were earmarked for peerages, if the House of Lords needed to be 'packed' to ensure the passing of the Great Reform Bill. It shows a pleasant sense of self-mockery in JM that, when his family later asked him what title he would have chosen, he said with a laugh, "Lord Luggins, of course." 'Luggins' was the local pronunciation of Lugden's Bottom, the most obscure bog on the Forest edge. He served long enough to be included on the extreme edge of Sir George Hayter's great picture of the Commons in 1833. The family has the fine watercolour portrait of him, on which the picture was based. This shows him as a sharp featured, self-confident man with a power of command and the traces of the former dandy in the neatness of his dress.

1833 shows that JM was considered a man to be trusted by his influential contemporaries. White's Club was sliding into decline owing to the intemperate rejection of all prospective members by a small coterie. A special committee was set up to sit for a year and empowered to elect any candidate they chose as well as amending the rules. The committee consisted of four well-known peers and three commoners, of which JM was one. They elected one hundred new and acceptable members and created new black-balling rules which still stand today.

His brief period in the Commons had brought him back on the London social scene, for in 1835, at the age of 46, he courted and married Sarah Charlotte Micklethwait (1813-1869) aged 22. Her portrait by Sir Francis Grant shows her to be a beauty, but JM was gambling on very long odds if she was his choice as 'the prettiest heiress in London.' Six brothers were based at the family home of Taverham Hall in Norfolk, with property there, in Suffolk and Sussex. However, his long odds came unexpectedly home in 1903 when the last of the childless brothers died and the Mills son of Sarah Charlotte, the eldest daughter, became heir to the East Anglian property. It is interesting to note that her mother had been Lady Charlotte Rous, the sister of Ensign John Rous, later the 2nd Earl of Stradbroke, of the Coldstream, who served in the Peninsula at the same time as JM and whose letters have been published as *A Guards Officer in the Peninsula*, (Edited by Ian Fletcher, Tonbridge Wells, 1992).

In 1836, the elder son, John Mills IV (1836-1899) was born. After education at Eton and Christ Church, Oxford, he immersed himself totally in squiratical duties and country pursuits. With beagling experience at Oxford, he hunted a useful pack of harriers and later converted them to hunting the fox over the Western New Forest. The Avon salmon fishery was developed in his time, but, with the advent of breech-loading guns and modern cartridges, pheasant and wildfowl shooting became his great hobby, later pursued from a chair bolted to a cart as gout set in. He followed his father in planting woods but sadly introduced Rhododendron, which his great nephew has spent 50 years controlling.

The eventual heir was the second son, the Reverend Cecil Mills (1839-1908), who was Rector of Barford between 1864-1900, with whose descendants we shall finish our story.

JM continued to take snuff and he and Sarah Charlotte strongly disapproved of smoking. They nearly cut off their sons' prospects by issuing a potentially terminal ultimatum, that if John IV and Cecil cared to smoke, they would only be allowed to do so in the gunroom. This had prudently been built 200 yards from the house because of the volatile nature of the black powder stored there. One feels the shrubberies and earth closets, the sanitation up until 1900, proved a more discreet venue.

JM became High Sheriff of Hampshire in 1839 and a Verderer of the New Forest, as well as a Deputy Lieutenant for the County and had been a JP for Ringwood since his twenties. However, he and Sarah Charlotte worked closely together on many Bisterne projects. She designed an elaborate and elegant formal garden, of which a simplified form still exists. The Regency bow window, which JM added to the library, from which to admire the garden, caused him problems, for he could not match the mellow Tudor brick of the rest of the house. JM chose a radical solution, for which his heirs have reason to be grateful, in covering the whole house in thick golden stucco, which with age makes the whole house glow as if built of Cotswold stone.

It also obviated the need to point the old brickwork, and to ensure the stucco's integrity JM forbade climbing plants against the house, although ancient magnolias now clothe the south side. The old kitchen garden, now restored, was several hundred yards from the house, whose parks and their sheep and horses had come up to its walls. With the creation of the formal garden a Regency summer house was built and a ring of protective shrubberies, lawns and specimen trees from many countries were planted. Sadly, many of the trees have reached the end of their life, but Sarah Charlotte's pattern remains intact.

A good network of brick farmhouses had been established for the tenants by the later Comptons and William Mills. Sarah Charlotte designed a model bungalow for a labourer which was modern enough to be used as a pattern in the next century. She founded the excellent primary school and provided cloaks for the children, toiling down the lanes in all weathers.

With the rising agricultural and estate population the 3-mile journey to Ringwood church became tedious. William II recorded in 1808 that he had gone there with his nine children, no doubt through a morass of mud and puddles — asphalt arrived in the 1920s. In 1843 the little church of St Paul's, Bisterne, was dedicated, although the family prayer books are dated 1842 in anticipation. The initials erroneously cut as 'TM' by the printer must have infuriated JM, who had the 'T' converted to the Latin I. He had contributed the land, had the oaks felled to make a clearing and his £3,000 had ensured that the church was a neat building in Early English style.

JM was forward-looking in the interests of the neighbourhood. In the late 1840s he encouraged the South Western Railway to press on over the New Forest through his land to Ringwood, to promote the trade of that market town, and became a Director and subsequently Vice-Chairman. However, he obstructed its extension to the rural town of Christchurch until he received good compensation for his land over the Avon.

William, the soldier in India, had died in 1838, and no heirs now survive his only son. The heir of Charles, the banker, and Baronet, became Lord Hillingdon, but that Barony is now extinct. The last direct descendants of Edward left their original Mills silver back to the family. Charlotte and Henry Compton brought up ten children to maturity to remain in close touch with Bisterne. JM had a younger sister, Selina Mills, too young to appear in the Letters, who, nicknamed Sigma, became a close friend of her fellow Hampshirewoman, Florence Nightingale. She and her husband, as the childless Mr and Mrs Bracebridge, chaperoned Florence on her voyage to Scutari in 1854 and joined her in pioneering nursing work. Their friendship had developed when they took Florence to Italy in 1847 and up the Nile in 1849. Florence called Sigma, 'more than a mother to me.'

Sarah Charlotte died in 1869, but JM remained active to the end. He enjoyed the forays he had started in the Peninsula with the muzzle loader and black powder of his youth. The earliest game book shows him shooting as many walked-up partridges as pheasants, wildfowl on the river and a few blackcock in the hedgerows across the river. His last memorial was the planting of copses of larch and Scots pine on the edges of the estate, which he had rationalised in a major way by exchanges of land with his Morant neighbour to ease administration and farming. The boundaries he left still stand. JM died on February 28th 1871 and his remains lie with those of his wife in the crypt of the little church they built across the park, with its cedars planted by them.

The story of the Bisterne he loved can be quickly told, for two successive Mills named after him have spanned the 20th Century — Sir John Digby Mills and Major John Micklethwait Mills.

Sir John Digby Mills (1879-1972) was brought up at Barford as the son of the Reverend Cecil Mills, served with the Warwickshire Yeomanry in Gallipoli and France, in World War I, and was Colonel of the New Forest area Home Guard in World War II. He was MP for the New Forest and Christchurch 1932-45, 2nd Church Estate Commissioner, Deputy Lieutenant, Verderer, JP, Chairman of the Police Authority and engaged in a myriad other Hampshire and local voluntary good works. He was possibly proudest of his work for the Avon and Stour rivers and relished his days in the Bisterne countryside. His wife, Carola, of a distinguished Virginian and Maryland legal family, became Chairman of both the Ringwood bench and Juvenile Court among local authorities.

John Digby's eldest son, Major John Micklethwait Mills (1919-), served in the Hampshire Territorials, 7th Commando and the Warwickshire Yeomanry. His work for Wessex rivers has been recognised with an OBE, and he has been active in many other fields, but at Bisterne his 50 years of clearing and planting trees and the splendidly productive farms, including the efficient use of maize, while protecting the environment, would particularly appeal to JM. His younger brothers, Giles and Julian, have retired as a Major General of Green Jacket origin, and former Resident Governor of HM Tower, and a Director of Hill Samuel respectively.

If JM, his great grandfather, could jog today around the farms and woods on the shade of 'Docktail' or sit at ease over a glass of wine and a pinch of snuff, looking out at the great plane tree, under which he threatened to bivouac on his return from Spain, he would find himself content with the preservation and enhancement of all which he cared for or created in the 19th Century.

Appendix 1

OFFICERS OF THE 1ST BATTALION
COLDSTREAM GUARDS
IN THE PENINSULA, 1811
January to December unless otherwise stated

LIEUTENANT COLONELS

Joseph Fuller
 March onwards, having been posted from 2nd Battalion
Hon. Henry Brand
 January 1st to April. Posted to 2nd Battalion
James Philips
Sir George Stirling Bart
George Smyth
 From January 1st to July 3rd. On leave to England upon resignation
Thomas Braddyl
 October to December 3rd. On leave to England upon resignation

CAPTAINS

Edward Dalling (Major)
 January 1st to July 31st when he died
Lucius Frederick Adams (Major)
George Collier
Sir Henry Sullivan, Bart
 January 1st to November. Sick leave to Lisbon
William Henley Raikes
Henry W. Vachell
 January 1st to September. Promoted to 2nd Battalion
Thomas Barrow
Hon. William George Crofton
 From February, having joined from England
Daniel Mackinnon
 January 1st to August 15th. ADC to Stopford, then sick leave to England
Hon. John Walpole
 From June 25th, having joined from England

Thomas Steele
>*From February, having joined from England*

Edward Harvey
>*From March, having joined from England*

George Bowles
>*From October, from 2nd Battalion*

Thomas Sowerby
>*From November, from 2nd Battalion*

James Vigors Harvey
>*January 1st to March 30th. Promoted in 2nd Battalion*

ENSIGNS

William Lovelace Walton
>*January 1st to April 23rd. Promoted to 2nd Battalion*

William Lockwood
>*January 1st to May 22nd. On leave to England upon resignation*

Hon. John Wingfield
>*January 1st to May 4th, when he died*

Paulet St John Mildmay
>*January 1st to November 30th. Promoted to 2nd Battalion*

Alexander Wedderburn
>*January 1st to December. Promoted to 2nd Battalion*

Charles White

Thomas Bligh

Charles Shawe

George Henry Macartney Greville
>*From June 25th, having joined from England*

John Talbot
>*From October, having joined from England*

George Harvey Percival

William Stothert
>*January 1st to May 5th, when taken prisoner at Fuentes de Oñoro*

Walter George Baynes

John Stepney Cowell

Wentworth Noel Burgess
>*From February having joined from England*

John Mills

James Bradshaw
>*From March having joined from England*

Francis Love Beckford
>*From October having joined from England*

Frederick Vachell
>*From October having joined from England*

ADJUTANT

John Fremantle (Captain)

QUARTERMASTER

John Holmes

SURGEON

Charles Coombe

ASSISTANT SURGEON

Thomas Rose
Edward Nixon
   From March, having joined from England

Appendix 2

OFFICERS OF THE 1ST BATTALION COLDSTREAM GUARDS IN THE PENINSULA, 1812
January to December unless otherwise stated

COLONEL

Joseph Fuller
January 1st to May 31st, promoted to 2nd Battalion

LIEUTENANT COLONELS

Hon. Henry Brand
June to October 6th. From 2nd Battalion, sick to England October 6th
James Philips
January 1st to December, when ordered to 2nd Battalion
Sir George Stirling Bart
January 1st to February 28th. Retired by sale of his commission
Alexander Woodford
James Macdonnell
From May, having exchanged with a Lt-Col of a garrison battalion

CAPTAINS

Lucius Frederick Adams (Major)
January 1st to April. Promoted to 2nd Battalion
William Henley Raikes
Sick between end of January and August
Thomas Barrow
On leave to England between February 10th and July
Hon. William George Crofton
Daniel Mackinnon
June to September, otherwise recruiting in England

Hon. John Walpole
    January 1st to November 19th. Sick wounded, on leave to England
Thomas Steele
Edward Harvey
    January 1st to October 18th, when killed at Burgos
William Burroughs
    From July, formerly Adjutant
George Bowles
Thomas Sowerby
Edward Lascelles
    From April, having joined from England
Patrick Sandilands
    From April. Joined from England after being wounded at Talavera
Charles Mackenzie Frazer
    May to October 5th. Sick leave to England after wounded at Burgos

ENSIGNS

Charles White
    January 1st to April. Promoted to 2nd Battalion
Thomas Bligh
    January 1st to April. Promoted to 2nd Battalion
Charles Shawe
    January 1st to June. Promoted to 2nd Battalion
George Henry Macartney Greville
    January 1st to November 1st. Promoted to 2nd Battalion
John Talbot
    January 1st to December. Promoted to 2nd Battalion
George Harvey Percival
Walter George Baynes
John Stepney Cowell
Wentworth Noel Burgess
    January 1st to October 18th, when killed at Burgos
John Mills
James Bradshaw
    January 1st to October 28th. Joined 2nd Battalion
Francis Love Beckford
    January 1st to October 3rd. Sick leave to England
John Charles Buckeridge
    January 1st to October 7th, when killed at Burgos
John Lucie Blackman
    From April, having joined from England
William Grimsted
    January 1st to October 3rd. Sick leave to England

Beaumont, Lord Hotham
April to July, then November 30th onwards Sick leave in between
Hon. John Rous
From July, having joined from England
Windham Anstruther
From June, having joined from England
Charles Shirley
From December, having joined from England
Frederick Vachell

ADJUTANT

John Fremantle (Captain)
January 1st to November. Afterwards ADC to Wellington

QUARTERMASTER

John Holmes
January 1st to May 8th. Joined 2nd Battalion
Thomas Dwelly
From October 15th, having joined from England

SURGEON

Charles Coombe
Sick from January 1st onwards

ASSISTANT SURGEONS

Thomas Rose
January 1st to October 5th. Leave to England
Edward Nixon
January 1st to December 3rd. Leave to England
Thomas Maynard
From October, having joined from England

OFFICERS OF THE 2ND BATTALION COLDSTREAM GUARDS WHO EMBARKED FOR HOLLAND, 24TH NOVEMBER 1813

Lt.Col. L. F. Adams
Lt.Col. H. Loftus

Capt. W. L. Walton (Acting Adjutant)
Capt. Thomas Bligh
Capt. Charles Shawe
Capt. John Talbot
Capt. G. H. Percival
Capt. W. G. Baynes

Ensign John Mills
Ensign T. S. Duncombe
Ensign F. Eyre
Ensign T. Powys
Ensign H. Gooch
Ensign A. Culyer

Adjutant, Capt. C. A. F. Bentinck
Acting Adjutant Capt. W. L. Walton
Assistant Surgeon George Smith
Assistant Surgeon Sept. Worrell

Appendix 3

Fellow Officers of the Coldstream Guards mentioned by JM in his Letters and Diaries

BAYNES, Walter George. Ensign, April 6th 1809; Lieutenant, June 1st 1813; Retired from the army October 4th 1820.

BECKFORD, Francis Love. Ensign, January 25th 1810; retired from the army, December 29th 1813. Awarded Military General Service Medal with clasp for Ciudad Rodrigo.

BLIGH, Thomas. Ensign, April 21st 1808; Lieutenant, February 13th 1812; retired from the army, May 14th 1823.

BOWLES, George. Ensign, December 20th 1804; Lieutenant, February 1st 1810, Brevet-Major, June 18th 1815; Captain, May 27th 1825; Brevet Lieutenant-Colonel June 14th 1821; Major-General November 9th 1846. Lieutenant of HM Tower of London. Awarded Military General Service Medal with clasps for Talavera, Ciudad Rodrigo, Salamanca, Vittoria, Nivelle, Nive. Served at Waterloo. His letters were printed in volume two of *A Series of Letters of the First Earl of Malmesbury*,

BRADSHAW, James. Ensign, January 4th 1810; retired from the army, December 16th 1812. Like JM, he became a dandy in Regency London society and was a friend of Beau Brummell.

BRADDYL, Thomas. Exchanged into the Coldstream as Captain on December 7th 1799, from the 17th Regiment; Captain, December 22nd 1808; retired from the army on November 6th 1811.

COWELL, John Stepney. Ensign, May 18th 1809; Lieutenant, September 9th 1813; Captain, June 15th 1830; Brevet-Major, February 17th 1820; Retired from the army, June 21st 1832. Awarded Military General Service Medal with clasps for Fuentes de Oñoro, Ciudad Rodrigo, Salamanca and Vittoria. Served at Waterloo. His memoirs were published in 1854 as *Leaves from the Diary of an Officer of the Guards*.

CROFTON, Hon. William George. Exchanged into the Coldstream as Ensign, December 7th 1803 from Lieutenant in the Royal Fusiliers; Lieutenant, March 10th 1808. Was wounded at Burgos, October 18th 1812, and was killed during the sortie from Bayonne on April 14th 1814. Is buried in the Guards Cemetery at Bayonne.

FULLER, Joseph. Ensign, August 1st 1792; Lieutenant, January 22nd 1794; Captain-Lieutenant, June 18th 1801; Captain, May 25th 1803; Major-General, June 4th 1813. Removed from the Coldstream on July 25th 1814, being a General Officer.

FRAZER, Charles Mackenzie. Exchanged into the Coldstream as Lieutenant on August 16th 1810 from Captain in 50th Regiment; wounded at Burgos on September 22nd 1812. Retired from the army on March 16th 1814. Awarded Military General Service Medal with clasp for Salamanca. His portrait can be seen in *Gentlemen's Sons*.

GREVILLE, George Henry Macartney. Exchanged into Coldstream as Ensign, September 8th 1808, from Ensign in the 9th Regiment; Lieutenant, September 24th 1812; exchanged to Captain in the Royal Fusiliers, September 23rd 1813.

HARVEY, Edward. Ensign, May 24th 1808; Lieutenant, August 17th 1809; wounded at Fuentes de Oñoro on May 5th 1811 and was killed at Burgos on October 18th 1812.

HULSE, Richard. Born 1773. Ensign, March 24th 1790; Lieutenant, April 25th 1793; Captain-Lieutenant, September 23rd 1799; Captain, May 9th 1800; Major General, January 1st 1812. Died at Arevalo, Spain, September 7th 1812. Hulse was the brother of Sir Charles Hulse, 4th Baronet of Breamore House, near Fordingbridge, Hampshire, where the family still resides. The friendship between the Mills and Hulse families continues today.

MACKINNON, Henry. Exchanged into the Coldstream as Lieutenant on October 9th 1793 from Captain in an Independent Company; Captain, October 18th 1799; Major-General January 1st 1812; Killed whilst leading the 3rd Division at the storming of Ciudad Rodrigo on January 19th 1812 and is buried there. The uncle of the famous Daniel Mackinnon, his memoirs were published posthumously shortly after his death as *Journal of the Campaign in Portugal and Spain*.

MILDMAY, Paulet St John. 1791-1845. Joined the Coldstream as a Gentleman Cadet from the Royal Military College as Ensign, May 14th 1807; Lieutenant, October 3rd 1811; retired from the army on April 22nd 1812. Mildmay was the second surviving son of Sir Henry Paulet St John Mildmay, 3rd Baronet of Dogmersfield Park, near Fleet, Hampshire. Educated at Winchester College. Did not go to university but joined the Coldstream Guards. He was twice MP for Winchester, 1818-34 and 1837-41, and thus served England in another capacity. A great friend of JM he also appears with him in the painting by Sir George Hayter of the House of Commons in 1833.

PERCIVAL, George Harvey. Joined the Coldstream as a Gentleman Cadet from the Royal Military College as Ensign, March 16th 1809; Lieutenant, March 23rd 1813; died on November 11th 1815. His letters are deposited at the National Army Museum, London.

RAIKES, William Henley. Exchanged into the Coldstream as Lieutenant, June 13th 1805 from Captain in the 66th Regiment; Captain, June 3rd 1813; Junior Major, May 27th 1825; retired from the army on June 21st 1826. Awarded Military General Service Medal with clasps for Talavera, Busaco and Fuentes de Oñoro.

ROSE, Thomas. Assistant-Surgeon, March 31st 1804; Surgeon, November 26th 1812; appointed Surgeon in 64th Regiment on April 30th 1818.

SHAWE, Charles. Ensign, May 26th 1808; Lieutenant, April 23rd 1812; Captain, April 28th 1825. Was wounded at Bergen-op-Zoom on March 9th 1814. Awarded Military General Service Medal with clasps for Busaco, Fuentes de Oñoro and Ciudad Rodrigo.

SOWERBY, Thomas. Ensign, February 28th 1805; Lieutenant, June 27th 1810; Captain, May 14th 1817. Retired from the army, April 16th 1823. Awarded Military General Service Medal with clasps for Talavera, Salamanca, Vittoria, Nivelle and Nive.

STEELE, Thomas. Ensign, March 17th 1804; Lieutenant, June 1st 1809; Captain, January 18th 1820; Brevet Lieutenant-Colonel, December 29th 1814; exchanged to half-pay, unattached, June 1st 1829.

SULLIVAN, Sir Henry, Bart. Appointed to Coldstream as Lieutenant on December 3rd 1803 from Captain in 66th Regiment; Captain, September 24th 1812. Killed before Bayonne on April 14th 1814 and is buried in the Guards Cemetery, Bayonne.

WALPOLE, Hon. John. Ensign, February 18th 1804; Lieutenant, June 23rd 1808; Captain, July 25th 1814. Wounded at Burgos, October 18th 1812. Retired from the army on April 27th 1825. Awarded Military General Service Medal with clasps for Barrosa, Ciudad Rodrigo and Salamanca.

Bibliography

MANUSCRIPT SOURCES

THE MILLS FAMILY

The Letters and Diaries of John Mills, of Bisterne, Ringwood, written to his Family from Spain, 1811 and 1812, while serving with the Coldstream Guards, and from Holland, 1813 and 1814.

THE NATIONAL ARMY MUSEUM, LONDON

23 MSS Letters of 29 Sept. 1810 to 11 June 1814, written to his aunt Mrs Charles Drummond in London, by Lt. & Capt. G.H. Percival, Coldstream Guards, from the Peninsula, 1810-11 and the Low Countries, 1813-14.

The Letters of John Lucie Blackman, Coldstream Guards, 1812-15.

PUBLISHED SOURCES

ANGLESEY, Marquis of. *The Capel Letters; Being the Correspondence of Lady Caroline Capel and her daughters with the Dowager Countess of Uxbridge, from Brussels and Switzerland, 1814-17* (London, 1955).

BEAMISH, N. Ludlow. *History of the King's German Legion* (London, 1833).

Blanco, Richard L. *Wellington's Surgeon General: Sir James McGrigor* (Durham, NC, 1974).

BOUTFLOWER, Charles. *The Journal of an Army Surgeon during the Peninsular War, August 1809-May 1813* (Manchester, 1912).

BRETT-JAMES, Anthony (Ed). *Edward Costello; the Peninsular and Waterloo Campaigns* (London, 1967).

BRETT-JAMES, Anthony. *General Graham, Lord Lynedoch* (London, 1959).

BRETT-JAMES, Anthony. *Life in Wellington's Army* (London, 1972).

BRUCE, H.A. (Ed). *Life of General Sir William Napier* (London, 1864).

CASSELLS, S.A.C. (Ed). *Peninsular Portrait, 1811-1814. The Letters of Captain William Bragge, Third (King's Own) Dragoons* (London, 1963).

COWELL, John Stepney. *Leaves from the Diary of an Officer of the Guards* (London, 1854).

DONALDSON, Joseph. *Recollections of the Eventful Life of a Soldier,* (London, 1856).

FLETCHER, Ian (Ed). *A Guards Officer in the Peninsula. The Peninsular War Letters of John Edward Cornwallis Rous, Coldstream Guards, 1812-1814* (Tunbridge Wells, 1992).

FLETCHER, Ian & POULTER, Ron. *Gentlemen's Sons — The Foot Guards in the Peninsula and at Waterloo, 1808-1815* (Tunbridge Wells, 1993).

FLETCHER, Ian (Ed). *Letters from the Front: The First World War Correspondence of Lieutenant Brian Lawrence, Grenadier Guards, 1916-17* (Tunbridge Wells, 1994).

FLETCHER, Ian. *Craufurd's Light Division* (Tunbridge Wells, 1991).

FLETCHER, Ian. *In Hell Before Daylight. The Siege and Storming of the Fortress of Badajoz, 1812* 2nd Edition. (Tunbridge Wells, 1994).

FORTESCUE, The Hon. J.W. *History of the British Army* (London, 1910-30).

FRASER, Edward. *Soldiers Whom Wellington Led* (London, 1913).

GLEIG, George. *The Subaltern* (London, 1825).

GLOVER, Michael. *Wellington's Army in the Peninsula* (Newton Abbott, 1976).

GLOVER, Michael (Ed). *A Gentleman Volunteer: The Letters of George Hennell from the Peninsular War, 1812-1813* (London, 1979).

GRATTAN, William. *Adventures with the Connaught Rangers, 1809-1814* (London, 1902).

GURWOOD, Lt.Col. John. *The Despatches of Field Marshal The Duke of Wellington, during his various campaigns in India, Denmark, Portugal, Spain, the Low Countries and France from 1799 to 1818* (London, 1834).

GUY, Alan (Ed). *The Road to Waterloo* (London, 1990).

HAMILTON, Sir F.W. *The Origin and History of the First or Grenadier Guards* (London, 1874).

HASWELL, Jock. *The First Respectable Spy; The Life and Times of Colquhoun Grant, Wellington's Chief of Intelligence* (London, 1969).

HAYTHORNTHWAITE, Philip J. *Wellington's Military Machine* (Tunbridge Wells, 1989).

HAYTHORNTHWAITE, Philip J. *Armies of Wellington* (London, 1994).

JENNINGS, Louis J. (Ed). *The Croker Papers, The Correspondence and Diaries of the late Right Honourable John Wilson Croker, Secretary to the Admiralty from 1809 to 1830* (London, 1884).

JONES, Lieut.Col. John T. *Journal of the Sieges carried on by the Army under the Duke of Wellington in Spain during the years 1811 to 1814* (London, 1814).

KINCAID, Captain J. *Adventures in the Rifle Brigade, in the Peninsula, France and the Netherlands, from 1809 to 1815* (London, 1909).

LARPENT, Sir George (Ed). *The Private Journal of F. Seymour Larpent, Judge-Advocate General, attached to the Headquarters of Lord Wellington during the Peninsular War, from 1812 to its close* (London, 1853).

LEACH, Lieut.Col. J. *Rough Sketches of the Life of an Old Soldier* (London, 1831).

LESLIE, Major John H. (Ed). *The Dickson Manuscripts, being Diaries, Letters, Maps, Account Books, with various other papers of the late Major General Alexander Dickson, Royal Artillery.* (Woolwich, 1907).

LIDDELL HART, Captain B.H. (Ed). *The Letters of Private Wheeler, 1809-1828* (London, 1951).

LLOYD, Peter. *French Are Coming! The Invasion Scare of 1803-05* (Tunbridge Wells, 1991).

MACKINNON, Major General Henry. *A Journal of the Campaign in Portugal and Spain, containing Remarks on the Inhabitants, Customs, Trade, and Cultivation, of those Countries, from the year 1809 to 1812* (London, 1812).

MACKINNON, Colonel Daniel. *Origin and Services of the Coldstream Guards* (London, 1833).

MALMESBURY, Earl of. *A Series of Letters of the First Earl of Malmesbury, his Family and Friends from 1745 to 1820* (London, 1820).

MCGUFFIE, T.H. (Ed). *Peninsular Cavalry General (1811-13). The Correspondence of Lieutenant-General Robert Ballard Long* (London, 1951).

NAPIER, Colonel W.F.P. *History of the War in the Peninsula and in the South of France, from the Year 1807 to the Year 1814* (London, 1889).

OMAN, Sir Charles. *Wellington's Army, 1809-1814* (London, 1913).

OMAN, Sir Charles. *History of the Peninsular War (Oxford, 1902-30).*

OMAN, Sir Charles. *Oman, Studies in the Napoleonic Wars* (London, 1929).

PAGE, Julia (Ed). *Intelligence Officer in the Peninsula* (Tunbridge Wells, 1988).

PERCIVAL, George. MSS letters

PERRETT, Bryan (Ed). *A Hawk at War; The Peninsular War Reminiscences of Cap-tain Thomas Brotherton, CB* (Chippenham, 1986).

PORTER, Maj. Gen. Whitworth. *History of the Corps of Royal Engineers* (London,1889).

RAYMOND, John (Ed), *The Reminiscences and Recollections of Captain Gronow, Being Anecdotes of Camp, Court and Society, 1810-1860* (London, 1964).

REGULATIONS AND ORDERS FOR THE ARMY, 1811

ROUSSEAU, I.J. (Ed). *The Peninsular Journal of Major General Sir Benjamin D'Urban, 1808-1817* (London, 1930).

RUDORFF, Raymond. *War to the Death: The Sieges of Saragossa, 1808-08* (London, 1974).

STANHOPE, Philip Henry. *Notes of Conversations with the Duke of Wellington* (London, 1888).

STOTHERT, Captain William. *A Narrative of the Prinicpal Events of the Campaigns of 1809, 1810 and 1811, in Spain and Portugal; interspersed with Reamrks on Local Scenery and Manners. In a Series of Letters* (London, 1812).

THORNTON, James. *Your Obedient Servant* (Exeter, 1985).

THOUMINE, R.H. *Scientific Soldier. A Life of General Le Marchant, 1766-1812* (London, 1968).

TOMKINSON, James (Ed). *The Diary of a Cavalry Officer in the Peninsular and Waterloo Campaigns 1809-1815* (London, 1894).

VERNER, Colonel Willoughby. *History and Campaigns of the Rifle Brigade, 1800-1813* (London, 1919).

WARD, S.G.P. *Wellington's Headquarters. A Study of the Administrative Problems in the Peninsula* (London, 1957).

WELLER, Jac. *Wellington in the Peninsula* (London, 1962).

WROTTESLEY, Lt.Col. The Hon. George. *Life and Correspondence of Field Marshal Sir John Burgoyne,* (London, 1873).

INDEX